Current Perspectives in Psychology

Affirmative Action Is Dead; Long Live Affirmative Action

Faye J. Crosby

YALE UNIVERSITY PRESS   NEW HAVEN AND LONDON

Set in Adobe Garamond type by The Composing Room of Michigan, Inc.

Printed in the United States of America by R.R. Donnelley, Harrisonburg, Virginia.

Library of Congress Cataloging-in-Publication Data

Crosby, Faye J., 1947–

    Affirmative action is dead : long live affirmative action / Faye J. Crosby.

       p.   cm. — (Current perspectives in psychology)

Includes bibliographical references and index.

    ISBN 0-300-10129-5 (alk. paper)

    1. Affirmative action programs—United States.   2. Discrimination in employment—United States.   3. Discrimination in education—United States.   4. Race discrimination—United States.   I. Title.   II. Series.

    HF5549.5.A34C76 2004

    331.13′3′0973—dc22

                                        2003019187

A catalogue record for this book is available from the British Library.

The paper in this book meets the guidelines for permanence and durability of the Committee on Production Guidelines for Book Longevity of the Council on Library Resources.

10 9 8 7 6 5 4 3 2 1

To Yuki and Matthew
and
Molly and Tim
with love, hope, and admiration
and to Pat Gurin
for her courage and wisdom

Contents

Series Foreword

Current Perspectives in Psychology presents the latest discoveries and developments across the spectrum of the psychological and behavioral sciences. The series explores such important topics as learning, intelligence, trauma, stress, brain development and behavior, anxiety, interpersonal relationships, education, child-rearing, divorce and marital discord, and child, adolescent, and adult development. Each book focuses on critical advances in research, theory, methods, and applications and is designed to be accessible and informative to nonspecialists and specialists alike.

Affirmative Action Is Dead; Long Live Affirmative Action is a careful, comprehensive, and engaging examination of the many facets of affirmative action. The guiding questions of the book are What are the benefits of affirmative action in the United States? and Why is public support for the policy shrouded in ambivalence? To address these questions, Faye J. Crosby draws from multiple disciplines, including psychology, law, political science, education, sociology, social policy, race relations, African American studies, and women's studies. Through the use of empirical findings, case studies, and analyses of court cases, she elaborates affirmative action and its underpinnings in individual belief systems, social practices, and policy and law.

The book carefully defines and describes affirmative action in theory and practice, examining the arguments for and against such action. Reviews of classic federal and state rulings are presented to convey key issues and provide a historical perspective. The arguments for the necessity of affirmative action, what it can and cannot accomplish, and the effects of such action are carefully articulated. Crosby explores core concepts such as prejudice, racial bias, quotas, discrimination, and merit, detailing many specific practices in which these concepts emerge—for example, the use of psychological testing, college admissions practices, and hiring in business and industry.

Three features of Crosby's treatment of affirmative action are especially noteworthy. First, the book draws heavily on empirical research in such areas as prejudice, perceptions of justice, and the impact of expectations on performance. Second, Crosby provides a balanced view, giving careful treatment to different sides of debates and opposing views. In her presentation of key Supreme Court decisions, for example, she discusses the dissenting views and their merit as well as the majority view. Finally, she goes beyond mere description and evaluation of practices and policies to explore their underpinnings and how such practices have been integrated into society. In order to be effective, Crosby argues, affirmative action, like any other policy, must take into account core beliefs of individuals as well as implicit cultural views with which it might be in conflict.

In *Affirmative Action Is Dead* Crosby offers a readable, accessible overview that at the same time contributes significantly to scholarly research and conceptualization of key issues in the affirmative action debate. Thanks to her authoritative analysis and integration of this critical topic, we can see with fresh eyes how affirmative action fits with deeply held views about bias, fairness, and justice and think about how these can be reconciled.

ALAN E. KAZDIN
Series Editor

Preface

Every book is produced over a long period of time, but this book has had an even longer gestation period than most. I sent the first draft to Yale University Press in September 2002, and it was working its way through the production process when, in December, the Supreme Court declared that it would hear two landmark affirmative action cases, *Grutter v. Bollinger* and *Gratz v. Bollinger,* both of which challenged race-conscious admissions policies at the University of Michigan. The Press and I decided to hold back the book so that I could revise it after the Court had rendered its decisions.

On June 23, 2003, the Supreme Court decisions were handed down. Although they contain good news for race-sensitive admissions policies in education, they are framed in such a way that we are likely to see years of continued debate about the fairness of affirmative action and other attempts at diversity. At the core of this book is the question of why a policy that is sensible, even unremarkable, in so many ways has nonetheless occasioned so much controversy over the years. Thoughtful scholars are still left to wonder why affirmative action has not elicited unwavering support from either the American public or America's public servants. Yet since its inception in 1965, it has produced controversy. It is my hope that this book can help Americans become better informed about the policy and practice of affirmative action.

Many people deserve thanks for their part in bringing this book into being. An enormous thank-you goes to Valerie Jenni for her assistance at every step along the way. Had it not been for Valerie's good-humored, capable presence, I would still be sharpening my pencil and waiting to begin. Thanks also to Jesse deFrank, Dianne Lessman, and Alfreda Brock for making me feel that, yes, it really was their job to make my life as easy and hassle-free as they could and that, no, they never had anything else to do or anyone else to help on the days I needed them. And thanks to Tom Allen for rescuing me when I was stranded away from Jesse, Dianne, Alfreda, and Valerie.

Great is my gratitude to Fred Pincus for sharing his work with me and encouraging me. To Cliff Daigle, David Mastros, Bob Newman, Danielle Obinger, Marilyn Patton, and Zev Reiner for their help in research and manuscript preparation, I say thank you again and again. I owe a great debt to Stephen Reysen for his ability to find any and all materials and to Julia Tomasilli for her acumen and skill. I am deeply thankful for the compulsive care Jamie Franco lavished on the manuscript during a particularly hurried time. Her investment in the work mattered more to me than I can express.

For reading and commenting on the manuscript, special recognition goes to Myrtle Bell, Marc Bendick, Jr., Madeline Heilman, Alison Konrad, David Kravitz, David Rose, Paul Sniderman, and Colette van Laar. They all helped and guided me with excellent suggestions. Ellen McCambley also has my everlasting appreciation for reading and commenting on the entire manuscript. Her observations were both wise and smart. I feel profound respect and gratitude for Mary Crawford, who astonished me first with her spontaneous and generous offer to edit the book and then later with the grace and clarity she tried to inject into the prose.

Students in my University of California in D.C. classes on affirmative action deserve to be acknowledged for their input. Their actions and reactions all contributed to this book. Thank you Esmeralda Aguila, Shari Doi, Sara Eckhorn, Elizabeth Glick, Sonia Hansra, Ching-Gi Ho, Alyson Hong, Ming Ling Hsieh, Brittany Jensky, Alicia Levenson, Gening Liao, Alex McNair, Lys Mendez, Maria Mercado, Kim-Yen Nguyen, Christina Oh, Vanessa Pereda, Jamie Sae Koo, Camellia Sanford, Troy Thomas, and Fredricka Ung.

Finally, the University of California has made it possible for me to write the book by sending me to its Washington Center, where the mist off the Potomac kept me chained to my word processor. Over a critical six-month period, I led a privileged existence. Larry Berman and Karen Akerson in D.C. and Dan Wirls and Martin Chemers in Santa Cruz helped engineer the professional experience, while friends like Ellen Kimmel and Doug Turk, Shari Miles, Anne Tashjian, Dickran Tashjian, and most of all Marilyn Patton were able to create a wonderfully supportive environment for me in those oh-too-few hours when I stepped out of the library or away from the office. For all I have been given I feel thankful and joyful.

1

The Nature of the Beast

There is no reason for us to be at each other's throats when there is so much on both sides of the argument from which all can learn.

Stephen L. Carter, *Reflections of an Affirmative Action Baby*

In October 1997, two White residents of the state of Michigan, Jennifer Gratz and Patrick Hamacher, filed a lawsuit in federal court against the University of Michigan. They had been denied admission to the undergraduate college. Because applicants of color with lower test scores and grades than theirs had been admitted to the school, Gratz and Hamacher argued that their constitutional rights had been violated. Two months later Barbara Grutter filed a similar case against the law school at the University of Michigan.

The cases wound their ways through the courts, and in December 2002, the Supreme Court announced that it would hear both *Gratz v. Bollinger* and *Grutter v. Bollinger.* Oral arguments occurred on April 1, 2003. On June 23, 2003, the Supreme Court handed down its decisions.

In the case of *Gratz v. Bollinger,* the Court found that the university had indeed erred. At fault was a numeric system by which applicants who had attended a predominantly minority high school or who were themselves members of a minority received an automatic 20 points out of a possible 150. By awarding points uniformly to applicants of color, the university was making an impermissible distinction between citizens on the basis of ethnicity or race.

To reach its decision, the Court paid particular attention to a legal precedent known as "strict scrutiny." According to this decades-old principle, whenever the government or its agents make distinctions on the basis of race or ethnicity, those distinctions must be held to the high standard of strict scrutiny, to satisfy which a program must both serve a compelling state interest and be narrowly tailored. The majority decision, written by Chief Justice William Rehnquist, declared that Michigan did indeed have a compelling interest in ensuring racial or ethnic diversity in its student body but that the numeric system (with the offending 20 points) was not narrowly tailored. Thus, even though the Court found in *Gratz v. Bollinger* that the specific admissions system used by the university violated the Equal Protection Clause of the Fourteenth Amendment of the Constitution and Title VII of the Civil Rights Act of 1964, it was careful to declare that it "rejected petitioners' argument that diversity cannot constitute a compelling state interest."[1]

The state's compelling interest in fostering diversity of the student body was also central to the determination of *Grutter v. Bollinger,* for which Justice Sandra Day O'Connor wrote the five-person majority decision.[2] Alluding to social scientific research, O'Connor emphasized the importance of having a critical mass of minority students. Only when the student body contained that critical mass could the minority students feel free to express opinions without fear of being stereotyped. A critical mass of minority students was also considered crucial for the ending of racial stereotypes, for with sufficient numbers would come diversity of opinion among minority students. Given the obvious importance of a law degree from a top-ranked school for the assumption of a leadership role in public life, furthermore, the Court referenced an *amicus* brief filed by a group of retired generals and another filed by a conglomerate of corporations, noting, "In order to cultivate a set of leaders with legitimacy in the eyes of the citizenry, it is necessary that the path to leadership be visibly open to talented and qualified individuals of every race and ethnicity."[3] The Court also looked favorably upon the holistic approach of the law school, in which every aspect of an individual applicant was considered, finding such an approach to be narrowly tailored.

The next morning the *New York Times* announced in banner headlines: "Justices Back Affirmative Action by 5 to 4, but Wider Vote

Bans a Racial Point System." A front-page article by Pulitzer Prize–winner Linda Greenhouse carried its own set of headlines: "Colleges Relieved" and "U. of Michigan Ruling Endorses the Value of Campus Diversity." A jubilant Mary Sue Coleman, president of the University of Michigan, was photographed standing in front of the Supreme Court. Certainly, good feeling ran high among the many supporters of affirmative action who had feared that the Court might declare unlawful not only race-sensitive admissions policies but also affirmative action in employment.

Within two weeks, however, some observers noted that the victory was not as complete as it may have first appeared. The front page of the July 4 issue of the *Chronicle of Higher Education* noted, "Affirmative action survives, and so does the debate." A special twenty-eight-page section contained all the Court's opinions, majority and minority, and in-depth articles by veteran affirmative action reporters Peter Schmidt, Jeffrey Selingo, and Sara Hebel, among others. One article noted that while the Court endorsed race-sensitive admissions policies in principle, it did not require them. Thus, any governor could, like Jeb Bush of Florida, sign an executive order banning affirmative action in admissions. And the electorate of many states could, like those of California and Washington, pass referenda outlawing race-sensitive admissions policies. Another potential point of conflict concerned race-specific scholarships. Could such scholarship programs now withstand legal challenge? In the days to come, as the proponents of affirmative action try to push the limits, its opponents will try equally hard to find the loopholes.

In the court of public opinion, the battle over affirmative action is likely to continue unabated. Yes, the Supreme Court of the United States has now definitively given its stamp of approval to race-conscious admissions policies. But the grounds on which it made its decision—that the state has a compelling interest in diversity—may not prove convincing to many Americans, who will be wondering whether diversity is being bought at the price of fairness.

Another aspect of the Michigan cases is likely to lead to confusion. Although the press has characterized the Court's decisions as concerning affirmative action, never once in the Court's written opinions does the term "affirmative action" appear. To be sure, a race-conscious admissions policy is one type of affirmative action, but both the policy and the practice of affirmative action involve much more than race-conscious admissions. While they are monumentally important for what they say about the permissibility of the state making use of racial or ethnic differentiations, the Michigan cases say nothing directly about affirmative action in employment or procurement. Did the Court deliberately avoid using "affirmative action" to ensure that its decisions were not construed as being more far-reaching than intended?

What Is Affirmative Action?

In the recent flood of publications on affirmative action, few writers have paused to define their terms. All too often, people have hurled headlong into debates over the value of affirmative action without stopping to clarify what they intend by the words they use. Thus, commentators have characterized affirmative action as a policy "designed to right the wrongs of the past,"[4] as a quota system, or as a set of remedial programs aimed to compensate for the inadequacies of people of color or of women.[5] Such writers tend to see affirmative action as colliding with values like fairness and self-reliance, and as encouraging big government, and interpret opposition to the policy as an indication of America's devotion to fair play. Other commentators have envisioned affirmative action as a policy that aims to correct deficient systems, not deficient people. Given the extent to which present systems of judging merit are skewed to disfavor the disempowered and valorize those whom birth has privileged with the "right" color or sex, proponents of affirmative action argue that the policy is one of the nation's fairest ways to overcome the lingering effects of racism and sexism.[6] Such writers sometimes see resistance to the policy arising less from a genuine concern with justice than from a need to justify the present structures or a desire to hide the ways the United States currently deviates from its own meritocratic ideals.[7]

Before entering into pitched combat over the fairness or unfairness of affirmative action, perhaps the combatants should check to make sure they agree on their terms.[8] What appear to be clashes over principles might turn out to be nothing more than semantic disagreements.

The nontechnical definition of affirmative action is this: Affirmative action is the expenditure of energy or resources by an organization in the quest for equality among individuals from different, discernible groups. The general definition enjoys surprisingly wide acceptance among both the opponents and the proponents of affirmative action. It is based on federal publications and has been reaffirmed by both Republican and Democratic administrations. Roughly the same definition has been offered by such nongovernmental groups as the American Psychological Association (APA), a nonpartisan alliance of more than a hundred thousand practitioners and academic psychologists. In a pamphlet entitled *Affirmative Action: Who Benefits?* published by the APA's Public Interest Directorate, affirmative action is defined as "both voluntary and mandatory efforts undertaken by federal, state, and local governments; private employers; and schools to combat discrimination and to promote equal opportunity in education and employment for all."[9]

Affirmative action differs in important ways from the present construction of another policy that also grew out of the Equal Rights Movement of the 1960s: equal opportunity.[10] Equal opportunity assumes that individuals are to be considered only as individuals and not as representatives of a demographic group. Equal opportunity, furthermore, tends to assume that when unfairness occurs, it is either intentional or traceable to conscious prejudices. Finally, unlike affirmative action, equal opportunity assumes that those who are victimized by unfairness will come forward on their own behalf. Thus, while affirmative action implies a *pro-active* stance against discrimination, equal opportunity implies a passive or *reactive* one.

Affirmative action and equal opportunity represent two different mechanisms for achieving the same purpose. Affirmative action requires organizations to take cognizance of the demographic characteristics of their constituents, and equal opportunity does not. Affirmative action calls for more government involvement in education and employment than equal opportunity. Yet while equal opportunity and affirmative action differ substantially in their methods, they hold the same goal: to decrease, or eliminate if they can, discrimination against individuals.

Of course, affirmative action exists as a legal fact and not just as a principle. At the federal level, there are between 150 and 200 laws and regulations that concern affirmative action.[11] Most of the these are of the type that lawyers call "precatory," meaning that they express a sentiment or wish but specify neither the means of implementing the wish nor the sanctions for failure to follow it. For example, some laws concerning the transfer of agricultural funds from the federal government to state governments contain clauses expressing the wish that state agencies develop mechanisms to identify and use banks that are owned by women or minorities.

From time to time, a Senator or a U.S. Representative vows to bring to an end the one federal law with teeth: Executive Order 11246, which established "classical" affirmative action. On March 3, 1995, for example, Sen. Jesse Helms of North Carolina introduced an anti–affirmative action bill into the Senate. The initiative failed to gather momentum, perhaps in part because of a study commissioned by Sen. Robert Dole that proved that no affirmative action measure involved quotas.[12] Not a single one. Indeed, the study, conducted by the Congressional Research Service, showed that the number of regulations and laws involving monitoring was greater than the number that mentioned preferences or set-asides.[13]

Most of the laws concerning affirmative action relate to business. The imbalance between employment and education is consistent with the observation that affirmative action in employment affects many more citizens than does affirmative action in education. Currently, there are about 11.5 million Americans attending four-year colleges and universities. Educators estimate that no more than half of the four-year institutions are selective. The rest admit everyone who applies. Thus, issues concerning college admissions relate, at most, to about 6 million Americans. In contrast, about six times as many people are affected by affirmative action programs in employment.

How Does Affirmative Action Operate?

The concept of affirmative action in employment typically refers to a system that was initiated by President Lyndon Johnson in 1965 when he signed Executive Order 11246 and later strengthened by President Richard Nixon and revised by President Bill Clinton. At the heart of

Executive Order 11246, sometimes referred to as "classical" affirmative action,[14] is the requirement that firms of a certain size doing a certain amount of business with the federal government institute a way of monitoring their hiring practices. In essence, employers check their own records to make sure they are employing qualified people from specified targeted classes—such as women or African Americans—in proportion to their availability in the work force. If the organization finds a discrepancy between incumbency and availability, it must devise a sensible plan for corrective action and show a good-faith effort to remedy its deficiencies. No inference of prejudice, maliciousness, or discriminatory intent is made from the finding that a company does not employ enough qualified people from targeted groups. But if an appropriate plan for correcting the problem is not devised or not followed, the organization is subject to penalties imposed by the Office of Federal Contract Compliance Programs (OFCCP), which is part of the Department of Labor. As with tax returns, only a small percentage of affirmative action employers are audited by the federal government. Both systems operate on the assumption that employers are generally honest in their self-monitoring efforts.[15]

The example of a research university can illustrate how classical affirmative action works. Most research universities conduct business with the federal government—contracting, for example, to develop products for government use. Because they are federal contractors, the universities are of necessity affirmative action employers. They keep records of how many women and how many ethnic minorities they employ in a number of job categories. Working in coordination with the OFCCP, the university also calculates the availability of qualified workers for the different jobs, which are presumed to draw from pools of different sizes. The relevant talent pool for professors, for instance, is usually considered to be the entire United States, and qualifications usually include a doctorate in the appropriate discipline. The relevant pool for clerical workers, by contrast, is presumed to be residents of an area within reach of the campus, and qualifications may be an associate's degree or even a high school diploma.

Imagine that University X wished to determine empirically what percentage of its social science faculty ought to be women. It would look at the proportion of Ph.D.s in the social sciences granted to women during the years (including the current year) in which its faculty were obtaining degrees. From such data University X would calculate the availability figure. Having determined availability, the university would then look at its professorial ranks and note the percentage of social scientists who were women. Imagine, now, that the university calculates that it ought to have a social science faculty in which 30 percent of the professors are women but that it actually has one in which only 10 percent are. University X would then need to devise sensible plans to increase the number of women. It could not legally fire any of the male faculty simply to make room for women. Nor could it bar men from applying for any job. But it could make an extra effort to locate and recruit talented women. It could also use gender as a tie-breaking factor if two candidates appeared equally qualified.

Now what if, while University X was in the process of increasing the number of women faculty, a compliance review were conducted by the OFCCP? Basically, as long as University X could demonstrate that it was making a good-faith effort to increase the number of female social scientists no adverse action would result, even if the gap between incumbency and availability were quite large. No contracts would be canceled. No damages would be sought.

With the exception of the federal government (the nation's largest employer) employers that do not wish to monitor their work force are not required by federal law to do so—as long as the employer does not obtain a federal contract and as long as it has not been specifically ordered to undertake affirmative action as a consequence of a judicial finding of discrimination. Those who think that classical affirmative action is cumbersome, inefficient, or constraining are free to avoid the system simply by refraining from doing business with the federal government.

An additional type of federal affirmative action—set-asides for procurement—has developed over the years. In 1953 the Small Business Act introduced into the economy the practice of setting aside a percentage of government contracts for entities within specific categories (in this instance, small enterprises). President Nixon later signed Executive Order 11458, which created the Office of Minority Business Enterprises and made minority-owned businesses a subcategory within "small business." Both the Public Works Employment Act of 1977 and Public Law N. 95-507 authorized set-aside programs through which minority-owned businesses could enter into procurement contracts.[16] In 1988 set-asides were extended to women by the Women's Business Ownership Act.[17]

More recently the legality of set-asides has been called into question. President Clinton's reform of affirmative action eliminated several set-aside procurement programs in the military and elsewhere. In a series of decisions, ending with the case of *Adarand Constructors v. Pena* (1995), the Supreme Court has severely curtailed the operation of set-aside programs.[18] Unlike the classical affirmative action programs established by Executive Order 11246, those which use set-asides often appear to pluck their numbers from thin air. On what grounds does a municipality decide to set aside 10, 20, or 30 percent of its construction contracts?

Currently, about one in five employed people in the United States works for either the federal government, a federal contractor, or a large subcontractor. In other words, 20 percent of the American work force is estimated to be covered directly by mandatory affirmative action programs. Many more workers, of course, are covered by voluntary programs.

Affirmative Action in Education

Affirmative action in university admissions follows essentially the same logic as affirmative action in employment. Colleges and universities take stock of the availability of individuals qualified to become college students. A state university might, for example, calculate that the top 12.5 percent of high school seniors in the state constituted the pool of qualified students.[19] It would then look at census and other figures to determine how many of those who were qualified came from the underrepresented groups: African Americans, Hispanics, and Native Americans. The next step would be to compare the percentages of qualified African Americans, Hispanics, and Native Americans available with the percentage who actually matriculated. In addition, it might look at the percentage who graduated. If the matriculation or graduation figures were substantially lower than the pool of qualified potential students, the school would need to find the reason for the problem and correct it.

The recent landmark cases involving the University of Michigan have concerned race-conscious admissions programs that were put into place because the university noticed that it had fewer persons of color in attendance than expected, given the number of talented minorities in the state. Even in the case of the undergraduate college, where the majority of justices found the point system to be unconstitutional, the Court noted that the university had not admitted unqualified applicants of color.

Why Is Affirmative Action Needed?

In the recent cases of *Grutter v. Bollinger* and *Gratz v. Bollinger,* the Supreme Court posed the question Why are race-conscious admissions policies needed at the University of Michigan? The answer it gave was that race-conscious policies were needed because they would help the school enroll a critical mass of ethnic minority students. Alternative plans for increasing diversity, such as a lottery system for admission, would have diminished the quality of the school. Race-sensitive admissions policies guaranteed not only that the student body was ethnically diverse but also that all who were admitted were capable of doing the demanding work.

The Supreme Court did not address the broad issues of fairness. For the Court, questions of legality trump all other questions. The Court is only interested in determining whether practices conform to the Constitution of the United States and federal statutes. Legal scholars may deem the practices that conform fair and those that do not unfair; the Court tends to remain mute on the topic of fairness. "Justice" and "fairness" are not words one often encounters in the Court's opinions. In any event, the words never appear in the decisions handed down on June 23, 2003.

General Issues

So even as we acknowledge that some forms of affirmative action are useful to achieve diversity, we may be left wondering whether any are needed to ensure fairness. The answer, I think, is that affirmative action is essential to ensure fairness. Fairness is achieved through sensible and good decision making, and affirmative action enables sensible and good decisions.

Several elements make affirmative action an eminently sensible policy. Like any good policy in business or education, affirmative action revolves around informed decision making. And like most good business policies, affirmative action is results oriented.

Compare how a firm conducts its affirmative action programs with how it seeks a profit. If the firm makes several products and distributes them to different markets via a number of outlets, the smart executives at the firm are likely to ask for data that show the costs of making and distributing each product, the revenues obtained from each product, the rate of sales from each outlet, and so on. Market studies are commonplace in business. Intelligent executives and managers who have devised or inherited a process usually check to see whether the process is working well. When examining results, formal data-gathering mechanisms almost always prove superior to unsystematic information collection, and both are better than anecdotal data.

Data are arranged in categories, and having the appropriate categories assists sensible decision making. Sometimes, for example, a retailer may wish to know the volume of sales from specific stores; sometimes that retailer may even wish to know the volume of sales from specific shelves in each store. It is inefficient to collect data that are too fine-grained but foolish to keep the categories overly general.

In classical affirmative action programs, individuals in specific jobs are classified along the axes of gender and ethnicity or race.[20] Tracking how well organizations perform with regard to the hiring and promotion of individuals in different gender and ethnic categories is really no different, from the point of view of accounting procedures, from tracking the volume of sales of various brands in different locations in a grocery store. In both cases, the effectiveness of the process is gauged by results. In neither case is there a substitute for good, hard numbers.

Some, including Justices Antonin Scalia and Clarence Thomas and Chief Justice William Rehnquist, would no doubt object to the assertion that race or ethnicity can function as a variable like any other in a decision-making equation. According to Rehnquist, Scalia, and Thomas, the Constitution prohibits differentiation according to race or ethnicity.[21] Others, like Ward Connerly, Shelby Steele, Thomas Sowell, and Stephen Carter, all of whom are African Americans in the public eye, also object to the enumeration of race or ethnicity on ethical grounds.[22]

But many conservatives seem to be swayed by the simple administrative logic of counting results by categories. President George W. Bush, for example, has pinned his intended educational reforms to the concept of affirmative action, even as he has steadfastly shied away from the label. One hallmark of Bush's education bill is that every school district will track separately the results of its efforts for White students and for underrepresented students. Specifically, Section 441, b (2) (G) of P.L. 107–110 ("No Child Left Behind Act of 2001") states that measurement and reporting shall "include information on special groups, including, whenever feasible[,] information collected, cross tabulated, compared, and reported by race, ethnicity, socioeconomic status, gender, disability, and limited English proficiency."[23]

As a general rule in administration, a certain level of detachment aids in good decision making. It is also true that intentions count for little until they result in action. Woe to the executives who think that simply because they personally *wish* their company to make a profit, money will flow in faster than it flows out. And woe to the executives who imagine that their organization will become instantly nondiscriminatory simply because they *wish* for all employees to be treated equally.

There are many reasons why it is difficult to transform an imperfect organization into a bastion of nondiscrimination. One reason might be the malicious resistance of those who have benefited from the injustices. Certainly, wickedness exists; but selfishness and greed may not be the cause of current unfairness. Ironically, good motives may be the cause of many problems. Bluntly put, one reason it is difficult to transform organizations is that people like to think that the organizations they are involved with are already governed by the rules of fairness. Add to the motive to see the world as a just place the assumption that most unfairnesses which occur are intentional, and then stir into the mix what cognitive psychologists now know about the systematic biases in person perception, and it is evident that even the most pure of heart may fall far short in their efforts to find out whether their own institutions are discriminatory.[24] As long as people are unable to gauge the extent of discrimination, they are hampered in their efforts to create and sustain fair institutions.

Can Impartial Judges Detect Discrimination?

We can hardly overstate the significance of bias in human reasoning. When it comes to functioning as logical thinking machines, we humans are imperfect. As everyone knows, emotions cloud our thinking and prejudgments impair our reasoning. There is also another problem, known to research psychologists but unrecognized by most laypeople: people are notoriously poor at drawing appropriate inferences about groups on the basis of information about individuals.[25]

A good demonstration of this can be found in a series of studies some colleagues and I performed. The studies were undertaken over a number of years at a number of different institutions using different sample populations. Typically in the experiments we provided participants with information about a certain company, which we called Company Z. The information described the situation of two groups— usually women and men—in Company Z. We then assessed how well the research participants understood the information. We told the participants in the original experiment, for example, that their job was to determine the extent of sex discrimination in Company Z and to let us know how certain they felt about their determinations.[26]

Into the materials we embedded data showing that Company Z discriminated against some of its workers on the basis of a group characteristic like gender. We noted that the two groups had the same work-related characteristics, but one group earned only 80 percent of what the other group earned.

Sounds like an easy task, right? We complicated matters by presenting the information in two different ways. The content of the information was constant; but half the time participants encountered it in one format and half the time in another. In the first format, participants saw information in aggregate form, assembled on a single page. We called this "The Aggregate Condition." In this format, the page would have ten rows for the ten divisions in Company Z.

Columns contained the "inputs" and the "outcomes" of women and men in the ten divisions. Inputs included

- educational background,
- years of work experience,
- managerial level, and
- (unbiased) performance ratings.

The outcome was salary. Subjects were told that the outcome was determined by the inputs, but they were not told how much to weigh any of the inputs. The Aggregate Condition represented the systematic assembly of data required by affirmative action. Indeed, in the original experiment, conducted in 1984, the formatting of the materials in the Aggregate Condition was modeled on reports I consulted at the university's Office of Affirmative Action and Equal Employment.

In the second format the information was presented in disaggregated form, forcing the participants to make separate judgments about ten separate comparisons. In any one of the divisions, the women might be more qualified than the men on one input qualification but less qualified on another.

The data for Division D, for example, showed that the female managers, on average,

- had a bachelor's degree,
- had twenty years of seniority,
- worked at level 13 in the hierarchy, and
- were rated as "excellent" in terms of motivation.

Meanwhile the male managers in Division D, on average,

- had completed some postgraduate work,
- had twenty years of seniority,
- worked at level 13 in hierarchy, and
- were rated as "good" in terms of motivation.

On average, the female managers in Division D earned $56,000 a year while the male managers earned $60,000.

In the original experiment, we called the nonaggregate condition "The Dribble Condition" because it resembled the anecdotal and incomplete way that people usually obtain information in organizations: it dribbles in. Unless you are a human resources officer, you usually hear about possible sex discrimination in an organization by learning how this or that woman did not obtain a particular promotion or was dissatisfied with her raise. The natural tendency when information dribbles in seems to be to compare the specific women to specific men who did obtain promotions. In all but the lowest level of jobs, the individual men and women are unlikely to be matched on every input characteristic, allowing for the possibility that one or another specific characteristic was the deciding factor in who got the promotion or the raise.

We found in our first experiment that intelligent people were generally able to detect the discrimination if they were in the Aggregate Condition but surprisingly unable to detect it in the Dribble Condition. In other words, people were good information processors under optimum conditions (with all the information spread on a single sheet) but poor information processors when they encountered the same information in a nonsystematic format. The default presumption was that things were operating fairly.

The original experiment used male undergraduates at Yale as participants. When questioned, some of the young men described themselves as feminists (that is, people in favor of equal opportunities and equal rewards for women and men) but most did not. Importantly, the tendency to underestimate discrimination in the Dribble Condition did not depend on the participant's feminist leanings. The few ardent feminists were no more likely than the rest to detect the discrimination when they encountered the evidence piecemeal. And the few misogynists were just as likely as other participants to detect the discrimination when they encountered evidence in aggregated form.

Follow-up experiments showed that we had uncovered a general phenomenon.[27] A study at Smith College, where the participants were decidedly more feminist than at Yale, showed the same results as the original study.[28] Importantly, the same pattern was found when the evidence was said to concern Plant A and Plant B in Company Z rather than women and men. When asked to evaluate the experience of being in the

Table 1.1
Hypothetical Data About Company Z

| | Men | | | Women | | |
Branch	Years	Level	Salary	Years	Level	Salary
A	11	12	37,000	10	12	40,000
B	12	16	47,000	12	14	50,000

Note: Company Z has two banches, A and B. In Company Z two input variables are supposed to determine salary: years of employment and level of management. The longer the
employment, the higher the salary. The higher the level of management, the higher the
salary.

study, participants who read the original materials about sex discrimination rated the experiment interesting while those who read about Plant A
and Plant B admitted to being bored. Nonetheless, participants who
studied Plant A and Plant B were able to detect discrimination in the aggregate condition but not in the piecemeal condition, just like participants who studied women and men. Once again, attitudes had no effect
on the participants' ability to see the discrimination or not.

Unwilling to base all our conclusions on undergraduates, my colleagues and I tested our concepts further with a sample of MBA students taking a course on good decision making at the Kellogg School
of Management at Northwestern University.[29] At the time of our
study, *U.S. News and World Report* considered Kellogg the most competitive business school in the United States, ahead of Wharton and
Harvard. As in the earlier studies, some of the participants were presented with information in aggregated format while others received
the information piecemeal. In the piecemeal presentations, we sometimes made the discrimination conspicuous and sometimes did not.
When the discrimination was conspicuous, we arranged the inputs
and outcomes so that the disadvantaged group (men for half of the participants and women for the other half) exceeded the advantaged
group on both relevant input variables but received less pay. Thus, participants who received data on a conspicuous case of anti-male bias saw
data similar to those in table 1.1. All the participants judged that Company Z discriminated against men when they encountered the information in this format. But participants who encountered the same

Table 1.2
Hypothetical Data About Company Z

Branch	Men			Women		
	Years	Level	Salary	Years	Level	Salary
A	12	16	47,000	10	12	40,000
B	11	12	37,000	12	14	50,000

Note: Company Z has two banches, A and B. In Company Z two input variables are supposed to determine salary: years of employment and level of management. The longer the employment, the higher the salary. The higher the level of management, the higher the salary.

data arranged so that the discrimination was less conspicuous were significantly less likely than their colleagues to detect the discrimination we had built into the system.

To understand why the certifiably smart and business-savvy students at Kellogg performed with less than perfect logic, look at the information presented in table 1.2. Now compare the information in table 1.2 with the information in table 1.1. By simply reversing the men's input lines for Branch A and Branch B in table 1.2, the discrimination (against men) seems magically to disappear.

The clear conclusion from our laboratory studies echoes the work of many other research psychologists. The people we studied—and perhaps all human beings—had a difficult time being completely logical. We are all imperfect judges of data. We have special weaknesses when we seek to cross-tabulate information about groups and individuals. Most people make poor inferences about the situations of groups on the basis of information about individuals.[30] It is as though we have two chambers in our brain: one for the knowledge we keep about individuals and one for the knowledge we keep about groups.

Sensible administrative structures are those that acknowledge human frailty. The most effective systems are those that deliver to people what they want but that do not require of people more than humans are capable of doing. Granted how much Americans care about justice and how hard it is for Americans to detect unfairness from nonsystematic data, affirmative action—with its monitoring function—is, in principle, an especially efficacious policy.

But what, we might ask, about the victims of injustice? Certainly people must notice when they are being treated unfairly. Even if others do not detect injustices, the victims themselves will surely look out for their own interests. Such is our assumption about how people operate in employment situations.

Common sense makes us imagine that adults want to watch out for and are capable of watching out for their own interests. Imagine a work situation in which a number of new employees start in equivalent jobs in the same year. Let's assume that some of the new hires are women and some are men. After a year some of the men and women leave the firm but others stay, and some are promoted. Would it not make sense to assume that any given woman would notice if her male counterparts were promoted more rapidly than she? Would it not be normal to expect the woman—rather than her co-workers or her supervisor or her subordinates—to watch out for her own interests and to complain when men who were no better qualified than she obtained more rapid promotions?

The expectation that people will be their own watchdogs is buttressed by a substantial amount of social scientific research showing that people tend to overestimate their own capabilities and to underestimate the capabilities of others.[31] We notice the mote in the eye of our colleagues and fail to perceive the beam in our own. In light of the strength of the self-serving bias, isn't it logical to expect that people will jump forward with complaints about how they have been mistreated even if they are insensitive to the mistreatment of others?

Indeed, the expectation that people will watch out for their own interests forms a cornerstone in the anti–affirmative action rhetoric. Consider the thinking of conservative powerbroker Linda Chavez:

> At a National Press Club panel discussion . . . [William] Raspberry drew an analogy he thought would put the issue in focus. Suppose, he said, that during halftime at a basketball game it is discovered that the referees allowed one team to rack up sixteen undeserved points. The referees are expelled from the game, but that doesn't fix the score. What to do?
>
> My response . . . was simple: Compensate the victims of

discrimination. . . . Wherever we can, in basketball or in
society, we should apply specific remedies to specific victims of discrimination. The antidiscrimination laws of this
country already allow us to do just that. Courts are empow-
ered to force employers to hire or promote victims of discrimination. . . . Similar tools are available to redress discrimination in housing, schools, and contracting.[32]

Chavez never considers the possibility that the victims of injustice
might remain silent about their mistreatment. Yet at least one large-
scale systematic study has shown that only a tiny proportion of people
who consider themselves to have been the victims of discrimination
ever engage in remedial legal action. Indeed, people are less willing to
pursue a claim of discrimination than to lodge a complaint in a contract dispute.[33] Many victims of systematic unfairness understand the
risks of registering complaints and feel pessimistic about what they can
achieve through their own actions.[34] Even liberal college students tend
to view with suspicion anyone who complains of mistreatment.[35]

The problem is not simply one of conscious self-censorship.
Conservatives like Chavez assume that victims always have perfect access to knowledge about the forces that affect them, as well as a perfect
understanding of them. Chavez's view may sound reasonable at first,
but it turns out to be naive. Numerous studies have shown that people
behave differently from the way we might expect. There are many
things that most people do not want to know or to admit to themselves. One of those things is how they are mistreated. Even among
people who acknowledge that other people just like themselves—their
own in-group—are discriminated against, we find an inability to admit personal disadvantage.

More than twenty years ago we stumbled upon the finding that
people tend to underestimate the extent of their own personal disadvantage. At the time I was conducting a large-scale empirical test of a
social scientific theory known as relative deprivation. The theory states
that people generally feel deprived not according to what they possess
in some objective sense but rather relative to some standard, such as
their expectations or their neighbor's possessions. The test of the theory involved in-depth interviews with about four hundred individuals

living in a suburb of Boston.[36] The employed women and men in the sample had been matched with each other in terms of their jobs and a number of job-related characteristics, such as hours worked, job training, and psychological investment in the job. The respondents answered questions pertinent to their home lives, their work lives, and the work lives of women generally.

Their answers produced some surprises. We found that the employed women in the sample earned significantly less money than the employed men even though they were matched on all the characteristics relevant to earnings, such as the level of their jobs. We had not expected to find that the women in the sample were discriminated against, but that's just what we found. Another surprise concerned the women's reactions to the discrimination. The employed women knew that women as a whole were discriminated against, and they resented sex discrimination. Yet, by and large, they did not show the slightest awareness of their own disadvantaged position. It seemed as though most of the women imagined themselves to be the one lucky exception to the pervasive sex discrimination. We called the phenomenon denial; other researchers relabeled it minimization.

Subsequent studies have underlined just how common denial or minimization is. Less awareness of personal disadvantage than of group disadvantage has been documented among Canadian working women as well as working women in the United States.[37] Denial or minimization has also been found among ethnic minority residents of the Toronto area,[38] linguistic minorities in Quebec,[39] and inner-city African Americans in Miami.[40] It has surfaced among immigrants,[41] among Black MBAs,[42] among undergraduates,[43] and among welfare mothers.[44] It has appeared in samples of homosexuals.[45] Minimization has even appeared among a national probability sample of Black and White workers interviewed by a major newspaper.[46]

The implication is clear: people are reluctant to see themselves as victimized. They do not like to think that bad things can attach to the self.[47] This specific reluctance, combined with the general inability of people to detect systematic unfairness on the basis of anecdotal information, demonstrates how hard it is to detect (let alone correct) problems until the problems are too large to be ignored.

One goal of affirmative action is to force institutions to make rel-

atively benign adjustments before the problems assume large proportions. Little improvements stave off major conflicts, which can be
costly to the individuals and institutions involved and especially costly
to society as a whole.

Why Is Support Not Stronger?

Both on and off college campuses I have noticed an interesting phenomenon whenever I give a talk on affirmative action. Again and again
people remark with great surprise on the noninflammatory nature of
the policy. Like any standard administrative practice, affirmative action appears to be routine, uncontroversial. I agree with my audiences,
and I wonder how such a sensible policy has come to be so controversial.

It is a puzzle. Why does affirmative action not enjoy stronger
support in the United States? What is it about affirmative action that
so irritates some members of the intelligentsia and some leaders of
public opinion? If the policy is as good as it appears to some of us who
study it closely, why does it not look better to more people?

Maybe, as some political scientists claim, the leaders of public
opinion are really the followers of public opinion—astute readers of
the general mood of Americans giving voice to what Americans really
feel. If so, the question changes, but not very much. We are left to wonder why Americans display so much ambivalence over affirmative action.

Public support for affirmative action is uneven. In 1991 Louis
Harris found that 70 percent of those he polled favored affirmative action.[48] A poll conducted in 1995 asked, "Do you favor or oppose affirmative action?" More than half the Whites favored the policy while 36
percent opposed it.[49] Five years later, a survey conducted by Princeton
Survey Research Associates found less positive results. The Princeton
survey asked, "Thinking about future appointments to the Supreme
Court, please tell me whether you would like to see justices appointed
who would rule in favor of or against affirmative action?" Thirty-six
percent of the participants wanted to see justices who would rule in favor of affirmative action, and 56 percent wanted to see justices who
would rule against it.[50]

A year later 58 percent of Americans contacted by the Gallup Polls thought affirmative action had been good for the country, while 33 percent thought it had not. Asked in the same survey, "In general, do you think we need to increase, keep the same, or decrease affirmative action programs in this country?" 24 percent elected the first option, 34 percent thought the programs should stay the same, but 35 percent thought they should decrease. Fifty-six percent declared themselves in favor of "affirmative action programs for minorities and women for admission to colleges and universities," and 58 percent declared themselves in favor of "affirmative action programs for minorities and women for job hiring in the workplace."[51] Yet in 2003, at the time the Supreme Court was considering the Michigan University cases, a poll by *Newsweek* found that 68 percent of those questioned, including 56 percent of minority respondents, were opposed to preferences for Blacks.[52]

As for college students, the findings depend on how you ask the questions. Phrased one way, affirmative action garners their support; phrased other ways, it does not.[53] Fewer White students endorse affirmative action than do students of color.[54] One recent study, conducted at Cornell University, found that only 27 percent of the students supported affirmative action while 46 percent opposed it.[55]

The question of American ambivalence over affirmative action lies at the heart of this book. Why does the policy of affirmative action, which appears reasonable to many social scientists, attract so much negative comment? Why do Americans as a nation have so little shared acceptance of the necessity and the worth of affirmative action? Given the apparent value of the policy and its close fit to Americans' concern with social justice, why aren't the endorsement figures at 75 percent, 80 percent, or 85 percent? What accounts for the apparent disconnect?

The puzzle deepens when we realize that affirmative action is not really very different from many other government programs that operate to protect citizens and keep society functioning without major upheavals.[56] Consider transportation. Every state in the nation requires the operators of motor vehicles to obtain licenses. Licenses can be revoked if the citizen engages in actions that are likely to harm others, either individually or collectively. Anyone who finds the system too confining or philosophically aberrant has the option of not driving a motor vehicle; but no one has the (legal) option of driving without a license.

Less apparent, perhaps, to ordinary citizens—but no less confining—are the regulations imposed by the Food and Drug Administration. Food is essential to life, but it has not always been highly regulated. One hallmark of an industrialized nation is the standardization of food production and consumption. In the United States today a number of restrictive rules govern the production and distribution of food. The restrictions around food transportation operate more tightly than those of affirmative action, but they go all but unquestioned. Few national policies raise any outcry of public criticism for the ways they appear to sacrifice justice or personal liberty in the name of another value, such as diversity or safety.

Of course, people's reactions to regulations may be different when their lives are at stake than when the issues concern matters of justice without life-and-death implications. Yet when it comes to nonvital concerns like the regulation of telephone and radio communications or the governing of corporate affairs, important justice-related issues fail to arouse controversy. What is going on?

Is Practice the Problem?

Could it be that affirmative action is less fervently embraced than one might expect, given the American love of justice, because it has so often been put into practice in a negative way? There is evidence to show that the average person endorses the principles of affirmative action without necessarily endorsing the way it is implemented.[57] Perhaps Americans would like the policy if they had not had bad experiences with the programs.

To say that Americans would love affirmative action were it not for the misapplication of the policy seems implausible for a number of reasons. First, most opinion polls ask about affirmative action generally. The polls, in other words, are pulling for people's reactions to the policy overall, not asking about specific practices. Some respondents may use their specific experiences with various affirmative action programs (or with something that they interpret as an affirmative action program) as the basis for their attitude toward the general policy, but others may not. Many people I've met at public lectures have expressed well-formed opinions about affirmative action and then admitted that they have had no personal experiences with the policy. Similarly, many business people confess to having little firsthand experience with affirmative action but claim to base their reactions on what they think they heard about someone whom a friend once met.

Second, it is just as likely, maybe even more likely, that the causal arrow shoots in the opposite direction. People interpret what they "see" in light of what they think generally. A mountain of social psychological research and plain old common sense tells us that people's interpretations of events are generally guided by their preexisting opinions.[58] Those who endorse the concept of affirmative action may dismiss problems in its implementation as atypical and concentrate on its positive effects. Those who dislike the concept may attribute its positive consequences to other causes, such as the Civil Rights Act, the women's movement, the Equal Rights Movement, or a healthy economy. And they may assume that what they admit to be a well-intentioned policy is uniformly misapplied.

It also seems that when people do not fully endorse the concept of affirmative action they support it haphazardly and thus contribute to its ineffectiveness, but when they believe in affirmative action they produce positive results.[59] Rebecca Warner and Brent Steele conducted a study of the practices in 280 major American cities for hiring female police officers in the period from 1978 to 1987. Police chiefs who made it a top priority to hire women were able to find capable female officers, and they did so at a much greater rate than police chiefs for whom gender diversity was not a priority.[60] A more recent study conducted by the U.S. Merit Systems Protection Board in December 1994 illustrates the same point. The government-wide survey of federal supervisors and managers, stratified by grade level, occupational category, and race or national origin, investigated efforts to increase workforce diversity. Respondents were asked about their behaviors and their attitudes. Analysis of data from nearly 6,000 supervisors and managers targeted the recruitment of Hispanics, the only ethnic minority group that was still underrepresented in the federal system.[61] The analysis showed that both Hispanic and non-Hispanic supervisors who thought diversity contributed to the productivity of their workgroup were likely to recruit Hispanics, while supervisors who did not believe in diversity were not. Similar results were also found for the hiring of Blacks in six cities in Florida.[62]

An in-depth analysis of the building of the Atlanta airport from 1973 to 1980 provides insights into the ways in which interested parties can make an affirmative action program effective.[63] By 1970 Atlanta's population was more than 50 percent Black. Three years later Atlanta elected its first Black mayor, Maynard Jackson. Jackson was determined to include the African American community in the major construction project involving the city's airport. White politicians and business leaders opposed Jackson's plan, arguing that it was unrealistic to expect to find capable African American and minority contractors and workers. After a bitter struggle, in which the *Atlanta Constitution* accused Jackson of illegal and unfair behavior, Jackson appointed a well-trusted White administrator, George Berry, to the post of director of airport administration and development.

Berry informed the community that anyone who wished to bid on any aspect of the airport expansion would need to pre-qualify. Pre-qualification was a standard practice, and construction firms were accustomed to submitting papers on their capital accumulation, bonding status, and so on. But Berry further required construction firms operated by Whites to outline their plans for African American and minority partnering and employment as part of the pre-qualification process. No bids could be submitted without pre-qualification on all the required dimensions. Once bids were submitted, Berry selected the lowest bid for the proposed work. Through grit and ingenuity, Jackson and Berry were able to engineer an outstanding success. All phases of construction included substantial African American and minority involvement, and the $500 million project was completed within budget and on schedule.

Just as pro-diversity attitudes can be self-fulfilling, so can anti-diversity attitudes. An anecdote circulated throughout academia in the 1970s that a White male candidate for a job had received the following rejection letter: "I am sorry to report that although our department saw you as our top candidate, we will not be able to make you an offer for our new position. Our university is an affirmative action employer and the department must attempt to fill the new position with an individual from a recognized oppressed minority." The department in question eventually hired a candidate who was less well qualified than the rejected candidate. Was the person hired a White woman or a member of an ethnic minority? Not at all. Perhaps not surprisingly, he was a White male from the same graduate school as the chair.[64]

This anecdote illustrates both the fears of many who oppose affirmative action and the groundlessness of those fears. Those who are convinced of a paucity of talent among the targeted groups end up finding few qualified female candidates or few qualified candidates of color for their job openings. Those who believe the opposite have the opposite experience.

Any government program has aspects that some people question. And any government program can be misapplied. What is excellent in principle may be less than excellent in practice. But in many areas, misapplications of a policy do not occasion a reexamination of its fundamental value. The corrupt policeman who accepts a bribe to fix a speeding ticket may be chastised without calling into question the policies surrounding road safety. The venal food inspector may be reprimanded without strong public outcry to reverse the FDA's system of labeling beef. But any flawed affirmative action program appears to ignite a public outcry against the policy of affirmative action.[65] Why?

How Else Might We Understand Resistance?

Affirmative Action Is Dead; Long Live Affirmative Action examines possible causes for the less-than-perfect endorsement of affirmative action policy in the United States. Seen from certain angles, American ambivalence toward affirmative action is a puzzle. The point of my book is to probe the mystery. There are many factors that contribute to the relative unpopularity of the policy of affirmative action, and the central chapters of *Affirmative Action Is Dead* examine numerous social scientific studies to explore five explanations for why Americans grant only limited acceptance of the policy of affirmative action.

Standing back from the empirical studies, we also catch a glimpse of another, as yet untested, reason for American ambivalence about affirmative action. In Chapter 7, I move beyond the data of earlier chapters to offer a speculative explanation. I argue there that the controversy over affirmative action grows out of something uniquely American: an idealization of justice. I propose that as Americans we are emotionally invested in the concepts of merit and individual reward for merit. We long for simple justice and are upset with affirmative action for what it forces us to recognize about justice. One unpalatable conclusion has to do with the hypocrisy of using a merit-based reward system when the chances of demonstrating and developing merit are unevenly distributed among different groups. Equally disturbing is the revelation that even in a country far beyond the injuries of racial and sexual oppression, justice is neither easy nor simple. True justice is a messy and complicated affair.

If I am correct in my speculations, it is a matter of extraordinary importance for Americans to come to terms with the issues surrounding affirmative action. Not only do they need to rethink their attachment to notions of individual merit, they also need to hone their appreciation of the complexities of justice in a contemporary multicultural world. It is a psychological truism that one sign of maturity is the replacement of idealized views of the world with realistic views. That is why, ultimately, I believe that Americans will benefit from seeing affirmative action for what it is—a policy that is both imperfect and utterly reasonable and necessary.

Bridges

This book is not for those who want a quick rhetorical fix. Not only do I recount in explicit detail the conclusions reached in numerous academic studies; I also go into some depth about the methods by which scholars have reached those conclusions. In an area as contentious as affirmative action, it is often crucial to know what questions were posed to respondents or what materials presented to research subjects. How the questioner frames an issue has a substantial effect on respondents' reactions. So as we study the dynamics of the reactions, we need to know how the issues were framed.

Despite my scholarly concern with details of methodology—or perhaps because of it—I have tried to strip my prose of academic jargon. Without sacrificing accuracy or simplifying complications, I wish to open contentious and often misunderstood issues to the interested reader. It is my hope that this book may help the educated general reader, as well as the expert on or student of affirmative action, participate intelligently in a national discussion on an issue of continuing importance. Only with informed and civil debate can our democracy truly flourish. "Education," as the Supreme Court noted, "is the very foundation of good citizenship."[66]

2

Reverse Discrimination?

Why discriminate against someone to make up for the past? What's past is water under the bridge. Don't punish me for my grandparents' mistakes.

White student in an urban university

Thirty years of solid research in the social sciences confirm what two and a half centuries of observations have suggested: Americans love justice. Americans may or may not love justice more than other people on the planet; but they certainly are more devoted to fairness than any cynic would expect.[1]

Perhaps it would be more accurate to say that Americans love the *idea* of justice. Social psychologists have repeatedly shown that human beings have a strong motive to believe that ours is a just world, a world in which people are rewarded or punished according to their deeds. We wish to envision our world as one where fair and honest procedures dominate and where self-serving corruption enjoys no stronghold.

Of the major criticisms of affirmative action, perhaps the biggest of them all is that it is unfair. Many people see affirmative action as nothing more than reverse discrimination. Unjustified preferences and quotas are certainly unfair, and affirmative action may appear to many to be only a step away from these.

The criticism of affirmative action on the grounds of injustice has a ring of truth to it. How, after all, can it be fair to hire a woman in the place of a man with higher scores in the screening test? How can it be fair to admit a student of color to college while rejecting a White student when the former has lower SATs than the latter? Where is the justice in giving a Black applicant to law school a 234.5 times better chance of admission than a White applicant with the same LSAT scores and grades?[2] Does not affirmative action go against the American ideal of giving everyone an equal chance, which is considered the essence of fairness?[3]

Focusing their attention on issues of diversity, many of the major proponents of affirmative action in education have remained silent about the justice or fairness of affirmative action. Part of the reason that proponents have attended so closely to diversity is that the Supreme Court, in *Bakke,* declared that the state has a compelling interest to achieve diverse student bodies in its institutions of higher education.[4] But as educators trained their sights on arguments that were intended to pass constitutional muster, the average citizen may have been left with the impression that they were avoiding issues of fairness. Certainly, the landmark decisions in the Michigan cases, framed entirely in terms of diversity, have not dispelled the fear that many forms of affirmative action are willing to trade the rights of White individuals for the attainment of diversity.

Some commentators have suggested that affirmative action creates a set of micro-injustices, whereby a particular White person or a particular man pays a small price for the privileges of Whites or men in the past. Some scholars see the micro-injustices as necessary minor evils, rendered acceptable by the greater good affirmative action aims to accomplish.[5]

My argument takes a different form. Instead of picturing affirmative action as a trade-off between micro-injustices and macro-justice, my account focuses on the ways affirmative action can be seen as more fair to all individuals than equal opportunity. Close scrutiny reveals that the apparent trade-off between justice and diversity is not as simple as the critics of affirmative action contend. Whenever the issue of standards arises, it behooves us to ask, What are the purposes of having standards? Are they intended to acknowledge and reward past performance or are they intended to predict future performance? Either way, additional complexities arise because the methods used to set these standards may give readings on some but not all the relevant qualities. And the readings they render can be more or less accurate. Test bias poses huge headaches for those who construct the standards.

Current Concepts of Justice

Philosophers have concerned themselves with issues of fairness from ancient days. Aristotle had a lot to say about what makes a society fair or unfair. So did the Enlightenment philosophers—Voltaire, Rousseau, Diderot, and the like. Nor were the utilitarians, especially Jeremy Bentham, silent on the topic of fairness.

In contemporary philosophical discussions of fairness, one scholar towers above the rest: the late John Rawls of Harvard. For three decades, Rawls's massive, dense, and obscure text, *A Theory of Justice*, has dominated academic discussion.[6] No self-respecting book on the topic of justice can be published without the obligatory citation to Rawls. No scholarly article would be taken seriously without a reference to the master.

At the hub of Rawls's complex web of ideas and constructs lie a number of fairly simple propositions. The most basic precept is this: if you want individuals to devise fair rules of common governance, they need to construct those rules before they know their position in the society or organization. When people select rules while they are still behind the "veil of ignorance," they don't know whether the rules will benefit or harm them. But once people know what their social position will be, self-interest interferes with fairness.

Imagine that you and I are about to play a game and we need to decide how to distribute the winnings. I propose that players take a part of the prize in proportion to their score. You propose the rule "winner takes all." According to Rawls, the procedure of deciding allocations will be more fair if we engage in it before we start to play rather than after we know who has more points. Imagine further that there are three of us playing, and you have a score of 100, while your brother has a score of 50, and so do I. My distribution rule would give you half of the kitty; yours would give you all of it. Obviously, it would be difficult for us to decide what the distribution rule should be after the fact, because everyone would want to act in his or her self-interest.

Although Rawls's theory has come in for some pretty severe criticism for its failure to anticipate real-world considerations, it has obvious appeal.[7] (At least, it appeals to anyone who has ever played a game with a sibling or a rival.) All Monopoly players know that major trea-

tises could be written on the question of how to allocate the money in
Free Parking.

From his basic observation about the veil of ignorance, Rawls developed a proposition that all fair societies take care of their poor. It is
axiomatic, according to Rawls, that people will wish for a distribution
that supports the least well off because, in advance of play, it is only rational for us to recognize that we could be that least-well-off person. To
fail to provide a safety net for the poorest members of society thus goes
against our own self-interest—before the start of "play."

While Rawls and other philosophers are in the business of arguing, inductively or deductively, that one system is more fair than another, psychologists like myself content ourselves with documenting
people's feelings about fairness. Determining justice is beyond the
scope of the social scientist. In contrast, our job is to determine regu-
larities in people's perceptions of justice, judgments of justice, and justice-related behaviors.

By mapping people's conceptions of justice, social psychologists
and sociologists have observed a number of points of agreement. First,
people do care about justice. Some need more than others to believe
that they live in a just world; but most people, most of the time, like to
think of themselves, their families, and their friends as just or fair people. People will engage in a number of strange behaviors and think a
number of strange thoughts simply to preserve the delusion that the
world is a fair place and that they themselves are fair-minded people
interacting with other fair-minded people.[8]

Moreover, even though people may not have the vocabulary to
describe what they are doing, they seem to use certain common rules to
determine what constitutes fairness. Just as we all apply the rules of
grammar to our writing, we seem to apply rules of fairness to our actions. A linguist can listen to you talk and write down the grammatical
rules governing your speech; you may recognize them even if you are
unable to articulate them spontaneously. Similarly, social psychologists
can detect patterns in your judgments and behaviors, patterns that feel
familiar to you when you hear them listed but that you would not necessarily have been able to outline without prompting.

One well-known rule for psychologists is the equity rule. First
proposed in 1965 by an industrial psychologist, J. Stacy Adams, the eq-

uity rule has been the topic of intensive study by a number of psychologists, including especially Elaine Hatfield Walster.[9] In algebraic form, equity obtains when:

$$\frac{O_A}{I_A} = \frac{O_B}{I_B}$$

In the equation, O stands for outcomes, I for inputs, and A and B for people (person A/Person B). In other words, when the outcomes relative to the inputs of person A equal the outcomes relative to the inputs of person B, equity obtains. When the ratio of outcomes to inputs favors A, A may feel guilty and B angry or envious. Similarly, when the ratio of outcomes to inputs favors B, B may feel guilty while A is angry or envious.

A moment's reflection reveals how commonly we apply the equity formula to our everyday encounters and social exchanges. The student who writes what he knows to be a mediocre paper (input) unquestioningly accepts his grade of C (outcome). But when he learns that his roommate's equally undistinguished paper was awarded an A, he feels ripped off. A woman gives her all at a job (input) for a salary of $30,000 a year (outcome) and feels positive about her situation because she compares herself to her equally talented and hard-working sister who earns only $25,000 a year.

Arguments about equity often involve disputes over the appropriate values to assign to different inputs and outcomes. The student who complains, "But I worked hard on this paper," assumes that hard work is a relevant input in decisions about grades. The teacher who replies, "But I grade on results, not effort," disagrees.

The arguments can be expanded to include the question of reparations. Reparations are the outcomes in the equation; past harms suffered are the inputs. The greater the harms, the greater the reparations. How one calculates reparations to living individuals for harms done to their parents and grandparents can evolve into something quite contentious.[10] As much as Americans care about equitable outcomes, furthermore, they also care about an aspect of social transactions that is not captured by the equity formula: the manner in which the exchanges take place. Many surveys and experiments have shown that people want fair procedures, not just fair outcomes.[11] A good outcome achieved by improper or unjust means galls as much as a bad outcome.

Exactly what constitutes a fair procedure has not yet been well mapped out, but some of the elements of procedural fairness do seem to be commonly accepted. Impartiality is important. When an authority figure metes out punishments equally to all, not sparing her friends, she gains a reputation for fairness. When she doles out rewards without favor, she solidifies her position of authority. Consistency also matters. Changing the rules in the middle of the game provokes anger, especially among those whose outcomes are diminished by the change.[12] Allowing people to express their opinions also enhances perceptions of procedural fairness, even when the opinions are expressed after a decision has been made.[13]

Disputants in an ideological battle may sometimes underestimate their opponent's attachment to justice. We see ourselves as just. We know our opponent disagrees with our opinions, so we conclude that the opponent, the other side, must be unjust. We are the champions of fairness; our opponent is the scoundrel who stomps on fairness through selfishness or blind prejudice.

In the intellectual mud-slinging over affirmative action, each side has pointed out what it sees as the shortcomings of the other side. Opponents of affirmative action have sometimes seen its proponents as Machiavellian political actors, ready to sacrifice justice in some ill-conceived quest for diversity. Proponents, meanwhile, have sometimes been quick to dismiss critics of the policy as disingenuous in their references to just procedures, especially in view of the link between prejudice and opposition to affirmative action.

As a proponent of affirmative action, I believe that one possible conclusion we can draw from the literature on prejudice and reactions to affirmative action is that resistance is sometimes linked to sexism and racism. But I do not believe that there is any evidence to support the assertion that opponents of affirmative action care less about justice than proponents do. People oppose (or support) the concept of affirmative action for a number of reasons and with a number of motives. Just because some opponents are disingenuous does not mean all are. Even racists and sexists, furthermore, may genuinely appeal to concepts of fairness as they oppose the policy.

Arguments Against Affirmative Action

A number of public figures who oppose affirmative action claim, in essence, that affirmative action violates the equity rule. Ward Connerly is a Black businessman whose land-use consulting firm in Sacramento, California, proved wildly successful and who then parlayed his business success into political clout. Connerly captured the public ear by portraying affirmative action as unfair. As one of the Regents of the University of California, and the organizing genius of the fight to pass California's anti–affirmative action Proposition 209, Connerly has commanded national attention. As he wrote in 1995: "Most of us want to think of ourselves as fair-minded people. We want an equitable and inclusive society. We want to stamp out racial and gender discrimination. We want to expand opportunities and we want those opportunities to be equally accessible to all. Affirmative action has become a major detour in our journey to a fair and equitable society. We need to give affirmative action, as a system of preferences, a decent burial, and the digging should start at the University of California."[14] "I won't be defined as an affirmative action businessman," Connerly further declared; "I want to be judged by the quality of my work."[15] With contracts and opportunities as outcomes, Connerly wants the inputs to be assessed without regard to ethnicity or race.

Nor is Ward Connerly alone in his anti–affirmative action fight. The powerful and well-funded Center for Individual Rights (CIR) has argued that it is unfair to admit minority applicants to universities when majority applicants with better test scores are denied admission. A hard-driving organization, CIR has underwritten the costs of several legal challenges to university admissions policies. They were instrumental in the *Hopwood* case, which forced the University of Texas to change its admissions policies, and they were also a major force in the Michigan cases, which they characterize on their Web site as "the Alamo of affirmative action."[16]

Public Critics in and out of Academia

Some social scientists have echoed the critiques proposed by Connerly and the CIR. Two influential psychologists, for example, wrote in a professional journal: "Civil rights legislation is supposed to be color blind and not color favoring, that is, favoring one race, African Americans, at the cost of another race, the majoritarian White. . . . It is repugnant in the view of many to achieve nondiscriminatory benefits and a level playing field for one race by unjustly discriminating against another race."[17]

Similar sentiments have been voiced by the philosopher Lou Marinoff. Marinoff blasts affirmative action because, in his view, it "sets implicit or explicit biological quotas, and thereby asserts that it is just preferentially to employ certain people (e.g., females of color) on the basis of criteria irrelevant to the position (i.e., skin pigment and sex chromosomes) and preferentially to exclude certain other people (e.g., white males) from employment on the basis of criteria irrelevant to the position (i.e., skin pigment and sex chromosomes)."[18] Translated into the language of the equity formula, the politicians, psychologists, and philosophers are arguing that there is an imbalance in the relative ratios of outcomes and inputs. The imbalance derives from the inclusion of inappropriate inputs, like color and gender.

The temptation exists to cast as a relevant input all indignities and abuses that people of color have suffered at the hands of Whites, past and present. Shelby Steele recounts an anecdote about a young Black man who was going to college. In anticipation of his departure, his mother counseled him, "They owe us this, so don't think for a minute that you don't belong there."[19] The problem with the mother's logic, says Steele, is that "Blacks cannot be repaid for the injustices done to the race, but we can be corrupted by society's guilty gestures of repayment."[20] Thus, while reparations may appear at first glance to be just, they actually violate the equity rule. Past sufferings, say the critics of affirmative action, are what the pro–affirmative action people focus on, but past sufferings are not permissible inputs. A Black person who thinks she deserves to be admitted to college because her grandparents or great grandparents suffered is no better than the student who thinks he deserves to get an A because he owns the books for the course.

Affirmative action appears to violate more than just the equity rule of distributive fairness. It also seems to fly in the face of fair procedures, the hallmark of American democracy. Confusing affirmative action with quotas, Paul Roberts and Lawrence Stratton write: "Considering the headway that equality of results has made in undermining equality before the law, the pervasiveness of quotas, and the lack of understanding of their origin and implications, the fight to reclaim law from privilege has barely begun. Ultimately, either quotas will go or democracy will, because legal privileges based on status are incompatible with democracy's requirement of equal standing before the law."[21]

Procedural justice dictates that similarly situated people should receive similar treatment. When some people are treated one way and others another, procedural justice is breached. How can it be fair to have one set of rules for women and another for men? How can it be fair to have one procedure for people of color and another for White people? Just because life used to function that way doesn't mean that it is the right way. What happens to impartiality? To consistency?

The apparent trade-off between equality in results and equality of treatment puts into stark contrast the difference between distributive and procedural justice. In the words of Charles Canady, Representative from Florida, who introduced into the U.S. House of Representatives an anti–affirmative action bill in 1995: "Is American equality about guaranteeing equality of results? Is equality only meaningful if, at the end of the day, all Americans are equal not merely in right, but in fact? Or does equality consist primarily of the equal application of the laws, such that each citizen has an equal opportunity to advance, regardless of racial or gender considerations?"[22]

Not only does affirmative action apparently call for people of color to be treated differently from White people, it also calls for people of color to be treated one way in some situations and another in other situations. Edward Blum and Marc Levin, writing for the conservative *Washington Times,* enlarge on the theme of inconsistency:

> The critics of racial profiling by police officers are correct in their analysis: using race as a proxy for criminality is wrong. It offends the very meaning and purpose of the Constitution and an entire body of civil rights law. Skin color and ethnicity are meaningless qualities within the American judicial system. Equal protection under the law is built on colorblind principles.
>
> It is baffling, however, that so many of the critics of po-

lice racial profiling encourage schools and universities to engage in the very same racial stereotyping when it involves admissions and curriculum.

Apparently, the civil rights groups decrying police profiling by race believe that it is "bad" stereotyping, but when universities profile applicants by race, that is "good" stereotyping. Well, they can't have it both ways. Either skin color tells us something about how a person should be treated in society or it doesn't.[23]

Nor is affirmative action consistent, according to its critics, in how it approaches the issue of skin color and disadvantage. At one time Asian Americans were considered a targeted group; now Asian Americans often suffer because of their phenomenal academic and professional successes, successes achieved through hard work and dedication. Many consider that it is harder for an Asian American student with excellent grades and high test scores to gain admission to elite universities than it is for a member of any other group.[24] The skin tone of Asian Americans has not changed, but their affirmative action status has. Meanwhile, many—but not all—recent immigrants benefit from affirmative action policies as soon as they obtain U.S. citizenship. Writers like Steven Holmes have pointed out the inconsistencies of helping recent arrivals "who came to the United States voluntarily and may or may not have suffered from discrimination" through "a policy meant to help the descendants of slaves who were forcibly brought here."[25] And where is the logic in helping some dark-toned people (African Americans) and not others (Arabs and many other Middle Easterners)? Why are some "grievance groups" afforded special privileges while others need to conform to rules and regulations that limit their options? Is it procedurally fair to bestow "sovereignty," that is "the power to act autonomously," on some but not all?[26] Surely not!

White men who suffer reduced chances for selection appear to be the direct victims of attempts to achieve diversity. But, say the critics of affirmative action, they are not the only victims. Also unfairly disadvantaged is the general public. This point has been made by Linda Gottfredson in her scathing critique of the examination put in place by Nassau County, New York, to select police personnel. The test, according to Gottfredson, has been stripped of any cognitive content and otherwise manipulated in an attempt to eliminate disparate impact. Those who will ultimately pay for the ill-advised attempt to level the playing field are the citizens of Nassau County, for it is they who will lack a competent police force.[27]

Two prominent critics of affirmative action sum up their opposition to the policy with reference to a variant of the equity formula. Say Frederick Lynch, author of *Invisible Victims,* and William Beer, professor of sociology at Brooklyn College, "Treating people differently because of their race, origin, or gender violates what Harvard's George Homans termed the law of distributive justice. According to this principle, people feel that their rewards should be proportional to their 'investments'—educational level, grades, test scores, seniority, experience, and other measurable qualities. If others with less training, ability, or education are granted equal or superior rewards, frustration and anger are the likely outcomes."[28]

Does the Person on the Street Think the Same as the Public Critic?

What about the average American? Do average American citizens, be they students or workers, think that affirmative action entails reverse discrimination? Or do the data reveal a gap between the opinions of the public intellectuals and the opinions of the person on the street, in the factory, and in the classroom?

The data are mixed. Opponents of affirmative action like Lynch and Beer report what seems to be widespread disgust with the unfairness of affirmative action. The numbers of disgruntled men and disgruntled White people reported by the proponents of affirmative action seem much less impressive. Probably the most cautious conclusion is that some people, whether prominent opponents or average citizens, are adamant in their condemnation of affirmative action as a violation of justice principles, while many suspect, without total conviction, that unfairness plays a part in most affirmative action plans. People's assumptions about reverse discrimination are more pronounced when the questions deal with generalities than when they get down to specific cases.

Consider a study conducted by Myrtle Bell and her associates. They asked two samples of respondents—sixty-five students in a class on organizational behavior and sixty-four randomly selected managers—to answer three questions anonymously. The first question asked respondents to list the disadvantages of affirmative action programs, the second asked them to list advantages. The third asked simply, "What else comes to your mind when you think about affirmative action programs?" Bell and her colleagues sorted the 479 phrases produced by respondents into 13 categories. The most frequent disadvantage, mentioned by almost 1 in 5 respondents, was "causes employers to hire less qualified employees and reject more qualified employees."[29] Opponents of affirmative action might stress the finding that the most common spontaneous association people made to the term "affirmative action" was with reverse discrimination; but proponents might note that less than 20 percent of respondents characterized affirmative action in such a way.

Several studies have focused on general attitudes and assumptions about how college admissions and the labor market work. A comprehensive study of the attitudes of Americans using a probability sample in 1980 found that 73 percent of White respondents thought Blacks had opportunities at least equal to those of Whites, and 53 percent thought Blacks benefited from reverse discrimination. The two beliefs, furthermore, were strongly related. Whites who saw Blacks as free of discrimination understood social and economic programs like affirmative action as a form of unfair preference.[30]

The passage of time has changed the pattern only slightly. More than a third of the White people in a media poll in 1997 thought that reverse discrimination was a greater national problem than discrimination.[31] Similar anti–affirmative action sentiments also surfaced in recent qualitative studies on university campuses. Typical is this statement by a White person at a large urban university: "I don't think that special treatment of minorities or giving them preference is any answer . . . [to past discrimination]. Just because someone is a woman or black or whatever doesn't mean they should get an advantage. That is reverse discrimination, and is just as bad as discrimination."[32]

The same thinking is evident in this statement by a White student at another large university, the University of Michigan: "I'm all for helping whoever needs help, but I don't think it should be based on a history of oppression. I know a lot of bad things happened in history to minority groups, but . . . my generation did not inflict any of this on to your generation. . . . I really believe that [college admission] should be based on meritocracy . . . on who's more qualified."[33]

Moving from generalities to specifics, the figures change dramatically. Only 10 percent of White males polled in a telephone survey in 1984 claimed to have personally experienced reverse discrimination.[34] National probability samples drawn from the 1970s to 1995 show that between 5 and 12 percent of Whites think they have lost a job or a promotion because of race. (Meanwhile, 33 percent of African Americans think the same.)[35] Only 3 percent of Whites surveyed in Los Angeles claimed to have ever experienced ethnic discrimination in pay or promotions.[36]

Judicial statistics also show that fears about reverse discrimination may be grossly exaggerated.[37] Although White men are not shy about suing on the grounds of discrimination, bringing 80 percent of the age discrimination suits, they are unlikely to file reverse discrimination charges.[38] Five percent of discrimination cases heard in the circuit courts of the federal judiciary system between 1965 and 1985 involved reverse discrimination.[39] Four percent of discrimination complaints filed with the Equal Employment Opportunity Commission between 1987 and 1994 charged reverse discrimination.[40] Two percent of cases heard in federal district and circuit courts between 1990 and 1994 claimed reverse discrimination.[41]

Similarly, a government study has found that few contractors felt pressured to impose quotas or enact other forms of reverse discrimination. In 1994 the Employment Standards Administration surveyed 641 federal contractors about their experiences with the Office of Federal Contract Compliance Programs (OFCCP). Two percent thought the regulations were enforced in such a way as to create reverse discrimination. That leaves 98 percent who did not.[42]

The gap between reality and rhetoric has been interpreted in different ways by different scholars. In the pattern of data, supporters of affirmative action like John Dovidio and Samuel Gaertner see proof of the existence of covert racism. Given an opportunity to show disrespect for Black people without having to confess to it, the racist White person gives vent to generalized statements about reverse discrimination. Detractors of affirmative action, meanwhile, perceive in the same pattern of data evidence of the way reasonable White people are forced to muzzle their fully justified resentments unless they have a shield of anonymity.

Going Deeper

Persuasive as it may at first sound, the rhetoric of people like Shelby Steele and Ward Connerly is flawed. Two main problems interfere with their argument that affirmative action is unfair. The first is misrepresentation. The critics often misrepresent the reasons for affirmative action, and they mischaracterize its operation. Second, the critics' treatment of justice issues is superficial and incomplete.[43]

Affirmative action does not consider gender and race or ethnicity because of *past* wrongs. It examines gender and race or ethnicity because of *present* wrongs. The present wrongs may or may not be produced by present prejudices. Structural imbalances produce problems that are probably far more numerous at many levels of society than the problems produced by mere racism or sexism. The structural imbalances may have been produced by prejudices in former years. Yet they are real, and they create injustice.[44]

How do structural imbalances operate? A homely but true example may illustrate the issue. For years I have taken graduate students or advanced undergraduates with me to professional conferences. There can be career advantages for students who have the opportunity to follow new developments and make personal contact with experts in their field. In order not to bankrupt the students or myself, I usually share my conference accommodations with them. Because I am worried about appearances, I virtually never invite a male student to share my room. Much as I want to help the careers of my male students, I do not want to risk being brought up on sexual harassment charges. You may note nothing very radical here; everything sounds reasonable.

But take this reasonable-sounding practice and consider the consequences for a male student if virtually all the faculty are female. Similarly, females become excluded from important networks of information and trust when all senior staff are male and when off-site arrangements call for employees to share accommodations. The exclusion does not come about because evil men are sitting around dreaming up ways to undermine the career progress of women. The exclusion occurs because good men may be too busy to think through the gender-asymmetric consequences of neutral-sounding practices.

When a monitoring system like affirmative action is in place, someone becomes responsible for determining whether males and females advance in their careers as rapidly as they ought, given their qualifications. If females are found to advance more slowly than similarly qualified men, someone has to think about the reasons why. People search for the mechanisms that hold women back. Innocent-seeming practices that have a disparate impact on males and females can be modified or eliminated.

To rephrase the process in terms of procedural justice, the issue is whether operating procedures that appear to treat everyone equally do in fact treat everyone the same. Cast in terms of distributive justice, the issue is whether men have obtained outcomes (a chance to talk personally with the boss, for example) that may have been denied women with equal inputs. Unless someone is monitoring the situation, imbalances may be hard to detect.

Nor do all the imbalances relate to gender issues. In ethnic or racial terms, people of color can—and do—face hurdles not faced by equally qualified Whites. Dark skin in the United States invites more problems than a light skin does in many areas of life—social, educational, and economic.

Some of the current problems are the direct result of past prejudices. For example, the anti-Black bias of White bankers and the racist covenants in White neighborhoods thirty or forty years ago meant that many responsible Blacks were unable to purchase and retain their own home. Blacks were less able to build up equity than Whites. Black parents have therefore had less to loan or otherwise transfer to their children and grandchildren. And therefore, when banks today impartially follow federal guidelines about loans, many more Blacks than Whites fail to qualify for a mortgage.[45] The seemingly neutral operating practices of today perpetuate racial or ethnic asymmetries that arose because of prejudice in the past, even despite the absence of current prejudice. Such is the nature of structural racism.

In view of previous discrimination, the question arises about the fairest way to determine who ought to receive such benefits as bank loans. Currently, accumulated capital is one of the relevant inputs that goes into the formula. But perhaps the raw amount of capital is not as impartial an input as would be the rate of capital accumulation. In other words, perhaps it's not how many dollars you have saved but how much you save each month that ought to determine loans. Banks should not be in the business of rewarding past economic behavior (especially when the market unfairly favored some to the detriment of others). Rather, banks should use the past only as a predictor of future economic behavior.

One could cast the dilemma in terms of the equity formula. Assume that a local bank makes a lot of mortgage loans. Let's assume further that the bank is under obligation to make the loans fairly. Accept the proposition that fairness means being fair to the community and not just watching out for the bank's or its stockholders' narrow interests. So now let's imagine that two applicants come to the bank, each wishing to buy a home costing $200,000. The homes both pass the appraisal test. One of the applicants has $20,000 (given by her parents) for a down payment and wishes to borrow $180,000. The other has only $14,000 and needs $186,000. Both have good incomes that will allow them to meet the mortgage payments. Would it be unfair of the bank to bend its requirement of a 10 percent down payment for the second applicant and give mortgages to both, especially if the bank knew that its own discriminatory lending practices had contributed to the lack of capital accumulation in the family of the second applicant? If we take a rigid, narrow approach to the definition of mortgage inputs as "10 percent of the house value," any bending of the rules is unfair. But if the rules themselves seem unfair, modification may be the only way to attain justice.

Similarly, the hypothetical example can be analyzed in terms of procedural fairness. We can agree that a fair procedure is one that treats everyone the same. But what does it mean to treat everyone the same? Is similar treatment achieved by mechanically imposing a 10 percent rule on all applicants? Or is similar treatment achieved by asking whether the applicants have demonstrated that they are capable of making their mortgage payments and repaying the loan? If one adopts the narrow definition of similarity, then background factors are irrelevant and should not be considered. If one adopts a more expansive definition of "similar treatment," on the other hand, then it is appropriate to consider background characteristics, especially as they shed light on a person's motivation and ability to pay the mortgage.

If my mortgage example seems far-fetched, consider another kind of capital that is transmitted across the generations—human capital. Increasingly, education is the ticket to an economically comfortable life in America.[46] Prejudice has given some Americans much less access to education than others. My white skin has been a definite advantage to me.[47] The white skin of my parents has also brought me, not just them, benefits. When I was a girl we lived in the town of Manhasset, New York, which had three elementary schools for its three sections: Plandome, Munsey Park, and the Valley. Because we were White, my parents were able to buy a home in the area served by Munsey Park Elementary School.[48] Had we been Black, we surely could not have lived in any section of Manhasset in the 1950s other than the Valley. Less town money went to the Valley school than to the two other elementary schools, with the effect that virtually no Black students placed in any honors courses in high school and only a portion of the Black students took the college-bound curriculum, although virtually all the White students did. In hindsight, I feel that many of the Black students had more drive to succeed than the Whites. Given a chance to make up for lost preparation, they could have achieved as much or more than I and my White classmates.

In the equity formula, college admission could be the outcome and "academic qualifications" the input. But what is the best way to gauge academic qualifications? Should motivation to overcome obstacles be considered? Does the B average of a pampered White girl denote the same drive to succeed as the B average of a Black girl who overcame the handicap of having gone to Valley Elementary School? Probably not.

What if a student has been incorrectly promoted to an accelerated class or incorrectly relegated to a slower track? Should the student be expected to pay the price for mistakes made by the teachers or the guidance counselor? And what are we to do when inquiry reveals that not one or two isolated students but an entire cohort of students with brown skin has been incorrectly assigned or poorly counseled?

As Donald Stewart of the College Board points out, the question is not simply rhetorical. Indeed, a study of schools in California revealed that Latino and Black students were twice as likely as Whites to be incorrectly assigned to low-track classes and were much less likely than Whites to have well-informed guidance counselors. From the start of elementary school through the final years of high school dark skin led to "a harsh sorting, not done on the basis of academic merit."[49]

And who determines how much each criterion should count? In the late 1990s three researchers at Texas A&M University reviewed the records of 439 people who had applied to the College of Medicine at Texas A&M in 1996.[50] They looked at two factors that determined admission: a composite measure of previous academic success and a measure of such personal qualities as communication skills, motivation, intellectual capacity, and social service orientation that was derived during the interview. The researchers then calculated who would have been admitted and who would have been rejected using three different algorithms. Different algorithms produced different lists of acceptances. In the absence of research showing how much success in medical school and after depends on early academic achievement and how much depends on personal qualities, how can we know which algorithm to use?[51]

Medicine is not the only area where uncertainties arise. Most law schools accredited by the Law School Admissions Council base admission on two factors: scores on the law school admissions test (LSAT) and undergraduate grade-point average (UGPA). Typically the LSAT counts 60 percent and the UGPA 40 percent in determining a composite score for admission to law school. These percentages are used despite the studies showing that women, on average, score substantially higher than men on UGPA and slightly worse than men on the LSAT. If UGPA counted 60 percent and LSAT 40 percent, instead of the other way around, significantly more women would be admitted to law school.[52] Indeed, for a change to occur, all that is required is for UGPA to count 50 percent.

Arguments in Favor of Affirmative Action

Once problems are detected, solutions can be found. Affirmative action promotes the effective detection of problems through the regular and systematic review of information. Affirmative action also encourages effective solutions.

Sometimes the solutions are less than perfectly fair while still being more fair than so-called "equal opportunity." Another example plucked from my academic life may illustrate the point.[53] Years ago the chairman of the psychology department at a major research university took his responsibility to help increase minority representation among graduate students seriously. Like any good scholar, he began his attack on the problem by conducting a little study. In the course of his study, the chairman—let's call him Professor B—focused on the consequences of a standard practice which, up to that point, had escaped notice. Specifically, he noticed that the department's method of screening applicants put those who came from unrenowned schools at a disadvantage.

Because of its overwhelming number of applicants, the department had instituted a procedure that appeared to be impartial and efficient and that also allowed each of its subareas (clinical psychology, developmental psychology, and the like) the proper measure of autonomy. In the first phase of screening, each faculty member was assigned a large number of dossiers without regard to subarea. The faculty were instructed to sort the dossiers into three piles: very likely to succeed, very unlikely to succeed, and uncertain. The dossiers were shuffled and reshuffled so that each dossier was independently rated by three faculty members. In the second phase, the dossiers were sent to the subarea, whose faculty then selected predetermined numbers of applicants. For most of the areas, the number of applicants who had received three "very likely to succeed" votes far exceeded the number of slots, so that applicants with even one "uncertain" rating were never discussed. All this seemed procedurally fair and equitable until Professor B noticed that some faculty members had the habit of giving a rating of "uncertain" to applicants who came from small colleges or had letters of recommendation from little-known scholars. It also turned out that a great proportion of the applicants of color were from small schools and that few had advisers who were known to the faculty at the research institution.

Professor B devised a plan. He appointed a faculty member to take all the dossiers of minority applicants that had received one or more rating of "uncertain" and one or more rating of "very likely to succeed." The faculty member then contacted as many of the references as she could so she could form her own judgment of the qualifications of the applicants. She then submitted the top one or two applicants of color in each area to the area for consideration along with the other top applicants.

In a perfectly fair world, with infinite resources, the faculty member would have contacted all the references of all applicants, no matter what their ethnic or racial background. But the resources were far from infinite. So a compromise was implemented. The result was an increase in the number of graduate students of color in the department with no loss in quality. If one sees the telephone calls as special treatment, the compromise may appear unfair. But if one sees that the original screening procedure had built-in biases that operated to the detriment of minority students, one would have to conclude the extra effort was not special treatment but rather an equalizing of the treatment.

Note that the short-gap compromise measure instituted by Professor B was a remedial plan. Professor B was attempting, with success, to compensate for deficiencies in the existing system. Perhaps the plan might have been misinterpreted as one that adjusted for deficiencies in people rather than one that adjusted for deficiencies in the operating system. In an attempt to minimize the chances for misinterpretation, the chairman and his helper made sure that the grade-point averages and test scores of the applicants of color were no lower than those of the White applicants. Extra effort had been expended to locate students of color equal in measured abilities to the White students, but no change in standards could be alleged.

Acceptable Moves

Many, but not all, affirmative action plans operate in a fashion similar to the one I've just described. Plans like these involve only differential expenditures of time, effort, or money with no adjustment of test scores or other "objective" indicators of a candidate's qualifications. Recruiters visit all the schools likely to produce qualified applicants of color but only a fraction of the schools likely to produce qualified White applicants. Qualified applicants of color are offered all-expense-paid trips to graduate schools and businesses while qualified White applicants are invited to pay their own way.[54] Qualified applicants of color at private schools (though not state schools) are offered fellowships and scholarships that are more lucrative or involve less labor than the fellowships and scholarships offered to White students.[55] Special affinity groups are granted seed monies or other forms of support not available to clusters of White men. Special mentoring programs are established for women and for men of color.[56]

Unlike "reserved" scholarships or fellowships, affirmative action programs that simply involve extra efforts rarely generate dissent. Indeed, when organizations go out of their way to be inclusive, praise is often heaped on them and on their members who make the special efforts. Outreach is likely to garner awards, not condemnation. Special mentoring programs make for good publicity, not controversy.

One reason special efforts gain praise denied to other forms of affirmative action is that they do not call into question the status quo. Professor B was not questioning the usefulness of grades and test scores when he instituted the measures to make sure that no talented applicant of color had been overlooked. His program necessitated no questioning of the underlying belief in merit or in the means that were used to judge it. Professor B improved upon the system; he did not seek to overturn it.

Much more hullabaloo accompanies affirmative action programs that entail a change in, or even a questioning of, the standards by which merit is judged.[57] If we are really attached to the idea of merit—and Americans certainly are—we need a way of measuring it. The concept without the instrumentation is ineffectual, while serious questions about instrumentation challenge the concept.

In particular, any attempt to make adjustments for test scores is likely to provoke a great deal of resistance. For a police department to hire a female applicant with a mediocre score on a test of physical endurance while turning away a man with an excellent score smacks of reverse discrimination. Reverse discrimination or preferential treatment appropriately elicits strong condemnation.

But what happens when someone discovers that the test itself operates in a sexist or racist way and is irrelevant to the job at hand? What if the test of physical endurance is really a test of lung capacity and not an accurate test of how long the applicant can sustain physical work at a certain level? To show that selected female applicants do less well than rejected males on a certain test is not to show reverse discrimination if the test has nothing to do with the qualities needed for the job or if it is biased.

Issues of fairness in testing have reached the Supreme Court, which decided in 1971 the case of *Griggs v. Duke Power Company.* Duke Power Company was using a written test as a hiring tool for nonmenial jobs, and many fewer Black applicants than White passed it. The company was unable to demonstrate that the test measured qualities necessary for the jobs in question. Without a demonstrated business reason for the tests, they were declared unconstitutional.[58] The *Griggs* ruling allowed many other cases to be brought. The New York Fire Department, for example, underwent extensive changes when it was discovered (through legal confrontations) that many of the tests it used were unrelated to the job of fighting fires while other qualities, needed for a cohesive fire-fighting team, went unassessed.[59] In the parlance of equity theory, the existing tests failed to measure some of the appropriate inputs while measuring other, unrelated inputs.

Tests and Their Purposes

People in the United States spend billions of dollars each year on tests. Testing is big business. One of the best-known and largest testing organizations is the Educational Testing Service (ETS), which serves industries and agencies in close to 200 countries. In fact, ETS develops and annually administers more than 12 million tests worldwide. Through a partnership with the computer-based testing service Thompson Prometric, ETS provides computerized testing to individuals, schools, colleges, and businesses. Although ETS is a nonprofit agency, Prometric earned revenues of $7.2 billion in 2001. Prometric delivers more than 6 million standardized tests per year for more than 200 clients, in more than 25 languages in over 140 countries.[60]

Despite the ubiquitous nature of testing in America—or perhaps because of it!—until recently few public discussions displayed the same cynicism toward the testing industry as they did toward the policy of affirmative action. Among the general, nonexpert public, standardized tests have been reified. Large debates, for example, arise over the reasons for racial differences in standardized test scores with little reflection devoted to either the philosophy or the mechanics of testing.

The public inattention to the philosophy and mechanics of testing does not stem from an equal lack of debate among scholars, however. In part as a reaction against the practice of race norming, the National Academy of Science conducted a review of more than seven hundred studies that used the General Aptitude Test Battery (GATB), which had been a standard in both industry and the government for screening job applicants.[61] In 1998 the Brookings Institution published an important compendium of articles on testing edited by Christopher Jencks and Meredith Phillips.[62] Two years later the scholarly journal *Psychology, Public Policy, and Law* devoted an entire issue to the question of testing and educational policy.[63] Similarly, the flagship journal of the American Psychological Association, *The American Psychologist*, regularly carries articles describing the ways tests are created and utilized.[64] Yet with few exceptions, the knowledge of the researchers remains out of the hands of the general public.

How can one bridge the information gap?

A good place to start any inquiry is to ask what tests are for. Two broad purposes can be discerned. Tests can reward past behavior or mark a historical moment. They can also be used as predictors of future behavior.

History-marking tests are common. A wrestling match, for example, might be held to determine the best wrestler or a chess match to determine the world chess champion. An exit exam could be held in a school and the student with the highest score proclaimed the best student. A race is run, and someone goes down in the books as the winner.

History-marking tests help build a sense of community. They foster civic pride. They temporarily divide people into opponents, but they unite everyone who agrees to abide by the rules of the tests. In the Olympic Games, for example, fierce national rivalries exist, but ideally global unification also comes because all the nations agree to conform to the regulations of the games.

When the rules and regulations are violated, the sense of community is threatened. An obviously biased judgment by an Olympic judge provokes an outcry worldwide, not just from the nation that loses the gold medal. Every fan calls for impartial judgments from the referees, and even fans of the winners feel disgusted if they learn that a referee "handed the game" to their team. When a contestant in a history-marking match is unfairly judged, either through mechanical failure of the tools of assessment (the stopwatch broke; the scoring grid was misaligned) or through foul play, remediation and compensation appear to be the fairest course of action.

The second general purpose of tests is to predict the future. The choirmaster wants to build a harmonious choir, so she holds auditions. The military wants to know who has the potential to lead the troops, so it administers entrance exams. When a corporation wants to know who will make a good computer analyst, it does not just ask applicants about courses taken but rather sets them to solving problems of logic and computer challenges. A college wants to see who will be able to carry a heavy workload, and it looks at the scores obtained on a series of different tests.

Predictive tests allow people to make predictions about how much an individual person or an individual team will achieve or accomplish. They also allow predictions about how much an individual person or an individual team will contribute to the well-being and success of the greater entity. The distinction is rooted in whether one looks to the individual or to the greater entity.

The functions of tests can best be explained in baseball terms. Like most sports, baseball is filled with tests. The World Series, for example, determines whether the American League team or the National League team emerges as the champion in any given year. The games of the World Series make up a history-marking test. Quite different in function are tryouts for a team. Regardless of whether an athlete has been identified by a scout and asked to try out, the athletes who go to spring training tryouts are subjected to a set of tests intended to predict their future performance. A man who throws a variety of pitches at 100 miles per hour with great accuracy is likely to be a first-rate pitcher during the playing season. Although any aspirant player is probably most interested in making a name for himself, the team owners are more interested in the contributions the players can make to the overall success of the team than in each player's individual achievements. A player with a fabulous batting average on a losing team is of less interest to the team owner than a player with a decent batting average who helps the team win.

As with baseball, so with life. Consider public education. An individual student is likely to experience acceptance to or rejection from the university of her dreams as a history-marking event. Acceptance makes her feel that she has been rewarded or recognized for her accomplishments. Rejection makes her feel that her accomplishments have not been great enough. But the university sees the matter differently. The university is, in essence, betting on the future.[65] It looks at past behavior not because it seeks to reward or punish the applicant but as a clue to the future. The university, furthermore, accepts those students it believes are likely to contribute to the education of all students, including themselves. An incredibly brilliant paranoid schizophrenic who refuses to take medication may be a bad bet for the school. He may accomplish a lot while putting other students in harm's way. An outstanding violinist with mediocre high school grades, on the other hand, may be welcomed at the university for the contribution that he will make to the cultural education of his classmates.

In business, too, organizations can use tests to estimate the skills of applicants and then decide to employ applicants with complementary sets of skills. A corporation cannot hire only accountants or only lawyers if it needs both accountants and lawyers. It is fair to hire people who have the talent needed, not simply to hire people because they are talented.

Sometimes women and people of color are invited to attend a school or hired to work in an organization because the school or the organization realizes that the women or the people of color can make a contribution, even though a White man may score higher than they did on tests of specific attributes. The contributions have to do with differential experiences in society, not with differences in any essential characteristics. Like the boy in the fable of the Emperor's New Clothes, a person who has been on the fringes can bring a valuable perspective to any organization for she or he is likely to question the Emperor's outfit in a way that a longtime insider might not.

Tests and Their Biases

The mechanics of testing are as vital to any consideration of fairness as are its purposes. Here again the detailed discussions among experts are rarely echoed in the more public discussions.[66] What most people know is that in America Blacks score significantly worse than Whites on standardized tests of cognitive functioning. But they do not know how to interpret the difference in scores. To make matters worse, books like *The Bell Curve* (which claims to show that racial differences in scores on intelligence tests derive from genetic differences between Whites and Blacks) purport to bring highly scientific materials to bear on social issues, but are often quite selective in what they include and what they leave out. Despite all its statistically heavy material, for example, *The Bell Curve* made the embarrassing mistake of confusing within-group variation and between-group variation. Many psychology and sociology textbooks have by now pointed out the mistake (and other mistakes) to introductory students, but the general public may have been left with the impression that Harvard professor Richard Herrnstein and his co-author Charles Murray were making a credible argument.[67]

Tests are made by human beings and so are theoretically subject to the biases and logical lapses of human beings. When researchers find—as they consistently do—differences in the average test scores of different ethnic groups, the challenge is to determine whether the differences represent differences in groups or are a function of test bias.[68] Denying the possibility of bias is as silly as denying the possibility of true differences.

One way psychometricians assess test bias is by looking at the reliability of a test. "Reliability" refers to whether the test is consistent. One type of reliability is "test-retest reliability," which essentially means that the test produces the same reading over time. If a person scores extremely well on an intelligence test on Monday but looks like a cretin in the same test on Tuesday, the test lacks reliability. Another common form of reliability is "split-half reliability." When split-half reliability is high, the score that results from marking the even-numbered questions closely approximates the score that results from the odd numbers. Still another way to calculate reliability is to see whether a person's array of scores on any one item is similar to the array of scores on other items. But looking at the relative lineup of scores, statisticians calculate what is known as an alpha-coefficient. Alpha-coefficients that are too low indicate low reliability.

If a test is reliable for Whites but not reliable for others, one can infer test bias. Similarly, if the reliabilities for Whites are very different from the reliabilities for others, test bias is the likely explanation. An early and extremely influential review of test bias was conducted by Arthur Jensen.[69] Jensen concentrated on racial differences in intelligence (I.Q.) tests and found that the tests were generally reliable, and equally reliable for majority and minority samples. Subsequent to Jensen's examination, Valencia and Suzuki also conducted a comprehensive review of cultural bias in testing. Like Jensen, they concluded that in terms of reliability, the evidence speaks against strong biases in intelligence tests.[70] Similarly, the National Teacher Examination, the SAT, the ACT (American College Test), and the GRE (Graduate Record Exam) all appear to be relatively free of threats to reliability.[71]

Validity differs from reliability. A reliable test may not necessarily be a valid test. Reliable tests are simply consistent tests. Valid tests are tests that measure what they claim to measure.

Robert Sternberg, one of the nation's foremost experts on intelligence and president of the American Psychological Association, points out that validity is always dependent on cultural values, for our cultural values determine our conceptual definitions.[72] In contemporary America musical ability is not considered a component of intelligence. Nor is athletic ability. Yet in some other cultures, those who are capable of manipulating sounds and those who can remember complicated action sequences are thought to be as intelligent as the people who can manipulate mathematical symbols and the people who can remember long sequences of syllables.

In other ways, too, validity can be compromised by culture. Researchers distinguish among many different types of validity, but two have traditionally been of central importance in discussions of group differences: predictive validity and discriminant validity. A test that has good predictive validity is, as the name implies, a test that enables accurate and fairly precise predictions. Discriminant validity is high when a researcher can demonstrate that the test measures one attribute and not another.

According to most, but not all, contemporary experts few cognitive tests have an anti-minority bias in predictive validity. Tests of knowledge, reasoning, and other forms of thinking predict the job and school outcomes of Blacks with the same degree of accuracy, according to most experts, as they do for Whites. The ethnic gap in scores, furthermore, occurs even when time limits are relaxed and when Blacks receive coaching.[73]

For a number of years, liberals assumed that standardized tests penalized ethnic minority students by underestimating their grades. In fact, recent analyses show the opposite. Looking at the records of 10,558 students who entered eleven selective universities and colleges in 1989, Fredrick Vars and William Bowen found that the SATs overpredicted grades for Blacks relative to Whites.[74] Thus the average Black student with a combined score of, say, 1100 on the SATs earned lower grades in college than the average White student with the same scores.

What about discriminant validity? Issues of discriminant validity are central to the attacks on tests that claim to measure "aptitude." Often what is touted as a test of innate intelligence or cognitive ability turns out to be indistinguishable from a test of exposure to specific knowledge. Says Mark Cohen:

> The overt biases of earlier tests astound us now. In an era before widespread radio and television, for example, illiterate rural Americans and brand-new immigrants were asked to identify baseball players—as a measure of inherent intelligence, not cultural knowledge. Poor people were asked to complete unfinished drawings of a tennis court (where a few, at best, might have served as ballboys). Immigrants to the United States were asked to identify attractive faces; the "correct" answer was a northern European ideal, while some other options looked much more like many of the immigrants themselves. These questions were administered seriously by professional testers of intelligence.[75]

Even today for many tests it is impossible to discriminate between "intelligence" and social class. Most studies of ethnic or racial differences in test performance do not take social class into account. When social class is considered, according to some experts, "the mean difference in intellectual performance between Whites and minorities is reduced and in some cases is negligible."[76]

Selective System Bias

Let us assume for the moment that most tests of cognitive and other abilities are reliable and valid, for both majority and minority applicants. Does that mean that no bias exists? Some say yes and therefore condemn affirmative action for the way it appears to disregard merit.

But others disagree. Their dissent derives from the empirical observation, disputed by none, that even reliable and valid tests may explain very little of the variation in later performance.

In most jobs, many different factors contribute to performance. "Street smarts," charm, judgment, drive for success, and other personality factors determine much more than does simple cognitive ability. Even with a valid measure of cognitive ability, we cannot perfectly predict job performance. Studies show that valid tests like the GATB account for only about 15 percent of the variations in supervisors' ratings of workers.[77]

In college, too, the quality of students' work depends on many factors other than sheer brain power. Students with good study habits perform better than students with poor study habits. Students with good social skills achieve more than students with poor social skills. How much any one factor influences a student's grades remains something of a mystery. What is well known, on the other hand, is that SAT scores have predictive value only for the first year of college, and even then the value is slight.[78]

The relatively small amount of predictive power that can be wrung from cognitive and other tests allows for the possibility of another type of bias: selective system bias. "Selective system bias [arises] whenever the standardized racial gap in job performance is smaller than the standardized racial gap in test performance."[79] If people of color do much less well than Whites on an entrance exam but only a little less well than Whites in the job or at school, it would be unfair to use the test as the main screening tool for the job or the school. People who could do the work would be unjustly disqualified.[80] In the words of Jencks and Phillips, our reliance on standardized tests "forces blacks to pay for the fact that social scientists have unusually good measures of a trait on which blacks are unusually disadvantaged."[81]

Several elaborate and carefully conducted studies—including a major national study of the test scores of teenagers and their educational attainment fifteen years later—have shown that Blacks and Whites differ much more in their cognitive test scores than in their educational attainments. Similarly, Blacks who score much lower than Whites on standardized tests of ability perform only slightly worse than Whites on the job.[82]

When the opponents of affirmative action see it as unfair to select a person of color for an educational or employment opportunity instead of a White who has scored better on a standardized test, they are implying that the test is fair. But biases in the selection system make the test unfair. Psychologists James Amirkhan and his colleagues put it well when they noted: "A moral and political tension exists in contemporary America between the ideal of meritocracy, wherein achievement is based on individual effort, and the reality of societal injustice, wherein whole groups of individuals have been denied an equal opportunity to pursue the meritocratic ideal."[83]

Bridges

Treat same the same. Such is the essence of procedural justice. Reward people in proportion to their contributions. So goes the golden rule of distributive justice's equity formula. How, then, can the typical affirmative action program be fair when it enjoins an organization to hire the third-ranked candidate over the first-ranked simply because the third-ranked is a woman and the first-ranked is a man? How can a program be fair when it encourages a school to admit applicants of color with lower scores than White applicants? These questions fan the flames of many debates about affirmative action.

At first glance it may appear that the only logical answer to the question is, no fair program could enjoin an organization to hire the third-ranked candidate in place of the first or to admit those with lower scores in place of those with higher. The apparently inescapable conclusion is that affirmative action is unfair. And that perception of unfairness accounts for why so many people are ambivalent about or downright opposed to affirmative action.

Upon reflection, however, we see that the apparently logical answer makes some very illogical assumptions. It assumes highly predictive measures of merit. It assumes that those who develop the tests and measures, as well as those who implement them, are fair and unbiased.

Marc Bendick, Jr., an economist who has served as a consultant to industry and government, recounts a true story that illustrates how dangerous it is to assume that all measures of merit operate in an unbiased fashion. The story concerns a "company [that] promoted forklift drivers from among warehouse laborers who were 'qualified,' meaning they had forklift experience. . . . But the qualifications could be acquired with only a single day's experience, usually gained at the company itself by filling in when a regular driver was absent." Interestingly, although the company employed many Blacks in the warehouse, only Whites were promoted to forklift driver because only they were given the fill-in jobs.[84]

Biased rankings or biased screening tests undermine the whole proposition of fairness. Given our inability to predict with much certainty who will succeed and who will fail, it behooves us not to rely too much on any predictive measure on which groups of people are known to score differently from other groups. Years of scientific effort have led to the creation of highly reliable cognitive tests that are equally reliable for majority and minority test takers and for women and men. There are now also tests that are relatively free of ethnic or gender bias in their predictive validity. But even if a test could be a perfect index of the quality being measured, it should not function as the only gateway to an opportunity unless the qualities tested are the *only* qualities needed for success.

The truth is that we have yet to develop accurate and sensitive measures that account for success in school and on the job. Given the multitude of factors that determine success, the goal seems remote. In the meantime, the fact that different groups have differential success rates on our selection tests poses a major dilemma in terms of fairness.

Considering the problems of quantifying merit, some commentators and researchers have examined the White claims of injustice with a jaundiced eye. As the eminent jurist Derrick Bell claims, "As presently administered, the scores on standardized tests more accurately measure the economic status of the test takers than they measure their potential for success in school or on the job."[85]

Could it be that the claims of injustice are just a cover for prejudice?[86] In an email message to me, the industrial psychologist Myrtle Bell questioned how a concern with merit plays out for "sons and daughters who got into Yale because of privileges they didn't earn from ancestors who weren't slaves but were slaveholders." Is there, wondered Bell, more "'merit' in being the heirs of slaveholders rather than of slaves?"

Myrtle Bell is an expert on affirmative action. Her studies are among those cited here and elsewhere. She has thought long and deeply about the issues involved. She knows how the policy operates. Perhaps the problem for those who waver in their support of affirmative action is not some prejudiced or self-interested interpretation of justice. Perhaps they, unlike Myrtle Bell, do not really understand how affirmative action works. How much does misinformation account for opposition to affirmative action? It is to that question that I now turn.

3

Semantics Versus Substance

Every policy is contested in a symbolic arena. Advocates of one or another persuasion attempt to give their own meaning to the issue and to events that may affect its outcome.

W. A. Gamson and A. Modigliani, "The Changing
Culture of Affirmative Action"

In the 1980s the media hardly mentioned affirmative action, and the number of books on the topic could be counted on two hands. Some people had strong opinions, to be sure. But generally the term "affirmative action" produced more indifference than interest in the media.

Now everything has changed.

Several factors contributed to the increased media attention. One major impetus was President Bill Clinton's comprehensive review of affirmative action. From the voluminous, detailed report delivered to him on July 19, 1995, by George Stephanopoulos and Christopher Edley, Jr., Clinton popularized the issue with a highly quotable soundbite: "Mend it, don't end it."[1] The same month University of California Regent Ward Connerly, with the backing of Governor Pete Wilson, persuaded the other regents to ban consideration of race, ethnicity, or gender for applicants to the university. In December 1995 Connerly assumed the chairmanship of the California Civil Rights Initiative, and within a year California voters had approved Proposition 209 by a margin of 54.6 percent to 45.4 percent. Although it made no mention of affirmative action, and although 27 percent of those who voted for Proposition 209 wished to support affirmative action, the proposition was widely touted as an anti–affirmative action law.[2] The law added section 31 to Article I of the California constitution, stating, among other provisions, "The state shall not discriminate against, or grant preferential treatment to, any individual or group on the basis of race, sex, color, ethnicity, or national origin in the operation of public employment, public education, or public contracting."[3] On November 3, 1998, the voters of the state of Washington passed their version of the law, Initiative Measure 200 (I-200).

Several prominent court cases have also kept affirmative action on the front pages. On March 18, 1996, in the *Hopwood* case, the Fifth Circuit Court decided that the University of Texas had violated the U.S. Constitution in allowing race to be used as a factor in admissions. After almost four years in court, on May 29, 2001, the Ninth Circuit Court ruled that the University of Washington Law School's race-sensitive admissions program did not violate the Constitution. (Owing to the passage of I-200, however, the university could not continue using its program.) The Eleventh Circuit Court ruled on August 27, 2001, that the University of Georgia's admissions policy was unconstitutional. The Eleventh Circuit had no problem with the use of race as a criterion but thought the university's program was not narrowly tailored enough to pass constitutional muster.

Perhaps most famous of all the cases are the two recent suits brought against the University of Michigan. In October 1997, Jennifer Gratz and Patrick Hamacher filed their class-action suit against the university, claiming that the College of Literature, Science, and the Arts (LSA) had violated the Equal Protection Clause of the Fourteenth Amendment and Title VII of the Civil Rights Act when it awarded 20 bonus points to applicants of color. In December 1997, Barbara Grutter began a similar action against the university when she sued the law school on virtually identical grounds.[4]

Although the plaintiff's claims in *Gratz v. Bollinger* and in *Grutter v. Bollinger* were similar, opposite judgments in the two cases were rendered at the district level. In December 2000, federal judge Patrick Duggan ruled that while the admissions policy in place from 1995 to 1998 was unconstitutional, LSA's current policy did pass constitutional muster. He reasoned that the state had a compelling interest in obtaining a diversified undergraduate student body, that the admissions policy was in fact narrowly tailored to suit the need, and that the university was not under obligation to consider a race-neutral alternative to the system they used. Four months later, Judge Friedman, in the same district as Judge Duggan, ruled that Michigan's law school had violated the constitutional and the statutory rights of Barbara Grutter. Diversity, according to Friedman, was not a compelling state interest, and even if it were, the law school's admissions program was not narrowly tailored enough to be considered constitutional.

The two Michigan decisions were both appealed. In an unusual move, the full panel of judges for the Sixth Circuit Court considered arguments about both cases at the same time. The Sixth Circuit Court heard oral arguments on December 6, 2001. Constrained by legal precedent, the court reversed the district court decision in the *Grutter* case, stating that the university followed guidelines for the consideration of race in admissions set forth by Justice Powell in the *Bakke* case. The Sixth Circuit gave no decision in the *Gratz* case. In December 2002, the Supreme Court announced that it would hear both *Grutter v. Bollinger* and *Gratz v. Bollinger.* More than sixty amicus briefs were filed on the side of the university, and two dozen were filed on the side of the plaintiffs. On April 1, 2003, with demonstrators ranged outside, the Court heard oral arguments. Internet services provided avid spectators with live streaming of the sessions. The *New York Times* took orders for transcripts. Three months later the Court handed down its decisions. National newspapers flooded their pages with coverage, and television and radio joined the media blitz.

The media have not been the only ones to shower attention on affirmative action. Since the 1990s, affirmative action has also become an increasingly fashionable topic for research. During those years there has been a significant increase in the attention given to affirmative action by academic writers. Among the many books to appear on the topic were several especially influential ones. In 1990 Shelby Steele in his beautifully written *The Content of Our Character* argued that affirmative action was the product of White guilt and simply helped erode the self-respect of Black students. The next year Stephen L. Carter, a professor at Yale University Law School, attested to the very sentiments described by Steele in his widely acclaimed *Reflections of an Affirmative Action Baby.* Strong anti–affirmative action arguments were put forward by Stephan and Abigail Thernstrom in their massive study of race relations, *America in Black and White,* published in 1997.[5]

On the pro–affirmative action side appeared the moving and provocative *Alchemy of Race and Rights* by Patricia Williams, and other scholarly books by Barbara Bergmann, Christopher Edley, and Barbara Reskin. Equally influential was the authoritative study of race-sensitive admissions policies presented by William Bowen and Derek Bok in their 1998 *The Shape of the River.* Also important was the nonpartisan study of culture and politics written by John David Skrentny, *The Ironies of Affirmative Action.*[6]

Meanwhile, a staggering number of articles have appeared in scholarly journals in the different social sciences. The articles primarily include data gathered in systematic studies on the need for affirmative action, the effects of affirmative action, and the opinions of Americans toward the term "affirmative action" and toward aspects of the policy. When I stacked the scholarly articles on my desk, they reached more than three feet high.

How Knowledgeable Are People?

A reasonable person might think that all the attention recently devoted to affirmative action would mean that most Americans are now knowledgeable about the issues. Since only a hermit could have escaped the barrage of media coverage, it seems logical to expect the average citizen to be confident about his or her understanding of the term and to speak knowingly about what affirmative action is and how it operates.

But expectations and reality diverge. A substantial proportion of the people I've encountered at events focusing on affirmative action have only a vague idea of what the policy entails. Unless they are human resources professionals, many people admit to being confused about the specifics of affirmative action in both education and employment. The confusion exists even among highly educated and motivated individuals—including those so motivated to learn about affirmative action that they have come to attend a lecture on the topic.

Readers may object that I must travel in particularly uninformed circles. Perhaps the people who already know something about affirmative action are not the ones coming to the lectures and the rallies. Maybe when I ask people how much they know about affirmative action they are being cagey or modest. Perhaps—but I think the problem goes deeper, and other experts agree with my assessment.

A Simple Test

Fred Pincus of the University of Maryland has developed a test that gives an objective measure of how knowledgeable people are about affirmative action. When I administer this test to students, professors, and other professional workers, the results indicate a need for remedial education on the subject, with some audiences averaging nine or even eight correct answers. With Professor Pincus's permission, I reproduce the test here. An A goes to anyone who correctly answers at least fourteen of the fifteen questions. Thirteen or twelve correct answers would earn a B. Readers may be sobered by their own poor performance.[7]

Test of Affirmative Action Knowledge

Questions 1 through 5 pertain to federal affirmative action guidelines that are administered by The Office of Federal Contract Compliance Programs (OFCCP) of the U.S. Department of Labor.

1. Who is legally required to have a written affirmative action plan?
   a. All employers with at least 25 employees
   b. All federal contractors, regardless of size
   c. Federal non-construction contractors with 50 or more employees and $50,000 or more in contracts
   d. Federal construction contractors with 100 or more employees and $100,000 or more in federal contracts

2. Affirmative action plans must include "goals and timetables." This means that by a specific date, employers who are covered by affirmative action guidelines and whose labor force falls below a specified percentage of women and/or minorities must
   a. actually hire a certain number of minorities and women, whether they are qualified or not;
   b. actually hire a certain number of minorities and women, but only if they are qualified;
   c. try to hire a certain number of women and minorities, whether they are qualified or not;
   d. try to hire a certain number of women and minorities, but only if they are qualified.

3. After formulating their affirmative action plans, employers are required to
   a. submit them to the OFCCP for approval;

b. keep them on file in their own offices and be ready to submit them to OFCCP if they are requested;

c. have a majority of their women and minority employees approve the plan;

d. All of the above.

4. The OFCCP conducts "compliance reviews" where they investigate employers whom they believe may be violating affirmative action guidelines. In any given year, what percentage of employers covered by affirmative action guidelines undergo compliance reviews?

a. Less than 5%

b. 11%

c. 24%

d. More than 50%

5. Employers who violate affirmative action guidelines and fail to take corrective action can lose their existing federal contracts and be declared ineligible to receive others. This is known as being "debarred." Between 1972 and 1995, how many employers have been debarred?

a. 0

b. 39

c. 197

d. More than 1,000

Questions 6 through 8 are based on federal law and U.S. Supreme Court decisions as of January 1, 1996.

6. Which of the following policies may any employer legally use for hiring and promotion decisions without first getting the approval of a federal court?

a. Decide to hire or promote a black or hispanic for a particular position even though a white is clearly better qualified

b. Decide to hire or promote a woman for a particular position even though a man is clearly better qualified

c. Use race or gender as one of many factors in considering hiring and promotion

d. All of the above are legal

7. In order to attract more black and hispanic students, any college or professional school may legally:

a. offer special minority scholarships that whites could not apply for;

b. set aside or reserve a certain number of seats for black and hispanic students;

c. require the admissions office to visit all predominantly black high schools in a 50 mile radius to talk about the college;

d. None of the above are legal.

8. According to the U.S. Supreme Court, under what conditions can a lower fed-

eral court require an employer to hire and/or promote a certain number of qualified women and minority group members?
a. The proportion of minorities and women employees is lower than the proportion of minorities and women in the United States.
b. The judge suspects that the employer has discriminated in the past.
c. Either a or b would be sufficient.
d. None of the above would be sufficient.

Questions 9 through 11 are based on the results of national public opinion polls that were administered in 1995.

9. National public opinion polls of white Americans in 1995 show that:
   a. more than 90% are opposed to affirmative action;
   b. they have different feelings about different kinds of affirmative action policies;
   c. they are surprisingly supportive of affirmative action;
   d. None of the above.

10. National public opinion polls show that black Americans:
    a. generally support affirmative action;
    b. are neutral toward affirmative action;
    c. are opposed to affirmative action.

11. National public opinion polls show that women have:
    a. more positive attitudes toward affirmative action than men;
    b. the same attitudes toward affirmative action as men;
    c. more negative attitudes toward affirmative action than men.

12. One hears a lot of discussion these days about reverse discrimination against white males because of affirmative action. Recent income data for college graduates who are year-round full-time workers show that white males earn:
    a. about the same as white females;
    b. slightly less than black males;
    c. more than black females;
    d. All of the above.

13. Two studies of law suits by white males, which allege reverse discrimination, show that these suits:
    a. are becoming almost as common as discrimination suits brought by minorities and women;
    b. are less likely to be successful than suits brought by minorities and women;
    c. are more likely to involve charges of race discrimination than sex discrimination;
    d. All of the above.

14. In considering whether or not to admit students, elite universities like Harvard, Yale, and Princeton:
    a. consider only measures of academic skills such as grades, class rank, Scholastic Assessment Test (SAT) scores and teacher recommendations;
    b. give special preference to the children of parents who graduated from that university;
    c. have never discriminated against blacks, Jews, or Asians;
    d. None of the above.

15. After 15 years of affirmative action, blacks received _____% of the medical degrees and _____% of the law degrees during the 1992–93 academic year.
    a. 5.8 and 5.7;
    b. 9.8 and 10.5;
    c. 19.2 and 21.7;
    d. 30.2 and 28.3.

Answers:
1. c; 2. d; 3. b; 4. a; 5. b; 6. c; 7. c; 8. d; 9. b; 10. a; 11. a; 12. c; 13. b; 14. b; 15. a.

Do Systematic Surveys Reveal the Same Level of Ignorance?

What about surveys of large groups of citizens? How do they perform? As it happens, despite the flood of research on attitudes toward affirmative action, few researchers have attempted to assess general knowledge of the subject. A protracted search by two of my students and me yielded only a handful of formal surveys, some rather old.

In the fall of 1975 and the spring of 1976, Audrey Noble and Richard Winett conducted a case study of the operation of affirmative action at the University of Kentucky.[8] They sent a survey to all department chairs—about a hundred people in all—and to everyone who first assumed an academic position at the university in the fall of 1974 or later. Both questionnaires contained an item concerning penalties for the failure to reach affirmative action goals. Among the new hires, one in five people thought that a department could be penalized if it failed to meet its affirmative action goal. Clearly, 20 percent of those hired misunderstood how affirmative action operates, for, as we saw in Chapter 1, organizations can be penalized for their failure to follow the proper procedures, but they cannot be sanctioned for an inability to meet goals. Among the department chairs, most of whom had been responsible for hiring new members in their departments, the percentages were similar: four out of five department chairs knew the correct answer, but one in five did not.

Around the time that Noble and Winett were collecting their data, researchers on the West Coast were interviewing midlevel managers in a city that had recently developed an affirmative action plan. Before the research all managers had been invited to a training session on affirmative action, but only a third had accepted the invitation. The level of understanding among the managers was fairly dismal. One manager even confused affirmative action with a new sewer plan for the city.[9]

Ten years later, managers in the same city were interviewed again about affirmative action. By 1983 the city had instituted a program whereby advancement to the level of supervisor required attending a course on affirmative action. As a result, reported the researcher, "the managers had become much more sophisticated."[10] Nonetheless, at least 20 percent of those interviewed admitted to being unfamiliar with how affirmative action worked. Had they, perhaps, been sleeping during the mandatory instruction sessions?

The next case study of people's understanding of affirmative action occurred in the late 1980s. In 1988, a little before affirmative action became a burning public issue, Smith College became an affirmative action employer. Although faculty at the elite women's college had long been recipients of federal grants, no one at the school had obtained a federal contract before the late 1980s. Then a professor in one of the natural sciences became the subcontractor on a project concerning acid rain, and in order for the professor to accept his subcontract, Smith College had to become an affirmative action employer. Some controversy erupted on campus—enough that the alumnae magazine carried an article about affirmative action.

With the cooperation and assistance of the administration at Smith College, my students and I undertook a small study.[11] After identifying four constituencies at the school—students, staff, faculty, and administrators—we carefully obtained representative samples of each constituency and arranged to conduct interviews with sixty-two individuals. The interviews (each of which lasted about a half an hour) were tape-recorded and transcribed.

The survey examined self-rated knowledge as well as more objectively rated knowledge. The second question on the interview schedule read, "Would you say that you know a lot or a little about what affirmative action is and how it operates?" The respondent assigned herself or himself a number ranging from 0 (*I know very little*) to 10 (*I know very much*). A set of additional open-ended questions allowed us to gauge each respondent's knowledge for ourselves. One item asked the respondent to "imagine that a friend from out of town learned that the college has become an affirmative action institution and asked you: What is affirmative action? Based on the information you have gathered, what would you say?" Another item asked, "What, if anything, is the difference between being an equal opportunity employer and being an affirmative action employer?" From the open-ended questions, a highly trained rater, conversant with the workings of affirmative action, graded each respondent on a 7-point scale ranging from −3 (totally misinformed) to +3 (totally well informed).[12]

We found a lamentable lack of knowledge among the students and staff. While the faculty and administrators were significantly better informed, they too had at best a rudimentary understanding of the policy. According to our ratings of the transcripts, support staff obtained an average score of −1.1, and students obtained an average of −0.2. Meanwhile, administrators scored 0.5, and faculty scored 1.1. Our ratings were generally consistent with the participants' self-ratings.[13] On a 0 to 10 scale, staff placed their expertise at 2.8; students at 3.6; administrators at 4.7; and faculty at 5.8. That means that even the best-informed group gave themselves less than a passing grade in terms of their knowledge of affirmative action.

Several years later, David Kravitz and Judith Platania carried out what may have been the first comprehensive study of people's beliefs about affirmative action.[14] Their sample included about 350 students, aged 15 to 75, attending Florida International University (FIU), an ethnically diverse college in Miami. Kravitz and Platania asked the students to evaluate twenty-four potential components of affirmative action plans and estimate the likelihood that such components formed a part of affirmative action. The components included various forms of proportional hiring, preferential treatment, and additional efforts in the form of extra recruitment or extra training.

The students in Kravitz and Platania's sample displayed a poor understanding of affirmative action. Quotas—which were and are illegal—were judged to be quite likely components. At the same time, most of the respondents thought it unlikely that affirmative action was required of organizations with government contracts, which, as we have seen, is the heart of classical affirmative action policy.

In a very different setting, another study also found strong evidence of a common misunderstanding about affirmative action. In 1993 my associates and I entered questions on an omnibus telephone survey of a randomly selected sample of adults living in and around the greater Chicago metropolitan area.[15] Only 14 percent of those contacted refused to participate in the study. Our final sample included 631 women and 422 men.

One question was of special interest. It read, "There is a lot of talk about affirmative action today, but not many people define it. Using a scale from 0 to 10, where 0 means you know very little and 10 means you know a lot, how would you rate how much you know about what affirmative action is and how it operates?" Approximately 8 percent of the sample rated themselves a 10, but 18.6 percent gave themselves a 0. All told, only about 42 percent of the respondents fell above the midpoint on the scale of self-rated knowledge.

Once again, objective indicators paralleled subjective ones. Another question asked the participants which of two definitions matched their own definition of affirmative action. The question went on, "The first definition is: Affirmative action occurs when an organization monitors itself to make sure that it employs and promotes qualified minorities and White women in proportion to their numbers. The second definition is: Affirmative action occurs when the government forces organizations to meet quotas for minorities and White women." Fewer than 12 percent of the respondents said "neither of the above"; 40.4 percent saw affirmative action as a quota system; and 48 percent saw it as a monitoring system. In other words, fewer than half the respondents selected the correct definition from the choices offered.

As most of us know, it is harder to generate correct answers than simply to recognize them. If only half the Chicago residents could choose the correct definition when presented with choices, what would result from a harder test of knowledge? Answers to a poll conducted by CBS and the *New York Times* in April 1995 showed the general lack of knowledge in the United States. More than a third of all the White participants in the poll (and 55 percent of those without a high school diploma) could not come up with a word or phrase in response to the term "affirmative action."[16]

Nor had matters improved a lot by 1997. Between March and June of that year—a year in which voters narrowly defeated an anti–affirmative action initiative—the residents of Houston were polled by telephone. The telephone interviewers asked the ninety-eight English-speaking participants who agreed to be in the study about the likelihood of six different measures being included in the "typical" affirmative action program. The six measures were:

- giving information to the government about the company's work force
- making extra efforts to get members of targeted groups to apply for positions
- setting aside jobs for target group members
- providing extra training for target group members
- taking actions to eliminate discrimination against target group members
- hiring less-qualified target group members in the place of more-qualified other workers.

The respondents thought set-asides and preferential hiring were as likely to be included as any of the other measures. On a scale from 1 ("very unlikely") to 4 ("very likely"), the Houston citizens gave an average rating of 2.8 to both preferential hiring and the elimination of discrimination, and a 2.9 to set-asides.[17] No wonder ballot Proposition A was defeated by only a narrow margin.

Around the same time that David Kravitz and his colleagues were assessing knowledge about affirmative action among Texans, Kimberly Jacob Arriola and Elizabeth Cole were surveying students at Northeastern University in Boston.[18] Jacob Arriola and Cole found that 38 percent of their sample of 176 White undergraduates were unable to define affirmative action or were misinformed about what the policy entailed. Interestingly, the Northeastern study was conducted at a time when an affirmative action case in which a White student challenged the race-sensitive policies at Boston Latin School was dominating the news in Boston. Apparently controversy did not translate into knowledge.

The current familiarity with the philosophy and mechanics of affirmative action is shockingly low in the United States. The average citizen does not know what affirmative action is or how it operates. College students seem no more or less educated on the topic than other citizens. Even those in charge of decisions about affirmative action—supervisors, college administrators, and high ranking officials—may be fuzzy about the policy.

What Do Americans Think of Preferences?

The confusion of affirmative action with unjustified preferential treatment or with quotas would not be a problem were it not for the fact that many Americans, particularly White Americans, strongly dislike quotas and preferential treatment. If you were running a popularity contest, quotas and preferential treatment would win the booby prize—at least in the United States.[19]

What Do College Students Think?

Much of the research documenting our relative dislike of preferential treatment, like the study conducted by Kravitz and Platania in 1993 that we have already encountered, has been carried out on college campuses. Kravitz and Platania not only asked respondents to estimate the likelihood of twenty-four potential aspects being part of affirmative action; they also instructed participants to evaluate each aspect. Most popular among the students was "elimination of organizational barriers that limit women, minorities, and the handicapped." Out of a possible maximum endorsement score of 5, this procedure earned an average score of 4.2. The students also rallied around other procedures, each with average scores above 4:

- disregard status
- set up training programs for women, minorities, and the handicapped

- do your best to have qualified women, minorities, and handicapped people apply
  - make sure potential applicants know about positions
  - refuse to consider demographic status unless the applicant is qualified.

Least popular, in order of the strength of the dislike, were:

- requiring an organization to hire unqualified women, minorities or handicapped people
- giving preferential treatment to women, minorities, and the handicapped
- requiring demographic status to be considered in employment decisions
- deciding in favor of a woman, minority, or handicapped person over an equally qualified man, nonminority, or nonhandicapped person
- hiring women, minorities, and handicapped people in proportion to their representation in the applicant pool
- using quotas.[20]

Kravitz confirmed his survey findings in a study that used an experimental methodology.[21] Instead of asking all participants to rate different aspects of affirmative action programs and quotas, Kravitz systematically varied what the participants learned about affirmative action and then studied their reactions.

The first page of the instructions informed participants that decisions about hiring are regulated by the federal government. The text went on to say that as a consequence of the Civil Rights Act, after a history of discrimination against Blacks in the United States many organizations had instituted affirmative action plans. The opening materials explained that the investigator was "studying people's reactions to affirmative action" and stressed, "There are no right or wrong answers; the only 'right' answer is an accurate statement of your beliefs."[22] Following a series of questions about the effects and value of affirmative action, whether true opportunity exists for all, and opinions concerning Blacks, Kravitz divided the sample into eight groups of roughly the same size. Each group was asked to evaluate one specific type of affirmative action:

- affirmative action as the elimination of information about the applicants' race
- affirmative action as the elimination of racial discrimination
- affirmative action as the special recruitment of Black applicants
- affirmative action through special training programs for Black applicants
- affirmative action as assurance that the proportion of Blacks hired equals the proportion of qualified Black applicants
- affirmative action as the assurance that the quota of Blacks hired equals the proportion of qualified Black applicants
- affirmative action as the hiring of a Black applicant over a White applicant when the two have identical qualifications
- affirmative action as the hiring of a Black applicant over a White applicant when the White applicant has slightly better qualifications.

Some of the participants in Kravitz's experiment expressed a marked dislike of affirmative action. Which ones? Those who had been randomly assigned to learn about affirmative action plans that involved the hiring of a Black applicant rather than an equally or slightly better qualified White applicant. Although all Blacks were dropped from the sample, Kravitz included a large proportion of Hispanic students. Both White and Hispanic respondents rated preferential procedures unfair and a threat to their own interests and the interests of people like themselves. When the plan was described as striving for a quota of qualified Black applicants proportional to the applicant pool, participants were neutral in their evaluations. For all other plans, the participants expressed positive attitudes.

Kravitz's study revealed more than a dislike of quotas. It also showed how easily people's opinions are influenced. No doubt the pliable nature of people's attitudes has come as a by-product and remains as an indicator of the general public's relative lack of knowledge about affirmative action.

Nor is Kravitz the only investigator to document such malleability. Indeed, among some populations, the mere mention of the phrase "reverse discrimination" appears to produce a devaluation of affirmative action. Myrtle Bell and colleagues conducted an experiment, masquerading as a survey, in which 367 students and 367 employed adults were randomly assigned to one of three conditions. All the participants completed a so-called survey about affirmative action. For a third of the sample, the survey started out with these neutrally phased instructions:[23]

> Unlike any time in the last 25 years, there is now a strong national debate about the need for and effectiveness of Affirmative Action Programs in employment. On the next pages, please give *your* opinion about Affirmative Action Programs in employment.

A third of the participants encountered the following positive statement immediately after the neutral opening sentence:

> Despite acknowledged problems, these programs can still have positive effects. Recent articles in *The Wall Street Journal, Business Week, Forbes,* and *U.S. News and World Report* suggest that Affirmative Action Programs have been successful in reducing discrimination against minorities and women. They also concluded that such programs are still needed to help "even the playing field." However, not everyone agrees. On the next pages, please give your opinions about Affirmative Action Programs in employment.

And for the last third came this:

> Despite acknowledged advantages, these programs can still have negative effects. Recent articles in *The Wall Street Jour-*

nal, Business Week, Forbes, and *U.S. News and World Report* suggest that Affirmative Action Programs have sometimes resulted in reverse discrimination against whites and men. They also concluded that while Affirmative Action Programs may have served a purpose for a time, they are no longer needed. However, not everyone agrees. On the next pages, please give your opinions about Affirmative Action Programs in employment.

Among the White participants in Bell's study, the disparaging words at the outset of the questionnaire resulted in lower evaluations of affirmative action than came from Whites who received the neutral instructions. The positive words did not affect participants' opinions about affirmative action. When the researchers repeated the study with a fresh sample of undergraduates, the same results appeared among Whites. Among students of color, the derogatory message had no effect, but the positive message did. Students of color who filled out the survey after reading that the *Wall Street Journal* and other authorities praised the policy gave it even higher ratings than those who read only the neutral version.

What Do Other Samples Show?

A question arises. Does the pattern of findings that researchers obtain on college campuses match that among other adults? Studies of students are well and good. But students may not represent the public at large.

The answer is not hard to find. For more than thirty years, pollsters and academics have asked Americans about their opinions concerning preferential treatment, quotas, and nonpreferential forms of selection and reward. Across a variety of polling methodologies, Americans consistently show that they do not prefer preferences.

A 1995 Gallup Poll, for example, revealed as much. A randomly selected group of individuals across the nation was asked by Gallup to "please tell me whether you generally approve or disapprove" of nine different practices including, in the exact words of the survey:

1. providing job training programs for minorities and women to make them qualified for better jobs

2. providing special educational classes for minorities and women to make them better qualified for college

3. companies making special efforts to find qualified minorities and women and then encouraging them to apply for jobs with the company

4. favoring a well qualified minority candidate over an *equally* well qualified white applicant when filling a job in a business that has few minority workers

5. requiring a certain percentage of government contracts to be awarded to businesses owned by minorities and women

6. establishing quotas which require schools to admit a certain number of minorities and women as students

7. establishing quotas which require businesses to hire a certain number of minorities and women

8. making a certain number of scholarships at public colleges and universities available only to minorities and women

9. favoring a minority applicant who is *less* qualified than a white applicant, when filling a job in a business that has few minority workers.[24]

In 1995, as in 1977, Mr. Gallup found that preferential treatment was dramatically less popular than equal opportunity. Ninety-four percent of Black participants and 80 percent of White participants, for example, endorsed the first option. Meanwhile, only 22 percent of Blacks and 11 percent of Whites endorsed option nine.[25]

Like Gallup, pollster Louis Harris has documented the public's dislike of preferential treatment. In a pair of polls conducted in 1991, Harris found that more than 70 percent of Americans favored laws requiring "affirmative action programs," but less than 50 percent endorsed "racial preference programs." Harris also asked his respondents how they reacted to the terms "racial preferences" and "affirmative action." He then coded the reactions as being either positive (for example, "doing something good for people") or negative (for example, "hiring minorities who are unqualified"). Eighty percent of the responses to the prompt "racial preferences" were negative, but 80 percent of the responses to the prompt "affirmative action" were positive.[26]

Pollsters like Gallup and Harris apply rigorous methodological controls in their work. But they also operate outside the university context. It is instructive to find out whether the same results are found by university researchers.

In 1991, with generous support from the National Science Foundation, the Survey Research Center at the University of California, Berkeley, conducted the "Race and Politics" study. Using a random-digit dialing procedure, professional interviewers contacted more than two thousand people nationwide. About nine hundred Whites were presented with this item:

> Some people say that because of past discrimination, qualified blacks should be given preference in university admissions. Others say that this is wrong because it discriminates against whites. How do you feel—are you in favor [of] or opposed to giving qualified blacks preference in admission to colleges and universities?

Meanwhile another nine hundred or so White people heard:

> Some people say that because of past discrimination, an extra effort should be made to make sure that qualified blacks are considered for university admission. Others say that this extra effort is wrong because it discriminates against whites. How do you feel—are you in favor [of] or opposed to making an extra effort to make sure qualified blacks are considered for admission to colleges and universities?

In response to the question about preferential treatment, 40 percent of the sample were strongly opposed and another 34 percent weakly opposed. Sixteen percent were weakly in favor and a mere 10 percent were strongly in favor. Responses to the item about extra effort were quite different: 13 percent were strongly opposed, 22 percent weakly opposed, 38 percent weakly in favor, and 27 percent strongly in favor. Thus only half as many Whites were opposed to a mild form of affirmative action as were against preferential treatment.[27]

Another source of excellent data is the series known as the National Election Studies (NES). Conducted by the University of Michigan every even-numbered year since 1952, the NES is thought to set the standard for scientific studies of public opinion. Meticulous sampling, standardized face-to-face interviews conducted by highly trained professionals, and well-designed interview schedules all contribute to the extraordinary quality and utility of the information gathered in the NES.

In an important and beautifully written book, *Divided by Color,* Donald Kinder and Lynn Sanders of the University of Michigan analyzed data gathered in 1986, 1988, and 1992.[28] Kinder and Sanders distinguished between questions that assess people's attitudes toward equal opportunity and questions that assess people's attitudes toward preferential treatment. One question about equal opportunity asked, "Some people feel that if Blacks are not getting fair treatment in jobs, the government in Washington should see to it that they do. Others feel that this is not the government's business. Have you been interested enough in this question to favor one side over the other? [If yes] How do you feel? Should the government in Washington see to it that Black people get fair treatment in jobs or is this not the government's business?"[29] Another question, worded in a parallel fashion, asked about whether the government in Washington should see to it "that White and Black children go to the same schools."

Meanwhile, two other questions asked about preferential treatment in employment and education. One question asked, "Some people say that because of past discrimination against Blacks, preference in hiring and promotion should be given to Blacks. Others say preferential hiring and promotion of Blacks is wrong because it gives Blacks advantages they haven't earned. What about your opinion—are you for or against preferential hiring and promotion of Blacks?"[30] And the other: "Some people say that because of past discrimination, it is sometimes necessary for colleges and universities to reserve openings for Black students. Others oppose quotas because they say quotas give

Blacks advantages they haven't earned. What are your opinions—are you for or against quotas to admit Black students?"[31]

Averaging across the three years studied, Kinder and Sanders found that 46.2 percent of White citizens endorsed equal opportunity policies in employment, and 35.6 percent in education. Meanwhile, only 15.4 percent approved of preferential hiring, and 29.7 percent of quotas in education. All forms of corrective action were more highly endorsed by Black Americans than by White Americans, but like Whites, Blacks valued equality over preferences. Ninety percent of Blacks favored equal opportunity through government action in employment, and 82.9 percent in education. In contrast, 67.7 percent favored preferential hiring and promotion, and 79.7 percent endorsed quotas in education.

Does Dislike of Quotas Influence Attitudes Toward Affirmative Action?

No study is perfect. No one data source can provide a complete picture. The studies by Kravitz and others that involve college students may not generalize to other groups. The thoughts and feelings of Joe and Josephine College may not mirror those of Joe and Josephine America.[32] Meanwhile, the polls taken by Gallup and the University of Michigan allow us to claim with a fair degree of certainty that Americans like equality of opportunity and dislike quotas, but they do not explicitly link not liking quotas with not liking affirmative action.

Fortunately, we have more pieces of the puzzle. Another study, also imperfect in its own way, demonstrates the link between quotas (presumed to be disliked) and other forms of affirmative action (presumed to be liked) on the one hand and attitudes toward affirmative action on the other. It is time to rewind the reel to the Chicago study discussed earlier in the chapter.

Recall that in the Chicago study we allowed respondents to select one of two definitions of affirmative action. One definition equated affirmative action with quotas. The other equated the policy with monitoring. About 12 percent of the respondents chose neither definition. Of those who did select a definition, 54 percent defined affirmative action as a monitoring system while 46 percent thought of it as a quota system.

Analysis of all the data showed that there was a strong association between the definition chosen and people's attitudes about affirmative action. Those who thought of affirmative action as a monitoring system gave, on average, an endorsement score of 6.8 to affirmative action on the 0–10 rating scale, while those who saw the policy as a quota system averaged more than a point lower in their approval rating. Using a statistical technique known as multiple regression, we were able to determine that how people defined affirmative action influenced their rating of it even after all the other factors relating to those people were taken into account. To be sure, factors like gender, ethnicity, and political orientation affected what people thought about affirmative action.[33] However, a respondent's *understanding* of affirmative action mattered *over and above* the other important factors. For example, women who thought of affirmative action as a monitoring system approved of the policy much more than did women who thought of it as a quota system; the same was true among men, among Whites, and among people of color.

Similar results were obtained in two separate studies of student opinion, one conducted in the South and one in the North. David Kravitz and his colleagues found that people who thought affirmative action included set-asides and preferential hiring disliked the policy. The less likely such actions were perceived as being part of affirmative action, the more positively affirmative action was viewed.[34] Similarly, in the Boston sample of Jacob Arriola and Cole, those who envisioned affirmative action as preferential treatment were less favorable toward the policy than were others.[35]

Is Opposition to Affirmative Action Simply a Matter of Ignorance?

The evidence is incontrovertible. Americans don't know much about affirmative action. Many Americans still think that it is a quota system, a system of unjustified preferential treatment, or a form of reverse discrimination. Reactions to affirmative action are contaminated by our aversion to preferential treatment.

For some time I have had no doubt that much of the resistance to affirmative action is based on misconceptions about the policy. Years of writing, lecturing, and teaching on the topic have shown me the surprising levels of ignorance about the policy and the practice of affirmative action among people who ought to know better: highly educated professionals and otherwise well-versed educators. My experience has also shown me that opposition can vanish in the face of accurate information. Consistent with my observations are the results of studies like the Chicago survey I undertook or the studies of David Kravitz showing a link between an accurate understanding of affirmative action and endorsement of it.

The policy implications of this conclusion would seem to be clear. Just teach people how affirmative action really operates, and controversy will die down. And some influential people do believe in the power of education to change attitudes. Interviewed in the newsletter of the American Association for Affirmative Action, Miranda Massie, the lead attorney for the student interveners in the University of Michigan lawsuits, expressed confidence in the efficacy of education. Asked, "Do you agree with the 'conventional wisdom' that this is a conservative time and most people do not support affirmative action?" Massie replied, "We believe that the majority of Americans believe in the principles of integration and racial equality, and when affirmative action is explained in these terms, most people support it."[36]

How very simple.

Or not.

One tip-off that the situation may not be as simple as it appears is the way the media treat it. In the wake of the Michigan cases, the media heaped attention on affirmative action. But they sometimes did so in ways that produce more heat than light. Around the time President Bill Clinton was conducting his review of affirmative action, a colleague and I did a search of all articles concerning affirmative action that appeared in the *New York Times,* the *Washington Post,* and *USA Today.* During the months of June, July, and August 1995, less than 6 percent of the 176 articles we uncovered offered a definition of affirmative action. Many of the others simply (and wrongly) equated affirmative action with reverse discrimination or preferential treatment.[37]

In the media frenzy concerning the Michigan cases at the Supreme Court, few journalists pointed out that race-conscious admissions policies are only one form of affirmative action in education. Nor did they inform their readers, viewers, or listeners that affirmative action in employment, where preferential selection occurs less often than in education, affects six times as many people as does affirmative action in education.

Why have the media not been more informative? Part of the reason is that reporters and journalists may themselves have had difficulties getting at the facts. Affirmative action has taken a number of different forms in both education and employment. Even President Clinton—famous for his encyclopedic knowledge of government and his elephantine memory—publicly declared himself to have been poorly informed about affirmative action before he immersed himself in the review that George Stephanopoulos and Christopher Edley prepared for him.[38]

Yet perhaps the problem is more than just lack of knowledge. The media's treatment of affirmative action, like their treatment of related topics, may reflect a measure of self-interest. Interesting stories sell papers, and conflict provokes interest. From a practical point of view, then, a story that defines affirmative action may be less saleable than one that does not. From a psychological point of view, too, journalists and reporters may have a vested interest in upholding traditional values of meritocracy, especially as applied to universities.[39]

Nor would it be in the journalists' professional self-interest to inform at the expense of entertaining. A study conducted by Stephen Klineberg and David Kravitz tracked public opinion about affirmative action in Houston over a five-year period, including the year when the mayor campaigned hard in favor of the city's procurement program. Newspaper coverage was heavy. Yet only in the short term did the campaign have much effect.[40]

What Is the Role of Self-Interest?

You don't need to be a journalist to be motivated by self-interest. Human beings inherently see the world through the lens of their own experiences and their own position in the world.[41] Self-interest plays a role both in how the ordinary person understands affirmative action and in how, given that understanding, he or she reacts to it.

An excellent demonstration of the importance of self-interest can be found in three studies conducted by Donald Truxillo and Talya Bauer.[42] Each included nonstudent samples: 213 applicants for a law-enforcement position in a large southeastern city in Study 1; 459 applicants for a police position in a medium-sized southern city in Study 2; and 125 applicants for promotion in the police department of a large southeastern city in Study 3.

Truxillo and Bauer explained the concept of "banding" to the participants in their study. In banding, scores on an exam are grouped into bands; all the scores in one band are considered equivalent. Thus, scores from 90 to 100 might all be designated "excellent," and scores of 80 to 89 might all be considered "good." An evaluator would distinguish between excellent scores and good scores, but all scores within a band would be counted the same. Thus, an A differs from a B, but all As are treated as equivalent to one another, and so are all Bs.

Truxillo and Bauer measured participants' reactions to banding. Participants were asked whether they thought banding would benefit them personally, whether it would help the organization achieve its affirmative action goals, and whether it was fair.

Applicants who thought that they would benefit personally from banding tended to evaluate the practice as much fairer on a number of dimensions than did applicants who thought they would not benefit personally. Also, to the extent that African American applicants thought banding would further the organization's affirmative action goals, they endorsed banding. Among Whites, no such relation was visible. Whites' endorsement of banding did not depend on whether they thought the practice would help or hinder affirmative action.

Further proof of the importance of self-interest was provided by Kimberly Matheson and her colleagues.[43] In their experiment, male and female students, tested in mixed-sex groups, took an exam in which they wrote stories, purportedly to measure their level of creativity. Highly creative individuals, they were told, would be given interesting work and big rewards, while the other students would have to settle for more boring, less lucrative work. After the exams were allegedly scored, the experimenter explained that they had reason to suspect bias. Far too few women were passing the exam, said the experi-

menter. The experimenter then announced that remedial action would
be taken.

Different groups were told different things about the type of remedial action that would be taken. In the "passive nondiscrimination"
group, participants were told, "We are hoping that if the experimenter
who scores the stories doesn't know who wrote them, gender won't
make a difference. This is why we've asked people to place their student
number on the story and recall sheet. Therefore, we won't know people's gender, and so hopefully the selection criteria didn't work against
women."[44]

In the "preferential treatment" group, participants were given
this explanation: "We selected into the high-creativity group any of the
females who passed the necessary cutoff point for being labeled highly
creative. Although some males may have scored higher, we only selected males if there weren't enough females that passed the minimum
cutoff scores. Therefore, we're hoping the selection won't work against
women."[45]

Matheson and associates did not use the term "affirmative action," but their "preferential treatment" group closely resembled a
fairly common form of affirmative action, declared legal in 1987 by the
Supreme Court in the case of *Johnson v. Transportation Agency.*[46] After
describing the remedial action taken to correct for the suspected gender bias, the experimenter returned the exams to the students. Some of
the students were told they had passed and some were told they had
not. The participants then filled out a long questionnaire assessing
their perceptions of the procedures and of their own talent and motivation.

Both the female and the male students rated the corrective procedures as more fair when they involved passive nondiscrimination than
when they involved preferential treatment. These results indicate that
reactions to affirmative action are influenced by people's understanding of what the policy involves. But self-interest also played a strong
role. Both the women and men who passed the exam rated the procedures as more fair than those who flunked.

Survey research corroborates the role of self-interest. A telephone
poll was conducted in Houston that included random samples of
about 400 Whites, 400 Blacks, and more than 150 American-born His-

panics. Asked to rate the typical affirmative action plan and the special case of a tie-breaker (in which preference goes to the person of color when two candidates are otherwise indistinguishable), White respondents liked best the tie-break plan while Blacks and Hispanics liked best the typical affirmative action plan.[47]

Another indicator of self-interest is the finding that well-educated people tend to be more liberal than poorly educated people, except when the issues concern preferential admissions to colleges and universities. Those with more education may give special value to education and may worry about how increased competition will affect the chances of their own family members to gain admission to institutions of higher education.[48]

Given the importance of self-interest, it would be foolhardy to imagine that we can eliminate all the controversy about affirmative action simply by educating people about the policy and its practice. Education can be embraced or resisted. Educational messages are filtered through the preconceptions and the needs of those who receive them. To educate is vitally important; but education alone is not the answer.

What Is the Role of Other Attitudes?

Another factor complicates the results we can expect from instructing people about the true nature of affirmative action. Attitudes toward and knowledge about affirmative action do not exist in a vacuum. People who have attitudes toward and knowledge about affirmative action also have attitudes toward and knowledge about many other aspects of society. They "know" something about how discrimination works. They "know" something about how organizations function. They "know" something about the nature of humans, and may believe that they "know" something about how different types of human beings (say, males and females; Blacks and Whites) differ. Their knowledge of and attitudes toward society and its workings influence how they react to affirmative action generally and to different specific aspects of affirmative action.

Especially informative in this regard is a campus study conducted by Truxillo and Bauer.[49] Truxillo and Bauer asked students enrolled in business courses how they felt about affirmative action. The researchers also asked for background demographic information. The respondents, some of whom were graduate students, were older and had more work experience than student samples in most studies. After they gave their opinions, the students were asked to imagine that they were applicants at Company X and that they had taken a multiple-choice test as part of the application procedure. The students were then randomly divided into three groups and given one of three explanations of how Company X scored the tests and selected the successful applicants.

Subjects in the "top-down" group were told: "Company X uses the *top-down method*. In this method, the organization considers hiring each applicant in the order of their test score. Thus, an applicant with a 98 on the test would be considered before one with a 97, an applicant with a 97 would be considered before an applicant with a 96, and so on, without regard to race or gender."[50]

Subjects in the "banding/random-selection" group were told: "Company X uses the *banding method*. In this method, test scores are grouped into 'bands.' All scores within each band are considered statistically equal. For example if the band width were calculated to be 5, the top band would be from 96–100, and the scores within this band would be regarded as tied. Company X will hire applicants *randomly* from within the top band to increase the chances of hiring people from protected classes (e.g., women, minorities). In other words, by randomly selecting from a *range* of top scores, Company X may increase its changes of hiring female or minority applicants."[51]

Finally, subjects in the "banding/preference" group were told: "Company X uses the *banding method*. In this method test scores are grouped into 'bands.' All scores within each band are considered statistically equal. For example if the band width were calculated to be 5, the top band would be from 96–100, and the scores within this band would be considered tied. Company X will hire applicants who are in the top band. However, Company X will at first pass over (not hire) applicants in the band from nonprotected groups, such as White males. Instead, Company X will hire applicants in the band from the protected groups (e.g., women, minorities) who might have received lower test scores, only hiring White males in the band if there are enough job openings. Using the above example, if a female or a minority applicant scored a 96 on the test, Company X would hire that applicant rather than a White male who got 100. Company X may thus increase its chances of hiring people from protected classes."[52]

Truxillo and Bauer asked participants to evaluate the fairness of the selection procedure and the attractiveness of Company X as an employer. They expected to find the highest evaluations for the top-down method and the lowest for the banding/preferences method. To their surprise, they found little difference in the overall evaluation scores. Truxillo and Bauer then divided participants into two groups: those who endorsed affirmative action and those who did not. Among the students with relatively unfavorable attitudes toward the policy of affirmative action, the predictions now held true: the top-down method seemed more fair and more attractive than the banding/random-selection method, which, in turn, seemed more fair and more attractive than the banding/preference method. Among fans of affirmative action, however, the predictions did not hold true. Indeed, proponents of affirmative action found the banding/random-selection method slightly more fair than the top-down method and considered that the banding/preference method made Company X most attractive.[53]

Truxillo and Bauer's small study has large implications.[54] The study demonstrates that attitudes cluster together. Supporters of affirmative action probably have a different worldview from that of their opponents. It would be nice to assume that all we have to do to increase acceptance of affirmative action is educate citizens in the way it really operates. But one implication of Truxillo and Bauer's findings is that people will differ in how they receive the information.

Are Attitudes Influenced by Framing?

An assumption that White opposition to affirmative action springs from a single cause would be naive. White Americans hardly form a monolith. Some are Republicans, others Democrats. Some fear for their own position in society, others do not. Some are racist or sexist, many are not. Some are well educated about political matters, most are poorly educated. It should hardly be surprising to find that different motives operate among different constituencies.

To test the idea of differential motivations, Kinder and Sanders analyzed data collected in 1985 in conjunction with the 1984 National Election Study.[55] The sample included 380 participants, all of whom were asked two questions about affirmative action (one concerning employment and one concerning college admissions) and a series of additional questions about background characteristics and other attitudes. The affirmative action questions were presented in the traditional mode of survey research. Generally speaking the formula ran: "Some people say affirmative action is good; others say it is bad; what do you say?" For half the participants, the anti–affirmative action justification added, "because it discriminates against whites."[56] For the other half, the justification added, "because it gives blacks advantages they haven't earned."[57]

How the justification was framed did not affect the strength of opposition. But the framing affected mightily the factors that were associated with White people's opinions, especially if the people were not politically sophisticated. Under the reverse-discrimination frame, the interests of self and peers tended to determine attitudes toward affirmative action. The more threatened a person felt, the more negative his or her attitude toward affirmative action. Under the frame of undeserved advantages, self-interest mattered little, but racial sentiments mattered a lot. Whites who disliked Black people also disliked affirmative action when opposition was justified by reference to unearned advantages. Framing opposition to affirmative action in terms of unearned advantages also increased the influence of negative emotions, especially disgust, on the statements about their attitudes given by Whites.

Are Attitudes Affected by Personal Experiences?

Self-interest and attitude clusters are surely part—but not all—of the reason White citizens endorse affirmative action less strongly than Black citizens do and part—but not all—of the reason men endorse affirmative action less strongly than women.[58] Differences in how people understand affirmative action and differences in experiences with discrimination might also account for some of the variations in attitudes that exist among demographic groups.[59] Certainly experiences with discrimination help explain varying levels of support for affirmative action among Blacks. Blacks who know that they have borne the brunt of discrimination endorse affirmative action; Blacks who believe they have avoided discrimination support affirmative action only if they are ideological liberals.[60]

Whatever the reason, racial differences are large, ranging from the merely substantial in some surveys to the truly gargantuan in others.[61] Steeh and Krysan gathered polls concerning racial issues that have been conducted by a number of different organizations.[62] Yearly, from 1987 to 1994, the Times Mirror Center for the People and the Press asked a national representative sample of adults whether they agreed or disagreed with the statement "We should make every possible effort to improve the position of Blacks and other minorities, even if it means giving them preferential treatment." Percentages of those in agreement were:

	Blacks	*Whites*
1987	64 percent	18 percent
1988	70 percent	20 percent
1989	not broken out by race	
1990	68 percent	17 percent
1991	not broken out by race	
1992	67 percent	29 percent
1993	not broken out by race	
1994	62 percent	25 percent

Year by year the percentages fluctuate. But they do not fluctuate much. The racial gap is constant and pronounced.

Other surveys reviewed by Steeh and Krysan show the same persistent divide between Black and White opinions. For a number of years, pollsters asked citizens about "preferential hiring and promotion of Blacks." They provided a set of responses, including "oppose strongly," "oppose but not strongly," "favor but not strongly," and "favor strongly." For each year of the study, far more White than Black respondents expressed themselves in strong opposition. And for each year of the study, far more Black than White respondents expressed themselves strongly in favor.

Not surprisingly, Gallup shows similar results to those of the other pollsters. African American citizens in his sample were twice as likely as White citizens to endorse quotas for schools, quotas for business, reserved scholarships, and the hiring of less-qualified Black persons. Similar patterns divided by ethnicity and gender have been found in other small surveys.[63]

Or revisit the National Election Studies data analyzed by Kinder and Sanders. More than twice as many Black citizens as White citizens endorsed government action to ensure equal opportunity in employment and education. Two and a half times as many Blacks as Whites favored quotas, and four times as many endorsed preferential hiring. In extended analyses of the data from the National Election Studies, Kinder and Sanders document the myriad ways White and Black opinions have diverged, especially concerning issues related to race.[64] More than half the African Americans sampled in the 1986, 1988, and 1992 NES surveys supported increased federal spending on food stamps, while only 18 percent of Whites did. Nearly three-quarters of Blacks thought solutions should be found for the problems underlying urban unrest, while less than half of Whites did. Forty-five percent of Blacks wanted stronger sanctions against the apartheid government of South Africa, while only 26 percent of Whites did. And while a paltry 17.6 percent of Whites agreed that there should be increased "federal spending on programs that assist Blacks," an overwhelming majority of Blacks—74.6 percent—thought so.[65]

Differences in attitudes show up among people working within the same organization as well as among the public at large. Such is one finding to emerge from a large, multistage research project conducted by Alison Konrad and Frank Linnehan.[66] Konrad and Linnehan asked managers in four large companies in an eastern metropolis to evaluate a set of twenty-six personnel practices. Some of the practices were identity-conscious, others were not. Examples of identity-conscious practices included "insuring that some women and minorities are included as candidates for management," "tracking the percentage of women and minorities in jobs that lead to management," "aggressive recruiting of women and minorities for management," and "affirmative action plan." Examples of identity-neutral practices were "informing all employees of all management job vacancies," "providing management training to employee management candidates," and "system to identify candidates for promotion into management." White men,

White women, and managers of color were equally (and very) enthusiastic about the identity-neutral practices. The identity-conscious practices received much stronger endorsement from White women and from people of color than from White men.

Bridges

Americans are not well informed about affirmative action. Few citizens claim to have a great deal of knowledge about its policy or practice. A sizable minority equates affirmative action with unjustified preferential treatment, which is extremely unpopular in the United States.

Perhaps a campaign of education would increase the acceptance of affirmative action among Americans. Several experts have emphasized how important it is to demystify affirmative action whenever a new program is being implemented within an organization.[67] The expectation is that with knowledge comes acceptance.

While misunderstandings of affirmative action certainly must account for some of the resistance, they probably don't account for all of it. The profound divergence of opinions along racial or ethnic divisions highlights another possible explanation for the lack of popularity of affirmative action in the United States. Social scientists like Kinder and Sanders have seen in the pattern of data support for the suspicion that prejudice contributes powerfully to the nation's ambivalence over affirmative action. The possibility is unsettling. Perhaps the reason Americans are so uninformed about affirmative action is that, at some level, they do not want to know how fair and sensible the policy really is.

Given the rampant misconceptions about affirmative action, it would not be surprising to discover that the policy has had limited effectiveness. People who are ignorant about affirmative action can find reasons to take issue with it. Then, citing the (putative) unfairness or ineffectiveness of the (misconceived) policy, they can shy further away from learning more about how affirmative action can and does operate.

If people in positions of authority persist in their misconceptions about affirmative action, it is unlikely that it will be able to fulfill its potential to help affect social change. A legitimate reason to dislike the policy would be its ineffectiveness. Perhaps the costs of the policy out-weigh the benefits.

Yet if those responsible for implementing affirmative action are better informed about the policy than the general public, they may have been able to make it work more effectively. The effectiveness of the policy is an important issue, furthermore, for if it turns out that af-firmative action *has* been effective, then the opposition to it takes on a new cast. We would then have to wonder whether White citizens sometimes disliked the policy not because they don't know what it is but, on the contrary, because they do know what it is, and they do know that it works well for people of color. In the same vein, maybe some men resist affirmative action programs for women because they are uncomfortable with the idea of gender equity.

The effectiveness of affirmative action in employment and edu-cation is an empirical question. Fortunately, it is a question on which there are many data. Those data form the heart of Chapter 4.

4

Effectiveness

The [affirmative action] policies I have recommended for minimizing workplace racial and gender bias . . . will lead to more effective use of human resources and [will] improve organizational performance. So what's holding things up?

William Bielby, "Minimizing Workplace Gender and Racial Bias"

Maybe the problem with affirmative action is that it doesn't work. Perhaps people have less than solid enthusiasm for the policy because the policy has not succeeded in bettering the lives of those whom it intends to benefit. Could it be that people dislike affirmative action because they doubt it has had concrete results in either business or education?

If affirmative action policy has produced little change in the American scene, then it may not be worth the controversy it provokes. Fortunately, a large number of studies, many undertaken by economists, using a variety of ways of assessing effectiveness, have by now resulted in a significant body of knowledge. As a detailed examination of that literature will reveal, affirmative action does work. In exclusively material terms, the benefits of the policy have far outweighed the costs.

Procurement Programs

A good place to start the examination is with set-asides—an aspect of affirmative action that was once legal but is generally not now. The concept of setting aside some government contracts for minority business enterprises (MBEs) or women-owned enterprises (WBEs) developed during the presidency of Richard Nixon. The idea had a certain logic, given that economists estimate that government contracts (at the federal, state, and local levels) account for about 10 percent of the gross domestic product.[1]

When set-asides were still legal, various scholars and public figures examined their effectiveness. Activist attorney Anthony Robinson found procurement programs—as set-asides are sometimes called—very effective. Robinson highlighted the success story of the Terry family. In 1960 the family founded Terry Manufacturing Company, which made work clothes. A decade or so later Terry Manufacturing Company joined the MBE program and obtained a contract with the Department of Defense. By 1985 the company had graduated from the program, having obtained contracts with McDonald's and Champion.[2]

Although not all minority-owned businesses enjoyed the phenomenal success of Terry Manufacturing, the policy is generally thought to have helped minority businesses obtain contracts and clients. Economist Darrell Williams looked at small businesses in the state of California in the late 1980s.[3] He found that the vast majority of WBE and MBE business involved sales to private, nongovernmental clients. In fact, only 7.2 percent of WBEs and 12.6 percent of MBEs sold goods or services to the state or local government, compared with 16.4 percent of other small businesses. Yet the WBE and MBE firms that did business with the government relied more heavily on procurement dollars than did the nonminority firms. Similarly, 6.6 percent of the total revenue of MBEs came from state and local government procurement contracts, in contrast to 3.1 percent for the firms owned by White males.

Another economist, Tom Larson, looked closely at the city of Los Angeles, where Directive 1-B established set-asides in 1983 and Directive 1-C modified the program in the wake of *Croson v. City of Richmond* (which declared set-asides in a Richmond, Virginia, program unconstitutional).[4] Larson documented the amazing effectiveness of the Los Angeles program. MBEs obtained only 2.2 percent of Los Angeles's billion dollars in contracts before 1983, and 11.8 percent after Directive 1-B. For WBEs, the corresponding figures were 0.3 percent and 8 percent—a 2,400 percent increase!

While the strong leadership of Tom Bradley, the famous mayor of Los Angeles and a Black man, may have energized the Los Angeles program, similar results have been shown in studies around California and elsewhere in the United States.[5] In Tallahassee, for example, the percentage of city contracts awarded to MBEs rose to 24 percent from 0 percent after the establishment of a set-aside program.[6] New Haven, Connecticut, went from awarding 1 percent of its contracts to women- and minority-owned businesses to giving 25 percent.[7] A study by the Urban Institute in 1998 compared fifty-eight cities around the country. In cities without procurement programs, MBEs captured only 45 per- cent of the contract dollars they should have gotten based on the num- bers of MBEs among all contractors. In cities with affirmative action programs, MBEs captured 57 percent of the expected amount.[8]

Other states boast statistics similar to those in California. In 1993, 8.3 percent of government contracts in Texas went to "underutilized groups." Women captured nearly half those contracts.[9] Similarly, in 1993–94, New York State granted 205 federally funded engineering subcontracts, of which 127 went to Asian Americans, showing that not only African Americans and Hispanics gained contracts through tar- geted procurement programs.[10]

Of course, as economist Marc Bendick, Jr., has pointed out, the real success of a procurement program is not measured simply by look- ing at the business brought to minority-owned or women-owned busi- nesses in any one year. To be really successful, set-aside programs must foster development among minority firms to the point where the firms no longer need economic shelters. Excellent procurement programs are those that train minority businesses, help solidify connections be- tween minority businesses and financial institutions, and then require the minority businesses to "graduate" from the program, moving away from sheltered markets.[11]

Successful procurement programs also create jobs for ethnic mi- nority workers. As Timothy Bates has documented, some firms that claim to be minority owned are really shells for White investors, and other minority-owned businesses are so small and economically fragile that they do nothing to help revitalize inner cities or other locations with a large constituent of ethnic minority workers. Nonetheless, in a sophisticated economic study of procurement programs in twenty- eight metropolitan areas in the 1980s, Bates was able to show that many Black businesses thrived and that, furthermore, they helped increase employment among minority workers in urban centers. Especially effective were programs in cities where the mayor was Black[12] and programs with procedures in place to inhibit fraud and help MBEs overcome problems associated with bonding requirements and insufficient capital assets.[13]

Costs of Set-Asides and Other Procurement Programs

Programs cost money. According to Kweisi Mfume the federal MBE program in 1994 cost taxpayers about $20 million.[14] Such a tab is not negligible. Yet expenses may be less in fact than they appear at first glance. If federal WBE programs helped women stay off the welfare rolls, for example, then money spent on one program saved money that would have been spent on another. Sometimes, too, the expenditures generate other revenues. One program that appeared to be expensive was the 1994 auction of narrow-band radio licenses. That year women- and minority-owned businesses were allowed to purchase up to thirty licenses at half-price. The program was decried as a "huge giveaway," but appearances turned out to be deceptive. By opening license purchase to enhanced competition, the program actually forced nondesignated bidders to pay more than they had previously done. The result was a $45 million increase in government revenues—an increase of about 12 percent.[15]

Fate of Set-Asides

In January 1989 the policy of set-asides suffered a major defeat in the Supreme Court decision of *Croson v. City of Richmond.* The Court decided that the city's set-aside program violated the Equal Protection Clause of the Fourteenth Amendment by requiring White contractors to employ minority subcontractors even when the subcontractors submitted somewhat more expensive bids. The Court found unpersuasive the documented pattern of historical discrimination and chided the city for having selected a target figure (30 percent of the subcontracts had to go to MBEs) without appropriate study. Another blow to set-asides came in June 1995 when the Supreme Court decided the case of *Adarand Constructors Inc. v. Pena.* A set-aside program, the Court mandated, needed to be narrowly tailored and subject to strict scrutiny. After *Adarand*, President Bill Clinton ordered the military and other units in the government to reduce or eliminate affirmative action in procurements. The passage of Proposition 209 in California in 1996 sounded the death knell for set-asides there at the state and local levels, as did the passage of I-200 in the state of Washington two years later.

Positive Effects of Executive Order 11246

More extensively documented than the effects of procurement programs are the effects of hiring policies. Many economists have measured the effects of Executive Order 11246 (the law signed by President Johnson in 1965 that established classical affirmative action) and comparable state and local directives, and they have done so using a variety of methods and a number of indicators. Some scholars have looked at who is hired while others have concentrated on what they're earning. Some have contrasted government employment with employment in the private sector; others have compared federal contractors with non-contractors.

Effects in Government Hiring

The federal government, state governments, and many local governments are required by law to monitor workforce figures and correct the disparities they document. If affirmative action is effective, we should find that government workforces contain a higher proportion of women and minorities than does the private sector. If, on the other hand, the government has not increased the percentage of its workforce that are women or people of color, then E.O. 11246 is a policy that exists only on paper.

Several studies have documented the employment of women and minorities in government jobs. Consistently, the studies show just what the proponents of affirmative action would predict. As sociologist Barbara Reskin notes, small but detectable advances have been made by Hispanics, African Americans, and women in overall government employment since the creation of affirmative action.[16] One study conducted in the mid-1980s also found that women especially gravitate to the state and local levels of government and people of color to federal jobs.[17] Another study found that public universities hired ethnic minorities for administrative positions in greater numbers than private universities.[18] Yet another study documented how important the federal government has been as a source of administrative jobs for Blacks. The number of African American managers and professionals in government increased 275 percent from 1960 to 1970 and another 200 percent from 1970 to 1980. For Whites, the comparable percentages were 82 and 29.[19] A late-1990s study concentrated on the state of California. There economist M. V. Lee Badgett found that White men made up 32.1 percent of the workforce in the private sector but only 28.3 percent in state government jobs and 27.9 percent in local government positions.[20]

Of course, having a job, just any job, is not necessarily an indicator of success. If affirmative action has been effective, it should help women and minorities rise to management positions. Badgett's in-depth analysis of employment trends in California is again instructive. Badgett showed that more women and people of color attained management positions in California's state and local governments than in the private sector. Women especially benefited. In the dry prose of an economist, Badgett recounts:

> In 1970, a 38-year-old married white woman with some college, English proficiency, U.S. citizenship, and no disability was 15 percent less likely than a white man with the same characteristics to be in a managerial or professional position in the private sector, but she was only 4 percent less likely to hold one in the public sector. . . . By 1980 she was only 4 percent less likely to hold a managerial job [in the private sector], and by 1990 her chances were roughly equal. But in the public sector in 1990, this representative white woman was roughly 5 percent *more* likely than a similar white man to be in the top occupational category.[21]

Similar statistical patterns also appeared for Black men: in 1970 a college-educated Black man had ten times more chance of becoming a manager in a government job than he did in the for-profit sector. And, as one might expect given the correspondence between job level and earnings, gender and racial gaps in compensation are smaller in public-sector jobs than in private.[22]

We should remember that not all government agencies welcome women and minorities. Police departments have been particularly resistant to the inclusion of women. Soon after the passage of the Equal Employment Law of 1972, many departments instituted height and weight requirements designed to exclude women. Common is the lore that declares women unfit for police work. The percentage of women in the civilian police ranks is one-third the percentage of women in the ranks of the military police.[23] While voluntary affirmative action programs have been helpful to women in some police departments,[24] the primary engine for change in 1980s was anti-discrimination litigation.[25]

Hiring by Federal Contractors

What about more-direct evidence of the value of affirmative action to women and ethnic minority men who seek jobs? Even a highly controlled comparison between hiring in the government and in the private sector, of the type undertaken by Badgett, might be comparing apples and oranges. Perhaps the people who are drawn to bureaucracies differ from entrepreneurs.

A number of econometric studies have compared federal contractors with other employers. The comparisons are usually made over time and usually take into account other factors, like the sector of the economy. To understand why the economists need such complicated formulas, remember that the labor force is segregated along both ethnic and gender lines. Few women are employed in manufacturing concerns, many in retail sales. Federal contractors are more likely than noncontractors to be in manufacturing and less likely to be in retail.[26] Thus, if you just compared the percentage of women in the workforce, the federal contractors would look worse than the noncontractors. The crucial comparisons are those that look at changes over time and those that control for such factors as whether the organization is in the manufacturing sector. Most of the econometric studies that compare federal contractors and others, furthermore, rely on data filed annually by all firms employing more than a hundred workers.[27]

The conclusions of the economists are fairly, but not completely, consistent.[28] Breaking up the findings into different periods lends a certain clarity to the data. Basically, affirmative action seems to have had steady, and increasingly positive, effects from its inception in 1965 until the presidency of Ronald Reagan in 1980. In the Reagan-Bush years, the effectiveness of affirmative action decreased.

Conclusions drawn for the early years come from several studies that use somewhat different data sets and methodologies. An early study by Orley Ashenfelter and James Heckman looked at employment data from 40,445 firms sampled in 1966, one year after E.O. 11246 was signed, and again in 1970.[29] They found that the growth in employment for African American men, relative to White men, over the four-year period was 3.3 percent greater in the federal contractors' firms than in other firms. Even more dramatic, federal contractors that were all White in 1966 had a much greater chance than unintegrated non–affirmative action firms of having at least one Black worker by 1970.[30] In contrast to Ashenfelter and Heckman, two other economists found little change in the job share of women and ethnic minorities in the early years of E.O. 11246.[31]

It is possible, especially in those early years, that affirmative action produced greater effects in some parts of the country than in others, and such differences could explain inconsistencies in the national data sets. Looking at 3,700 firms in the Chicago area between 1970 and 1973, Heckman and Kenneth Wolpin found somewhat greater effects on employment growth for minorities than for women. Minority men made special gains in blue-collar jobs at contractor firms.[32] In a highly detailed study of Black employment patterns in South Carolina during the 1960s, Heckman and Brook Payner were able to demonstrate the critical role played by E.O. 11246.[33] By breaking down the data into counties, Heckman and Payner were able to dismiss several alternative explanations for Black prosperity, such as the tight labor market and the shift away from agriculture. Heckman and Payner demonstrated that it was the involvement of Black workers, both women and men, in the textile industry, and the close monitoring of the industry by the Department of Defense in accordance with E.O. 11246, that produced the marked improvement in Black earnings in South Carolina. At that time, Black workers—both women and men—were deeply involved in the textile industry. In counties where Blacks were not employed in monitored industries, improvements were slower.

One of the most prolific scholars to track the employment effects of affirmative action is Jonathan Leonard of the Haas School of Business at Berkeley.[34] In one of his first studies, Leonard examined the records of 68,000 establishments in 1974 and 1980, with records on 16 million employees.[35] He found that the share of jobs going to Black workers and women increased more dramatically among federal contractors than among other firms. Establishments that underwent compliance reviews were especially likely to increase the number of ethnic minority males and females. Federal contractors that were expanding or growing over the period also experienced especially rapid growth in their percentages of minority employees. As with employment, so with earnings. Among all employers, the ratio of Black male earnings relative to White male earnings increased by 2.3 percent, from 0.684 to 0.700, between 1974 and 1980. Among federal contractors, the percentage increase was almost three times as great.

After 1980, however, Leonard noted a marked difference. During the Reagan years, according to Leonard's research, affirmative action was poorly enforced.[36] Sanctions for noncompliance were not applied. President Reagan even considered dismantling the OFCCP office. Finding virtually no advances for women working for federal contractors during the 1980s, Leonard concluded that the Republican administration was just "going through the motions."[37] According to some analyses, Black workers actually fared slightly better among noncontractors than among federal contractors in the 1980s,[38] but other studies find that minorities did better with federal contractors than with noncontractors even during the 1980s.[39]

Other scholars have been more optimistic than Leonard, in part because of the regions they have studied and in part because matters improved again during the Clinton presidency.[40] William Rodgers III concentrated his focus on ethnic disparities in California. Looking at files from 1979 to 1994, he contrasted federal contractors and comparable other employers.[41] Given the importance of the defense and energy industries in California, Rodgers made sure to take industry sector into account. His detailed analyses showed that federal contractors tended to employ Blacks and Asian Americans in greater proportions than

their counterparts who were not federal contractors. White males lost
1.7 percentage points of their advantage in 1982 and 1 percent in 1994.
While the decrease for Whites was tiny, the advantage to Blacks and
Asians, who constituted 7 percent and 11 percent, respectively, of the
California workforce, was enormous. The one anomaly in Rodgers's
findings concerned Hispanics. Perhaps because he had no way to account for immigrant laborers (both legal and illegal), Rodgers found
that federal contractors were less likely than other comparable firms to
hire Hispanics. The Hispanics in the non–affirmative action firms
tended, Rodgers found, to work at low-level jobs.

More-Precise Comparisons

Comparisons between federal contractors and other firms are likely to
underestimate the true impact of affirmative action for two reasons.
First, as economist Barbara Bergmann has shown, federal contractors
differ in their application of affirmative action.[42] Second, many firms
have voluntary affirmative action programs. Thus, when federal contractors are compared to noncontractors, the latter group may include
organizations that have vigorous affirmative action programs of their
own. The most accurate comparisons occur when pollsters ask participants if their firms are affirmative action employers. Such comparisons
show unequivocally the effectiveness of affirmative action.

   One such study was done by Cedric Herring and Sharon Collins.[43] Herring and Collins examined information from two studies—
the 1990 General Social Survey and the 1992 survey of Chicago adults.
In both surveys, participants were asked, "Does the place where you
work have an affirmative action program, or make any special effort to
hire and promote minorities?"[44] Dividing the samples into firms that
were affirmative action employers (either by law or voluntarily) and
those that were not, the investigators found that the former employed
significantly more Blacks and women than the latter. Seven percent of
those working for affirmative action employers declared that no Blacks
worked at their firms. In contrast, 33 percent of those working for other
employers declared the same. For women, the figures were 2 percent
and 20 percent, respectively.

   Not only are women and minorities more likely to be employed by affirmative action organizations; they are also likely to find better jobs with affirmative action employers than with others. Indeed, all of the respondents in the surveys—including White men—tended to have more prestigious jobs if their employer was an affirmative action employer. The gain was especially marked for racial minorities and for those who grew up in poverty.

Given the differences in job status, it seems only logical to expect a difference in earnings. And that is what Herring and Collins found. Among people of color, employees earned $1,200 a year more at a small affirmative action organization than at a small non–affirmative action organization and $6,000 a year more at a large one. In contrast, Whites earned considerably less at small affirmative action organizations than at other small organizations, but about $3,000 more at a large affirmative action organization than at other large organizations.

Similar to the Herring and Collins study was one conducted by Harry Holzer and David Neumark, both of Michigan State University. They undertook a massive and elaborate econometric study of eight hundred employers in Atlanta, Boston, Detroit, and Los Angeles. Individual phone interviews were conducted with human resource officials over a two-year span, from June 1992 to May 1994. Each participant was asked a series of questions about the firm's most recent hire and was also asked whether "Affirmative Action or Equal Employment Opportunity Law play any role in your recruiting activities for this position" and "play any role in whom you actually hire."[45]

Sixty percent of the establishments claimed to use affirmative action in recruiting and 45 percent in hiring. The researchers asked about the educational qualifications of the most recent hire as well as about the educational requirements, line of work (for example, sales, clerical, operative), and starting salary of the job. They also noted the type of work done by the firm, its size and location, and the ethnic and sexual composition of the work team, the supervisor, and the client base. They obtained an assessment of the worker's job performance. And, of course, they asked what the sex and ethnicity of the employee was.

Holzer and Neumark found that White males stood a 6 percent greater chance than White females of being hired by firms that did not practice affirmative action. Reasoning that affirmative action firms and non–affirmative action firms differed in many ways, including especially their average size and the percentage of the workforce covered by collective bargaining, the economists undertook additional comparisons in which they statistically equated the affirmative action firms with the others on all relevant characteristics, such as size of workforce. If the original difference was due to these other factors, the controlled test would have found no difference in the probability of White males being hired relative to the other demographic groups. Rather than flattening the effect, the controls increased the effect! With all the controls in place, the White male advantage in the non–affirmative action companies increased. Detailed analyses showed that White women and Black men increased their chances of being hired by 15 percent when they sought employment at an affirmative action employer.

Targeted studies of specific organizations also document the effectiveness of affirmative action, whether legally required or voluntarily undertaken. In the early 1970s, General Motors began an "aggressive affirmative action plan" that elevated the share of management jobs going to women and minorities by 4–5 percent.[46] After a review by the OFCCP in 1978, Cleveland's five largest banks increased the number of women at the upper levels by more than 20 percent.[47] After a discrimination suit, BankAmerica promoted so many capable ethnic minorities and White women to managerial jobs that the company ended by significantly exceeding industry averages.[48]

In the 1990s, Alison Konrad and Frank Linnehan examined information from a hundred-plus employers in the Philadelphia area and found that those with formal affirmative action plans had more women in management positions than did other firms.[49] Kul Rai and John Critzer have documented how affirmative action directives have helped White women advance in the professorial ranks and attain virtual parity in educational administration and have helped open the ranks of the professorate to men of color.[50]

The effectiveness of affirmative action in helping women and people of color find good jobs has also been documented by self-report. Gwyned Simpson obtained questionnaire information from 238 Black women lawyers; she also interviewed 20 of these in depth.[51] A large portion of the women claimed that they had been helped by affirmative action. More than half of the women gained admission to law school through affirmative action programs. Although affirmative action played a large role in helping the women, 87 percent of the sample indicated that they had still been discriminated against at work. The majority of the sample found work in housing and labor specialties, often in government employment, and were unable to make the leap to the more lucrative private sector.

The Costs of Executive Order 11246

Every coin has two sides. Let's admit that affirmative action has had its successes among people who were previously excluded from employment opportunities. Even so, it may be a bad policy. Maybe all the advantage to women and people of color comes at a cost to the establishments where they work.

Speaking in 1980, Sen. Orrin Hatch gave voice to the fears of many: "Affirmative action is a net cost to the economy. . . . And the true dynamic effects—the opportunity cost of all this expense and effort, the diminution of competition, inefficiencies due to the employment and promotion of marginal labor and the consequent demoralization of good workers—can only be a matter of conjecture, although they are clearly the most important of all."[52]

Senator Hatch was referring to two types of costs. First, firms have to pay to maintain their affirmative action plans, including the salary of an affirmative action officer. Second, affirmative action may inflict hidden costs on firms if the policy forces them to hire people of inferior talents. Reverse discrimination is bound to result in a loss of productivity, not just because of the resentments of White men, but also because of defects of the unqualified new hires.

Direct Administrative Costs

What do the data show about the direct administrative costs? There are certainly costs associated with having an affirmative action plan for any company that is a federal contractor.[53] The U.S. Office of Management and Budget estimates that a new federal contractor will need to spend about 180 hours—more than four working weeks of full-time professional work—developing its initial affirmative action plan. A compliance review can also be time consuming. Every year, the

OFCCP conducts compliance reviews on approximately 2 percent of the contractors around the nation. That means that between 3,500 and 4,000 firms a year must fill out a set of forms and answer a set of questions. If the initial responses are not satisfactory, more protracted contact results. Organizations that are found not to be in compliance with the law, furthermore, must carry the further costs of correcting the imbalance. In 2001, the OFCCP recovered $30 million in back wages and salaries due individuals from the targeted classes.

Adding together the customary paperwork and the sometimes extraordinary time commitment needed for a review, how much does a firm spend on affirmative action compliance? Jonathan Leonard has calculated the costs to companies that arise when they are federal contractors. "The direct administrative costs of affirmative action," concludes Leonard, "are comparable in magnitude to the cost of giving each employee a New Year's turkey or two."[54] An early Business Roundtable study placed the costs of compliance at about a tenth of 1 percent of revenues for forty large federal contractors.[55] Other estimates ranged from $278 per employee to $12.40 per employee in 1992 dollars, with the lower figure being the one adopted by Senator Hatch's Labor Committee.[56] A survey of "customer satisfaction" conducted in 1994 by the OFCCP found that more than 85 percent of contractors had no complaints about the amount of paperwork.[57]

Costs of Lawsuits

Ours is a litigious society. Traditionally, one of the major reasons that some large employers have embraced affirmative action is to prevent female workers or workers of color from having just cause for a lawsuit. The existence of a well-designed and carefully enforced affirmative action program goes a long way toward persuading judges and juries that an organization does not discriminate.

In recent years some have come to see affirmative action programs as a double-edged sword. Employers have expressed the fear that an aggressive affirmative action program could open them to legal challenge from angry White men.[58] Given the apparent power of angry White men like those who gave birth to California's Proposition 209, such fears may seem reasonable.[59]

Data from the Equal Employment Opportunity Commission (EEOC) show that these reasonable fears have not, however, been realized. According to Eleanor Holmes Norton, Chair of the EEOC between 1987 and 1994, less than 2 percent of the discrimination charges filed at the EEOC were by White men claiming reverse discrimination.[60]

The small number of reverse-discrimination suits brought by White men was not due to some testosterone-induced reticence about appearing demanding. Indeed, in 1994, of 8,026 age-discrimination suits filed with the EEOC, 6,541 came from White men. "It is unlikely," observes Norton, "that white men, who understood age discrimination, would have any reluctance to file complaints if they believed they were victims of other forms of discrimination."[61]

Possible Loss of Efficiency

Even if the administrative costs are low, firms may suffer from loss of efficiency or effectiveness, especially if they are hiring people who do not achieve the top scores on the entrance criteria. Many affirmative action plans allow an organization to hire the person who ranks third, fourth, or fifth in entrance criteria, so long as the person scores above threshold. Hiring that person instead of the first-ranked person might compromise the competitive edge of any company.[62]

There is another way that affirmative action could jeopardize productivity. It could provoke conflict. By bringing in women workers where they are not wanted, affirmative action could produce a hostile backlash among male workers. By bringing in people of color, no matter how talented, where they are disliked, affirmative action could evoke negative reactions among White people. Conflict is never good for business.

But it is also possible, according to economists, that justified and limited preferential hiring of the type permitted by affirmative action will not affect profits. Assuming that there is no marketplace discrimination, in times of less than full employment, the practice of hiring someone within a band of an identified width, whether at the top or the bottom of the band, could have no impact on the firm's performance, assuming that everyone within the band-width has the capability to do the job. Unemployment means that there is a surplus of qualified workers. When unemployment figures are greater than zero, employers can "use criteria other than merit in hiring workers with little effect on profits."[63] Consider, for example, the professor who needs an excellent research assistant—someone with an A average (that is, within the band-width of 10 percentage points). As long as some A-average student workers are unemployed, the professor will have the luxury of selecting from among a number of A-student applicants. In such a situation, the professor can select someone for reasons that have little to do with academics and suffer no ill consequence in the research program.

The assumption of a marketplace free of discrimination seems starry-eyed to some social scientists. But if one believes that people of color or White women have been discriminated against, one might conclude that policies like affirmative action can actually improve the profitability of companies. Artificial barriers have kept out talented people; removing the barriers would raise the level of talent working at the firm.

Another way that good affirmative action policies can raise efficiency and profitability is by helping firms retain the talented women and talented men of color they have hired. Paul Osterman found that women employees are less likely to quit jobs in industries that receive the attention of the OFCCP than in other industries.[64] Talented people like to know that their opportunities are not being blocked.

In theory, then, one could argue that affirmative action will decrease productivity, and one could also argue that it will increase productivity. How can we settle the issue? My preference would be to do so as we have settled so many others—through empirical data. Fortunately, there are empirical studies available. Three very careful studies in particular all bear directly on the question.

Jonathan Leonard approached the issue by looking at the number of women and minority workers in various industries between 1966 and 1977 and then examining whether the industry's output changed as the percentage of women or minority workers changed. In his calculations, Leonard took into account the region, the capital stock, and the percentage of the industry that was blue-collar. He concluded that neither the change in the percentage of women nor the change in the percentage of minorities in the workforce had any effect on productivity.[65]

Cecilia Conrad repeated the type of analysis done by Leonard, but looked at data from 1984 to 1989, a period when affirmative action was particularly strong. Like Leonard, Conrad found no effect on productivity through increased percentages of women or people of color in the workforce. The negative impact predicted by the critics of affirmative action simply did not materialize. Neither did the large positive effect that some of the more radical proponents might have expected.[66]

Both Leonard's and Conrad's analyses have limitations. Because they are dealing with large data sets, where the information has been aggregated at a very general level, both analyses rest on inferences that, while reasonable, should curtail the confidence with which we draw conclusions. For both sets of data, for example, we have to assume that regional variations are not large. Worse, we have to assume no substantial difference in the productivity of women working for affirmative action employers and women working for other employers. The same assumption needs to be applied as well to ethnic minorities.

Another study helps to fill the inferential gaps left by Leonard and by Conrad. In their survey of eight hundred employers in Atlanta, Boston, Detroit, and Los Angeles, Holzer and Neumark not only obtained information about the ethnicity and sex of people hired; they also looked into the employees' qualifications and their on-the-job performance.[67] Holzer and Neumark first divided the sample into firms that used affirmative action in recruiting and firms that didn't. No differences could be detected between the two types of firms in terms of the qualifications of those hired. They then took a second pass at the sample, dividing it into two groups: the highly committed firms that used affirmative action in *hiring* and those—the majority—that used it in recruiting. The gap between the credentials of White males on the one hand and women and people of color, on the other, was significantly greater in the firms that used affirmative action in hiring than in the other firms. Affirmative action employers hired women with lower qualifications than men and hired people of color with lower qualifications than White people. Yet when it came to performance, no differences were detectable. White women and people of color performed just as well on the job whether they worked for a committed affirmative action employer or elsewhere.

As the American economic environment becomes more receptive to diversity, companies might realize another benefit from having strong affirmative action plans: attracting capital. Similarly, organizations that are known to practice ethnic or sex discrimination, in today's ideological climate, may have a hard time finding investors.

Such was the logic of Peter Wright, Stephen Ferris, Janine Hiller, and Mark Kroll, who published the results of their investigation in the prestigious *Academy of Management Journal*.[68] Wright and colleagues looked at fluctuations in stock prices of companies that were either known to be outstanding affirmative action employers or known to be discriminatory. The sample of outstanding affirmative action employers was derived by using the list of winners of the EVE (Exemplary Voluntary Efforts) Award, approximately six of which are given annually by the OFCCP. For the thirty-four companies that won the award between 1986 and 1992, stock prices jumped up at the time of the announcement. Meanwhile, for thirty-five publicly traded companies that announced settlements of discrimination suits between 1986 and 1992, stock prices dropped significantly on the day after the settlement was announced in the *Wall Street Journal* or the *Dow Jones News*. At least for the very short term, good affirmative action is tacitly recognized by the business community to be good business.[69]

Other researchers have reported similar findings. Companies that are ranked as being very compliant with affirmative action by the EEOC enjoy an average return of 18.3 percent on their stocks, while companies that are ranked as being recalcitrant have only an average return of 7.9 percent.[70] From 1988 to 1992, according to one report, companies that ranked in the top fifth in terms of hiring women and people of color had stocks that outperformed the market average by 2.4 percent, whereas companies at the bottom fifth underperformed by 8 percent.[71]

Publicizing the Economic Effectiveness of Affirmative Action

In economic terms, the effectiveness of affirmative action has sometimes been exaggerated. Some have credited affirmative action with amazing effectiveness. One proponent notes that "affirmative action has been essential to the advancement of African Americans in job markets that were long out of bounds"[72] and goes on to credit the policy with some huge successes: "The result of affirmative action has been considerable achievement by the 'mobile strata' of African-Americans—stable working-class, middle-class, and upper-middle-class households. These now make up nearly 65 percent of black households. Family income data for 1990 show that some 246,000 black households earned $50,000 to $55,000; some 92,000 households earned more than $70,000; and some 8,000 earned more than $100,000."[73] It seems unlikely that affirmative action provides the whole explanation for Black advances. Certainly, other government interventions, like the civil rights legislation of the 1960s, should enjoy some of the credit. Market forces inside the United States and around the world are also surely part of the reason that the country has made some progress along the road to ethnic and gender equality.

More often, in the popular press, affirmative action has been vilified. Some conservatives have likened affirmative action to "a fungus that can survive only . . . in the dark," and have claimed that affirmative action has had a "stifling effect" on the economy. The claim has even been made that affirmative action has reduced our gross national product by 4 percent.[74]

The doom-sayers are probably ideological zealots, but many reasonable people entertain serious doubts about the effectiveness of affirmative action. Yet the strong consensus among economists and policy experts is that affirmative action has been effective. In economic terms, affirmative action has helped women and minorities get more jobs, get better jobs, and earn higher wages. The successes have not been constant, and some periods have shown fewer successes than others, but the overall record is good. The success, furthermore, has not imposed undue burdens on White men, especially on competent White men. Nor has it cost companies much.

Given how consistently the empirical data show that affirmative action is effective, why have scholars not done a better job of educating people about the facts? Why is it so hard for average citizens to learn the whole story? Why has the effectiveness of affirmative action been so often disputed?

Three explanations seem plausible. None is exclusively true, for different people's reactions to affirmative action may be motivated by different factors. But taken together, the explanations may clarify why the effectiveness of affirmative action, in economic terms, is still debated.

The first factor is the difficulty of penetrating the dense jargon of econometric treatises. Economists, with their talk of "residuals," "relative marginal productivity," and "logit models," are hard to understand. And the formulas can be forbidding for those who do not list advanced calculus among their credentials.

Yet journalists and scholars have been able to translate into understandable prose concepts that are much harder to grasp than the findings of economists. And the book-buying public has sometimes displayed a strong appetite for dry reading, encumbered with many references and formulas, as seen, for example, in the popularity of Dinesh D'Souza's lumbering *Illiberal Education* and Herrnstein and Murray's ponderous (and ultimately incorrect) *The Bell Curve.*[75]

A second possible reason it has been hard for justice-minded Americans to obtain a true reckoning of the economic costs and benefits of affirmative action is, in my opinion, the psychological price that comes with such a recognition. Asking why "the myth that affirmative action policies benefit minorities at the expense of qualified white men prevails," Cedric Herring and Sharon Collins reply, "We suspect that such a myth is founded in a tradition in which wealth, power, and prestige are acquired by severely limiting nonwhite and non-male competition. It may be that white men who object to affirmative action are less interested in social justice than in protecting their monopoly over these valuable social advantages."[76]

I imagine that another factor also contributes to Americans' continued ignorance about the economic consequences of affirmative action policy. Many Americans seem to confound the economic consequences of affirmative action and the educational consequences. More and more, educational attainments—and particularly a bachelor's degree—have a huge influence on an individual's life prospects.[77] With the decline of the importance of manufacturing in the national economy, it is no longer as common as it once was for a (male) high school graduate to earn a high salary as a skilled craftsman. Increasing numbers of young Americans are battling their way into college and, indeed, into graduate and professional programs. Because many White citizens may feel nervous about competition for prized positions among the collegiate student body, they may miss the difference between economic benefits and educational costs. But differentiating the two may be both sensible and important.

Affirmative Action in Education

What are the costs and benefits of affirmative action in education? Who reaps the benefits? Who bears the costs? These questions are of extraordinary importance.

As indicated in Chapter 1, aside from the relative disregard of gender issues in education and the relative concentration on ethnicity, affirmative action plans in education have followed the logic of affirmative action plans in employment.[78] Institutions—primarily universities—monitor the composition of the student body and compare what they observe to what would be expected if all students, no matter what their background, were provided equal access to the institution of higher education. When discrepancies are found, the institution seeks to take corrective action.

The University of California

The situation at the University of California in the 1990s illustrates how the logic may play out in concrete terms.[79] In 1965 the California legislature adopted what was known as the Master Plan for Higher Education for the State of California.[80] At the core of the plan is an acknowledgment that state of California has an obligation to educate its citizenry. A three-tier system differentiates between the University of California, the California State Colleges, and a network of community colleges. The University of California comprises ten separate campuses, of which nine are fully operational and one (Merced) is in its early development. Eight of the nine campuses include undergraduate as well as graduate education and one (San Francisco) exists almost exclusively as a graduate school. Among the campuses, Berkeley and UCLA are by far the most competitive in terms of undergraduate admissions.

Several factors distinguish the University of California (U.C.) from the California State Colleges (Cal State) and from the community colleges. Legally, the University of California is the only public university in the state that has the authority to grant doctoral degrees. From this distinction flow others. Although the Cal State schools include many prominent researchers in a number of fields in their faculty, the U.C. system is still considered the research university of California. U.C. is better funded than Cal State. The faculty teach a lighter load at the U.C. than at the Cal State schools. And, by law, U.C. is reserved for the "top" 12.5 percent of California high school graduates.

Determining who the top students are is complicated, however, because several different variables must be taken into account. Grades matter. So do scores on standardized tests. Table 4.1 provides the formula by which the university calculates academic achievement before taking into account such indicators of motivation and interest in schooling as extracurricular activities and a history of overcoming adversity. In calculating the grade-point average overall, an A in an advanced-placement course is worth 5 points, a B is worth 4 points, and so on. Meanwhile, an A in other courses is worth 4 points, a B is worth 3, and so on down the line.

In the late 1980s and early 1990s several senior administrators at the University of California, including the late Chancellor Chang-Lin Tien of Berkeley, started to publicize some anomalies.[81] They noticed that Hispanic and Black high school juniors and seniors were less likely than White and Asian American juniors and seniors to take the optional standardized tests (the SAT II exams in particular) and were also less likely to take advanced-placement classes. Generally the reason for the discrepancy had little to do with student motivation, preparation, or abilities and much to do with the schools the Hispanics and Blacks attended. Such schools were typically in the less affluent areas, and they lacked the monetary resources either to offer advanced-placement classes or to provide proper counseling to the students about the SAT exams. Clearly, the rules of admission were having systematic, although unintended, disparate effects on White students and students of Hispanic and African American heritage.[82] Discriminatory barriers were standing in the way of talented minority students making their way into the U.C. schools.

Table 4.1
Eligibility Index for U.C. Admissions
(California Residents)

Grade-point average	Test score total
2.80–2.84	4,640
2.85–2.89	4,384
2.90–2.94	4,160
2.95–2.99	3,984
3.00–3.04	3,840
3.05–3.09	3,720
3.10–3.14	3,616
3.15–3.19	3,512
3.20–3.24	3,408
3.25–3.29	3,320
3.30–3.34	3,248
3.35–3.39	3,192
3.40–3.44	3,152
3.45–3.49	3,128
>3.5	3,120

Note: Test scores consist of (SAT I) + (2x SAT II Writing score) + (SAT II Math score) + (3rd SAT II score).

What can be done about such a situation? Some remedies are long term and expensive. Others are more expedient. One long-term, costly remedy is to equalize availability of advanced-placement courses. Currently, the University of California is developing online advanced-placement courses. Another solution is to decrease the importance of expensive tests like the SATs, either by substituting other standardized tests that are free or by exempting a fraction of the top students from each school from the requirement to take the test. A system called Eligibility in the Local Context, approved by the Regents in 2000, currently allows the top 4 percent of every public high school in California to matriculate at U.C. on grades alone, without consideration of test scores. Much more expedient—quicker and less expensive to implement—was the system of taking into account a student's eth-

nic and financial background. By considering ethnicity and family fi-
nances, the university was attempting to neutralize the disparate impact of its (also admittedly expedient) admissions policies, a disparity
that it had noticed by monitoring the composition of its student body
relative to the composition of talented high school students.[83]

More Generally

While following the general logic of the employment policy, the policy
of affirmative action in education has taken three specific forms. First,
some plans concern adjustments to admission requirements. The second form centers around extra efforts to attract or retain students of
color through the selective use of scholarships and other financial in-
centives. Finally, as we saw in Chapter 2, affirmative action in education exists when institutions give special consideration to determining
whether students from designated groups actually meet the requirements.

Use of the last technique has come in for less criticism than either
of the other two. The admissions officer who makes an extra phone call
to determine whether the minority applicant is really as qualified as the
majority applicants does not seem to be violating the norms of impartiality in the same way as the admissions officer who awards extra
points to a candidate simply because the applicant comes from a minority background.[84] Perhaps because special inquiries seem inoffen-
sive, few critics have claimed that they are ineffective. In contrast,
many critics have asserted that race-conscious scholarship programs or
race-conscious admission standards are not only ineffective, they are
actually counterproductive.

Typical of the critics of affirmative action is Douglas Detterman,
a professor at Case Western University. In an essay entitled "Tests, Affirmative Action in University Admissions, and the American Way,"
Detterman claimed, "It is clear that, at least for the measures considered here, affirmative action has not had its intended effect. Blacks are
no better off today than they were 25 years ago. It might even be possible to show that they are relatively worse off. . . . At best, affirmative
action for college admissions has been inconsequential to the welfare
of minorities."[85]

He went on to announce: "Affirmative action was implemented because it seemed like the right thing to do. Like most social programs, it was implemented without any data to support its effectiveness. As far as I have been able to determine, there are still no data to support its continuation. If such data are not forthcoming, the program should be discontinued."[86]

Detterman is both right and wrong in his allegations. He is right that few data were available when affirmative action was instigated. But he is wrong when he claims that "there are still no data" about its effectiveness. Apparently, Detterman and others like him have somehow managed to avoid the highly publicized, critically acclaimed, monumental study *The Shape of the River,* published by Princeton University Press in 1998.[87]

The Shape of the River was written by two bastions of the educational establishment, "old boy" insiders William Bowen and Derek Bok. Bowen was president of Princeton University from 1972 to 1988, after which he assumed the presidency of the Andrew W. Mellon Foundation. Bok was president of Harvard University from 1971 to 1991. Their book was a scholarly, highly quantitative presentation of a beautifully conceived and executed study underwritten by the Mellon Foundation. Over a period of four years, the foundation assembled a massive database, which they called College and Beyond. It contained records of more than 80,000 students who had matriculated in 1951, 1976, and 1989 at twenty-eight top colleges and universities. The database consisted of two parts: the "in-college" component and the "after-graduation" component. The in-college information included test scores, rank in high school class, academic performance in college, extracurricular and athletic activities in college, and graduation status as well as sex and ethnicity. Subsequent information for many of the study participants included data about advanced degrees, occupation, family data, and participation in civic activities. Contacted through surveys (to which 80 percent of the 1976 matriculants and 84 percent of the 1989 matriculants responded), the participants reflected on their college years and described the degree of satisfaction with college life. The 1989 matriculants also answered questions about their experiences with members of other races.

Bowen and Bok concluded that many of the Black applicants

would not have been admitted to the schools had there not been race-sensitive admissions policies. Close examination of the rich data set led them to surmise that the race-blind admissions would have sliced in half the number of Blacks at the twenty-eight schools in the study. Thomas Kane performed similar statistical analyses on the College and Beyond data set for students who graduated from high school in 1982. Like Bowen and Bok, Kane concluded that at selective colleges and universities race-sensitive admissions policies gave Hispanic and Black applicants a significant boost—the equivalent of transforming a B average into an A— or of changing an SAT combined score of 1,000 to a 1,400.[88] Studies of other elite institutions, such as law schools and medical schools, have also reached the conclusion that race-sensitive admissions have increased and do increase the number of underrepresented minorities in professional schools.[89]

While affirmative action has dramatically increased the number of people of color in America's universities and colleges, it has not dramatically decreased the number of White students. Because Black students constituted a small proportion of the College and Beyond sample, changing their numbers by even 50 percent would not have influenced the numbers of Whites by more than a fraction. Indeed, Bowen and Bok determined that the elimination of race-sensitive admissions policies would have resulted in only a 1.5 percent change in a White person's probability of acceptance into one of the elite schools. Had there been no sensitivity to race or ethnicity, a White person's chances for admission would have increased from 25 percent to 26.5 percent. Meanwhile, separate studies have found that while affirmative action has increased the probability of a member of an ethnic minority entering Harvard, minority status continues to be dwarfed by legacy status. The children of alumni are three times as likely to be accepted at Harvard as are comparable nonlegacy applicants.[90]

Borrowing an image from Michael Nettles of the University of Michigan, William Bowen has likened the admissions figures to a fight over parking spaces. Imagine yourself in a large, overcrowded parking lot, unable to find a space and feeling more and more frustration. You spy three reserved parking spaces (set aside for the store manager and the handicapped). "Ah!" you think. "If only I could park there!" But if you could park there, so could any of the other cars that, like you, are circling the lot looking for a place to park. Chances of your getting those spaces are small indeed.

Admission to college is not the same as success in college. Many opponents of affirmative action bemoan the failures of Blacks once they are in college. Shelby Steele has written about what he sees as the devastating effect of affirmative action policies that entice ill-prepared Black students into a setting where they cannot compete.[91] Stephan and Abigail Thernstrom note that at least 50 percent more Black students drop out of college than White students, a statistic that even Bowen and Bok do not dispute.[92]

Yet in the College and Beyond sample, the dropout rate for Blacks was only 25 percent. The more selective the school, the lower the attrition rate—for Whites and for Blacks. The success of the most selective schools cannot, furthermore, be explained only in terms of the gifted students they attract. Bowen and Bok divided their samples according to intervals in the SAT scores. At each interval or band, the more selective the school, the higher the graduation rate—even when the students (Black or White) were at schools where most of their fellow students had much higher SAT scores than they. While Black students as a group earned lower grades than White students during college, furthermore, they were slightly more likely than White students to go on to earn an advanced degree. For the 1976 entering cohort, 87 percent of the Black students and 79 percent of the White students went on to earn a master's degree, a doctorate, or a degree in law or medicine. For the class entering college in 1989, the figures were 89 percent and 83 percent, respectively. So much for a cycle of failure!

Minority students were not the only beneficiaries of affirmative action admissions policies, according to data that Bowen and Bok collected from White graduates who had matriculated in 1989. More than 40 percent of the White graduates thought that it is very important to be able to get along with people of different races; and well over half of them credited their college experiences with having helped them develop the skill to do so.[93] Less than 10 percent of the White students said that they had no close Black friends at college, while 56 percent knew at least two Black students well. The higher the concentration of Black students at the school, the more likely it was that a White graduate had known at least two Black students well. Nearly three-quarters of the White students who knew two or more Black students well in college went on to make friendships after graduation with two or more Black people, but less than half of the White students without Black friends did. For White Americans wishing to learn how to get along in an increasingly multicultural world, affirmative action in college admissions is a decided boon.

Other research substantiates the findings of Bowen and Bok. Mark Chesler and Melissa Peet, researchers at the University of Michigan, conducted interviews with students there. Said one undergraduate, "I came from a place that was purely white . . . and I'm just totally culture shocked. Now I have friends of different cultures, different ethnicities, and I feel I wouldn't have done that if it weren't for the school I was at. If I'd gone to another school where diversity was not such a big deal I could stick to what I was comfortable with, but here you're forced to interact with these differences."[94]

Another student expressed thankfulness for affirmative action at the university "because without it we wouldn't be able to have diverse classes. I wouldn't be able to sit in a class on race and have students who are not white talk about their experience so I can learn from them. . . . [I've benefited from] learning to deal with people you don't get along with, who you can't understand and can't see eye to eye with, and how to function in those situations. . . . We'd never really understand other people's points of view without hearing them firsthand."[95]

Colleagues of Chesler and Peet at the University of Michigan, working under the leadership of Patricia Gurin, have corroborated their descriptive findings with hard figures, gathered in a set of rigorous quantitative studies. One of the studies was an experiment in which the "intervention" occurred during the students' first year and the results were tested during their senior year. During their freshman year, eighty-seven students assigned to "the experimental condition" took part in a special intercultural class in which they met weekly in small discussion sections with a mix of people. As seniors, the students were asked their opinions about their experiences. The researchers contrasted the experimental group of students with another group of students, matched on demographic characteristics, who had not participated in the program. The contrast showed that the students in the experimental condition had learned a lot. They understood constructive criticism, saw differences in outlook as consistent with America's democratic ideals, and showed a higher than average ability to take the perspective of the other person.[96]

Gurin has also looked at large data sets. In one study, she and her colleagues tracked 1,582 students at the University of Michigan over the four years of their college education.[97] More than 1,100 of the students were White. The more contact White students had with students of other backgrounds, the more they developed "active" and "engaged" thinking. Good judgment is an asset of value to any adult, no matter what his or her occupation, and apathy is no friend to democracy. The United States, and the individuals in it, benefit when its citizens nurture their capacity for critical thinking.

Were the results specific to the University of Michigan? Perhaps there was something unusual about the situation in Ann Arbor. After all, two lawsuits, both brought by rejected White applicants against the university, had the entire campus focused on issues of diversity and affirmative action during 2002 and 2003.

In a companion study, Gurin and associates have been able to demonstrate that the results generalize nationally. They analyzed data from 11,383 students (including 10,465 White students) at 183 different colleges and universities around the country and found essentially the same results. Contact with others unlike themselves helps students develop intellectually.[98]

The detractors may wring their hands and speak about the evils of affirmative action in education. But the data do not appear to conform to their dire characterizations. On the contrary, impressive data sets show that affirmative action in education has brought substantial benefit to students of color. The data also indicate that those White students who exhibit enough talent to gain entrance to colleges and universities reap the rewards of the race-conscious admissions policies of their schools. The major losers in the current situation seem to be the 1.5 percent of White students who are denied admission to the schools of their choice who might otherwise be admitted.

How one interprets the data from the social scientific studies may depend on one's politics. The majority of justices in *Grutter v. Bollinger*, for example, found the studies convincing. But some of the dissenters did not. And one justice, Antonin Scalia, who appeared to accept the methodology and conclusions of Bowen and Bok and of Gurin and colleagues, was nonetheless scathing about the premise that universities have a responsibility to teach good citizenship. Such tasks, wrote Scalia, are best left to the Boy Scouts.

At the Level of Society
Social Costs

Every rose has its thorns. No matter how effective the policy of affirmative action, it does contain some costs to society—and not simply in terms of the controversy it generates. When evaluating the policy, we need to weigh its demonstrated effectiveness against the problems it creates.

From the complaints of its detractors, we can identify three social costs of the policy, costs that would not be manifest in a strict accounting for an individual firm or school but nonetheless may fall on society or on segments of society. The first is the burden borne by taxpayers. As taxpayers, we bear the cost of staffing and operating the OFCCP, which employs about eight hundred people nationwide. The budget for the OFCCP is about one-quarter of the budget of the EEOC. In 1992, the budget was a mere $55 million; in 2002 it was still only $77.5 million.

Perhaps less evident but also more consequential are the problems that arise when incompetent people are hired for positions of public trust. In Linda Gottfredson's scathing 1996 indictment of hiring practices in the Police Department of Nassau County, the author claimed that the federal government, and specifically the Justice Department, had put unreasonable pressure on professional psychologists to help the county modify the tests that they administered for entry into the force.[99] The real impetus for the lowering of standards was, according to Gottfredson, a drive for ethnic diversity coupled with the inability of applicants of color to pass the original tests.

Of course, the fracas had a history. In 1971, in the *Griggs* case, the Supreme Court ruled that tests producing disparate impact were illegal unless justified by a compelling business interest. And in 1977 the Justice Department had sued Nassau County because its entrance exam had a disparate impact: many more White applicants than minority applicants passed the test. By 1994 a new test had been developed that showed no ethnic differences in the passing rate. A year later, the Justice Department was encouraging police departments around the nation to adopt the test.

The problem, according to Gottfredson, was that the test had been modified so much that it actually provided no screening at all. As an expert consultant to the Justice Department, Gottfredson had seen how the test omitted "virtually any measurement of cognitive (mental) skills, and she became disgusted."[100] The omission would have been fine only if, in the words of a vice president of the company that developed the test, "you assume a cop will never have to write a coherent sentence or interpret what someone else has written."[101] Relying on other educational credentials to ensure a competent police force would not help much, in Gottfredson's view, because research had shown her "that Black college graduates, on the average, exhibit the cognitive skill levels of White high school graduates without any college."[102] What appeared to Gottfredson to be a corrupt process would, of course, cause problems for the citizens of Nassau County. If Gottfredson is right, then they cannot rely on their police department to keep them safe.

That Gottfredson is at least partially correct appears to be shown in a detailed analysis of crime rates conducted by John R. Lott, Jr.[103] Lott examined data from comprehensive surveys conducted by the Department of Justice in 1987, 1990, and 1993. He limited his attention to city police departments employing a hundred or more officers. Nineteen of the cities had consent decrees imposed on them during the period, requiring that they change the composition of the force. On average the violent crime rate increased in cities after the police department was required to diversify. Crime rates increased as the number of Black officers increased. Lott inferred that the increase in crimes was due to the lowering of standards—for both minority and majority applicants—following the push for diversity.

But it is possible that Lott's explanation is wrong. Certainly, Lott's conclusions are not completely consistent with results of an earlier study by Brent Steel and Nicholas Lovrich.[104] Perhaps some other factor (such as increased poverty in the inner cities) accounted for the increase in crime, for the increase in police officers of color, and for the conflicts that led to the consent decrees. Without detailed knowledge of the histories of the nineteen cities with consent decrees, it would be hard to piece together the full story. Yet Lott's findings, in light of Gottfredson's worries, may signal that affirmative action sometimes results in burdens that will be carried by the public.[105]

A final potential cost of affirmative action for society is that it may act as a wedge within the Black community, dividing middle-class Blacks from impoverished Blacks. William Juris Wilson and Glenn Loury have both articulated the concern that affirmative action causes a split within the African American community.[106] Blacks with a good education who are relatively unencumbered by domestic responsibilities can take advantage of new opportunities opened by affirmative action in employment. Meanwhile, Blacks without a decent education or those who must stay home to care for their dependents are left behind—literally, as well as figuratively. As the beneficiaries of affirmative action move out of the inner cities and into the more affluent suburbs, the cities descend into deeper and deeper poverty.

Relying on figures produced by the ultraconservative Heritage Foundation, Robert Woodson, Sr., has echoed the worries of Wilson and Loury: "Since the inception of affirmative action programs, the gap between different economic tiers within the black community has steadily widened. From 1970 to 1986, black households with incomes above $50,000 increased by 200 percent as middle-income blacks moved into the upper income bracket. Yet, during the same period the number of black families with incomes below $10,000 continued to increase."[107]

Taking seriously the idea that affirmative action causes a split between Blacks, two colleagues and I set about to see whether national data showed such a trend.[108] If Wilson and Loury were correct, we reasoned, we would have found a greater bifurcation in wealth among Blacks following 1965 than among Whites. In fact, census data showed something different. For the past several decades, the United States has been traveling along an economic road that we used to think was true only of underdeveloped countries: the rich are getting richer and the poor are getting poorer. But the general trend is not influenced by ethnic categories; it is no more noticeable among Blacks than among Whites. Although a split is clearly detectable, affirmative action is not the cause. Perhaps it is because of data such as these as well as other epiphanies that Glenn Loury now embraces affirmative action.[109]

In sum, we need to be vigilant about the potential costs to society. Although affirmative action does not cost the taxpayers much, and although it has not divided the Black community economically, it may have contributed to problems among police forces around the country. How should we treat these problems? If we believe that the policy is unnecessary, unfair, or generally ineffective, the proper response to findings like Lott's would be to throw the policy out. If, on the other hand, we believe that the policy is necessary, fair, and generally effective, the best response would be to fix it. After his extensive review of affirmative action, President Bill Clinton coined the slogan "Mend it, don't end it." Adjustments and repairs must, I believe, be an ongoing process.

Social Benefits

For the sake of symmetry, let's not forget about the social benefits of affirmative action. One of the greatest social benefits is its role in helping African Americans and other ethnic minorities attain professional positions from which they contribute to society. In 1995 Bowen and Bok asked members of the matriculating class of 1976 in the College and Beyond sample about their volunteer activities. They divided the activities into ten categories:

- Community service
- Social service
- Youth service
- Educational work
- Cultural work
- Alumni/ae activities
- Religious
- Athletic
- Professional
- Environmental.

Among the alumni, for all categories except three—athletics, professional, and environmental—a higher percentage of Black men than White men were volunteers. In athletics, the percentages were the same. One-third of all male graduates volunteered their time and resources to athletic activities. For professional activities, 56 percent of White men did volunteer work, and 50 percent of Black men did. The largest difference appeared in community service. Black men were about twice as likely as Whites to be community leaders.

Among the alumnae, White women outpaced Black women in volunteer commitments in four categories. Women participated in civic activities less often than men, and the ethnic differences were smaller than the gender differences.

A strikingly similar pattern of results was found in a study of graduates of the University of Michigan Law School. Students who were admitted purely on the basis of test scores and undergraduate academic achievement gave less back to their communities in the years after graduation than did other students. Students who were admitted with an eye to their life experiences did as well professionally as the non–affirmative action admits, enjoyed their jobs as much or more, and involved themselves in volunteer activities.[110]

Nor is community-mindedness confined to after-hours volunteer work. Studies confirm that ethnic minority physicians are more likely to serve poor communities and ethnic minority communities than are White physicians. In an early study Nolan Penn, Percy Russell, and Harold Simon discovered that more ethnic minority graduates of the University of California, San Diego, Medical School worked in inner cities and rural areas than White graduates.[111] Another study, using quite a different sampling technique, relied on archival data to track 718 primary-health physicians in California in 1993.[112] The physicians worked in 51 different communities. Black physicians practiced in areas that had five times more Black residents than areas where other physicians worked, and Hispanic physicians practiced in areas with twice as many Hispanic residents. Not surprisingly, Black physicians were much more likely than others to care for Black patients while Hispanic physicians were much more likely than others to care for Hispanic patients. Black doctors took on a disproportionate number of patients on Medicaid, and Hispanic doctors took on a disproportionate number of uninsured patients. Two years later, another study found that Hispanic physicians in Colorado were much more likely than White physicians to serve Hispanic populations and to serve poor populations of all ethnicities.[113]

Andrew Brimmer, both when he was assistant secretary of commerce and later, prepared studies estimating the cost to the U.S. economy of discrimination against non-Whites. When Black men with college degrees in chemistry and physics are forced to work as postal clerks, the nation loses access to valuable talent. Brimmer found that race discrimination has resulted in between 1.5 and 2.2 percent loss of GDP between 1967 and 1993.[114]

Another advantage that society draws from affirmative action is that the policy, along with other liberal social and political policies, helps arrest the devolution of the United States into a stratified nation. After the racial riots of the mid-1960s, the Kerner Commission warned that the United States was becoming two Americas. White America was the land of abundant opportunities, rewarded talent, and hope. Black America was the land of increasing despair. In Black America the curtailing of opportunities was extreme. Huge numbers of African Americans were condemned to live in poverty with little hope of betterment. An explosion seemed ever more likely. Forty years after the Kerner Commission, Blacks in America still enjoy fewer opportunities than Whites. Black talent is still rewarded less consistently than White talent. Meanwhile, the gap between rich and poor is wider today than it was at the time of the Kerner Commission. Yet the dire fears of the commission have not been realized. The percentage of African Americans who attain advanced education and good jobs has increased. A strong Black middle class has developed. Blacks are more and more visible in positions of national leadership. Ruth Simmons heads Brown University, and Colin Powell serves as secretary of state. And it is not just Blacks who have made Oprah Winfrey one of the wealthiest, most influential television personalities today.

Bridges

Economists and other social scientists have accumulated a substantial amount of data on the effectiveness of affirmative action. In economic terms, the policy has directly benefited people of color and White women, giving them access to opportunities that would otherwise have been blocked. Businesses that use sensible affirmative action programs seem also to profit from the policy, as does society generally.

When it comes to education, where matters of affirmative action are played out almost exclusively in terms of race, rather than sex, and where fewer studies have been done, the issues seem especially fraught. Nonetheless, there are good data in this area as well, including one massive study published in 1998. And generally, the data demonstrate the positive outcomes of race-sensitive admissions policies for people of color and Whites alike.

Of course, some costs are hard to calculate in sheer material terms. Perhaps the policy of affirmative action has effectively opened opportunities to those who were previously denied them. Yet the benefits of affirmative action may have been bought at a price not measured in dollars and cents. To opponents of affirmative action the lowered self-respect of members of the targeted classes, combined with the increased resentment on the part of White men, does not balance the the benefits. In the next chapter, we shall explore how high these human costs really are.

5

Does the Medicine
Kill the Patient?

Young women currently being appointed to university positions are already suspect as a consequence of preferential hiring.

Doreen Kimura, "Affirmative Action Policies
Are Demeaning to Women in Academia"

The scholar William Beer adamantly opposes affirmative action. He asserts, "Social scientists have generally refused to study the effects of affirmative action in the United States. Although certainly it is one of the most controversial policies ever implemented, and abundant raw data on the subject are available, most researchers have been reluctant to study its consequences. This lack is particularly grievous because affirmative action's justifications rest on misconceptions that could be corrected by scrupulous scholars."[1]

Beer is partially, but not fully, correct. Scrupulous scholarship can certainly correct a number of misconceptions about affirmative action. But he is wrong in thinking that social scientists have not studied the effects of affirmative action. As we saw in the last chapter, research on the economic and social effects of affirmative action has been copious. Also abundant has been the research on the psychological effects of affirmative action.

Opponents of affirmative action have identified two potentially devastating psychological effects of the policy. Some see it as provoking strong resentments among the nonbeneficiaries. Others see the biggest harm as occurring among those who are supposed to be the direct beneficiaries. They claim that the well-intentioned policy is causing serious damage to the American psyche. If they are correct, the educational and economic benefits documented in Chapter 4 may come with an unacceptably high price tag.

Suspicions of Ill Effects

In May 1977 Congress enacted the Public Works Employment Act, authorizing a transfer of $4 billion from the federal coffers to state and local governments for use in building projects. The act included the Minority Business Enterprise (MBE) provision specifying that 10 percent of each state or local grant had to be spent on contracts going to minority-owned businesses, unless a waiver was granted. Waivers were granted when the municipality or state government could show that they had tried to meet the regulation but had been unable to do so.

On November 30, 1977, H. Earl Fullilove filed a complaint in federal court. As a White contractor, Fullilove felt that he had sustained economic injury because of the MBE clause. He claimed, furthermore, that the law violated the Equal Protection Clause of the Fourteenth Amendment and the Due Process Clause of the Fifth Amendment. About two weeks later, the district court issued a memorandum denying injunctive relief. The case went to the Court of Appeals for the Second Circuit, which, like the lower court, found that the MBE provision passed constitutional muster. Fullilove appealed, and on November 27, 1979, the Supreme Court heard oral arguments in the case of *H. Earl Fullilove et al., Petitioners v. Philip M. Klutznick, Secretary of Commerce of the United States, et al.*

The Supreme Court handed down its decision on July 2, 1980. It sustained the decisions of the district court and the appellate court, finding that the set-aside was not unconstitutional. "Congress," said the majority opinion, "after due consideration, perceived a pressing need to move forward with new approaches in the continuing effort to achieve the goal of equality of economic opportunity."[2] Examining the history of how the law had come to be written, the Court decided that Congress had a "rational basis" for concluding that without such a measure as the MBE set-asides, "subcontracting practices of prime contractors could perpetuate the prevailing impaired access by minority businesses to public contracting opportunities."[3] The existence of waivers, furthermore, meant that the law did not constitute an absolute bar to White contractors.

The majority opinion in the *Fullilove* case had six supporters: Justices Blackmun, Brennan, Burger, Marshall, Powell, and White. Chief Justice Burger wrote the majority decision, which was joined by Justices Powell and White. Powell also wrote a separate concurring decision. Justice Marshall wrote another concurring decision, which was joined by Justices Blackmun and Brennan.[4]

Justice Stewart wrote a dissenting opinion in *Fullilove,* and his opinion was joined by Justice Rehnquist. The dissent proposed that "[t]he Court's attempt to characterize the law as a proper remedial measure to counteract the effects of past or present racial discrimination is remarkably unconvincing."[5] Stewart and Rehnquist argued that any statute that accords a preference to some citizens on the basis of color or ancestry is likely to be unconstitutional. Recalling the infamous case that permitted racial segregation, they declared, "Today's decision is wrong for the same reasons that *Plessy v. Ferguson* was wrong."[6]

Equally strong was the language of Justice Stevens in his dissent. Stevens did not doubt that contractors had discriminated in the past, but he felt the "slapdash statute" did not rest on reliable evidence of current discrimination.[7] "[B]ecause classifications based on race are potentially so harmful to the entire body politic, it is especially important that the reasons for any such classifications be clearly identified and unquestionably legitimate."[8] Stevens continued, "Preferences based on characteristics acquired at birth foster intolerance and antagonism against the entire membership of the favored classes."[9]

Justice Stevens's observation—that preferences breed animosity—has been echoed in recent judicial rulings at both the district and appellate levels. The case of *Hopwood v. University of Texas* typifies a number of cases that challenged affirmative action policies in higher education in the 1990s.[10] In 1992 Cheryl Hopwood, Douglas Carvell, Kenneth Elliott, and David Rogers were denied admission to the University of Texas Law School. Hopwood, Carvell, Elliott, and Rogers were White. Ethnic minority students with lower scores than Hopwood on an amalgamated index known as the Texas Index (TI) were admitted. With Hopwood as the lead plaintiff, the group sued. At the time, the law school's admissions office screened applicants and put them into three categories: "presumptive admit," "discretionary zone," and "presumptive denial." It came to light that in 1992 a White applicant with a TI score of 192 was placed in the "presumptive denial" category, while a Black or Mexican American applicant had to have a TI of 179 or lower to be put in the "presumptive denial" category. Blacks and Mexican Americans with TI scores of 189 or better were placed in the "presumptive admit" category.

Both the district court and the Fifth Circuit Court ruled that the school's policy was in violation of the Equal Protection Clause of the Constitution. The circuit court noted, "Diversity fosters, rather than minimizes, the use of race. It treats minorities as a group, rather than as individuals. It may further remedial purposes but, just as likely, may promote improper racial stereotypes, thus fueling racial hostility."[11] In the court's opinion, the "government's use of racial classifications serves to stigmatize."[12] Classifications based on ethnicity, race, or color (and presumably sex as well) are unacceptable in the eyes of the Fifth Circuit Court and several other federal courts, not only because such classifications seem inconsistent with the courts' interpretations of the Constitution but also because they seem to be psychologically unsatisfactory, increasing stigma and animosity.

In his long and somewhat meandering dissent in the *Grutter v. Bollinger* case, Justice Clarence Thomas echoed the concern. Quoting from the *Adarand* judgment, Justice Thomas wrote, "Beyond the harm the Law School's racial discrimination visits upon its test subjects, no social science has disproved the notion that discrimination 'engender[s] attitudes of superiority or, alternately, provoke[s] resentment among those who believe that they have been wronged by the government's use of race.'"[13]

Does Affirmative Action Provoke Hostility?

Justice Thomas's pronouncements notwithstanding, what has appeared self-evident to some members of the courts has been treated by social scientists as an empirical question needing further study. Do racial and gender classifications, classifications based on characteristics "acquired at birth," lead to hostility and stigma? Do people from nonbenefited groups disparage women or minorities who are assumed to be the beneficiaries of affirmative action?

A number of social scientists have conducted experiments and surveys to find answers to these questions. Their methods as well as their findings merit a detailed discussion for two reasons. The first is the significance of the claim. It is extremely important to know whether either unjustified preferences or affirmative action, or both, cause the kind of mischief assumed and asserted by Justices Stewart, Thomas, and Rehnquist and by the Fifth Circuit Court of Appeals. Second, impartially and systematically collected data offer the best means of assuring ourselves that the assertions about stigma and self-doubt are not, themselves, simply the product of highly situated, possibly even prejudiced, thinking.

One of the most prominent researchers on the topic is Madeline Heilman, a professor of organizational psychology at New York University. Although Heilman has collected some data relevant to race relations, she has concentrated her considerable efforts mainly on gender issues. Heilman has been studying the unintended consequences of sex-sensitive and race-sensitive practices for nearly twenty years.

In 1992 Heilman, Caryn Block, and Jonathan Lucas published two studies showing that, yes, White men do stigmatize the recipients of affirmative action.[14] In the first study, a laboratory experiment, participants took part in what they thought was an investigation of employee selection procedures. Each participant read a packet of materials describing first a job and then a person who had applied for and gotten the job. Each participant then completed a series of rating forms. Participants were told that the purpose of the study was to match their ratings against the applicant's actual performance as a way of studying the predictive value of judgments.

Several factors were systematically (and randomly) varied in the materials presented to participants. For half the participants the job described was electrician; for half it was lab technician. One-third of the participants thought the job applicant was a man, while two-thirds thought the applicant was a woman. To emphasize the issue of gender, a photo of a White man or a White woman was attached to the file. Of special relevance for our purposes is the fact that half the participants who received materials about the female applicant thought she was an affirmative action hire, while the other half did not. The manipulation was effected by means of a section on the application marked "for clerical purposes only." Handwritten in the section was the phrase "Hire (affirmative action hiree)"—but only on the materials seen by a third of the participants. The other two-thirds of participants saw the word "Hire," but there was no mention of affirmative action.

The results were sobering. The rating forms included a measure of perceived competence. For the job of electrician, participants saw the man as the most competent, the nonaffirmative action woman as the next-most competent, and the affirmative action hire as the least competent. For the job of laboratory technician, the woman hired through affirmative action was again perceived as less competent than either the other woman or the man. Remember that there were no differences between the stated qualifications of the applicants. In fact, all participants saw identical information about the applicant with the exception of his or her sex and the affirmative action designation. The effects on rated competence between the "affirmative action" woman and the other two applicants were thus simply the product of the label "affirmative action." Those who were presumed to have been hired under affirmative action were also rated more negatively on a series of personal characteristics: hardworking versus lazy, energetic versus sluggish.

To see whether the results would generalize outside the university, Heilman and her colleagues approached White men in public places in New York and Chicago and asked them to complete a brief questionnaire. Nearly two hundred men took part in the study. The men were instructed, "Please take a few seconds to think of a specific co-worker, one who joined your unit in the past few years and is a member of a group who in the past did not typically have your type of job."[15] The study participants were then asked to assess the extent to which "this individual was given this position because of Affirmative Action Policies."[16] Later in the questionnaire, the participants rated the co-worker in terms of competence and other personal characteristics.

The more an individual was seen to be an affirmative action hire, the less the individual was seen to be competent. The negative association recurred for a number of different measures of competence, indicating that the findings of the laboratory experiment were accurate. The association between affirmative action and presumed incompetence was strong, especially if the co-worker was Black.

In later experiments, Heilman and colleagues demonstrated that the presumption of incompetence did not come only with the label "affirmative action." In one experiment, a woman who obtained a desirable job was told in the presence of the man who was chosen to be her subordinate that she had been selected either because of her superior scores or "because you are a woman."[17] In another study, conducted in an insurance company with managers serving as experimental participants, the target woman in the stimulus materials was sometimes said to have been selected "through [a] Women/Minority Recruiting Program."[18] Preferential treatment of any kind, not simply the term "affirmative action," triggered derogation.

Most alarming of all are the results of another experiment. It showed negative evaluations even though no indication was made that the specific woman had been given preferential treatment. Working with William Battle, Chris Keller, and R. Andrew Lee, Heilman conducted an experiment in which seventy-five MBA students looked at a packet of materials describing a woman who was being considered for promotion in a company. The students all read the same job description and the same description of the woman's background and qualifications. Where they encountered different materials was concerning the company's personnel policies. Just learning that a company had a preferential policy, without any indication that preferential treatment had been used in the specific case under consideration, was sufficient to produce some stigmatizing of the woman.[19]

While Heilman has shown that affirmative action, preferential treatment, and diversity-enhancing policies can provoke derogation of women among men, she has also been careful to investigate the boundaries of the connection she has so compellingly demonstrated. By varying certain aspects of the experiments she has explored whether derogation is inevitable. To do this, she has tracked the circumstances that limit the effect, as distinct from the circumstances that foster stigmatizing.

In the experiment where a woman (a confederate of the experimenter) was selected to serve as the supervisor of the male participant, Heilman and associates varied the qualifications listed for the woman. Sometimes, the woman was clearly superior to the man on the criterion test used to determine skill. Sometimes she was equal, and sometimes the man scored better on the test. In cases where the woman had scored as well as or better than the man, the decision of the experimenter to choose the woman as the leader on the basis of gender did not lead the man to underestimate her competence.[20] Along the same lines, two separate studies found that an indication that the woman had clearly performed well wiped out any effect on participants' judgments of competence due to whether the woman was or was not said to have been hired "through [a] Women/Minority Recruiting Program." It was only when the woman's performance was not clearly excellent that the notation in her file that she had been a special hire led participants to assess her work as less competent than that of other women or men.[21]

While preferential treatment produces more stigmatizing than merit-based evaluation systems, not all forms of "preferential treatment" are the same.[22] Some forms elicit less-negative reactions than others. In one study, Heilman's experimental procedure called for participants to assess the competence of a candidate for promotion at Corporate Paper Company and to guess at her future career success after reading materials about her and about the company's personnel policies. One-fifth of the participants learned that "Corporate Paper Company (CPC) is a quality employer and has a merit-based employment policy." Others learned that CPC "is an equal opportunity employer and has an affirmative action policy." Still others learned that CPC has an affirmative action policy such that "in all cases CPC gives primary consideration to hiring women and members of minority groups." The fourth group learned that CPC has an affirmative action policy and that "when applicants are determined to have the minimum job qualifications CPC gives primary consideration to hiring women and members of minority groups." The last group of participants learned: "When applicants are determined to be equally qualified, CPC gives primary consideration to hiring women and members of minority groups." Evaluations of the woman were highest when the company was described as having a merit system. Nonetheless, evaluations of competence and estimations of future career success were higher when participants had seen the words "equally qualified" than in any of the other preferential treatment programs. Not all preferential programs are equally damaging—at least in the lab. Indeed, in the program of research of the leading expert in the field, Madeline Heilman, the adverse consequences of judgments made on the basis of characteristics acquired at birth are contextual. That is to say, sometimes adverse effects occur, but equally often they do not.

Other Studies

Madeline Heilman is neither the first nor the most recent social psychologist to have documented the stigmatizing effects of preferential treatment through carefully conducted laboratory experiments. Indeed, the first study on the topic was conducted in 1977. In this experiment Marsha Jacobson and Walter Koch assigned men to work in groups headed by a woman. Half the time, the woman was selected through merit; half of time she was selected on the basis of her sex. The groups were given feedback as to whether they had succeeded or failed. When the woman had been selected on the basis of her sex, her male subordinates would blame her if the group failed, but they would not give her credit if the group succeeded.[23] Other early researchers found that highlighting affirmative action caused White participants to undervalue the résumés of Black applicants[24] and caused municipal administrators to recommend lower salaries for female applicants in a simulated personnel selection exercise.[25]

In 1998 Gregory Maio and Victoria Esses obtained some negative results among Canadian college students. Maio and Esses paid volunteers to take part in a study on "impressions and attitudes." The students were given what looked like a newspaper editorial on the topic of Surinamese immigration to Canada. The editorial portrayed the inhabitants of Surinam as hardworking, prosperous, and law-abiding. It described a (bogus) volcanic eruption in Surinam that had resulted in large numbers of Surinamers wishing to come to Canada. Half the participants saw the following text: "Besides being good neighbors, Surinamers should also be good job prospects: They will not be a burden to the economy of Canada. Once they arrive in Canada, they should be

able to obtain jobs in all sectors of our economy. As a result, Surinamers will be active in many different types of jobs, and they will contribute tax revenues to offset our federal and provincial deficits."[26]

For the other half of the participants, the text included twenty-
two extra words inserted in the middle of the text: "Besides being good
neighbors, Surinamers should also be good job prospects: They will
not be a burden to the economy of Canada. Once they arrive in
Canada, they will be a recognized minority. Consequently, they should
be able to benefit from our affirmative action and employment equity
programs. These people should be able to obtain jobs in all sectors of
our economy. As a result, Surinamers will be active in many different
types of jobs, and they will contribute tax revenues to offset our federal
and provincial deficits."[27]

The extra twenty-two words were enough to cause the students
to derogate Surinamers. Surinamers were evaluated in a more negative
light, liked less, and seen as possessing lower job skills when affirmative
action was mentioned than when it was not. Opinions about their immigration to Canada were less positive when affirmative action was
mentioned than when it was not. In fact, attitudes toward immigration in general were less positive among those reading the affirmative
action editorial than among the control group. Additional analyses revealed that the negative effects were most pronounced among students
who already had negative attitudes toward affirmative action policy.
"These findings," concluded Maio and Esses, "suggest that the consequences of affirmative action for intergroup attitudes should be seriously considered."[28]

Another recent pair of experiments has produced mixed results.[29] Students at a California state university devalued the competence of Hispanic workers who were said to have been hired through
affirmative action, relative to White workers and to Hispanic workers
hired without mention of affirmative action. Another set of students
from the same university did not, however, devalue the competence of
a Black worker hired through affirmative action.

More positive were the results of two experiments conducted by
Jacqueline Gilbert and Betty Ann Stead.[30] In their first study, Gilbert
and Stead followed the methodology of one of Heilman's experiments
and presented business students with materials about an applicant for

the job of electrician or laboratory technician. In a third of the materials, the applicant was a man. For half the women applicants, the words "affirmative action hire" were written on the documents. For the other half, no such designation occurred, but the description of the corporation included a long statement about how it embraced diversity as a business imperative. Respondents derogated the affirmative action hires but not women hired by the diversity-embracing company. In the second experiment, all the supposed applicants were male, and ethnicity was varied. Black and Hispanic applicants who were tagged "affirmative action hires" were not evaluated as positively as those hired by the diversity-embracing company.

Gilbert and Stead's study shows that one can eliminate or reduce stigma simply by changing the terminology and by explaining the business value of diversity. Such results are consistent with Madeline Heilman's observation that the pernicious effects of special privilege occur in some circumstances, but not in others.

If Gilbert and Stead's results give proponents of affirmative action some comfort, a recent study by David Evans should be a source of significant satisfaction.[31] Evans invited college students and businesspeople to analyze a worker who was described as either White or Black and as receiving either a positive or a negative evaluation. Evans also varied the description of the company's hiring policy. For a third of the subjects—those in the "equal opportunity" group—the policy was described thus: "We at First Federal Bank and Trust wish to emphasize that since 1991, we have given no preference to women and ethnic minorities in hiring applicants. Instead, our equal opportunity policy is designed to ensure that employment at First Federal is determined by qualifications alone, and it is not determined on the basis of race, color, religion, sex, or national origin (Civil Rights Act, 1991)."[32]

Another third read the following: "We at First Federal Bank and Trust wish to emphasize that since 1991, our personnel needs have required that we give slight preferences for qualified women and ethnic minorities, so long as they are as well-qualified and as highly skilled as other non-minority applicants. This affirmative action policy is designed to increase employment opportunities for women and ethnic minorities, and to insure diversity at First Federal that reflects the available work force (Civil Rights Act, 1991)."[33]

For the final third the statement read: "We at First Federal Bank and Trust wish to emphasize that since 1991, our personnel needs have required that we give strong preferences to qualified women and ethnic minorities, even if we must turn away better qualified or more highly skilled non-minority applicants. This affirmative action policy is designed to increase employment opportunities for women and ethnic minorities, and to insure diversity at First Federal that reflects the local community (Civil Rights Act, 1991)."[34] Although the final version represented a strong policy similar to the kinds enacted in some of the experiments by Heilman, it was, as Evans pointed out, not legal. Respondents in all the experimental conditions were asked to make judgments about the worker.

At the core of Evans's experiment was the question of whether subjects would derogate the worker in both types of preferential hiring or only when the policy was described in the strong—and in fact, illegal—terms. Results showed that the Black worker was stigmatized in the strong hiring condition but not when the hiring practices were described in the mild, legal form. The conclusion is clear: when affirmative action is implemented in ways permitted by the policy, its beneficiaries are not stigmatized by others.

Noncollege Populations in Real Work Settings

What about working people in actual organizations? Do White men really underestimate the value of women and people of color? And if so, is the negativity really due to affirmative action programs? Anecdotes abound of sexist men or prejudiced Whites. Stories circulate in every line of work about people who leap to the conclusion that any woman in their division or program must have been recruited through gender-sensitive programs or that any person of color got the job because of race-sensitive programs.

The vividness of such anecdotes can make us think the problem is common. But is it? Anecdotes are not a good way to measure the frequency of behavior. Systematic research is usually much more reliable than haphazard accounts, no matter how vivid the accounts.

One relevant study was conducted in 1989 by Paul Sniderman and Thomas Piazza.[35] The researchers telephoned nearly three hundred White residents of Lexington, Kentucky, and asked them to participate in a survey. Embedded within the survey was an experiment. The participants were asked how much they agreed with ten descriptions of African Americans, five of which were positive (for example, self-disciplined) and five of which were negative (lazy). Half the participants were asked their opinions before they were asked a question about quotas and half afterward. The question about quotas read, "In a nearby state, an effort is being made to increase dramatically the number of blacks working in state government. This means that a large number of jobs will be reserved for blacks, even if their scores on merit exams are lower than those of whites who are turned down for the job." Respondents were then asked, "Do you favor or oppose this policy?"[36]

The percentage of Whites who claimed that they see Blacks as irresponsible and lazy was reliably greater in the second group—those who had already been asked the question about quotas—than in the first group. Clearly, reminding people about quotas can "aggravate" the problems of prejudice.[37]

But what about legitimate affirmative action programs? Can we extrapolate from Sniderman and Piazza's findings about quotas to the dynamics of actual affirmative action? Do actual programs create or aggravate racial or gender animus? Does affirmative action make White men dislike or resent White women or people of color?

Survey research shows the problem of resentment to be much less common than has been suggested. Researchers from Northern Illinois University undertook a mammoth study of a large government agency with eleven sites around the country. Christopher Parker, Boris Baltes, and Neil Christiansen included in their study more than seven thousand individuals divided into four groups: White men, White women, Black and Hispanic women and men, and Asian women and men. The participants rated their organization and their jobs through twenty-one questions that clustered into six distinct concepts: satisfaction with the job, satisfaction with the possibility of career development, loyalty to the organization, the perception that the organization gives employees fair outcomes, the perception that the organization uses fair processes, and the perception that the organization promotes diversity and affirmative action. Three items gauged the last variable:

- The organization values cultural diversity (i.e., race, ethnicity, and gender).
- Senior managers are planning for a workforce that is culturally diverse.
- Senior managers emphasize AA/EO.[38]

As they expected, Parker and associates found that scores on the organization's promotion of diversity and affirmative action were higher among White men than among any of the other groups. Although they generally thought the organizations were doing a good job, White women and people of color were more dubious about the efforts of the organization than were White men.

But contrary to their expectations, Parker and colleagues discovered that White men valued the organization's commitment to diversity. Specifically, among their sample of 4,919 White men, the researchers found a positive relationship between perceived organizational support for affirmative action and all the other variables. The more a White man thought his organization emphasized diversity and affirmative action, the more satisfied he felt with his job and with how careers developed in the organization, and the more loyal he was to the organization. The more a White man thought the company emphasized affirmative action and diversity, the more he perceived the organization as fair in terms of its procedures and employee outcomes.[39] The researchers found no evidence of resentment among White men. Indeed, their data showed just the contrary.

Further confirmation of the positive findings of Parker and associates came from another study we have already examined that was conducted by Alison Konrad and Frank Linnehan. Like Parker and his colleagues, Konrad and Linnehan obtained opinions from White men and others who were actual employees.[40] Like Parker's study, Konrad and Linnehan's was a massive, multi-stage undertaking. Konrad and Linnehan first approached 138 vice presidents of medium to large companies in one metropolitan area, asking them about 119 specific practices related to equal opportunity and affirmative action. From this list, they then picked the 26 most common practices, which independent raters slotted into two types: identity-neutral and identity-conscious. Identity-neutral practices were such items as "providing management training to employee management candidates." Identity-conscious practices included items like "insuring that some women and minorities receive management training." Konrad and Linnehan collaborated with four different organizations (a food service company, an insurance company, an information services company, and an educational institution) to distribute questionnaires to White people and people of color at midlevel management ranks. Respondents evaluated each of the 26 practices.

When Konrad and Linnehan received the mailed, anonymous responses, they sorted the questionnaires into three piles: White men, White women, and people of color. They then calculated the average responses of each group to the identity-neutral items and the identity-conscious items. As discussed in Chapter 3, all groups of respondents evaluated the identity-neutral practices more highly than the identity-conscious ones. But no one actually disliked the identity-conscious practices. White women and people of color liked them, and White men were neutral about them.

Taken together, the small experimental studies by Gilbert and Stead and the large correlational studies by Parker and associates and by Konrad and Linnehan give us a sense of what is needed to combat the stigmatizing effects of affirmative action. When the policy is explained so that its fairness becomes evident, even those who do not directly benefit by it do not necessarily oppose it. Indeed, in studies of how people react to affirmative action—not to some misshapen caricature of it—White men do not appear to resent either the practices or the beneficiaries of affirmative action.

The pattern of empirical results also shows that it would be a serious tactical error for administrators to assume that the people who do not benefit in their organizations will automatically know that the policies are fair or that those promoted through the policies are qualified. In the absence of information, the men in Heilman's studies assumed that they were superior to the women on the characteristics that mattered for promotion.[41] Such an assumption would naturally lead men to conclude that promotion of women equaled preferential treatment. And as we have seen, Americans dislike preferential treatment. Clear information is needed to dispel unfounded assumptions.

Marlene Turner and Anthony Pratkanis are social psychologists who not only study affirmative action but also consult on the topic for organizations. On the basis of their experiences as well as their research, they have articulated a set of recommendations for those who would like to see affirmative action plans succeed.[42] Near the top of their list is the recommendation that administrators highlight the competence of women and people of color who are new to an organization or who have recently been promoted. Turner and Pratkanis also exhort administrators to explain to their workforces what affirmative action is and why it is fair. Declaring the policies fair by fiat gains nothing.

Turner and Pratkanis do not underestimate the difficulty of the task. Even cogent explanations can fall on deaf ears. Prejudiced individuals are unlikely to perceive the qualifications of a newcomer who does not match their own ethnic or gender group. Pratkanis and Turner discuss just how great the resistance can be in their historical studies of the career of Jackie Robinson and other great baseball players in the Negro Leagues. When Branch Rickey brought Robinson into the Brooklyn Dodgers, a number of scathing editorials accused Rickey of sacrificing quality on the altar of misguided liberalism. Blind to Robinson's talent, the critics cried, "Preferential treatment."

Can racial and gender classification systems of the type used in affirmative action allow covert and overt prejudices to flare into discriminatory words and deeds? Absolutely. Can such classification systems promote hostility or stereotyping even among people who are not extreme racists or sexists? Again, the answer would appear to be yes, as the several studies by Madeline Heilman and others have shown. Must the classifications engender hostility and resentment? No. Most people of goodwill appear not to be dismayed when qualified individuals are given a chance to succeed, even when that chance is offered by virtue of the individual's demographic category.

Does Affirmative Action Undermine Pride in the Group?

What about the opinions of those who are intended to be the beneficiaries of affirmative action or preferential treatment? How do women view other women who are said to have received opportunities and re-

wards by virtue of their sex? How do people of color view other people
of color who are the beneficiaries of either affirmative action or preferential treatment?

Again, the dominant researcher is Madeline Heilman, and the
majority of her empirical work concerns gender rather than race. Heilman's work makes it plain that women and men do not differ from
each other in how they view the beneficiaries of affirmative action or
preferential treatment. The studies by Heilman and her colleagues, described above, in which sixty-eight women and sixty-one men saw files
for job applicants, showed that no effects could be traced to gender.[43]
The same was true for the two experiments conducted in the insurance
company in which managers, not students, served as participants,[44]
and for the experiment conducted with the MBA students who read,
among other things, about a company's personnel policy.[45] In the absence of information about qualifications, female participants learning
about female affirmative action or preferential hirees devalue the hirees
as much as men do. This finding, replicated in other studies, is powerful in its implication that in the absence of actual information, people
presume that preferences, not merit, operate in instances of affirmative
action.

The devaluation process has a long reach. When high school girls
learned that some professions have increased their numbers of female
managers "as a result of pressures from legal regulations," they expressed little interest in having a career in those professions. But when
the girls learned that the increased number resulted from companies
actively trying to "recruit and promote competent women whose credentials and education enable success," the girls' interest increased.[46]

Does Affirmative Action Produce Self-Blame?

Knowing that people can sometimes devalue the recipients of affirmative action, it is natural to assume that the recipients might derogate
themselves. Do the intended beneficiaries of affirmative action interpret it as nothing more than preferential treatment? If so, do they feel
undermined by affirmative action?

In the public discourse, several men of color have written about
the deleterious effects of affirmative action on themselves and on oth-

ers whom they know. In his *Hunger of Memory,* for example, Richard Rodriguez discusses what it was like to grow up as a middle-class Hispanic in California, receiving good schooling at a private Catholic school. At the time Rodriguez attended college and graduate school, universities were beginning to develop race-sensitive policies. For the first few years of affirmative action Rodriguez accepted the label "minority," but this did not last.

> There was a problem: One day I listened to a government official defend affirmative action; the next day I realized the benefits of the program. I was the minority student political activists shouted about at noontime rallies. Against their rhetoric, I stood out in relief, unrelieved. *Knowing:* I was not really more socially disadvantaged than the white graduate students. *Knowing:* I was not disadvantaged like many of the new nonwhite students who were entering college, lacking good early schooling. . . . Slowly, slowly, the term *minority* became a source of unease. . . . I was not—in a *cultural* sense—a minority, an alien from public life.[47]

Rodriguez was not alone in his discomfort with affirmative action. White classmates expressed a hostility that, for Rodriguez, proved pivotal. In one conversation with a White fellow graduate student about teaching jobs, the White student expressed contempt for affirmative action. Even though he and Rodriguez were equally matched academically, the White student had received no job offers while Rodriguez was offered jobs at almost any school he desired. The only difference between them was ethnicity. Rodriguez was angered by his colleague's attack and tried to defend affirmative action: "After a minute or two, as I heard myself talking, I felt self-disgust. The job offers I was receiving were indeed unjustified. I knew that. All I was saying amounted to a frantic self-defense. It was all a lie."[48] Soon after his epiphany, Rodriguez left academia. Although he is now a highly successful writer, Rodriguez has apparently never completely come to terms with the insults, both external and internalized, of racial prejudice.[49]

A similar lament comes from Shelby Steele. Steele is a force to be reckoned with. His book *The Content of Our Character* took the country by storm in 1990 for its impassioned disavowal of affirmative action. "I am," he wrote, "a middle-class black, a college professor, far from wealthy, but also well-removed from the kind of deprivation that would qualify my children for the label 'disadvantaged.'" Theorizing that few Blacks, and probably no middle-class Blacks, actually face institutionalized racism, Steele decides that it is affirmative action that has created a sense of self-doubt among Blacks: "I think one of the most troubling effects of racial preferences for blacks is a kind of demoralization, or put another way, an enlargement of self-doubt."[50]

Colleges are microsocieties where unchecked self-doubt, fear, anger, and guilt can come to the surface for youths away from home for the first time. Having others, and themselves, think that affirmative action is the only way they got into college can be damaging for minority students, argues Steele.

> Under affirmative action the quality that earns us preferential treatment is an implied inferiority. However that inferiority is explained—and it is easily enough explained by the myriad deprivations that grew out of our oppression—it is still inferiority. There are explanations and then there is fact. And the fact must be borne by the individual as a condition apart from the explanation, apart even from the fact that others like himself also bear this condition. In integrated situations where blacks must compete with whites who may be better prepared, these explanations quickly wear thin and expose the individual to racial as well as personal self-doubt.[51]

Steele recounts how a young Black student at UCLA avoided sitting next to the other Black students in the class (who sat together in the back) because he did not want to be seen to be like them, "lazy, ignorant, and stupid. . . . [T]he terror in this situation for the black student I spoke with was that his own deeply buried anxiety would be given credence, that the myth would be verified, and that he would feel shame and humiliation not because of who he was but simply because he was black."[52]

Yale Law School professor Stephen Carter echoes the contentions of Rodriguez and Steele in his *Reflections of an Affirmative Action Baby.* The son of two professionals, Carter—like Rodriguez and Steele—was "unable to visualize [him]self as a victim of societal oppression"; "The programs were said to compensate for the present effects of past discrimination, and, even in 1977 . . . I was worried that there didn't seem to be any present effects in my life. No, I was more than worried: I was very nearly ashamed."[53]

Nor does Carter think himself alone in his worries. "So many Americans seem to treat receipt of benefits of affirmative action as a badge of shame." The policy, he believes, is a failure both because of the resentment it engenders among Whites and because of "the terrible psychological pressure that racial preferences often put on their beneficiaries": "Because so many people seem to assume that the beneficiaries of affirmative action programs are necessarily bound for failure, or at least inferiority, there is an understandable tendency for people of color to resist being thought of as beneficiaries."[54]

Like Steele, Carter sees affirmative action as implying Blacks' inferiority to Whites. If Blacks had the ability to compete with Whites, then, he poses, there would be no need for racial preferences. Already existing stereotypes set many affirmative action recipients up for "a double standard for the consequences of failure."[55] People who receive benefits from affirmative action are easily identified as a group, so when one of them fails to succeed despite the benefits, failure becomes expected of the rest of the group.

Empirical Studies in the Laboratory and Beyond

Public intellectuals like Rodriguez, Steele, and Carter may not be typical of all people of color. Shelby Steele and his twin brother, Claude Steele, the eminent psychologist, have had a famous falling out over affirmative action. Claude Steele, Chair of the Psychology Department at Stanford University, writes as vigorously in favor of affirmative action as Shelby Steele writes against it. Another well-known Black intellectual, Glenn Loury, recently made a dramatic about-face on the topic of affirmative action; but some years ago Loury asserted: "Affirmative action creates doubt about the qualifications of the blacks who benefit from it. . . . Racial preferences undermine the ability of black people to be confident that they are as good as their achievements would suggest. In turn, this limits the extent to which the personal success of any one black can be a source of inspiration guiding the behavior of other blacks." With age and experience Loury has come to see that collective action must supplement the actions of individuals.[56] He no longer dislikes affirmative action. He no longer claims that affirmative action engenders self-doubt.

Do the people on the street feel the same way about affirmative action that targets them as do Rodriguez, Carter, and Shelby Steele? Answers to this important question depend in part on who is the focus of the research. When people of color are the focus and ethnic divisions are in question, self-doubt appears less salient than when women are the focus and the spotlight is on gender differentiation. Also important is the empirical method used to find the answers. Experiments have yielded different data from those of surveys.

Pride of place among the experimenters goes again to Madeline Heilman. Heilman was the first to investigate the potentially deleterious effects of preferential treatment on women's psychological and behavioral functioning. Since 1984 she has conducted no fewer than seven experiments on the topic, all well-designed and beautifully executed.

In 1987 Heilman, Michael Simon, and David Repper asked men and women volunteers to report to the laboratory to participate in what they thought was a one-way communication task. Each time a woman was scheduled, a male confederate would arrive at the same time, posing as another participant. Each time a man was scheduled, a female confederate would show up. The experimenter greeted the real participant and the bogus participant (the confederate) and explained that they would first take a test called the Spatial Communications Skills Inventory, supposedly designed to determine their ability to communicate about spatial design. The test included items that tested, for example, whether it was easier to describe objects with straight or with curved lines. Although the test was bogus, the participants apparently believed in its predictive powers. After they took the test, the experimenter either "scored" it or conspicuously set it aside. When the experiment's script called for the test to be scored, the experimenter would take a few moments to score the tests of the participant and the confederate and then would announce, "Normally in situations like this, leaders are selected on the basis of skill and ability, which basically means that they are good at the task. We've been doing our selecting this way also, by using the Spatial Communications Skills Inventory that you just finished. It is a highly reliable measure of one-way communication skills developed by psychologists. So you [pointing to the participant], since you scored better on the inventory, you will get to be the leader for the task."[57]

But for some of the participants the experimenter had a different script. Instead of telling the participant that she or he had scored better, the experimenter said, "But today we are going to have to do things a little differently because there just haven't been enough male (female) subjects signing up so far. So, regardless of how each of you did on the inventory, you [pointing to the participant], since you are a man (woman), will get to be the leader for this task."[58] The experimental subject and confederate then were given a task in which they sat with their backs to each other and the leader (always the subject) described geometric figures which the follower (always a confederate) drew. The pair was then told by the experimenter that they had succeeded or that they had failed at the task. They then rated their own performance, their leadership ability, and their desire to persist as leader.

Regardless of whether they failed or succeeded, women participants gave themselves low marks in performance and leadership abilities and showed little interest in persisting as leader when they had been preferentially selected. Men, in contrast, were unaffected by the method of selection. If they were selected on the basis of merit, men thought of themselves as capable and as good leaders and expressed a desire to continue as leader. If they were selected on the basis of gender, men still thought of themselves as capable and good and still desired to continue in the leader role. Something about these men, their self-confidence or their sense of entitlement, made them impervious to the possible effects of stigma.

Negative thoughts and feelings can translate into behavior, or at least into behavioral intentions. A few years after Heilman, Simon, and Repper demonstrated the negative effects of preferential treatment on women's feelings, Heilman, Rivero, and Brett demonstrated that the effects extended to women's behavioral intentions.[59] Male and female participants reported to the laboratory for a dyadic interaction concerning financial services. After a bogus but plausible test of their managerial skills, the participants were assigned to be the manager either on the basis of their test scores (merit condition) or on the basis of their sex. They were then given the choice of two jobs: verifying the work of the subordinate (an easy task) or making loan decisions (a challenging task). Ninety-three percent of the women and 87 percent of the men who thought they had been selected on the basis of merit gravitated to the more challenging job, as did 100 percent of the preferentially selected men. Only 47 percent of the preferentially selected women took on the hard task.[60]

The self-limiting behavior of preferentially selected women can also be directed toward other women. As in the earlier studies, Heilman and associates brought women and men participants to the laboratory, paired them with a confederate of the opposite sex, and administered a test of their supposed abilities.[61] In this study participants encountered the "General Management Aptitude Test," and then were assigned to be the manager (with the confederate as the worker) on the basis of merit ("you did very well on the inventory . . .") or of sex (". . . but today we are going to do things a little differently"). The participant then engaged in a series of managerial tasks including evaluating two job candidates on the basis of their written dossiers and selecting one of the candidates for a job. The dossiers were accompanied by photos. One of the dossiers was for a man, the other a comparable woman.[62]

Female participants who had been assigned the management job on the basis of gender were much less likely to hire a woman than a man. They also rated the woman candidate as less competent than the man. Women and men hired on the basis of merit did not differentiate in their hiring recommendations or their evaluations. Men hired on the basis of gender did not differentiate either, presumably because they felt confident about their own abilities.

Considering Heilman's experimental findings as I have described them, one would be forced to acknowledge the sagacity of her concern that preferential treatment psychologically undermines its intended beneficiaries. If people confuse affirmative action with unjustified preferential treatment—and we have seen in Chapter 3 that many people do—then organizations that implement affirmative action may be causing unforeseen problems. Granted that affirmative action is a strong remedy for prevailing inequities, the question becomes one of side effects. Yes, affirmative action is economically effective. But is it also affectively lethal?

At the nub of the issue is this question: Does self-derogation inevitably occur for women who are singled out because of gender? The question is one for which Heilman provides data. As in her studies of how preferential treatment affects others' views of the target, so in her studies of self-evaluation has Heilman been careful to document the delimiting factors.

Heilman, Jonathan Lucas, and Stella Kaplow used the familiar strategy of assigning women and men to be leaders in a dyadic interaction either as a result of merit or as a result of gender.[63] They also gave the participants feedback on how well they had performed the experimental task. When women were given positive feedback, the crippling effects of preferential selection were wiped out.

Similarly, Heilman, Kaplow, Amato, and Stathatos found that they were able to nullify the effects of women's harshness to other women job applicants by providing the female participants with information about their success. Being preferentially selected, in other words, did not result in women being hard on other women when the selected women were confident of their abilities.[64] Also, in a study of different types of preferential selections, Heilman, Battle, Keller, and Lee found that giving women positive information about their qualifications staved off most of the detrimental effects of having been selected for a task on the basis of gender.[65]

In 2001 Heilman and Victoria Alcott published an experiment that assessed the effects of women's realizing that others viewed them as preferentially selected for a position.[66] The authors found that when women were uncertain about their ability on a particular task they responded timidly, were less likely to take risks, and reported feeling unhappy and dissatisfied. In contrast, when women were certain of their ability on that particular task, they responded boldly and attempted to refute stigma-based negative expectations. Again, the deleterious effects of preferential treatment were highly contingent on context.

Other Controlled Studies of Simulated Work Experiences

Do the results obtained in Heilman's laboratory replicate in the laboratories of others? A sine qua non of worthwhile findings in scientific inquiry is that independent investigators be able to produce similar results. While Heilman's results are compelling, her conclusions would be suspect unless other researchers found the same results.

As it happens, Heilman's elegant work has inspired many other researchers to test the effects of preferential treatment on the feelings and behaviors of its recipients. Some of the experiments have asked people to imagine themselves in different situations. Others have, like Heilman's, created experimental scenarios where participants are placed in a realistic situation rather than being asked to imagine one. Some of the studies have measured personality traits of the participants. Some have investigated the effects of preferential treatment on the basis of race as well as gender.

The most concise summary of the results of experiments conducted outside Heilman's lab is that although preferential treatment can negatively affect its beneficiaries, many factors limit the effect. Usually preferential treatment does not result in self-doubt. Here is an array of findings, including those that show the detrimental effects of preferential treatment to those that show the limits of those effects:

- Students who imagined that they were granted a job out of sympathy (because of past discrimination or physical impairment) expressed lower self-esteem and more negative affect than those who imagined they were granted the job on the basis of their qualifications.[67]
- Women who thought they were preferentially selected performed worse on a brainstorming task than did women who thought they were selected on the basis of merit when the task was said to require ability. But no differences occurred when the task was said to require effort.[68]

■ Students in an experiment were told that they had been selected on the basis of both sex and merit. This selection technique turned out to be equal to telling them that they had been selected on the basis of merit alone. The mere mention of merit took the sting out of the notion of preferential treatment.[69]

■ Students who thought they had been preferentially selected for a brainstorming task performed better, but felt worse, than students who thought they had been selected on the basis of merit.[70]

■ Students who were preferentially selected to join a group because they were told that they had a different style of thinking about problems felt better about themselves than did students who were told that they were selected at random.[71]

■ When asked to imagine themselves as preferential selections for a corporate job, participants liked the program better if there was an explanation justifying the preference than if there wasn't.[72]

■ Women participants who are confident of their abilities before arriving at the experimental laboratory do not exhibit the negative effects of preferential selection in their performance.[73]

■ Being informed that they had been preferentially selected for a program depressed women's performance on a math test except when the women were also told that they were just as competent as the men who had not been selected.[74]

■ African American engineering students and African American engineers both indicated that they would respond more positively to a race-conscious hiring policy than to a race-neutral one.[75]

■ Majority, minority, and international students were asked to imagine that they had obtained a scholarship at a university while scoring no better or worse than an unsuccessful candidate. The participants were asked to imagine, further, that the university had either a strong affirmative action policy or a weak one. While ratings of fairness were affected, imagined feelings were not.[76]

■ Students were asked to imagine themselves as the recipients of race-based affirmative action for which they did or did not have the qualifications. While women and minority participants were more sensitive to the manipulation of qualifications than were men and White participants, the type of affirmative action program described did not affect feelings.[77]

■ African American, Hispanic, and White participants in a role-playing experiment concerning racial affirmative action programs claimed they would be adversely affected by preferential treatment when given feedback of incompetence. Participants also claimed that without such feedback, or with feedback of competence, preferential treatment would not adversely affect them.[78]

■ A study with 201 students from a southern university reproduced the conditions of Heilman's studies but had different results. Preferential selection did not undermine the women in the study.[79]

As a whole, the laboratory results present a clear picture. Stark, unjustified preferential treatment produces self-stigmatizing. Yet many factors—including natural confidence and experiment-produced confidence in personal abilities—can change this attitude. In these regards the results of the experiments on self-stigmatizing match the results of the experiments on how nonbeneficiaries view direct beneficiaries. You can produce stigma; this much is sure. But you don't have to. You can avert stigma by reminding the beneficiaries of their capabilities.

Studies of Self-Doubt Among Workers

Are the results found in college laboratories consistent with what researchers find in the world of business? How common are the sentiments of Shelby Steele and Stephen Carter? How deep and pervasive is self-doubt among women or people of color when they know they are or may have been the beneficiaries of affirmative action? Does affirmative action have the crippling effects that some fear?

There are not many systematic studies. But their conclusions are consistent. The big news is that the beneficiaries of affirmative action in employment generally endorse the policy and do not feel stigmatized by the presence of gender-sensitive or race-sensitive policies. Only one study found evidence of stigma.

The one study to find stigma was published in the early 1980s. Thomas Chacko found that both satisfaction and commitment were lower among women workers who felt their sex (rather than their ability) was the reason they had been hired. Those who thought they had been hired because of their sex also experienced more role conflict than women who thought they had been hired because of their abilities.[80]

Very different results were obtained by Marylee Taylor in an analysis of the 1990 General Social Survey.[81] The survey asked participants, "Does the place where you work have an affirmative action program or make any special effort to hire and promote minorities?" Of the 1,372 Americans in the nationwide probability sample, 319 White women answered yes to the affirmative action question, as did 71 Black men and women.

Taylor's analytic strategy was simple. First she divided the White women into two groups—those who answered yes, their employer did have affirmative action or similar programs, in one group and those who answered no in the other. Taylor then compared the two groups on measures of job satisfaction, commitment, ambition, life satisfaction, health, and happiness. If affirmative action had the debilitating effect that Shelby Steele and others have claimed, the group saying yes should have been more dissatisfied, less happy, and certainly less ambitious than the group answering no. They were not.

Next Taylor turned to the information from Black respondents and divided them into four groups: Black women who worked for an affirmative action employer, Black men who worked for an affirmative action employer, Black women who worked for an employer without affirmative action, Black men who worked for an employer without affirmative action. Again, if Steele is correct, the Black women and men who worked for an affirmative action employer should have been less satisfied, committed, ambitious, or happy than the other Black women and men. And extrapolating from Heilman's work, the association between attitudes and feelings, on the one hand, and type of employer, on the other, should have been especially strong among Black women.

The self-stigmatizing hypothesis did not stand up to the data. For the two groups of White women—those who worked for an affirmative action employer and those who did not—the results were indistinguishable. When Taylor repeated her analyses of the data for White women figuring sophisticated statistical controls into the equation, the results remained constant: women who worked for affirmative action employers differed not at all in their job attitudes from women who worked for non–affirmative action employers.

As with White women, so with Blacks, or nearly. Black participants in the 1990 survey who worked for an affirmative action employer had the same attitudes and feelings, on the whole, as those who worked for other employers. The Black men and Black women reacted in the same way to affirmative action. Only one factor in the survey appeared to be affected by the presence or absence of an affirmative action program: ambition. Taylor measured ambition by noting how respondents ranked two items in an array of five listed when the interviewer asked them, "Would you please look at this card and tell me which one thing on this list you would most prefer in a job? Which comes next? Which is the third most important? Which is the fourth most important?" The higher the respondent ranked "chances for advancement," the higher his or her ambition score. The higher the respondent ranked "working hours are short; lots of free time," the lower the ambition score.[82]

The 1990 General Social Survey showed that Blacks working for an affirmative action employer were more ambitious than Blacks working for other employers. The results did not go in the direction predicted by Shelby Steele. They went in the opposite direction. Steele declares that affirmative action makes Blacks feel they are inadequate and saps their drive. But again, he is wrong. Blacks working for an affirmative action employer showed more ambition than Blacks who worked for non–affirmative action employers.

Entirely consistent with the 1990 General Social Survey findings were the results of a follow-up analysis of the 1986 National Election

Study.[83] The NES, as we saw in Chapter 3, has consistently shown large ethnic gaps in support for affirmative action. The data also show variations in support among both Whites and Blacks. Examining variations in support among Blacks, Terri Fine discovered that support for affirmative action increased among respondents with more education. She also found a strong positive association between the ethic of self-reliance and support for affirmative action. The more self-reliant the Black participant, the more strongly he or she endorsed affirmative action. Fine had expected the opposite pattern of results, but these results told her that "African Americans believe that their ability to succeed is tempered by discriminatory market forces thereby justifying the need for intervention."[84]

Nor were the anti–affirmative action forces correct about a 1995 Gallup survey. Pollsters asked more than seven hundred minority men and women, "Have you ever felt that your colleagues at work or school privately questioned your abilities or qualifications because of affirmative action or have you never felt this way?" Only 29 percent of the men and 19 percent of the women answered that they had felt this way.[85]

Another study involved MBA graduates of a small private university in the United States. Approximately a hundred female MBAs filled out a questionnaire sent to them by their alma mater. The questionnaire asked them four questions about the extent to which affirmative action worked in favor of women in their organization. The more a woman saw affirmative action as working for women in her organization, the more committed she was to the organization and the more satisfied she felt with her job.[86] Steele's predictions were thus further invalidated.

A fifth study also contradicts the assumption that affirmative action programs decrease the will to excel and make people doubt themselves and their ability to perform their jobs. In their large-scale study of federal employees discussed above, Parker, Baltes, and Christiansen found that 1,622 White women employees, 492 Black or Hispanic employees, and 195 Asian American employees all responded positively to being in workplaces that valued diversity and emphasized affirmative action. All respondents—especially White women and Black or Hispanic women and men—thought their organization was more fair and thought their own chances of promotion were greater when they also believed their managers cared about diversity and affirmative action than when they did not. Among most of the employees, furthermore, the more strongly a participant thought management endorsed affirmative action, the more satisfied and loyal he or she was.[87]

A slightly different methodological approach yielded the same general results. In the mid- to late 1980s a large busing company in Canada implemented an aggressive affirmative action policy mandating that 40 percent of all new hires be women and 25 percent be minority members. The company widely advertised its quantitative, bottom-line approach to diversity. About seven years after the start of the affirmative action program, Francine Tougas and colleagues sent questionnaires to all 451 women and 231 minority males who had been hired since the inception of the program.[88] Tougas and her associates questioned the employees (who were mostly bus drivers) about their hiring, their work situations, their views of affirmative action, and their views of themselves.

Two hundred and fifty-six questionnaires were mailed back to the researchers. Both the women and the men generally claimed that they had been hired for their qualifications and not because of their sex or minority-group status. The workers generally felt satisfied with their work and displayed high motivation. They judged their own abilities to be more than satisfactory. For the most part, the sample considered affirmative action a fair policy. The more fair they found the policy, the more motivated and satisfied they felt.

Quite different in method from any of the large surveys was a small, probing study conducted by Lea Ayers.[89] Ayers interviewed in depth thirteen women who publicly and unquestionably had been the direct beneficiaries of affirmative action. Some of the women had been granted race-specific awards. Others had been targeted for special assignments because they were women or because they were people of color. A couple of the women had been hired for jobs that were set aside for women of color. Here was a group of individuals who more than most had been confronted with real-life situations matching the extreme situations set up by experimenters like Heilman. If any research participants should have shown self-derogation, these women were those people.

Ayers tape-recorded the interviews she conducted with the women and transcribed the tapes. Given that the interviews ranged from thirty minutes to two hours long, the resulting stack of transcripts produced an armful. Ayers then extracted from the transcripts all statements that concerned any aspect of the fairness of affirmative action, and sorted these statements according to whether they concerned the policy of affirmative action or the practice of it. Coders then rated whether the statements were positive or negative. Altogether Ayers extracted 223 separate statements, 52 of which concerned affirmative action as a policy. Of these statements, 1 was negative and 51 were positive.

Ayers did find that the respondents had more qualms about the implementation of affirmative action than about its philosophy. One respondent complained about administrators who called for diversity without being willing to change the ways business was conducted, that is, without really valuing diversity. Said this respondent: "It is not a decision made purely on the basis of one's sex or race, but rather a redefining of what diversity will bring to enrich the university life and community. . . . [Affirmative action] may mean that a different approach may be taken to the process of recruitment and to the assessment of applicants. . . . [Affirmative action recognizes] that the enriching of the community is a responsibility that lies not just with the applicant, but with the institution."[90]

From the systematic studies of people in the workplace who have not been randomly assigned to different experimental conditions but rather have freely chosen their jobs, we would be hard pressed to conclude that affirmative action stigmatizes its beneficiaries in their own eyes.[91] Gender and ethnic classifications do not "serve to stigmatize." They do not create self-doubt. They do not create a "suspicion of inferiority" among their direct beneficiaries. They have been shown, in fact, to do the opposite.

Across Several Studies

If we fight our way through the tangle of empirical details into which I have led us, stand up on our hind legs, and survey the scene, a clear picture emerges. Here is what I see. In the carefully controlled conditions of the experimental laboratory, numerous research scientists have shown beyond reasonable doubt, an important truth consistent with aspects of the dissents in *Fullilove* and with the appellate court opinion in *Hopwood*. The truth is this: negative effects follow from preferentially selecting individuals for work tasks on the basis of demographic categories *rather than* on the basis of merit. In the laboratory, if the experimenter makes it explicit that he or she is replacing all considerations of merit with an exclusive interest in demographic characteristics, the results are harmful to all concerned.

Outside the laboratory, a few prominent individuals have made a career out of revealing the wounds inflicted on them by preferential treatment. The individuals have been eloquent, and personal testimonials can be persuasive. There seems to be something about the human animal that makes people remember and respond to a single vivid example over a wealth of systematic evidence. But this is a mistake. An emotionally wrenching example cannot substitute for the facts, especially when the examples are presented in a manner that glosses over the vast differences between unjustified preferential treatment and affirmative action.

Meanwhile, social scientists have discovered virtually no evidence of stigma in most employment situations. The social scientists have focused their sights on ordinary people, not extraordinary public commentators. White men are not angry and resentful. White women and people of color are neither crippled nor disgusted by affirmative action programs. Rather they are energized by working in establishments that value diversity and take positive steps to promote it.

The findings of researchers in the work world parallel some of the laboratory findings. Even researchers who most ardently stress the potential for stigma have indicated that there are boundaries to the problem. Assure people of the contributing role of merit in job and admissions selections, and the deleterious effects of categorical selections disappear.

It is when we confuse affirmative action with unjustified preferences that trouble arises. For many people, the confusion "naturally" exists, that is, the default option is to think of affirmative action as "unjustified preference." In laboratories, too, one can temporarily force

the two distinct terms to overlap. As soon as the forced overlap is removed, the pernicious effects persist for preferential treatment and dis-
sipate for affirmative action.

On the College Campus

What accounts for the differences between the experimental studies of
preferential treatment in the laboratory and the off-campus surveys of
employed people? The two lines of research differ in a number of ways.
One difference concerns the populations studied. Experiments typically use college students as participants, while the studies of employment behavior include as their participants mature adults with more
life experience.

Sensitivities of College Students

The emotional vulnerability of college students has been noted by
many. Richard Rodriguez articulated the anguished self-doubt that began when he was a student, and Shelby Steele's observations and anecdotes almost all concern college undergraduates. Both undergraduate
and graduate students devote a great deal of time and energy to the
pursuit of personality. Living in an intensely evaluative world, college
students are constantly engaged in one or another form of self-
scrutiny. Perhaps students are more susceptible than working adults to
the opinions of others. It is well and good to find the adults in the 1990
General Social Survey unfazed by programs that could be construed as
condescending; but are insecure students equally stalwart?

Two studies of minority graduate students, separated by about a
decade, show that students may be especially aware of how others view
them. In 1986 Joseph Ponterotto, Francine Martinez, and Davis Hayden distributed a questionnaire to sixty-five ethnic minority students
at a large public university on the West Coast.[92] The students were
strongly in favor of affirmative action programs, even though they saw
the programs as being only marginally effective. The students generally
expressed confidence in their academic abilities. Although they did not
feel undercut by affirmative action, the minority students acknowledged that others on campus had preconceived negative notions about

their capabilities. Affirmative action, they admitted, had made few inroads into the preconceptions.

Ten years later, writing in the *Harvard Educational Review,* Eric Margolis and Mary Romero described how graduate students in sociology are "socialized" into their professional roles. They quoted one woman of color whose treatment exemplified the worst aspects of the "hidden curriculum." Said the woman: "Coming in as a woman of color—there was always that stigma that you were an affirmative action student; that you got in because they LET you in . . . even some of the secretaries . . . would refer to me as OUR Indian student. I remember one guy coming up to me about my second year. He said, 'Geez, so you must be the affirmative action case.' I said, 'What the hell do you mean?' I happen to have seen his transcript . . . which was a C− or C transcript. My transcript was an A transcript. So I just said, 'No. As a matter of fact, my transcript is better than yours.'"[93] Neither the woman quoted nor the other students in the study by Margolis and Romero appeared to question their own abilities or the need for affirmative action. But neither, apparently, did they see affirmative action as bringing an end to the sort of prejudice that made graduate school uncomfortable.

Some of my own research has looked at the consequences of students' heightened awareness of the opinions of others. In 1996 a team of professors and students collected information from 155 Yale students and 196 Smith College students.[94] This was our first attempt to see how college students reacted to affirmative action. For the purposes of analysis, we divided the students into three ethnic categories: European Americans, Asian Americans, and Underrepresented students, including African Americans, Hispanics, and Native Americans. We also noted whether the students were male students at Yale, female students at Yale, or female students at Smith.[95]

We asked the students, "Have you ever wondered whether your peers think that you have been admitted to Yale [or Smith] because of your ethnicity and not because of your intellectual abilities?"[96] We repeated the question with regard to the views of the professors. Nearly three-quarters of the Underrepresented students claimed that they wondered what their peers thought, and about half (47 percent) claimed that they wondered what the professors thought. In contrast,

18 percent of the Asian Americans and 4 percent of the European Americans wondered what their peers thought; 15 percent of the Asian American students and 2 percent of the European American students wondered whether the professors thought they had been admitted on ethnic grounds rather than ability.

Meanwhile, all groups of students generally endorsed affirmative action. Students supported the theory of affirmative action slightly more adamantly than they supported its implementation. Yet among all groups of students, the average rating of affirmative action on four different scales and on one additional single-item measure was above the midpoint. Especially appreciative of affirmative action were students in our Underrepresented category. On a continuum stretching from 0 (strongly dislike affirmative action) to 10 (strongly endorse affirmative action), the African American, Hispanic, and Native American students averaged a score of 7.7. Underrepresented students envisioned affirmative action as giving them access to many opportunities, but European Americans did not see affirmative action as restricting their opportunities. Asian American students' responses to the question of opportunities fell between the European Americans' and the Underrepresented students'.

Why did the students of color endorse affirmative action even when they admitted that they thought their classmates and professors might be second-guessing their abilities? More than half the students in the Underrepresented category, but only one-quarter of the White students, felt that others judged their academic abilities on ethnic stereotypes. Support for affirmative action was greatest among students who felt that both professors and peers wondered about their abilities and least among those who felt that neither did. The extent to which a student thought that others wondered about the reasons for his or her admission to college—in other words, the extent to which a student felt stigmatized by others—statistically predicted support for affirmative action. We therefore concluded that the students at Yale and Smith, like the graduate students in the studies by Ponterotto and colleagues and by Margolis and Romero, were realistic about the nature of stereotyping.

The initial study at Yale and Smith gave us good information but left us with questions. First we realized that we needed a direct measure of the extent to which students of color questioned their own capabilities. We had asked whether they suspected that their peers and professors questioned the basis of their admission to college; but we had not asked whether they themselves questioned the basis of their admission. Second, and more important, we began to wonder which students of color, if any, disliked affirmative action. We wished to know what accounted for variations of opinion among students of color. We suspected that students of color who took pride in their ethnicity and in themselves would most strongly endorse affirmative action.

To find answers to our new questions, my colleagues and I conducted a second survey in the fall of 1997.[97] Our final sample included 181 Black college students from western Massachusetts. The students attended one of the colleges in a five-college consortium (Amherst, Hampshire, Mount Holyoke, Smith, and the University of Massachusetts). We asked the students about their attitudes toward affirmative action and about their sense of ethnic identity. Using an instrument developed by one of the collaborators on the project, Robert Sellers, we assessed several aspects of ethnic identity. To determine how central their ethnic identity was to their self-identity, we asked the students to respond to eight items. The items included statements such as "In general, being black is an important part of my self image," "My destiny is tied to the destiny of other black people," and "Being black is an important reflection of who I am." We also measured two factors we labeled "public regard" and "private regard." Public regard captured how students felt society views Blacks while private regard measured their own feelings as Blacks. Additional items measured four aspects of the students' ideologies, including whether they thought all oppressed people should band together.

Results from the 1997 study confirmed and extended what we had found the year before. Once again students of color endorsed affirmative action, seeing it as a good policy. Students in western Massachusetts thought that affirmative action enhanced opportunities for women and minorities, that the policy was still needed, and that it benefited society as a whole. They also believed, on average, that they themselves had personally benefited from the policy. As in the earlier study, the data collected in 1997 in western Massachusetts showed that students of color felt that other students and faculty second-guessed them. Seventy percent of the college students and 56 percent of the University of Massachusetts students thought their peers entertained doubts about them. Fifty-two percent of the college students and 49 percent of the university students thought the same about their professors. Meanwhile, 30 percent of the college students and 37 percent of the university students admitted that they themselves had doubts about their own intellectual capabilities.[98]

Of course, some students in the sample endorsed affirmative action more strongly than others. The most important predictor of how strongly a student endorsed affirmative action was how much the student felt personally benefited by it. Another crucially important influence on endorsement was the centrality of the student's ethnic identity. Students who considered their blackness to be central to their personal identity most strongly supported affirmative action. Those with a weak ethnic identity were weakest in their endorsement. Similarly, students who felt positive about being Black were the most ardent supporters of affirmative action. Students who felt academically confident supported affirmative action more strongly than did students who questioned their own abilities. Unrelated to the students' opinions about affirmative action were the students' views of how society envisions Blacks. Thus, support for affirmative action was not a "moving against" the dominant culture so much as a "moving toward" the cherished subculture.[99]

The final study in the series was conducted in the winter of 1999. It included 188 Hispanic students at the University of California, Santa Cruz.[100] All the students were asked their attitudes about affirmative action and their feelings of ethnic identity. Once again, ethnic minority students expressed strong support for affirmative action. Once again, the greater the strength of ethnic identification, the stronger the endorsement of affirmative action.

In sum, looking at the attitudes and opinions of undergraduate and graduate students in a variety of schools, there is scant evidence for the deleterious effects of affirmative action. Minority students are not shy about acknowledging the "chilly climate" of most predominantly White campuses. Nor are they blind to their stigmatized status. They do not conceive of affirmative action as a panacea. But neither does affirmative action cause them to cringe. On the contrary, they generally like affirmative action, and those who are most secure in themselves like it best.

Other Forms of Harm

The fact that both graduate and undergraduate students like affirmative action does not, of course, mean that affirmative action is actually good for them. Children like candy, not spinach. But spinach is good for them.

One impassioned spokesman for conservative America, Dinesh D'Souza, has railed against the liberals who, in his opinion, have created the modern version of the White man's burden, with predictably bad results. Claims D'Souza: "American universities are quite willing to sacrifice the future happiness of many young blacks and Hispanics to achieve diversity, proportional representation, and what they consider to be multicultural progress."[101] By admitting underqualified students of color, according to D'Souza, colleges and universities create a culture of failure. In this opinion, D'Souza is joined by many other critics of affirmative action, like Shelby Steele. Steele is particularly insistent that affirmative action trains young Black people to feel less self-reliant and self-assured than they would otherwise be.

Two recent studies show that we ought to pay close attention to D'Souza's warnings. Both indicate that there may indeed be some unpalatable consequences to race-sensitive admissions policies. Affirmative action can cause problems for ethnic minority students that they are not even aware of.

Ryan Brown and associates at the University of Texas administered a battery of questions to 370 freshman psychology students during their first week of classes.[102] The students in the sample had been admitted to the university before the *Hopwood* decision forced it to abandon its affirmative action admissions policy. In the sample were 14 Blacks and 55 Hispanics as well as 301 Whites and Asian Americans. The researchers placed the students in two groups: Majority (Whites and Asian Americans) and Underrepresented. They then asked the students what their SAT scores were. The students also rated their academic abilities relative to other students their age, to give a measure of their academic self-confidence. They were asked to guess "the extent to which you think that your race or ethnicity might have helped you get admitted to the University of Texas" on a 1 (did not help at all) to 7 (helped a lot) scale, which the investigators called the "suspicion of preferential treatment."

On all these measures, the two groups of students differed. Underrepresented students had lower SAT scores and lower academic self-confidence than the Majority students. Underrepresented students averaged a "suspicion" score of 3.03, while the Majority students scored 1.56, more than a minor difference.

The question of burning interest was: How did the students perform during their freshman year? With permission from the students, the investigators examined their official scores. As expected, Blacks and Hispanics, as a group, achieved a lower average GPA (around C+) than Whites and Asian Americans (around B−).

The investigators did not simply compare the two groups. They also looked within each group at the associations among several different factors. What factors were statistically predictive of GPA among either group of students? For both groups, SAT scores predicted GPA and so did academic self-confidence. The suspicion that ethnicity had been a factor in admission did not influence GPA. To the extent that students were laboring under a cloud of suspicion about their admission, that burden did not—at first glance—appear to influence academic accomplishments.

Further analysis changed this. Lumping together all the students in the sample, Brown and colleagues conducted a set of causal analyses. They first looked, among the total sample, at group differences in GPA. As already demonstrated, Underrepresented students had lower GPAs than Majority students. The researchers then showed, through a technique known as mediational analyses, that the causal path from group membership (Underrepresented or Majority) to GPAs ran through the variable of suspicion. In other words, being part of an underrepresented group led some students to suspect that they had been admitted because of ethnicity and, in turn, suspecting that they had been admitted because of ethnicity tended to depress their academic achievement.[103] In this further analysis, then, the doomsayers turn out to be right.

If the Texas study were the only one to document poor consequences of affirmative action programs, we might be able to dismiss the results as an anomaly. Certainly the sample in the Texas study was small. And the design of the study, without a post-*Hopwood* group of students, did not allow the researchers to make unambiguous attributions of the results to affirmative action.

But the results of the Texas study are not isolated. Other investigators, working at the University of California in Los Angeles had similar results.[104] At the time the data were collected, consideration of sex and race had not yet been banned in U.C. admissions. Colette van Laar and Shana Levin analyzed information that had been collected from all UCLA undergraduates in 1996. Their sample included 45 Blacks and 181 Hispanics. All of the students had been asked, "Do you feel you were admitted to UCLA because of affirmative action?" Sixty percent of the Black students and 70 percent of the Hispanics answered maybe or yes, and these students had lower GPAs than the Blacks and Hispanics who said no.

What explained the lower grades? Was preparation, as indexed by SAT scores, the only reason for the relative performance deficit among the students who thought that affirmative action may have helped them gain admittance? Or could there have been a psychological factor?

One likely contributor to poor performance, reasoned van Laar and Levin, is what Claude Steele has called "stereotype threat."[105] Stereotype threat is experienced by people in situations where they feel their performance might be judged in light of an existing stereotype. People experiencing stereotype threat are afraid that their performance will be used to confirm a negative stereotype either for themselves personally or for their group. Perhaps through distraction, perhaps through anxiety, stereotype threat has been shown to cause performance to decrease. For example, White men, a generally nonstigmatized group, experienced stereotype threat when they were presented with the information that Asian men typically outperform White men on math exams. Because of the activation of stereotype threat, highly able, math-identified White students expended more effort and got lower test scores than when the stereotype was not presented before the exam. This finding indicates that the underperformance was produced by evaluation apprehension associated with stereotype threat, rather than by lack of effort.[106]

Van Laar and Levin assessed stereotype threat with two questions. The first read, "I think about whether my academic performance will affect how others evaluate my ethnic group." The second read, "I think about whether the stereotypes of my ethnic group's intelligence are true for me." Van Laar and Levin found that the sting of affirmative action operates through the poison of stereotype threat. When a student was conscious of stereotype threat, the self-doubt that came from having been admitted through affirmative action contributed to a lowering of grades. But when the student had no consciousness of stereotype threat, even acknowledging that he or she might have been admitted because of affirmative action caused no ill consequences.[107]

Both groups of researchers point out that their empirical data provide a cause for concern. Brown and associates conclude their article: "In the real world, most preferential procedures use some version of gender [or race] plus merit. . . . However, it may be that the reality of preferential selection policies might not always matter as much as how these policies are perceived, both by beneficiaries and nonbeneficiaries. No matter how preferences are really used, beneficiaries' beliefs (or suspicions) that their selection may have been independent of their abilities might have a detrimental effect on performance."[108]

Bridges

To the extent that Americans misconstrue affirmative action as a system of unjustified preferential treatment, they may dislike the policy for its negative impact on mutual respect among people of different ethnicities or sexes. Even those who know that affirmative action is a monitoring system, rather than a quota system, may balk at a policy that draws attention to the immutable human characteristics of sex and race.

And even those who recognize the real achievements of affirmative action may think the policy's accomplishments come at too high a cost.

Acknowledging that perceptions and misperceptions are influential, the psychological research leads us to a fundamental policy question. Should we abandon the policy or significantly modify the programs? Or should we instead use affirmative action to try to change perceptions? Which course of action is better?

It seems to me that the most cautious answer is: We should do some of both. The administrators of any affirmative action program would, in the words of Brown and colleagues, "do well to be explicit about their belief in beneficiaries' abilities to succeed."[109] As Turner and Pratkanis and as Konrad and Linnehan have shown in the business context, clear messages from the top are not only helpful, they are downright necessary. Because affirmative action is currently justified most often in terms of diversity, not merit, there needs to be a change in how administrators talk about affirmative action. The change in emphasis may be particularly important among college students, whose self-esteem seems more fragile than that of older adults.

But to abandon or severely curtail affirmative action programs because of the fear of stigma would be to disregard the accumulated wisdom of the numerous studies conducted thus far. In a laboratory setting, we have seen the problems with telling respondents that they have been selected through preferential treatment without regard to merit. We have also seen how readily we can uncouple the pernicious connection between preferential treatment and hostility or doubt. In business, we have learned the positive effects that arise when organizations are active in promoting diversity and vigilant in recognizing talent in all its many shapes and colors. Without denying the importance of negative stereotypes, we have witnessed the support of college students for the policy.

For those still sitting on the fence, data from two additional research studies may help them decide. The first set comes from the landmark study of race-sensitive admissions policies presented in *The Shape of the River*.[110] Chapter 7 of that book, "Looking Back: Views of College," focuses on responses from women and men who matriculated in 1976 at one of the twenty-eight highly selective colleges or universities in the sample and who responded to a long retrospective survey done in 1996. From almost every detail a single story emerges: students of color enjoyed their college years and look back on them fondly. They express gratitude for and satisfaction with their college experiences and believe that college prepared them well for life. Naturally, some alumni of color had better experiences than others, had more positive things to say and fewer regrets. The same was surely true for the White graduates as well. But by and large, looking across a range of measures, the main response was one of satisfaction. Where, then, is the sacrifice of happiness? Certainly not here.

Also relevant, in a very different way, is a new study by Madeline Heilman.[111] Working with Steven Blader, Heilman presented 135 undergraduates with an evaluation task. The students believed that they were evaluating applicants who had been admitted to a graduate program in Urban Health Sciences. The school's admissions policies were described in one of three ways (affirmative action, merit only, and ambiguous). Sometimes the list of admitted students contained 1 woman and 7 men; sometimes it contained 4 men and 4 women; and sometimes it contained 7 women and 1 man. In ambiguous conditions, the participants made the assumption that the single woman was an affirmative action admit. They did not make the same assumption of a man. What a clear indication that the problem with preferential treatment lies as much, or more, in the observer as in the observed.

In her brilliant *In Defense of Affirmative Action,* economist Barbara Bergmann touches on the issue of stigma. Responding to the laments of Stephen Carter, Bergmann writes: "In thinking about this issue, we have to ask whether African Americans would be a less stigmatized group if there were fewer Black undergraduates at Yale, fewer Black Yale graduates, and fewer Black members of the Yale faculty. We also have to ask about those doing the stigmatizing. Has affirmative action created derogatory feelings about Blacks in people who would otherwise have had perfectly friendly feelings toward them?"[112] Bergmann's trenchant question leads us to the next chapter, where we look closely at people's reactions to affirmative action in light of their stereotypes, prejudices, and discriminatory behavior.

6

The Ugly Underbelly

I don't discriminate. . . . But naturally you'd distrust somebody who comes from a place like that.

White employer speaking about African American and Hispanic job applicants from a nearby housing project

Imagine that you are a young woman, filled with a righteous passion for justice and I am a pipe-smoking middle-aged man. Imagine that you are trying to convince me that much of the opposition to affirmative action derives from sexism. I am telling you that I am not sexist, but I don't like affirmative action, and I don't like you telling me that you think I am sexist. We check to make sure we have a shared understanding of what we mean by affirmative action. It turns out we mean the same things by the terms we use. We also have similar understandings of the effectiveness of affirmative action, and neither one of us believes that affirmative action harms the self-esteem of its direct beneficiaries. Yet we react in starkly different ways to the policy.

Or perhaps you are a young Black student, deep into your sociology major, and I am a well-educated White person with a certain sense of conviction about my beliefs. This time, you tell me that resistance to affirmative action is rooted in racism, and I tell you that I am not racist but I don't like affirmative action, and I resent your allegations. Again, we confirm that, yes, we do mean the same things by the term "affirmative action." And, yes, we both know that the policy has been effective, without damaging minorities. Yet we still disagree. The trouble is not misunderstanding of the policy or misinformation; the trouble is different conceptions of the world.[1]

How can we have a conversation? What could you possibly tell me that would persuade me? What could I possibly tell you that would sway you?

Being a middle-aged White woman who has come to see affirmative action as a necessary, fair, and effective system, I know that I can have little productive exchange with those of whatever age, race or ethnicity, or sex who are certain that affirmative action is unnecessary, unfair, and ineffective. I would have a hard time convincing affirmative action opponents, and am unlikely to be swayed by them either. Our starting premises are so different that we would both waste our breath in any attempt at persuasion.

In looking at how racism and sexism influence people's reactions to affirmative action, I must declare at the outset that my imagined audience includes few, if any, highly prejudiced people. A highly prejudiced person would not be reading a book like this one. In my mind's eye, I see the inquisitive friends of my parents and the classmates, colleagues, and friends of the two White men to whom I gave birth. In short, I envision myself talking to intelligent people who want to know whether there is any factual basis for the assertion that prejudicial thinking plays a part in objections to affirmative action.

To find an answer, we can break down the larger question into constituent parts. First, what is the status of sex and race discrimination and prejudice in the United States today? Discrimination occurs when people's demographic characteristics influence the treatment they receive. Prejudice is often, but not always, a component of discrimination. While discrimination concerns behavior, prejudice concerns attitudes or feelings. When prejudice takes a highly stylized form, people trade in stereotypes. If sexism and racism are things of the past, then it is unlikely that they motivate anti–affirmative action sentiment. But if the sexism and racism persist today, then it is only logical to assume that they are an aspect of some of the opposition to affirmative action.

If the evidence shows that sexism and racism persist, a second set of questions presents itself. Is there any circumstantial or direct evidence linking sexism and racism to feelings about affirmative action, one way or the other? Is the evidence the same for sexism as for racism? Finally, if some evidence does link prejudice and opposition to affirmative action, is the prejudice a matter of old-fashioned hostility or is it something else, something more subtle though perhaps no less damaging?

Does Sexism Still Exist?

Hierarchies exist. In every society on earth, some people are better off than others; some are at the top of the heap, others at the bottom. The steepness of the grade can vary. Sometimes a broad-based pyramid slopes gently up; other times the gradient is more severe. Whatever the variations, no culture escapes hierarchies.

Some hierarchies are arranged by sex. Men in some societies are, by and large, better off than women. Of course, men in one caste may be underprivileged relative to women in another caste, but in sexist cultures men at every level of society enjoy an easier life than women at the same level.

It is true that women in the United States are better off than women in many other countries.[2] After the attacks of September 11, 2001, every American schoolchild learned that the Taliban prohibited girls from obtaining an education. In many cultures around the globe, women have few or no rights. Life can be a misery.[3] Without dispute, American women are well off compared to many others.

It is also undeniably true that men in the United States have enjoyed privileges denied women. In the sexual hierarchy, men have traditionally lived at the top of the pyramid. Our Declaration of Independence proudly states that all men are created equal; but neither the Founding Fathers nor their progeny thought women were the equal of men. It was not until 1920 that women won the vote.

Women in the United States—or at least middle-class women—are better off today than at almost any time in the nation's past.[4] Many middle-aged women in the United States can recount stories illustrating how poorly we were treated in the past. I myself have such stories. In 1985, for example, I was required to enter the prestigious and elitist Alta Club of Salt Lake City via the side door because only members could enter through the front door and women could not be members. The fact that I was there as a representative of Yale University made no difference.[5] A year later, a bank in Northampton, Massachusetts, refused to grant me a mortgage without the signature of my husband. The money was my own, and I would have been granted the mortgage had I been a single woman. More to the point, the man who was then my husband would have been granted the mortgage with similar funding but without my signature had he requested it. In both incidents the sex discrimination was entirely legal. My hands were tied.

Many middle-aged women in the professional and middle classes can also crow over the improved treatment we seem to be receiving today. Again, I shall assume for a moment that I am typical. A few years ago, when I was purchasing a house in California, the developer appeared to be trying to cheat me out of something he had promised. I tried to reason with him, to no avail. Only when I threatened a lawsuit did I obtain satisfaction. My threat mentioned "fraudulent inducement to buy" and also the Unruh Act. The Unruh Act punishes sex discrimination in commercial dealings in California.[6] As the only single woman buying a house from the developer at that moment, I could claim that he was treating me differently from the way he was treating the men—something that was and is illegal in California. My life circumstances had certainly changed.

Stories like mine tell a tale of improvement in the condition of women in the United States. Do they also mean that sex discrimination is a thing of the past? After years of struggle, have we finally arrived at the point of true equality of opportunity and treatment?

Some would say yes. They would say that sex discrimination is now only a historical fact, that sex discrimination is no longer a present reality.

Take Diana Furchtgott-Roth, resident fellow at the American Enterprise Institute, member of the National Advisory Board of the Independent Women's Forum, and political appointee in both the first Bush administration and the Reagan administration. Along with Christine Stolba, Furchtgott-Roth has written a provocative little book entitled *Women's Figures* and subtitled "An Illustrated Guide to the Economic Progress of Women in America." Claim Furchtgott-Roth and Stolba: "The twentieth century has witnessed many changes to the legal, social, and economic status of women. The inequality of institutions that characterized the early years of the century [has] largely vanished. Policymakers have removed the legal barriers to women's entering and participating fully in jobs and professions. Equality of opportunity now reigns."[7]

Against the claims of Furchtgott-Roth and other conservatives comes the countercry of liberals. Scholars like Barbara Bergmann of American University and Barbara Reskin of the University of Washington would like everyone to know the true extent of sex discrimination in the United States. So would a host of feminist and women-friendly organizations, including the American Association of University Women, National Organization for Women (NOW), Catalyst, the Institute for Women's Policy Research, and the Feminist Majority.

Where does the truth lie? Trying to assess the extent of sex discrimination on the basis of personal experiences cannot deliver much value, not only because our own situations may not be typical but also because of the human tendency, discussed at length in Chapter 1, to overlook unpleasant aspects of our situations. To cloud matters further, women may exaggerate the extent to which women in general face discrimination while men minimize the existence of sex discrimination.[8]

Typically, social scientists use a number of methods to find an answer. One indirect way to assess the extent of sex discrimination is to measure sex stereotyping, also known as sex bias. A more direct way is to look at differences in treatment. To the extent that women and men are differentially treated, discrimination exists. Some studies look at differences in treatment in a specific situation or among the specific sample being studied. Others assess the degree of differential treatment with nationwide or regionwide data.

Each method has its evidentiary shortcomings. Even strong documentation of prejudice (which is attitudinal) does not mean that discrimination (which is behavioral) occurs. People are sometimes capable of leaving their personal attitudes at the office door. Specific studies of targeted organizations leave us wondering how widespread the discrimination problem might be. Finally, the problem with large sets of comparative data is that they rarely equate women and men on all the variables that might explain differential outcomes. Yes, hours on the job may be held constant, but what about level of education, years out of the labor market (to raise children), and so on?

While each method of assessing the extent of sex discrimination has shortcomings, together they allow a rather complete picture to emerge. The point is to look for converging evidence. When the same pattern emerges from different methods, we gain confidence in our conclusions. In the jargon of social psychology, good researchers "triangulate" on findings.

Sexist Thinking

People vary in the degree to which they are prejudiced. Prejudices, in the technical parlance of social science, refer to thoughts and feelings. Discrimination refers to behavior. At any one moment, the connection between feelings and behavior is imperfect, for even strong feelings do not always result in overt behaviors and equally often behaviors occur in the absence of strong feelings. Yet social scientists try to gauge the extent of prejudice because discrimination is generally more likely to occur when prejudice is high than when it is low.

One way to assess prejudice is to ask people their opinions. You might, for example, ask people to evaluate women and men on a variety of traits. Scholars try to reduce the effects of "response bias" by posing survey questions in ways that make all answers seem equally acceptable. Not many men or women today would respond, "Why, yes, of course I am," to the question "Are you a sexist?" or "Are you prejudiced on gender issues?" but many might reveal their biases when presented with reasonable-sounding alternatives.

It is a truism that what sounds reasonable will change over time and place. And that is the point. What sounds reasonable to a prejudiced person may sound outrageous to an unprejudiced person. Consider this question asked by Gallup in 1936, 1969, and 1976: "Do you approve of a married woman earning money in business or industry if she has a husband capable of supporting her?" As you can imagine, approval ratings increased dramatically over the forty years that the question appeared on the polls. In the Depression year of 1936, only 18 percent of respondents approved.[9] Yet by 1976, the question no longer sounded reasonable, even to the pollsters.

One aspect of prejudice is stereotyping. When people engage in sex stereotyping, they expect certain things of women and other things of men. Because of the differential expectations, they can inaccurately perceive or evaluate the behaviors of women and men.

Not all stereotypes are negative. Someone who thinks, for example, that women are kind, nurturing, soft, and loving has stereotypes that may be just as strong as the stereotypes of women as uncreative, unassertive, illogical, and self-absorbed. Such is the fundamental insight of one popular measure of sex stereotyping: the Ambivalent Sexism Scale. Developed by Peter Glick and Susan Fiske, the scale has two major components—hostile sexism and benevolent sexism.[10] Items tapping hostile sexism display the traditional antipathy of the war between the sexes. Typical items read:

- Many women are actually seeking special favors, such as hiring policies that favor them over men, under the guise of asking for "equality."
- Most women fail to appreciate fully all that men do for them.
- Once a woman gets a man to commit to her, she usually tries to put him on a short leash.[11]

The other component, benevolent sexism, is indexed by such items as:

- Women should be cherished and protected by men.
- Many women have a quality of purity that few men possess.
- Every man ought to have a woman whom he adores.[12]

The benevolent items may appear to be "woman loving," but they tend to reinforce the subordination of women. A sweet and gentle woman is not usually anyone's first choice as a competent leader.[13] In a massive research project involving fifteen thousand men and women in nineteen nations, Glick and Fiske found that benevolent and hostile sexism, while distinct, were related to each other, and that the two together predicted gender inequality more than hostile sexism alone.[14]

While some social scientists administer surveys to gauge the level of sexism, others perform experiments. In the 1960s and 1970s a couple of classic experiments revealed that their participants undervalued

women. Philip Goldberg gave his research participants essays purportedly written by either a John McKay or a Jane McKay and found that
they rated the essays by John as better written than those by Jane. Of
course, the essays were identical. That the students doing the evaluating were undergraduate women at a women's college signaled the
strength of the bias.[15] A few years later, Inge Broverman and associates
asked one-third of a sample of mental health professionals to pick adjectives from a list describing "a healthy, mature, socially competent
adult person." The researchers asked another third of the participants
to pick adjectives that described the healthy, mature, socially competent adult man and the final third to pick adjectives that described the
healthy, mature, socially competent adult woman. Broverman and colleagues found a great deal of overlap between the "adult person" and
the "adult man," but virtually no overlap between the "adult person"
and the "adult woman."[16] Such results show that sex stereotypes are
deeply ingrained in people's conceptions of personhood.

Goldberg's experiment and the experiment by Broverman and
colleagues captured the imagination of psychologists and sociologists,
and over the next several decades experiments on gender and sex-role
stereotypes proliferated. Since the 1980s a number of researchers have
been using a statistical technique known as meta-analysis to examine
whether sex-role stereotyping persists in its blatant early form. One
careful study found that Goldberg's results have not been consistently
replicated.[17] Should we, then, clap loudly and applaud the death of sex
stereotyping?

Not yet. While finding a decrease in the degree of blatant bias, researchers of sex stereotyping also found its persistence in some more
subtle—but no less pernicious—forms. One meta-analysis, for example, showed that men's successes are attributed to high ability, but
women's successes are not.[18] Other meta-analyses revealed that people
think of men, but not women, as leaders.[19] Still other research has
shown that women and men both have lower expectations for the performance of women than of men and set higher standards for women
to achieve than for men to achieve. The shifting standard of competence can erect powerful barriers for women.[20]

A new technology called the IAT—implicit associations test—
has also shown that stereotypes not only persist but often work outside

of consciousness. Developed by Mahzarin Banaji and Anthony Greenwald, the IAT is used in what are known as "reaction-time" experiments. In one type of reaction-time experiment, the participant, seated at a computer screen, is first presented with a word or phrase. The initial word is called a "prime." After the prime has faded from the screen, other words or nonwords appear on the screen and the participant is required to make a judgment about them. The participant might, for example, have to decide whether *he, she, it, me, is, do, as,* or *all* is a pronoun after having been shown the word *secretary,* and again after seeing the word *father.* People respond most rapidly to words that they consider associated—like *secretary* and *she* or *father* and *he.* Because reaction times are mapped in milliseconds, the process is instinctual and therefore not subject to the kind of conscious control that makes it hard to know whether respondents are telling the truth to a pollster or just trying to look unprejudiced.[21] Researchers can present participants with different words and, by timing their reactions, map the associations participants are implicitly making.

Some reaction-time experiments use a slightly different methodology. Down the middle of the screen appear a set of words. The task for the participant is to classify each word as belonging to one of the categories listed in a column to the left of the screen or to one of the categories listed in a column to the right. Two categories appear as column heads on the left, and two appear as column heads on the right. For example, on the left might be written the categories "Dog" and "Good" and on the right the categories "Cat" and "Bad." Down the middle might be such words as *bark, meow, kitten, puppy, loving, hateful, good,* and *bad.* A person who loves dogs and hates cats would be able to categorize quickly all the words when "Dog" and "Good" were paired together. The same dog-loving, cat-hating person would be slower in categorizing words when "Dog" and "Bad" were paired together and "Cat" and "Good" were paired together.

The IAT now exists in paper-and-pencil version as well as in a computer version. Figure 6.1 is a version of the IAT that Mahzarin Banaji helped me create to illustrate the general concept. If you were in an IAT experiment, your job would be to work as quickly as possible to categorize each word in the proper column by putting an X in the correct circle.

	CAT GOOD	bark	DOG BAD	
O		bark		O
O		healthy		O
O		bad		O
O		cat		O
O		loving		O
O		puppies		O
O		sweet		O
O		meow		O
O		sick		O
O		hateful		O
O		canine		O
O		dog		O
O		mean		O
O		feline		O
O		kitten		O
O		good		O

Figure 6.1
Implicit Association Test for Cats and Dogs

You can test the methodology yourself by using a stopwatch and perhaps enlisting the help of a friend. Take ten seconds to complete the chart shown in figure 6.1. Let a minute or so elapse and then look at the new chart in figure 6.2. Again, work as quickly as you can to categorize each word in the proper column. Again, with the help of a friend or a stopwatch, allow yourself exactly ten seconds. If you love cats and hate dogs, you will fill in more circles in figure 6.1 than in figure 6.2. If you love dogs and hate cats, you will fill in more circles in figure 6.2 than in figure 6.1.

During the 1990s, numerous studies have been conducted using the IAT. Indeed, millions of people have gone to the Web sites devoted to the IAT. You can check one out yourself at www.implicit.harvard.edu. Follow instructions at the Web site and then see how you do.

The conclusion from all the surveys and experiments? Gender

	CAT		DOG
	BAD		GOOD
O		bark	O
O		healthy	O
O		bad	O
O		cat	O
O		loving	O
O		puppies	O
O		sweet	O
O		meow	O
O		sick	O
O		hateful	O
O		canine	O
O		dog	O
O		mean	O
O		feline	O
O		kitten	O
O		good	O

Figure 6.2
Implicit Association Test for Dogs and Cats

stereotypic thinking may not be as robust as it used to be. Yet reports of its death are greatly exaggerated.

Sex Discrimination

Actions speak louder than words. Prejudicial thoughts and feelings, indexed by scales that are more or less opaque, matter only when they result in discriminatory behavior. What do studies—either of specific environments or of the regional or national trends—show?

One way to gauge economic sex discrimination is through the gender gap in pay. When women are paid less for a job than comparable men, sex discrimination is said to exist. Over the past few decades, economists and other social scientists have tracked gender differences in pay. Perhaps predictably, this area of scholarship is fraught with disagreement. Yet, everyone seems to agree on some basic points. First, all scholars agree that women earn less than men in the United States. Overall, there is a persistent gender gap in earnings and salaries. The conclusion rests on scores of studies. Typical are the following:

- Internal Revenue Service figures for 1998 show that nearly 60 percent of earners reporting less than $5,000 in income are women, but less than 7 percent of those reporting salaries of over a million dollars are.[22]
- Controlling for "human capital characteristics" like labor-force participation and education, women earned 71.5 percent as much as men in 1979 and 88.2 percent as much in 1988.[23]
- The National Adult Literacy Survey measured the cognitive ability of more than twelve thousand women and men across the nation with tests of prose comprehension, quantitative literacy, and business skills (such as the ability to fill out a form). By and large, European American women and men were equal in capabilities. Extensive analyses revealed that a woman earned 65 percent of what a man earned with the same level of parental education, labor-force experience, education, credentials, and competence. Among Hispanic Americans, a woman earned 75.9 cents for every dollar earned by a statistically matched male. Among African Americans, the figure was 85.7 cents.[24]
- A study of twenty Fortune 500 companies conducted in 1987 and 1988 found that women with equal credentials lagged behind comparable men in terms of promotions, job transfers, and salary.[25]
- Men and women who had graduated from the University of Michigan Law School in the years 1972–76 were surveyed about their earnings fifteen years later. The extensive survey asked about performance in law school as well as domestic and job characteristics since graduation. The men earned substantially more than the women. Taking into account factors like job setting, months spent out of the labor force, and so on, 13.2 percent of the male advantage was still

"unexplained" by any of the factors and could only be attributed to sex discrimination.[26]

■ In the entertainment industry, women managers earned 62 percent of what men earned in 2000; in communications, 73 percent, and in education, 91 percent.[27]

■ Statistically equating women and men in terms of seniority, credentials, and performance, women faculty members earn 88.5 percent of what men faculty members earn.[28]

■ Over a ten-year period, female graduates of the business school at the University of Pittsburgh received significantly lower salary offers than male graduates from the same school.[29]

Does the gap in pay necessarily mean sex discrimination? It does not. The second point of agreement among scholars is that some of the gender gap in earnings can be explained by differences in women's and men's qualifications or other characteristics, such as the sector of the economy in which women or men are concentrated. Noting a fair amount of variation among the findings of different economic studies, T. D. Stanley and Stephen Jarrell conducted a sophisticated mathematical analysis in which they were able to determine how much different characteristics of the studies accounted for the reported size of the gender gap.[30] They found, for example, that studies which took into account the number of weeks worked per year showed a smaller gender gap than studies which did not. The major conclusion of Stanley and Jarrell's investigation is that the gender gap in pay steadily declined in the 1990s. Publishing in 1998, the investigators surmised that if the rate of decline held steady, sex discrimination in pay would disappear in the United States by 2001.

Unlike Furchtgott-Roth, Stanley and Jarrell are careful not to claim that sex discrimination has disappeared. The attribution of pay differentials to characteristics like working experience and sector of the economy leads to the inference of sexual equality if, and only if, we can assume that women have the same access to good jobs as men do. If women have less access to jobs than do men, we cannot dismiss sex discrimination. Thus, one measure of sex discrimination is the rate of unemployment or underemployment among women relative to men. Typically, economists find that women are more likely to be unemployed or underemployed than men. According to figures released by the U.S. Department of Labor, for example, 6 percent of male workers heading households were unemployed in November 2001, while 8.3 percent of women heading households were.[31] The problem could not be traced to women having lower credentials or less education than men.

Another measure of discrimination used by economists and other social scientists is the degree to which women and men fall or are pushed into different jobs. Again, a finding that a woman is paid the same as a man in Job X spells sexual equality if and only if the woman has the same access to Job X as the man does. Both government researchers and university scholars have found high levels of sex segregation in the workforce:

- Using an index in which a score of 100 indicates a sexually segregated labor market and 0 indicates an integrated market, economists found that the United States moved from a score of 64 in 1960 to a score of 55 in 1990. After thirty years of struggle, then, the paid labor force was still more segregated than integrated.[32]
- Examination of individual jobs within occupational categories (for example, pediatrician versus surgeon) reveals more sex segregation than across occupations.[33]
- Department of Labor statistics for the year 2000 showed that only 27 percent of full-time wage and salary workers in executive, administrative, and managerial occupations were women. The study covered jobs at all levels from administrative assistants to CEOs.[34]
- A study prepared in 2002 for Congress by the General Accounting Office found that women made up half the workforce but only 12 percent of managers in the ten industries that employ the largest proportion of women.[35]
- The more gender-balanced a field or an organization, the less men enjoy working in that field or organization.[36]
- A study of 842 workers in a large federal bureaucracy found that men supported women when the women con-

stituted a relatively small percentage of the group but that men's support of women co-workers declined as women advanced in the ranks.[37]

■ An in-depth study of training programs for women leaving the welfare rolls across the nation showed that administrators shunted them into training programs for occupations in customer service, patient care, clerical work, and childcare work despite their interest in training programs in higher-paying jobs like carpentry, plumbing, electrical work, and truck driving.[38]

■ In an audit study of discrimination, three male and three female "testers" submitted résumés for server positions in restaurants in Philadelphia. Although the qualifications for the males and females were identical, in the higher-priced restaurants, males were significantly more likely than females to be asked for an interview and to be offered a job.[39]

Some conservatives claim that the extent of sex segregation in the United States reflects women's choices.[40] They argue, for example, that a working mother may choose to stay on "the mommy track." Meanwhile, liberals claim that women's choices are constrained, so that the high degree of sex segregation in the U.S. labor force presents an accurate picture of persistent discrimination. Given the circular nature of reality, in which people's circumstances control their choices, which, in turn, maintain the present circumstances or create new ones, it would be hard to calibrate exactly how much of the segregation is self-imposed; nevertheless, studies like the audit study of restaurants argue against the possibility that all the segregation is due to choices freely made by women.

Meanwhile, no one—not even the most rock-ribbed conservative—would wish to claim that more women than men actively elect to work under harsh conditions. Working conditions are the final measure of sex discrimination for social scientists. One aspect of working conditions is sexual harassment. Between 35 and 50 percent of women experience sexual harassment at some point in their careers.[41] Women are nine times as likely as men to quit a job because of sexual harassment.[42] During job training, too, gender disparities appear. A study published in the *Journal of the American Medical Association* reported that approximately nine in ten women had been subjected to sexual slurs while in training, and half had been the object of unwanted sexual advances.[43] Looking at the gatekeepers to the American justice system, we see that in the legal profession women are two to four times as likely as men to be subject to sexual harassment.[44] In fact, data from the 1990 National Survey of Career Satisfaction/Dissatisfaction conducted by the American Bar Association showed that nearly two-thirds of women in private practice and half of women in public or corporate settings had been subject or witness to sexual harassment on the job in the preceding two years.[45]

Sexism and Attitudes Toward Affirmative Action

With so much sexual prejudice and discrimination still alive in North America, it seems appropriate to ask whether sexual prejudice is linked to feelings against affirmative action. The two could be connected in a number of ways. One possible avenue is direct; men might see that affirmative action helps women get ahead, and sexist men might not want women to get ahead. Usually the path is more ambling. Sexist people—especially if they are of the benevolent type—may generally wish women well and yet underestimate them or undervalue their work. Such people might equate the hiring or promotion of women with the hiring or promotion of the "less qualified" and come thereby to dislike affirmative action as a form of what appears to be reverse discrimination.

The Canadian psychologist Francine Tougas has documented the connection between men's sexist attitudes and their resistance to affirmative action. Tougas and colleagues contacted Francophone men who were working in a variety of professional and managerial occupations. The men were then presented with different descriptions of an affirmative action program in which women were to be hired and promoted in occupations where they were underrepresented. Sometimes the description emphasized merit, sometimes it didn't. In one experiment, the occupation in question was bus driver. In another experiment, the occupations were managerial or professional.

The men also completed a scale developed by Tougas called "the neosexism scale." The scale included items like the following:

- Women should not put themselves where they are not wanted.
- It is difficult to work for a female boss.
- Women's requests in terms of equality between the sexes are simply exaggerated.
- Discrimination against women in the labor force is no longer a problem in Canada.
- Due to social pressures, firms frequently have to hire underqualified women.

For each statement, the participant indicated his level of agreement from 1 (totally disagree) to 7 (totally agree).

Tougas and colleagues found that men's evaluation of the affirmative action program varied as a function of their sexist attitudes. The more sexist the man, the less positive his general evaluation of the affirmative action program he read about. As to specific evaluations of the fairness of the programs, men's sexism did not affect their ratings of affirmative action in the experiment involving bus drivers. But how fair they perceived the programs for managers and professionals (like themselves) to be did depend on their level of sexism. The less sexist the man, the more fair he thought the program.[46]

Tougas does not claim that all of the men's opposition to affirmative action springs from sexism. The data do not support such a point of view. Indeed, Tougas and colleagues found that the descriptions of the programs exerted a marked effect on men's reactions. Men thought the programs were more fair and generally better when the descriptions included the pains being taken to ensure merit considerations. If sexism were the only motivation for resistance, such a pattern would not have arisen.

Nor does Tougas imagine that men are the only creatures ever to express anti-egalitarian sentiments. Women can be neosexists too. As a matter of fact, Tougas and associates have demonstrated the existence of neosexism among women working for a Canadian federal agency. Secretaries who had never made any attempts at upward career mobility were more sexist in their ideologies than were women at higher levels in the organization. The more sexist the women, furthermore, the less positive was her opinion of affirmative action.[47]

In Sum

Sexism is still a problem in the United States although surely it is less of a problem than in days gone by. The continuation of sexism undermines the argument that affirmative action has become obsolete. It also raises the possibility, borne out by survey data, that anti-woman prejudice motivates some of the opposition to affirmative action programs designed to benefit women.

Does Racism Still Exist?

Gender is not the only dimension along which hierarchies are constructed. Some hierarchies are color-coded. In many of these Whites live on top and in the middle. People of color live in the middle and at the bottom.

The social and economic pyramid in the United States has historically favored White people over Black people or other people of color. By some accounts, the nation was founded on genocide. European settlers systematically killed Native Americans. For more than 250 years there were large areas of the United States where White human beings could legally own Black human beings. According to the Founding Fathers, so wise in so many other ways, slaves officially counted as less than full human beings. We have not yet reached the sesquicentennial of the Emancipation Proclamation. Even during Reconstruction, Whites, both north and south of the Mason-Dixon line, no more thought of Blacks as equals than they thought of Asian immigrants and captives as equals. Symptomatic of the times, the building of the railroads by means of indentured Asian labor depended on and reinforced White hegemony.

Nor is the history all ancient. As recently as the 1950s and 1960s, Whites in the United States openly expressed racial prejudices. Donald Kinder and Lynn Sanders, describing the extensive racism of the United States in the 1950s and 1960s, note that the 1959 gubernatorial race in Mississippi turned on the issue of segregation. Candidate Ross Barnett declared, "I don't believe God meant for the races to be integrated. God placed the black man in Africa and separated the white man from him with a body of water."[48] White voters embraced Ross's philosophy and he won the election. No tiptoeing around. No veiled accusations. Just overt anti-Black sentiment on the part of threatened Whites. Vehement racial prejudice was not limited to a lunatic fringe.

Apartheid sentiments may have been more common among White people in the South than in the North, but not until the 1960s did such sentiments begin to be unfashionable throughout the country. As recently as 1978, half of all Whites questioned in a national survey believed Blacks were less ambitious than Whites, and one-quarter proclaimed Blacks less intelligent. A third imagined that Blacks were living on handouts and fomenting crime. In the late 1970s, 88 percent of White Americans endorsed at least some racial stereotypes.[49]

Some see the days of racial prejudice and discrimination as more or less over. Others believe that prejudices still exist but in a reduced form; they are no longer a major cause of discrimination. Such is the view of Stephan and Abigail Thernstrom, who in 1997 published their massive study of race relations in the United States, *America in Black and White.*[50] The Thernstroms fix their scholarly gaze on the progress made by Blacks in the United States in the second half of the twentieth century. Defining a middle-class income as being at least twice as much as the poverty line, the Thernstroms calculate that the percentage of White families who were middle class in 1940 was twelve times the percentage of Black families. By 1995 the percentage of Whites in the middle class was only 1.5 times as great as the percentage of Blacks.[51] Distinguishing between earnings and assets, the Thernstroms acknowledge the gap in wealth (as opposed to earnings), but explain it by noting that Black Americans have not had as long as White Americans to accumulate wealth and transfer it across generations.

Another aspect of Black success, according to the Thernstroms, is residential location. Scoffing at the prediction of the Kerner report that America was disintegrating into "two societies, one black, one white—separate and unequal," the Thernstroms document that America's largest cities are all multi-ethnic. Many Blacks have moved to the suburbs. There is still a lot of neighborhood segregation, but, say the Thernstroms, the segregation is not due to economic barriers or real estate bias. Rather, it is due to the fact that Blacks prefer to live in Black communities.[52]

What about Black poverty? It is not nearly the problem people think, according to the Thernstroms. Although Black poverty rates are "too high," most poor people are not Black. Nor do most Blacks live in poverty. Indeed, 1964 was the last year in which more than 50 percent of the Black population fell below the poverty line. Admitting that not much of the poverty has eroded since the 1960s, the Thernstroms claim that poor Whites have not made advances either. At issue are single mothers, kept by their domestic responsibilities from joining the workforce. "Poverty and employment are closely linked. . . . The vast majority of adults who are poor today—and this includes black adults—are people who do not work for a living or work part time."[53]

Where the Thernstroms make their boldest assertions is on the topic of crime. Crime has risen dramatically for all ethnic groups since the 1960s but nowhere more than among young Black men. The Thernstroms adamantly deny the charges of racial bias in the justice system. True, Blacks are overrepresented in arrests. But they are also overrepresented among those convicted and those who serve jail time, which the Thernstroms claim proves that the arrests could not have been biased.[54] Another indication that the system is not biased is that for twelve out of fourteen crimes, Blacks are as likely or more likely than Whites to be acquitted in state legal systems.[55]

The Thernstroms have an answer to the liberal accusation of racial bias in the death sentence. Liberals note that 20 percent of murder cases involving a Black defendant and a White victim result in the death sentence while only 4 percent of other cases do. The Thernstroms reply that the differential is produced by two factors: harsher sentences tend to be given when the victim is an official (like a policeman), and harsher sentences tend to be given when the crime is violent. Policemen and other officials tend to be White, and Black perpetrators are most likely, they say, to use violence.

The Thernstroms go farther in their argument than saying that racism is not the explanation for racial disparities in the crime rate. They contend that racial disparities in the crime rate are the explanation for many other differences in life circumstances that have been blamed on racism. Liberals think that poverty may cause crime; but the Thernstroms believe that "crime may cause poverty."[56] The cost of operating businesses in areas of high crime means that the businesses tend to move, leaving the local inhabitants without employers and places to shop. Other factors that contribute to low employment among Blacks in the inner cities are reliance on a welfare system,[57] the ill effects of incarceration,[58] and a lack of motivation to work.[59] The Thernstroms conclude their massive investigation by proposing, "The serious inequality that remains [between Blacks and Whites] is less a function of white racism than of the racial gap in levels of educational attainment, the structure of the black family, and the rise in black crime."[60]

Racial Gaps in Perceptions

While some commentators have dismissed the Thernstroms' claims as extremist, their provocative point of view demands careful attention for at least two reasons.[61] First, both authors are highly respectable academic scholars. Stephan Thernstrom is Winthrop Professor of History at Harvard University, and Abigail Thernstrom is a Senior Fellow at the Manhattan Institute in New York, as well as a commissioner of the U.S. Civil Rights Commission and a member of the Massachusetts State Board of Education.

Further, the views of the Thernstroms may not be far out of step with those of many mainstream White Americans. During the recent lawsuits against the University of Michigan, sociologists on the campus surveyed student opinion. Typical were the views of White students like the one who claimed,

> I think it is ridiculous to have affirmative action now that everything is equal—no one is being discriminated [against] anymore.
>
> I believe that black people have as much opportunity for advancement as we have. I feel like if you go out there and you go and find those opportunities that you'll have the same opportunity to advance that we do.[62]

How a person sees the issues of race or ethnic discrimination in the United States depends very much on the color of the person's skin. To be sure, some prominent African Americans and Hispanic Americans have publicly espoused the idea that in the United States any person with enough talent and dedication can succeed. And some prominent White people have decried what they see as "savage inequalities" in the system.[63] But if we look at the entire range of opinions and do not just focus on the extremes, we cannot help but see a yawning chasm between the opinions of Whites and Blacks on whether racial imbalances exist.

Whites and Blacks also differ in their explanations for how these racial imbalances come about. Whites more than Blacks offer accounts that include poor preparation, inadequate credentials, or low motivation on the part of Blacks. Blacks meanwhile, more than Whites include prejudice and discrimination as part of the causal narrative.[64]

The canyon between White and Black opinion, evident in the data discussed in Chapter 3, has drawn attention from a number of researchers. From their detailed examination of the National Election Studies from 1986 to 1992, Donald Kinder and Lynn Sanders conclude:

> To us, the most arresting feature of public opinion on race remains how emphatically black and white Americans disagree with each other. On the obligation of government to ensure equal opportunity, on federal efforts to assist blacks, and on affirmative action in employment and schooling, a huge racial rift opens up. Blacks and whites also disagree sharply over policy questions that are racial only by implication. They differ over how generous the American welfare state should be and over the integrity of American political institutions. They differ enormously in their partisan loyalties. . . . Black Americans are much more attracted by the claims of equality and much less apprehensive over the intrusions of the federal government than are white Americans. And they differ fundamentally in their view of race and American society. Whites tend to think that racial discrimination is no longer a problem, that prejudice is with-

ering away, that the real worry these days is reverse discrimination, penalizing innocent whites for the sins of the dis-
tant past. Meanwhile, blacks see racial discrimination as
ubiquitous; they think of prejudice as a plague; they say
that racial discrimination, not affirmative action, is still the
rule in American society.[65]

The gulf between Black and White opinion that Kinder and
Sanders described has been reconfirmed in a more recent study. In September and October 2001, researchers at the Center for Workforce Development at Rutgers University interviewed a thousand workers at
different levels of income. At all levels, Whites and Blacks provided
markedly different answers to a series of probing questions. Among the
entire sample, 10 percent of White workers felt that African American
workers were unfairly treated, while 50 percent of Black American
workers did. Among those in the top income brackets, 33 percent of
Whites and 56 percent of Blacks thought African American workers
faced discrimination. The contrast in opinions of those in the general
population and those at the top may indicate increased awareness on
the part of managers and administrators. It may also indicate that discrimination becomes more obvious as an African American employee
moves higher up the rungs of employment.[66]

Racial Discrimination

The problem for a researcher like myself in the area of race relations in
the United States is to provide evidence that persuades White readers
of the extent of discrimination. Convincing readers of color that discrimination persists poses few challenges. They are already convinced
of discrimination before ever setting eyes on my book.[67] But one aim
of scientific inquiry, including social scientific inquiry, is to persuade
the skeptics, not just the converted.[68]

As sociologist Lawrence Bobo and others have made clear, different worldviews are based in the different interests of various groups. It
is in the interest of privileged Whites to believe that social inequalities
arise from impartial forces in which the most able, hardest-working,
and most intelligent are rewarded; and it is equally in the interest of

underprivileged people of color to believe that social inequalities arise through a system of discrimination in which even the most able, hardest-working, and most intelligent people reap no rewards unless they are part of the "inner circle."[69]

Yet even admitting the potency of realistic group conflict, I maintain that an examination of the facts does permit people to understand the extent of racial and ethnic prejudice in the United States. To those who bear the brunt of prejudice, an examination of data clarifies the bounded nature of racism in the United States. For those who ride on the cloud of privilege, an examination of racial prejudice may illuminate the extent of its continuing sway.

One prong of the argument requires documentation of racial disparities. Such documentation abounds. Consider what studies have shown about racial disparities in how people are treated economically, socially, and politically.

- African American candidates for officer promotion were significantly less successful than White candidates across all branches of the military studied in 1988.[70]
- In a national sample of Black women lawyers, most of whom had graduated from law school between 1973 and 1983 and had been in practice between four and ten years, 87 percent of the respondents had experienced discrimination in law school, and the vast majority thought being a woman, an African American, or both had worked against them in at their firms.[71]
- A representative sample of more than twelve thousand youths across the nation showed that a high percentage of young workers felt they had faced job discrimination. White males were the least likely of any group to report discrimination.[72]
- Despite perceptions that Black athletes are highly paid superstars, a study of batting averages showed that in the 1990s Black baseball players had to out-hit and out-pitch White players in order to keep their jobs.[73]
- In the early 1990s a study by the Federal Reserve found that poor White applicants were more likely to ob-

tain mortgages than affluent minority applicants.[74] Hispanics and Blacks were denied loans substantially more often than equally qualified Whites.[75] A recent study by the Federal Reserve Board found that banks were still denying mortgages to Blacks while awarding them to Whites with similar incomes.[76] Similarly, a study of 1980s lending practices to small businesses found that, all things being equal, for every dollar that the small businessperson invested in his or her own business, banks awarded $1.79 in equity to White business owners but only $0.89 to Black business owners. The same study showed that adequate funding was a major determinant of business success.[77]

■ A study found that Asian American and Hispanic owners of established businesses were able to obtain bank loans only 90 percent as often as comparable Whites. For African Americans, the figure was 66 percent.[78]

■ Twenty government studies conducted between 1989 and 1995 found that Asian American businesses in California faced discriminatory barriers in their local contexts.[79]

■ Race segregation still occurs in the marketplace. In 1998 33 percent of Black and Hispanic workers were in jobs that had few White workers.[80]

■ According to the Department of Commerce, in 1989 Black men with a high school education earned an average of $20,280 a year while White men with the same education earned $26,510. College-educated Black women earned an average of $31,380 a year while college-educated White women earned $41,090.[81]

■ A study found that in 1990 Black professional workers earned 21 percent less than similarly situated Whites.[82]

■ In 1990 Mexican American men earned 81–89 percent of what White men with the same level of education earned. Overall, Mexican American men also obtained less education than White men.[83]

■ According to the bipartisan Glass Ceiling Commission, Asian American men earned between 83 and 90 percent of what White men with the same credentials earned.

For Asian American women, the figure was about 60 percent.[84]

■ Looking at personnel files from ten units of a U.S. financial firm from 1990 to 1993, investigators found that Hispanic and Black workers were 3 percent to 10 percent more likely than White workers in the same units with the same characteristics to be involuntarily laid off through reorganization or reduction in force.[85]

■ Blacks are more prone to kidney disease than Whites. Yet Black patients with kidney disease are only half as likely as White patients with kidney disease to receive a transplant, and of patients who are approved for a transplant, the wait is twice as long for Blacks as for Whites.[86]

■ Environmentally toxic neighborhoods contain a disproportionately large number of ethnic minority inhabitants relative to environmentally clean neighborhoods. One analysis of developments between 1987 and 1992 showed that in Ohio new toxin-emitting facilities were placed disproportionately in neighborhoods where people of color lived.[87]

■ A study published in 2002 by the Institute of Medicine reported pervasive race differences in the quality of health care received. Unlike earlier studies, the 2002 investigation was able to rule out insurance and income differentials as the explanation for race differences. Racial and ethnic minorities received poorer care than White patients even when income levels and insurance were the same.[88]

■ White detainees obtained better bail deals than did detainees of color in the state of Connecticut in the early 1990s. Judges set higher bail for people of color than for White people.[89]

■ A government study found "remarkably consistent" racial disparities in the application of the death sentence.[90] A separate study of two thousand murder cases in Georgia in which the victim was White found that the death sentence was returned 8 percent of the time when the perpe-

trator was White and 22 percent of the time when the per-
petrator was Black.[91]

■ In 1990, 60 percent of White voters in Louisiana
voted for David Duke for U.S. Senator. A former Grand
Wizard for the Ku Klux Klan, Duke overtly played the race
card.[92]

Taken alone, any one of the studies of ethnic imbalances might be
found to have methodological weaknesses and thus to allow for many
different explanations. Taken together, the studies paint a picture of
ethnic disparities that are most accurately described as discrimination.

Any remaining doubt about the existence of race discrimination
can be erased by consideration of experiments known as "tester studies," or "audit studies." In such studies, White actors are matched with
actors of color, and both groups are extensively trained. The actors
then try to obtain some good or service, while tabulating the responses
they receive. Tester studies show quantifiable racism. One audit study
conducted in more than twenty major U.S. cities in 1989 found that
Black and Hispanic couples were quite a bit less likely to be shown advertised real estate (for purchase or rental) than were identical White
couples[93] and that minorities who were shown properties were more
likely than Whites to be steered away from affluent all-White neighborhoods.[94] Another study revealed that employment agencies discriminated against minority applicants 20–25 percent of the time.[95] A
series of "tester studies" conducted between 1989 and 1992 sent
matched White, Black, and Hispanic actors to job interviews. Whites
received three to four times the number of job offers received by minorities.[96] Yet another tester experiment found that Chicago car dealerships charge Black and/or female customers higher prices than
White male customers, while an archival study of the records of car
dealerships in the Atlanta area found substantially greater mark-ups
when the customers were Black than when they were White, during
the period from 1990 to 1995.[97]

While people have a tendency, as we have seen in Chapter 1, to underestimate the probability that they personally suffer from the discrimination that affects their group, people of color are more likely than
White people to be aware of lost opportunities. Over the years, surveys

have shown that more than 33 percent of African Americans believe their skin color cost them a job or a promotion, while only 5 to 12 percent of White people think their color has worked against them.[98] Another survey of workers in Los Angeles discovered that 45 percent of African Americans, 16 percent of Hispanics, and fewer than 3 percent of Whites felt they had been discriminated against on the basis of race.[99]

Racist Thinking

Discrimination (unequal treatment), as we have noted, is not the same as prejudice (thoughts and feelings). In the absence of evidence of White prejudice, it is theoretically possible to argue that ethnic imbalances in treatment arise because of differences between Whites and ethnic minorities in terms of the work ethic, self-discipline, and so on. What we need is evidence on the extent of racial prejudice.

Social scientists have noted a dramatic decrease in the proportion of White Americans who express overtly hostile feelings or overtly derogatory thoughts about people of color. In 1948, for example, 63 percent of White respondents objected to having a Black neighbor, and 41 percent objected to having Mexican or Mexican American neighbors. By 1987 the objectors had dropped to 13 percent and 9 percent.[100] Support for integrated schooling grew from 42 percent in 1942 to 95 percent in 1983.[101]

Do the changes in the opinion polls reflect a true and abiding change in the private opinions of White people or might Whites be masking their true feelings in the hope of appearing politically correct? A study conducted in the Detroit area in 1992 suggests that some—but not all—of the apparent forward movement is really only lip service. White respondents reported much less positive feelings about affirmative action programs for Blacks in a mailed survey than in face-to-face interviews. They also expressed more reservations about open-housing laws when they could respond anonymously to a mailed survey than in face-to-face interviews. In the mailed survey, the Whites expressed the opinion that Whites now face reverse discrimination, a sentiment they hesitated to express face to face. On nonracial matters, such as relations with neighbors, White respondents were also less candid face to face than in the mailed survey.[102]

Similarly, a recent telephone survey of 1,663 Whites adults across the country showed that Whites admit that they would not like to live in neighborhoods that have Blacks and that the racial composition of the neighborhood predicts Whites' preferences over and above other reasons Whites provide to explain their choices.[103]

Skepticism was also voiced by scholars who mined the large national data set known as the Race and Politics Survey, to which I have alluded in earlier chapters. In the 1991 Race and Politics Survey researchers at the University of California applied an innovative technique called the computer-assisted survey method (CSM). With the CSM, a portion of the respondents are presented with questions phrased one way while another portion sees questions phrased another way. Looking at the differences between groups, researchers can calculate the importance of the wording changes. A group of survey participants, for example, was given a list of three items: increased gas tax, the high salaries of professional athletes, and corporate pollution of the environment. Another group was given the same list plus the item "black people moving into your neighborhood." Everyone was asked whether the items made them angry. Among Whites in the South, researchers found a large increase in reported anger when the items included "black people moving into your neighborhood." Indeed, the investigators calculated that 42 percent of the White southerners were angry about integration with Blacks. Yet only 7 percent of White participants admitted to feelings of anger about "black people moving into the neighborhood" if asked directly.[104]

Another tactic for testing whether Whites are privately as unracist as they publicly present themselves is to match actions to words. A review published in 1980 revealed that White Americans were, at that time, unwilling to voice racist-sounding opinions but willing to discriminate in behavior—so long as their poor behavior was private or sanctioned.[105] The more unobtrusive the measure and the more sanctioned the behavior, the more pronounced the discrimination. In one study, for example, White students, thinking they were taking part in an experiment on how people learn, were encouraged to deliver electric shocks to those who had given incorrect answers. White students gave longer or harsher shocks to Black learners than to White learners. Looking at the pattern of results from numerous studies, the authors of the review concluded that while White people were giving lip service to unprejudiced ideas, they had yet to internalize the beliefs.

Among those whose work was reviewed in the 1980 article was a White social psychologist, John F. Dovidio. Dovidio had grown up in a working-class Boston suburb and gone to college at Dartmouth. While there he spent a year as an exchange student at Wellesley College, a women's school. Dovidio's experiences as a token male sparked his interest in minority issues. Over a long and illustrious career, Dovidio has conducted scores of experiments on the workings of racial prejudice among Whites. The work has led him and his colleague Samuel Gaertner to develop a model of what they entitle "aversive racism," a form of modern racism: "According to the aversive-racism perspective, many people who explicitly support egalitarian principles and believe themselves to be unprejudiced also unconsciously harbor negative feelings and beliefs about blacks and other historically disadvantaged groups."[106]

As they describe it in a later work, "Aversive racists do not represent the open flame of racial hatred nor do they usually *intend* to act out of bigoted beliefs or feelings. Instead, that bias is expressed in subtle and indirect ways that do not threaten the aversive racist's nonprejudiced self-image. When a negative response can be rationalized on the bias of some factor other than race, bias . . . is likely to occur; when these rationalizations are less available, bias is less likely to be manifested."[107] The reason Dovidio and Gaertner call their model "aversive racism" is that the White people who harbor this prejudice would find it aversive to recognize the extent of their own racism.

A series of beautifully designed experiments has supported Dovidio and Gaertner's claim that aversive racism is common among young liberal Whites. In 1989 the researchers asked White college students to evaluate candidates for a position of resident counselor. The students each evaluated one candidate, indicating whether they thought the candidate should be hired and also the strength of their recommendation. In actuality, six sets of materials were prepared, each of which was evaluated by thirty or so students. A third of the sets showed a highly qualified candidate (endorsed by almost all the students who participated in a separate pretest) and a third showed an obviously unqualified candidate (rejected by almost all students in the pretest). The final third showed a candidate who was strong, but not unambiguously so. At each of the three levels of qualification, in half the cases it was clear that the candidate was White and in half it was clear that the candidate was Black. When the candidate was clearly well qualified, students strongly endorsed him or her, whether the candidate was White or Black. At the other extreme, students recommended in equal percentages against hiring the unqualified White and Black candidate. But when the candidate had the intermediate level of qualifications, the students recommended hiring the White candidate significantly more often than they recommended the Black candidate and felt more strongly about their recommendations for the White candidate than for the Black. Ten years later, Dovidio and Gaertner repeated the experiment with a new group of White students and got the same results. It is noteworthy that the students showed a noticeable decrease in the direct verbal expression of racial prejudice over the ten-year period. Thus, while White students became less racist in their rhetoric, their behavior remained unchanged.[108]

In a related study, Dovidio and Gaertner, along with other researchers, presented White students with information in a death-penalty trial. Pretests had allowed the psychologists to sort students into two categories: those who were overtly racist and those who were aversive racists. Students read a six-page summary of the trial, learning that a Black or a White defendant had attempted a robbery during which he had killed one policeman and wounded another. The experiment also included another complication. Each of the participants sat through a videotape in which three other jurors (whom they thought were other students) gave their verdicts and explained their reasoning. All the supposed jurors argued in favor of the death sentence. In half the tapes, one of the jurors was Black. In the other half, all the jurors were White.

Among the overtly racist students, Black defendants were judged much more harshly than White defendants, regardless of whether the videotaped jury included a Black person. Among the other students, sentences varied according to the race of the juror and the race of the defendant. When all the jurors were White, students treated the White defendant more harshly than the Black defendant. When one of the jurors arguing in favor of the death penalty was Black, however, the

White participants acted much more harshly toward the Black defendant than toward the White defendant. Dovidio and Gaertner interpreted the results as showing that White people will take pains to appear unracist until the situation gives them permission to express their hostility.[109]

Dovidio, Gaertner, and their associates are not the only experimental social psychologists to document the persistence of racial preferences among White people.[110] Additional evidence of continued White bias against people of color comes from Mahzarin Banaji's IAT studies. As described earlier in this chapter, the IAT helps measure people's stereotypes, generally free of conscious control. Reaction-time experiments show that White college students associate "White" with goodness, although they do not associate "Black" with badness. Reaction times for negative adjectives were the same whether the prime was "White" or "Black." But reaction times for positive adjectives were measurably faster after a "White" prime than after a "Black" prime.[111] Similar results were obtained in a reaction-time study of White attitudes toward Mexican Americans.[112] Still other experiments have shown that aversive racists (as measured by reaction times) tend to communicate their dislike of Blacks through subtle nonverbal means, such as avoiding eye contact.[113]

General Links Between Racism and Attitudes Toward Affirmative Action

The documented persistence of prejudice and discrimination is consistent with the argument that resistance to affirmative action springs in part from racism and sexism. Given how unfashionable it is in America today to espouse openly anti-minority or anti-female bias, the temptation is to transform hostility against minorities or women into socially acceptable forms. Perhaps, as Dovidio and Gaertner suggest, most prejudiced people do not want to confront themselves. Or perhaps some prejudiced people simply do not wish to face public condemnation.

Audrey Murrell and her colleagues presented 337 White college undergraduates with information about affirmative action programs. A third of the students learned that the programs were designed to help

Blacks; a third that they were designed to help the elderly; and a third that they were designed to help the handicapped. Attitudes toward the program were significantly more positive if it was said to be intended for the handicapped than for the elderly; programs intended for the elderly were more positively evaluated, in turn, than programs for Blacks. The lineup remained the same whether the description contained a justification for affirmative action or not.[114]

Susan Clayton asked students at two midwestern schools their opinions about categorizing people in terms of race, sex, religion, sexual orientation, and college major. She also specified that the categorization was to be used for different purposes, including identification, social support, political action, and college admissions. The students were most in favor of categorization in terms of college major and sex and least in favor of categorization in terms of race and religion. At both colleges, students of color were less opposed to categorizations than were White students, and sexual orientation as a factor in admissions was more strongly opposed than race. College major was seen as the most positive way to diversify admissions.[115]

In 2000 Stanley Malos asked students to rate seven different admissions policies in terms of fairness and related attributes. Malos never mentioned the term "affirmative action," but he told participants that "a given number of individuals would be admitted to the university and given financial support based on relevant criteria." For one policy the criterion was test scores, for another it was gender, for yet another, economic disadvantage, and so on. Policies using race or gender were rated as being less fair and less effective than policies using economic disadvantage, veteran's status, or disability. The concept of spots being reserved became noxious to the students only when the reservations were being made on the basis of sex or race or ethnicity.[116]

The patterns of findings in the studies done by Murrell and associates, by Clayton, and by Malos call to mind results obtained by researchers on the Davis campus of the University of California around the time that the famous *Bakke* case brought national attention to the race-sensitive policies of the Davis medical school. The researchers first conducted a campus-wide opinion survey in 1977, as the *Bakke* case was being argued at the Supreme Court. They conducted another survey in the fall of 1981, three years after the Supreme Court had judged that Davis's procedure for increasing the number of minorities in the medical school was unconstitutional. In 1977, 49 percent of the students surveyed agreed that "disadvantaged persons should have a certain number of spaces reserved for them in the University's graduate and professional schools." The same year 31 percent of the same students agreed with virtually the same statement when the word *minority* was substituted for the word *disadvantaged.* In 1981 the percentages were 46 percent in favor of spaces for disadvantaged people and 28 percent in favor of spaces for minorities.[117] Once again, the abstract idea of reserved spaces becomes palpably more negative when minorities will benefit from the procedure. If White reaction were simply a response to the procedure, then the percentages would remain constant no matter who the beneficiaries are.

There are, of course, several reasons why people might benignly treat racial categories differently from other categories. First, White students may dislike categories only when the categories refer to ascribed status, that is, to "characteristics acquired at birth." If so, the students would be in agreement with several justices of the Supreme Court of the United States who are increasingly adamant about their interpretation of the Constitution as prohibiting race-sensitive or gender-sensitive categorizations. It is also possible that the differential levels of endorsement for "Black" versus "poor" people is due to the students' desire that only needy people benefit from affirmative action. The students may not view professional and middle-class Blacks as needy; indeed, they may agree with people like Shelby Steele who consider the equation of "Black" with "needy" insulting.[118] Finally, it is possible that White students are naive about the extent of insults and micro-injustices suffered daily by African Americans. They may never have heard of the time the Black actor Danny Glover could not get a taxi to stop for him or other similar occurrences and may imagine that in American society Whites and non-Whites receive equal respect and equal welcome.[119]

Whatever the motivations underlying the students' reactions, student opinions have proven to be in line with those of the general public. In 1990 a nationwide General Social Survey asked participants how strongly they supported a number of policies designed to enhance opportunities. Among the 1,150 White respondents in the survey, support was always weaker for policies said to benefit Blacks than for the same policies when no mention was made of race. For example, the average endorsement score among Whites, on a scale going from 1 (strong opposition) to 5 (strong support) was 3.12 for this policy: "Giving business and industry special tax breaks for locating in largely black areas." In contrast the average endorsement score was 3.72 for "Giving business and industry special tax breaks for locating in poor and high unemployment areas."

Spending money on schools in Black neighborhoods garnered an average score of 3.65, while spending money on schools in poor neighborhoods rated 4.08. Scholarships for worthy students obtained an average rating of 3.65 when the question indicated that the students were Black and 4.24 when the question indicated the students were economically disadvantaged.[120] If White people were opposed to all forms of "preferential" treatment, wouldn't they dislike the programs aimed at helping the economically disadvantaged as much as they disliked programs aimed at helping Blacks?

A somewhat smaller but more recent study also provided evidence in line with the idea that a connection might exist between prejudices and dislike of affirmative action. In the 1997 telephone opinion poll conducted by David Kravitz and colleagues using a random sample of residents in Houston, the survey included an item asking respondents to enumerate the groups they thought the typical affirmative action plan was supposed to help. Attitudes toward affirmative action were less positive among White respondents who spontaneously mentioned Blacks or Hispanics than among other respondents.[121]

If White opposition to programs that benefit Blacks were simply a matter of White discomfort at categorizing people according to characteristics acquired at birth, then we would expect to find no difference in White support for racial or ethnic policies, on the one hand, and support for gender policies, on the other. All Whites, women and men, should dislike gender-sensitive programs as much as ethnic ones. Yet in a number of different instances, pollsters have determined that support for affirmative action programs that mention gender is greater among Whites than support for race-based programs. For example, a Harris poll conducted in June 1991 found 71 percent of White respondents in favor of "federal laws requiring affirmative action programs for women and minorities in employment and education provided there are not rigid quotas." A month earlier a *Wall Street Journal* poll had found only 57 percent of Whites in favor of "affirmative action programs in business for blacks and other minority groups." Such a discrepancy connotes what Gerald Horne calls "Afro-phobia."[122]

Specific Links Between Racism and Attitudes Toward Affirmative Action

What about direct evidence? Given the proliferation of studies offering circumstantial evidence of the link between prejudice—especially racial prejudice—and opposition to affirmative action, it may not come as a surprise that several additional studies have addressed the question in even more direct ways. These studies have quite clearly demonstrated a direct link.

The evidence is especially compelling—although not totally seamless—for race. A number of studies, conducted over several years in a variety of settings with various populations indicate that attitudes toward affirmative action on the part of Whites are reliably explained, in part, by their racial attitudes.

Studies can be differentiated by their methods. Some are qualitative, focusing on in-depth examinations of relatively small numbers of people. Others are quantitative, asking standard sets of questions to large numbers of people.

A good example of the qualitative approach is a study by Dana Ward. In 1976 Ward interviewed thirty men who were the children of men previously interviewed in a famous study by political scientist Robert Lane. Looking for generational differences, Ward intensively interviewed his respondents on their feelings about many racial issues including school integration and affirmative action.

Some of the individuals in Ward's sample were blatantly racist in the old-fashioned ways of their fathers. Quoted at length was one man, "Mike DeAngelo." Asked about racial issues, DeAngelo had this to say about Blacks: "I'm sick and tired of people telling me . . . 'it's because they're oppressed, they have no will to keep themselves up.' To me it's just a crock of shit. They're just lazy. They don't care and I'm sorry for them, but what can I say?" And about Puerto Ricans: "I don't particularly care for Puerto Ricans. . . . They scare me to be perfectly honest. . . . I don't have much use for them. I don't know that I would hire one if they came in. I don't know how to say this but to me they smell. They always seem to have that fish odor."[123]

Other participants expressed no antagonism when asked directly about racial issues, but then blurted out prejudiced opinions on other topics. Ward quoted a policeman whom he called "Whitney Woodside." Woodside opposed the program of racially integrating schools by busing children from different neighborhoods to a single school. His opposition appeared to hinge on his devotion to the American dream of upward mobility. Explained Woodside: "I think of my own family, friends and neighbors and so on and what it's like to really try hard and send your kids to a school that's . . . a little upgraded. . . . For me to work my heart out to move out to this area and then have my kids sent back into the city again, I mean it's a real bummer. It makes you feel like it isn't worth trying."

Off the sensitive topics of busing and race relations, and on the neutral ground of technology, Woodside showed a different way of thinking: "People who can't keep up get swallowed up. . . . Your blacks, your Puerto Ricans, the minorities, they are hostile and angry and lots of them do not even know why. The reason is they cannot keep up. In a lot of cases they do not have the mental capacity to be able to keep up. . . . In other cases they become victims of their own society."[124]

Quantitative studies tend to delve less deeply than Dana Ward did into the psyche of their respondents. Yet quantitative studies are as important, if not more important, than the in-depth qualitative studies. In quantitative studies the interpretation of data is less subjective than in qualitative studies. Also, many more people can be included in most quantitative samples than in the labor-intensive qualitative studies.

One data set of especial importance comes from the Race and Politics data analyzed by Laura Stoker. In the Race and Politics Survey a third of the participants were randomly assigned by the computer to hear the question, "Do you think that large companies should be requested to give a certain number of jobs to blacks, or should the government stay out of this?"[125] Another third heard virtually the same question prefaced with the sentence, "There are some large companies where blacks are underrepresented." The last group heard the preface, "There are some large companies with employment policies that discriminate against blacks." When White participants heard the questions in their mild form, without reference to discrimination, their attitudes depended on whether they believed in general that discrimination still exists. The less willing people were to concede that discrimination still exists, the less positively they felt about requiring set-asides. For the mild forms of the question, White people's feelings about Blacks did not influence their response. When, on the other hand, White respondents heard the question with reference to discrimination, their feelings strongly influenced their responses. The less racist and resentful the White person, the more she or he endorsed affirmative action.

How the study frames the issue was also an important determinant of the dynamics of White reaction to affirmative action programs in university admissions. The Race and Politics Survey showed that Whites more strongly endorsed programs that make an extra effort to be sure that qualified Blacks are considered in university admissions than programs that give preference to Blacks. The pattern of results was clear among unprejudiced Whites. Racial bigots rejected both forms of affirmative action on admissions.[126]

Among the most complete studies is a recent examination by David Williams and colleagues of data collected in 1995 in a probability sample of adults living in and around Detroit. Included in the sample were 520 White and 586 Black respondents. In face-to-face interviews, respondents were asked how much they agreed with the sentiment: "I would not mind giving special preferences in hiring and job promotions to blacks." Response options included 1. strongly agree; 2. moderately agree; 3. moderately disagree; and 4. strongly disagree. The interviewers also assessed a number of other factors, including

- a belief that Whites, as a group, have fared better or worse than Blacks as a group over the last five years,
- political orientation,
- belief in an ideology that values social dominance (winning matters most),
- a belief in hard work and individualism,

- traditional prejudice,
- modern racism,

as well as age, sex, education, and, as a proxy for social class, home ownership. The Michigan researchers also asked respondents about a racially coded issue, related to but distinct from affirmative action. From "strongly agree" to "strongly disagree," respondents could indicate their feelings about the statement: "The government should make every effort to improve the social and economic position of blacks living in the United States."

Analysis proceeded in phases. First, using a technique known as factor analysis, Williams and colleagues determined that the questions did, indeed, measure the different distinct concepts under study. Of particular concern, given recently scholarly turf wars, was the distinction between modern racism and traditional prejudice. Modern racism subsumes aversive racism and is often measured by the Modern Racism Scale (MRS) or by questions taken from the MRS. Developed by John McConahay, the MRS includes such items as "Many other groups have come to the United States and overcome prejudice and worked their way up; blacks should do the same without special favors," and "Blacks have a tendency to blame whites too much for problems that are of their own doing."[127] Modern racism is differentiated from traditional prejudice, which is assessed by such items as "God made the races different as part of a divine plan," and "Whites have more in-born ability than Blacks."[128]

Having established that the various factors in their survey were indeed distinct, Williams and associates then performed a series of multiple-regression analyses to see how the various factors statistically influenced attitudes toward preferential treatment and, separately, how they influenced attitudes toward government assistance for Blacks. A regression analysis is like a complicated correlational analysis. It allows researchers to gauge the simultaneous statistical influence of many different variables—say, political orientation, traditional prejudice, and modern racism—on a target variable such as attitudes toward preference. When researchers are interested in more than one target variable, they conduct more than one regression analysis. Thus, Williams and colleagues conducted one analysis with attitudes toward affirmative action as the target variable and another with attitudes toward government efforts as the target variable.

In both sets of regression analyses, modern racism predicted attitudes and did so *even after* all the other factors had been taken into account. Indeed, for both sets of analyses, but especially for affirmative action, modern racism explained more of the variation in attitudes than did other factors.[129] In other words, the most racist people disliked affirmative action the most, and the least racist people disliked affirmative action the least; and the differences due to attitudes counted more than any other factor, such as a belief in the work ethic.

The findings of Dana Ward, of Laura Stoker, and of Williams's research group are not isolated. An early, classic study showed the influence of racism on attitudes toward affirmative action among 1,673 non-Black citizens in the National Conference for Christians and Jews.[130] A 1986 survey conducted in the Bay Area of California found reliable associations between a White person's sympathy with Blacks and his or her endorsement of government programs that ensure equity on the job. More specifically, Whites who think that "Blacks on welfare should get a job" or that Blacks do not try hard enough tend to disapprove of programs like affirmative action.[131]

In 1993 another much-cited article reported the finding of the 1990 General Social Survey in which 1,150 White Americans and 159 Black Americans reported their opinions.[132] An independent analysis of the data showed the connection between prejudice and opposition to affirmative action. A large-scale survey, conducted in 1992, of 1,869 residents of Los Angeles County showed a connection between racist feelings and opposition to affirmative action.[133] Modern or symbolic racism trumped all other variables in explaining opposition to affirmative action and similar government policies in a sweeping study of the 1986 National Election Study focused on congressional elections, the 1992 National Election Study focused on the presidential elections, the 1994 General Social Survey, and the 1995 Los Angeles County Social Survey.[134] The large-scale studies have the particular conceptual advantage of reducing sampling error. With so many people selected through scientific sampling procedures, it would be hard to claim that the results are unrepresentative.

There is also a relation between racism and other public policies related to affirmative action. Mark Peffley and Jon Hurwitz delved into the Race and Politics Study mentioned earlier to explore some of the political consequences of racial stereotypes.[135] They discovered that Whites who held negative opinions of Blacks—seeing Blacks as lazy or aggressive—reacted differently to scenarios about welfare mothers and criminals from Whites who held positive opinions. For example, prejudiced Whites approved of the police stopping and searching two Black men using foul language, but they did not approve of searches of White men using the same language. Nor did they approve of the unprovoked search of well-dressed Black men. As Peffley and Hurwitz concluded, racial stereotypes shaped judgments of situations relevant to those stereotypes.

Not all the quantitative studies involve large representative data sets. Some have focused on smaller, more targeted samples. The smaller studies provide a useful complement to the larger surveys because they ask people about situations they face in their everyday lives.

Researchers at Tulane University leveled their sights on the employees of a specific company.[136] In that setting, the more racist the White employee, the more the employee resented Black success. Racist employees were most willing to imagine that being Black led to promotions and were most dissatisfied with their own opportunities.

Other investigators asked 739 upper-level psychology majors about their attitudes toward affirmative action and their feelings toward Blacks. Even after allowing for the students' tendency to answer in socially desirable ways, the researchers found a direct association between racism and negative attitudes toward affirmative action.[137] The same association, using different measures of the underlying concepts, was also found in a study of student reactions to the anti–affirmative action measure California Proposition 209,[138] in an elaborate study of 283 students at a southern university,[139] and in a study of nearly 200 students in Boston.[140]

In Sum

From the evidence, the conclusion seems inescapable: racial attitudes matter in how White people respond to affirmative action. Study after study has found a direct link. More than one review of the social scientific literature, including more studies than I have described here, has concluded that prejudice is a predictor of attitudes toward affirmative action.[141]

And Yet

Before anyone claims a complete victory in the culture wars, it would be wise to note that prejudice is not the only variable to predict opposition to affirmative action. Other variables, like self-interest or a belief in meritocracy, have also been found to be important, sometimes even more important than prejudice.[142] Thus, the finding that in many samples we can infer who is prejudiced by knowing his or her stance on affirmative action does not mean that we can make the inference among all samples.

Relevant here is a truly fascinating analysis conducted by Edward Carmines and Geoffrey Layman of some of the data from the 1991 Race and Politics Study.[143] Carmines and Layman looked at the associations between prejudiced thinking and policy endorsements among Whites in the sample, but they made separate analyses for Republicans and Democrats. They calculated prejudice for each respondent by looking at how much he or she agreed with negative and positive characterizations of Blacks. By and large, Republicans and Democrats were equally stereotypic in their thinking. The researchers then determined what respondents thought about government spending for programs to help Blacks get more jobs, welfare spending, government interventions to fight racial discrimination on the job, job quotas for Blacks, and preferential admissions to universities. Among Republicans there was no association between prejudice and support for the activist policies. Both prejudiced and unprejudiced Republicans disliked them all. Among Democrats, unprejudiced Whites supported activism while prejudiced Whites did not. From these analyses Carmines and Layman concluded that Republican opposition to policies that resemble affirmative action derives more from a dislike of government intervention than from racial prejudice.

Carmines and Layman found further corroboration of their conclusion by looking at the results of one of the computer-assisted-studies contained in the larger Race and Politics Study. With the computer randomizing the surveys, respondents were presented with one of three statements and asked if they agreed with it. A third of the participants heard, "Most poor people these days would rather take assistance from the government than make it on their own through hard work." Another third heard the same statement with the adjective "Black" replacing the adjective "poor," and the last third heard "poor Black people." Republicans who rejected racial stereotypes reacted more negatively to "poor people" or to "poor Black people" than to "Black people." Thus, even when handed an opportunity to disparage Black people, those members of the Republican Party who claimed to reject racial stereotypes really did reject them.

Other evidence also shows the importance of factors beyond simple prejudice in White people's discomfort with affirmative action. In the study of attitudes conducted by Williams and associates that I described a few pages ago, self-interest played a part in people's opinions, and economic individualism influenced attitudes toward preferential treatment. Whites who thought that White people had lost economic ground over the past five years agreed less than others with the idea that the government ought to have programs for African Americans. Participants who adhered to the ideals of economic individualism were less supportive of preferential treatment than were the other participants. In other studies, White citizens who have faith in the justice of federal laws and in the integrity of the federal government endorse programs like affirmative action more strongly than do the cynics.[144] Indeed, depending on how the facts are presented, racial attitudes can exert less direct influence on attitudes toward affirmative action than do feelings of justice.[145]

Equally important is the observation that ethnic and gender attitudes do not exist in a vacuum. About twenty years ago, James Kluegel and Eliot Smith published a brilliant analysis of how ideology and racism intertwine.[146] As Kluegel and Smith showed, it is hard to believe in policies that set about to dismantle discrimination if, for example, you do not think that discrimination still exists. And whether you see discrimination as still existing has a lot to do with your views of what or who has caused the discrepancies between, say, Whites and Blacks, which in turn has to do with your stereotyped beliefs about the abilities and attitudes of Whites and Blacks.

In 1994, Jim Sidanius, Felicia Pratto, and their associates looked at how attitudes are combined through societal myths or ideologies about power.[147] Every society, according to Pratto and Sidanius, develops myths or ideologies that help keep social conflict at a minimum.[148] Some ideologies legitimate and enhance hierarchies. Others attenuate hierarchies. The myth of meritocracy, stressing that some people are more deserving than others, is a hierarchy-enhancing cluster of ideas.[149] Beliefs in the universality of humankind and in the equality of all citizens are hierarchy-attenuating ideas. Within any one society, some people value hierarchy more than others. Such people are said to be high in "social-dominance orientation."

In the course of their studies, Sidanius, Pratto, and their associates examined data from a number of different sources, including undergraduates at the University of Texas, undergraduates at UCLA, participants in the 1986 and the 1992 National Election Surveys, and White respondents to the 1992 and 1996 Los Angeles Surveys. By and large, the results show that racist attitudes are associated with low support for affirmative action and with high scores on social-dominance orientation. Political conservatism, meanwhile, is also associated with opposition to equality-producing policies, especially among the politically sophisticated.[150]

Bridges

Some scholars have pronounced the death of sexism and racism in the United States. The data show otherwise. It seems that reports of the death of prejudice and discrimination are premature, to say the least.

Racism and sexism have been empirically connected to opposition to affirmative action. Racist and sexist people have been found to support affirmative action less strongly than others. The reasons why are not hard to imagine. Modern racists, including aversive racists, who disparage people of color without acknowledging their own prejudice may oppose affirmative action because they see people of color as less qualified than White people or because they imagine that racism is no longer a problem in the United States.[151] Similarly, modern sexists may assume that each new woman hired is less capable than each man and may fault affirmative action for causing a lowering of standards;

such a person may never realize that standards have not been lowered or that the real problem lies not in reality but in his own sexist views.

Less benignly, racists and sexists may dislike any policy that threatens to decrease their hegemony or to enhance the well-being of minorities and women. In Chapter 3 we saw that for some people opposition to affirmative action derives from a lack of knowledge about the policy. The evidence reviewed in the current chapter also suggests that the inverse may also be true. It may be, in other words, that for some White Americans the dislike of affirmative action grows not out of ignorance but rather out of knowledge. For overt and covert racists and sexists, the knowledge that affirmative action benefits those who have been previously excluded or oppressed may be what bothers them about the policy.

Some of us believe that prejudgments must be accepted as a fact of human life—that the human brain and heart seem to have been constructed in such a way that people will always irrationally favor some over others. "Every cockroach to his mother is a gazelle," or so the French side of my family tells me. As long as people have children, as long as families extend to clans and groups and nations, and as long as the human mind makes categories, people will prejudge some as better than others.[152]

Stereotypes are learned early in life, usually without formal instruction. The child observes the hesitations, fears, and suspicions that parents exhibit around certain categories of people (Jews, say) and the ease with which the parents interact with other people (Gentiles), and thus prejudice (anti-Semitism) is learned without one explicit phrase ever being uttered.[153]

How do we interrupt the negative effects of misogynist or racist prejudices? Two related paths have been identified. First, people can learn to control the judgments they make or the inferences they draw about people. Since the late 1980s, the psychologist Patricia Devine has cogently demonstrated the difference between automatic prejudicial thinking on the part of White people and controlled thinking, which can be either prejudicial or not.[154]

The second path is less individualistic, more structural. Here the trick is to configure the social and political arrangements in such a way that people's private preferences and prejudices do not result in structural discriminations. Progress has been made. Of this there is no question. But carefully collected and interpreted information shows us that people in the United States have not fully mastered the art of preventing prejudgments from causing grave inequities between women and men or between people of color and Whites.

Affirmative action can be understood as part of the system for interrupting the connections between prejudice and discrimination, between the natural valuing of one's in-group and the pernicious exclusion of others. By emphasizing rational accounting procedures, affirmative action can help correct for distortions in society wrought by the egregious sexism and racism of the past and perpetuated today through the more muted prejudices that exist largely outside of conscious awareness. With its insistence on self-monitoring, affirmative action offers America the most effective way to detect and neutralize practices that appear nondiscriminatory but are not. Affirmative action may be one of our nation's best weapons against the practices that masquerade as fair and yet leave the present baneful force of discrimination undiminished. In short, affirmative action may still help the nation attain the nondiscriminatory ideal to which so many Americans feel a real and abiding commitment.

7

Conclusions and Speculations

Affirmative action is one of the most controversial government interventions in the labor market since the abolition of slavery.

Jonathan Leonard, "The Impact of Affirmative Action Regulation and Equal Employment Law on Black Employment"

Some years ago the Southern New England Telephone Company (as it was then called) contracted me to conduct a study of managers' attitudes. On the basis of about four hundred hours of interviews, I prepared a report. Although attitudes toward affirmative action had not been part of the study, several managers spontaneously mentioned their discomfort with the company's new push for gender equity. I dutifully included the respondents' opinions in my report to the assistant vice president.

"What," he asked, "seems to be the objection?"

"Well," I replied, "it seems as if some people feel that the program has not been effective."

"Who feels that way more—the women or the men?"

Looking over my notes, I realized that the only ones who voiced objections were male managers.

"Don't you think," asked the assistant vice president, "that what may really be bothering these men is not that the program has been ineffective. Maybe it's been *too* effective for their tastes."

Recently I recounted the anecdote to my seminar students, who had read large portions of the draft of this book. A sophisticated student offered his reflections about the uses of explanations. Explanations, he suggested, are never neutral. They always serve the needs and interests of some people and not others. In scholarship, as in life, no one can escape her or his social and political context. Everything is seen from one point of view or another. In ways of which the scholars themselves may not even be aware, we all construct arguments that accord with our preconceptions and worldviews.

One unalterable aspect of bias is its invisibility to the holder of bias. This applies to everyone, even me. I'm not exempt from gravity, and I'm not exempt from bias. I acknowledged my human frailty to the class.

Another student weighed in: "Well, what bothers me is even more basic. Everything I've read in the book seems reasonable and convincing. But what about the excluded matter? We have no way of knowing if you are including only that part of the evidence that supports the wisdom of affirmative action." Turning to me, the student said pointedly, "Would we find your argument as persuasive if we knew all the facts—not just the ones you have selected to tell us?"

My response was to allow—really, to require—the student to conduct a search on her own for studies or findings that had been omitted (intentionally or otherwise) from the specific chapter that aroused her suspicions. She found none. To guarantee further the non-selective use of information, I undertook another step. I delivered a portion of the manuscript to someone who might be expected to have a very different outlook from mine, someone whose work is "deconstructed" in the text. Again, no trace of biased selection was detected in the materials. Even as I acknowledge that total objectivity is an illusion in the social sciences, I have not willfully misrepresented the empirical evidence, evidence that I have been collecting for years.

Unraveling Mysteries

Evidence is collected to answer questions, to solve mysteries. For me, the most puzzling mystery has been inconstancy of support for the policy of affirmative action. Why, I wonder, has affirmative action in employment and education not been universally and vigorously supported in the United States? Given how sensible the policy is, how can we account for the persistence of controversy surrounding it? What accounts for the popularity of books like *The New White Nationalism in*

America, by Carol Swain, in which academics of color declare their dislike for affirmative action?[1] What explains why substantial numbers of Americans appear to oppose programs that, upon inspection, are found to operate in a fairly humdrum (albeit effective) fashion?

Like any system of quality control, affirmative action is designed to ascertain the effectiveness of given processes by examining the results they produce. When the results match the template, no further action is needed. When the results fall short of expectations, the processes are subject to correction. Such a system seems hardly likely to spark controversy. What, one wonders, has generated all the fuss?

Opposition Because of Perceived Unfairness

The first probable explanation is that, for all its administrative rigor, affirmative action is socially unfair. Although many of the proponents of affirmative action have justified the policy on grounds of diversity, the opponents have attacked the policy for the way that it fails at fairness. The apparent unfairness makes the cost of diversity seem unacceptably high.

The recent decisions by the Supreme Court in the Michigan cases do little to unseat the perception of affirmative action as a mechanism for achieving diversity at the cost of some unfairness. Nowhere do the Court's opinions address the issue of whether it is fair to accept a minority applicant with lower grades or test scores than a rejected White applicant. Of all the separate opinions written in the cases, only the opinions of Justice Ginsberg even mention the issue of persistent discrimination against ethnic minorities in the United States, and even Justice Ginsberg avoids mention of bias in the assessment of merit.[2]

At first glance, there is much about affirmative action that smacks of "reverse discrimination." How, for example, can it be fair to hire or admit applicant A when applicants B and C score better on the entrance criteria? Isn't a system unfair when the highest-scoring Black to be hired or admitted has scored lower than many of the rejected Whites? Why should ethnicity or sex enter into the hiring or the admissions formulas? After all, is it not the essence of justice to have fair procedures, and is it not the essence of fair procedures to treat same the same?

Responses to allegations of unfairness require some thought. We need, first, to pause and inspect the hiring or entrance requirements. To the extent that the entrance criteria are themselves biased, reliance on them is also biased. The pressing question then becomes determining whether there is bias in the tests. Several reliable methods exist for measuring test bias, as I outlined in Chapter 2, and one of them, "selective-system bias," reveals consistent bias. Tests which predict little of people's actual performance in school or on the job and yet result in large discrepancies between the number of Whites (or men) who pass it and the number of people of color (or women) who pass them are poor tests. Even in the absence of intentional discrimination, even when the tests continue to be used through thoughtlessness rather than because of malicious intent to exclude some types of people, selection bias is unfair. It is also, in the case of employment, illegal. The *Griggs* case established that it is unlawful for employers to use tests that disparately impact different groups of people unless the tests constitute a compelling business necessity.

Affirmative action looks at results to determine whether procedures are operating fairly. The principle is the same as the one our family uses to see whether the toaster is working well. Rather than poke around at the coils, we monitor the toast. When it pops up burned or underdone, we adjust the dial. If adjustments in the dial fail to produce the intended result, we unplug the machine and resign ourselves to tinkering with its interior.

When women or candidates of color obtain fewer of the positions than expected based on sensible and formulaic predictions from well-accepted criteria, we can deduce that bias has slipped into the selection procedure and should take corrective action. When, for instance, many fewer women faculty are hired than would be expected from the number of well-qualified women who have obtained Ph.D.s in the relevant fields, the university deduces that bias has slipped into the system. Such a deduction triggers the setting of corrective goals, using well-tried procedures. To take another example: when fewer Hispanic students enroll in the University of California than would be expected based on the number graduating at the top of their high school classes and earning high SAT scores, the university scrutinizes its application procedures to see where the drop-off in Hispanics occurs. If it finds that the drop occurs because of certain nonessential elements of the admissions procedures (such as the failure of one group to take the expensive SAT-II tests required in the admissions process), the university may take corrective action (eliminate SAT-II as part of the admissions criteria or grant fee waivers).

The thought-provoking newspaper essay quoted earlier, "Racial Profiling: Wrong for Police, Wrong for Universities," points out an apparent inconsistency in the policies of the political left. The article first establishes that "the critics of racial profiling by police officers are correct in their analysis: Using race as a proxy for criminality is wrong."[3] The article then goes on to say: "Apparently, the civil rights groups decrying police profiling by race believe that it is 'bad' stereotyping, but when universities profile applicants by race, that is 'good' stereotyping. Well, they can't have it both ways. Either skin color tells us something about how a person should be treated in society or it doesn't."[4]

But there is a major flaw in the logic of the article. How do we know if we are racially profiling if we don't keep score? Introspection is not an accurate measure. Wanting to see ourselves as unprejudiced, we are likely to underestimate the extent to which we unconsciously differentiate between types of people. Focusing on individuals and their intentions, furthermore, we are almost sure to overlook many aspects of systemic discrimination—discrimination that results from practices that appear to be neutral but that in fact privilege some people over others. We might actually be profiling White men in admissions and hiring policies. Hiring procedures that rely on word of mouth to advertise available jobs, for example, always reinforce the dominance of the groups that already fill jobs at the organization and the exclusion of groups that might be out of earshot.[5] Impressionistic accounts of whether discrimination is taking place are highly unreliable. Much more trustworthy are systematic inquiries using quantitative means for measuring outcomes.

We cannot end racial or sexual or any other type of profiling simply by declaring our good intentions. We need to conduct careful counts if we wish to know how well we are succeeding in our goal of treating everyone equally, no matter what their categorical classification. Such counts are, of course, the first step in any good affirmative action program.

But what of the cry "treat same the same"? The formula sounds simple indeed—until we move beyond general slogans to the particulars. What, specifically, does it mean to treat everyone the same? Who decides whether treatment is the same and by what means do they decide?

Imagine that a multinational company decides to administer an entrance examination to all the job applicants. For the sake of universality and fairness, the company decides to select its local workforces on the basis of a single examination given in all nations to all applicants. Imagine further that there are more applicants in some nations than others and also that there are different numbers of job openings in different nations. In an effort to treat everyone the same, should the company apply an equal cut-off score in all nations? If so, some nations might need to borrow from the job pool of other nations. The result would be that in some nations, the company would adhere to its principle of local hiring and in other nations it would not, thereby treating the citizens of different nations differently.

Continuing with the hypothetical example, what are we to do about language? In what language should the examination be written? If everyone is to be treated the same, then a mechanical application of the rules would mean that everyone needs to be given the test in the same language. But which language? Sanskrit, Latin, or ancient Greek might be the fairest choices if one wanted to use a universal tool, universally applied. But not many applicants would pass the exam. And if it were given in English, the most common language worldwide, nonnative speakers would be at a disadvantage. An alternative would be to have everyone take the test in his or her native tongue. But words can't be translated "exactly" to another language—we can only find equivalences. And any translation, however "literal," will carry different cultural meanings to people belonging to different cultures. So, as this example shows, treating everyone the same on one level means treating people differently on another.

The difficulties of equal treatment multiply when justice seems to call for the rule of equity. The attempts to make outcomes proportionate to inputs are fraught with problems. Which outcomes count in the comparisons? Which inputs? How are they calibrated? What happens when people have different opinions about the value of their talents and their efforts?

Disputes can be minimized when inputs and outcomes are standardized. Everything is rendered in one currency. So many hours of work are to be compensated by so many dollars. So many thousands or millions of dollars in sales are to be rewarded with such and such a bonus. Such and such a test score guarantees entrance to such and such a university or to such and such a job.

But who then creates the standards and devises the units of calibration? Typically, standards represent codifications of existing practices and preferences. Such codifications always privilege those who already enjoy elevated positions in the social and economic hierarchies.

Yet without explicit standards and detailed record keeping, there is no check on the power accumulation of the socially privileged. The restaurateur of an upscale restaurant hires a competent male waiter over a more competent female because he wishes to cater to the expectations of his patrons. The contractor refuses employment to the competent woman carpenter because he wishes to sustain social harmony on the worksite. The college administrator turns a blind eye to reports of hostile work climates because he does not wish to perturb his senior faculty. And all the while, each man loves his wife and his daughters, and each would be horrified to think of himself as a sexist.

Fairness is no easy matter. In the attempt to treat same the same, we encounter numerous conundrums. Justice sounds so simple in the abstract. The devil is in the details.

Confusion

Most people don't know the details about affirmative action. Indeed, when people envision an unfair policy, it is often because they envision a policy that is not acceptable under affirmative action. Despite the outpouring of publications on affirmative action, ignorance and confusion abound.

It is possible that Americans' uneven acceptance of affirmative action arises from the fact that people are uninformed about the policy. Learning how affirmative action operates or probing the philosophy underlying it is no easy matter. Clear explanations of affirmative action crop up only infrequently in the media, while numerous journalistic accounts equate affirmative action with unwarranted special privilege, reverse discrimination, and even quotas.[6]

Empirical studies have indicated a clear link in some samples between accurate knowledge of affirmative action and support for it. Citizens who know that the policy functions as a monitoring system, for example, endorse it more avidly than other citizens. Those who mistakenly equate affirmative action with quotas dislike the policy more than others, even controlling for sex, ethnicity, education, and political orientation.

A lack of knowledge about affirmative action causes a number of problems in its acceptance. Those who are untutored about affirmative action may be forgiven, I think, for assuming that the policy undermines the confidence of its direct beneficiaries. Several prominent men and women of color—people like Richard Rodriguez, Shelby Steele, and Carol Swain—have described how affirmative action undermined their own sense of confidence and pride or the confidence of people they know. The media has showered attention on their laments, helping to create the impression that they speak for many people of color. Social scientists have contributed further to the problem by emphasizing the potential detriments of affirmative action. A number of carefully done studies have demonstrated that preferential selection programs harm their intended beneficiaries *only* when the beneficiaries have no means of knowing their true qualifications or doubt their own capacities. Yet the results of the studies have been reported as showing affirmative action harms beneficiaries *except* when they have an indication of their true worth. Reporting the glass as half empty seems much more newsworthy than reporting the glass as half full.

Lack of familiarity with affirmative action can also lead people to underestimate the effectiveness of the policy. A voluminous number of studies by economists and other social scientists attests to the profound positive effects of affirmative action for White women and for people of color, but few of the studies have been translated into lay language. The true effectiveness of affirmative action has not been adequately publicized. As a result, many citizens may doubt its worth.

Not Just Knowledge

Important as it is, familiarity with affirmative action does not seem to be the only crucial factor in people's reactions to it. At any given level of familiarity, differences among groups of people arise. Among those who mistake affirmative action for a quota system, Black citizens endorse the policy more strongly than Whites do. The same ethnic division appears among those who see affirmative action as a corrective for imbalances resulting from prejudiced thinking. Furthermore, for a number of advocates who, like myself, give lectures on the topic, it seems that some people soak up information about affirmative action while others more or less actively resist knowledge.

The imperfect influence of knowledge about affirmative action on attitudes toward the policy has a number of explanations. One problem is that many "facts" relevant to the topic allow different inferences. In a beautifully written article entitled "Why Women Need Affirmative Action," for example, Judy Lichtman, Jocelyn Frye, and Helen Norton note: "Women have moved into professional jobs previously occupied almost entirely by men—in 1993, 18.6% of architects were women, compared to only 4.3% in 1975, 47.6% of economists were women, compared to only 13.1% in 1975, and 22.8% of lawyers and judges were women compared to only 7.1% in 1975."[7] Lichtman and associates infer from such statistics that affirmative action has been a success and is thus a valuable and necessary policy. Yet it is from just such statistics that some opponents of the policy draw the conclusion that affirmative action is no longer needed.

Or ponder the assertion: "The major effect of such race-preferential policies [as affirmative action] has been a redistribution of black workers from small and medium-size firms to large companies and federal jobs. Black unemployment rates have remained twice those of whites."[8] What does one make of such an assertion, assuming it is true? Does one see in such statistics the failure of a system or its success? Or does one refuse to pronounce the policy either a success or a failure until one knows which types of jobs pay more, give more benefits, or have greater job security? As with so much else, the interpretation put on the bare facts depends a great deal on attitudes, attitudes that are then justified in light of the (interpreted) facts. Once an ideology is formed, even partially, it tends to affect how people see the information presented to them.

I would like you to consider, for the purposes of illustration, these data, put forward by proponents of affirmative action in two separate articles:

In 1993, 53% of African American men between the ages of
25 and 34 were either unemployed or, if they did have jobs,
earned too little to form or keep a family.[9]

A 1994 study of the U.S. Office of Personnel Management
found that African-American federal employees are more
than twice as likely to be dismissed as their White counterparts.[10]

What do these data prove? Do they illuminate Black incompetence or
do they illustrate rampant racism in American society? Those who oppose affirmative action tend to see in such statistics strong evidence of
its detrimental effect on Black morale. Those who favor affirmative action, in contrast, are prone to find in such figures a stinging condemnation of the inequalities of the current sociopolitical system.

Some proponents of affirmative action see in the persistence of
racism and sexism a resounding reason why affirmative action continues
to be needed. Meanwhile, some of the detractors of affirmative action see
in the existence of racism and sexism a reason to disband the policy. According to commentators like Shelby Steele, by drawing attention to
race, affirmative action only exacerbates hostility between people of different races and ethnicities.[11] Yet according to other giants on the American intellectual scene, we can ill afford the pretense that people's abilities
can be understood without reference to their situations or the delusion
that the situations of Americans occur independent of ethnicity or
race.[12] For people like Stanley Fish, the very label "reverse racism" be-
trays a deeply disturbing blindness to both history and current events.

Opposition Because of Prejudice and Discrimination

For many sections of American society, it has become unfashionable to
admit to overt racism and sexism. The typical White person finds it
unpleasant to think of himself or herself as racially prejudiced. The
typical man tries to avoid the perception of himself as a sexist. We find
it uncomfortable to recognize the many times in which we act in discriminatory ways.

Yet outside of conscious awareness, many Americans engage in both ethnic and sex discrimination. Even among people who harbor no negative thoughts, furthermore, there often exists a natural insensitivity to the realities of life for individuals whose circumstances differ from their own. White researchers, for example, may create questions that ask respondents about their reactions to Blacks being given advantages. The same researchers may never ask about the advantages given to Whites. What about students who were educated in the best schools? Perhaps they lived in the best school districts because of the inheritances their ancestors were able to leave them. And perhaps their ancestors were able to avoid some forms of discrimination that were visited on the ancestors of persons of color. As the industrial psychologist Myrtle Bell pointed out to me: "My great-great-grandmother was a slave. Anyone whose ancestors were not slaves has been given advantages that they didn't earn. But no one asks about this."

My observation—based on the substantial empirical literature presented in Chapter 6—that sexual prejudice, racial prejudice, and ethnocentrism explain why some individuals dislike affirmative does not mean that all individuals who dislike affirmative action are prejudiced, discriminatory, or ethnocentric. Some—perhaps many but certainly not all—of the people who claim that affirmative action gives unfair advantage to women or to people of color base their claim on untested and unflattering assumptions about women or people of color. Yet, even if we were to find that 100 percent of the people who object to affirmative action are racists or sexists, such a finding would not suffice to prove that affirmative action is a fair or just policy.

Complications of Fairness

In 1954 the psychologist Gordon Allport published his masterpiece, *The Nature of Prejudice*.[13] In it he examined various theories that had been advanced to explain why some people are so much more prejudiced than others. Allport observed that it would be naive to settle on any single explanation. According to Allport: "Multiple causation is invariably at work and nowhere else is the law more clearly applicable than to prejudice."[14]

The same applies to people's reactions to affirmative action. Individuals differ in the reasons for which they support or oppose affirmative action. While resistance to the policy might be due to ignorance in one individual, it could be due to prejudice in another, to a genuine concern for justice in a third, and to some combination of factors in yet other people.

Indeed, some combination of factors may explain any given person's reactions to affirmative action. Instructive in this regard is a set of studies conducted by Leanne Son Hing and colleagues at the University of Waterloo. Son Hing found that some students endorsed the principle of meritocracy (closely related to equity) less adamantly than others. Students also differed in how strongly they felt that discrimination inhibits the achievements of minorities. Students who endorsed the meritocracy principle and who perceived discrimination as widespread expressed favorable opinions about affirmative action, but those who endorsed meritocracy and thought discrimination was limited disliked affirmative action.[15]

There are many reasons, not one single reason, why Americans have stumbled so much in their support for a public policy that has proven effective in diminishing existing imbalances. Supplementing the causes for resistance which have been studied and dissected in the ways documented in this book, there is, it seems to me, another factor in the inconstant approval of affirmative action. That factor is America's national love affair with justice. America's infatuation with justice seems to me a major reason, perhaps the major reason, why affirmative action has not received unwavering support.

Note that I am not saying that affirmative action is an unfair policy or otherwise grossly flawed. Nor am I suggesting that the American appetite for anti–affirmative action literature or tolerance of anti–affirmative action political and government developments bespeaks conscious hypocrisy on the part of the American public. Most Americans are not conscious hypocrites. The problem is not that Americans are trying to pull the wool over someone else's eyes.

The problem, rather, is that Americans like their justice to be simple. In their infatuation with the concept of justice, Americans eschew subtleties and nuances. They assume stark contrasts between good and bad, between justice and injustice. Like someone who is newly in love, Americans show poor tolerance toward any suggestion that the object of their affection is less than perfect.

Meanwhile, affirmative action, in theory and in practice, offers several strong reminders of the imperfections of American justice. Like all policies that involve ethnicity or race, it calls to mind the nation's shameful history with respect to people of color. Americans are reminded by the policy that some very good people—people like the Founding Fathers and perhaps they themselves—have done some rather dreadful things.

The underlying premise of affirmative action, furthermore, is that we should not assume that America is now the land of equality. Americans are thus reminded by the policy that good intentions are insufficient to overcome social structures that create or perpetuate injustices. After all, if one could assume that everybody received equal treatment, there would be no need to monitor whether everyone was receiving equal treatment. And, of course, when the monitoring does reveal disparities, affirmative action illuminates how some of the so-called achievements of the privileged class derive less from talent and ability than from favored situations. Such reminders grate against the American version of equity in which individuals are rewarded in proportion to their natural talents. In the words of one commentator: "A moral and political tension exists in contemporary America between the idea of the meritocratic, wherein achievement is based on individual effort, and the reality of social injustice, wherein whole groups of individuals have been denied an equal opportunity to pursue the meritocratic ideal."[16] When those who are accustomed to privilege are made aware of how certain demographic characteristics work systematically in their favor, they are not uniformly overjoyed by the news. Men in America have an elevated sense of entitlement,[17] which they may be loath to admit. Indeed, one experimenter was able to depress men's sense of well-being simply by reminding them of the privileges they enjoy because of their sex.[18]

Even as affirmative action gnaws at the self-congratulations of society's privileged, it may also disconcert the underprivileged because of the way in which it provokes questions about distributive and procedural justice. Talk of "equal opportunity" seems to raise none of the questions about what constitutes "equality" that are raised by discussions of affirmative action. With "equal opportunity" we are not automatically reminded of the social dislocations that arise when resources are scarce and when harms require repair.

My speculation about the link between Americans' infatuation with justice and their unease about affirmative action is still a hunch. It has not been subjected to the same kind of empirical validation that has been applied to other explanations. Numerous studies have been conducted to test the proposals that a lack of familiarity, a strong sense of fairness, or deep prejudices influence people's reactions to affirmative action. Many additional studies have been done to test the effectiveness of the policy and to measure its effect on its direct beneficiaries. Not a single test has been undertaken to test the idea that uncertain support of affirmative action springs from a thirst for simplicity in matters of fairness.

Given the novelty of my proposal, we might wonder how it would be possible to test it. How could we test empirically whether the hunch were correct? Unless a theory can be translated into a form whereby we can articulate what pattern of data would support the theory and what pattern of data would refute it, the theory remains in the realm of philosophy.[19]

In fact, several means come to mind that could provide tests of the proposal. One way to test my speculations is to look at attitudes toward affirmative action among people with differing degrees of sophistication about justice. If I am correct, affirmative action should be most disliked by those who have a difficult time tolerating ambiguities, who see justice issues in black-and-white terms, or who assume that there is always one right answer to every dilemma of justice. Americans who understand the complexities of justice or who are tolerant of complications in the moral world should, if I am correct, generally be steadfast in their support of affirmative action. One way to test my speculations, then, is to measure the associations between attitudes toward affirmative action, on the one hand, and reasoning about justice issues, on the other.[20]

Correlational data are ill-suited to causal arguments. We could also conduct experiments to test my speculations. We could educate one group of Americans about the concepts of justice—pointing out the distinctions between distributive, procedural, and restorative justice and indicating how legitimate differences in focus or differences of opinion can result in different perceptions of events. No mention would be made of affirmative action. This group would be the "experimental group." The control group in my imagined experiment would be reminded about the nation's love of justice, about how American heroes have fought for justice. The control group would receive no materials that encouraged sophisticated conceptualizations about justice. If my hypotheses about Americans' infatuation with justice are correct, then the two groups should differ in their attitudes toward affirmative action. The experimental group should like affirmative action much more than the control group.

Some evidence already exists that is consistent with my speculations. As we saw in Chapter 3, a number of studies have shown that support for affirmative action increases with increases in levels of education. Assuming that people become more sophisticated in their reasoning as they attain more education, the evidence, while hardly definitive, is at least corroborative.

Some other, even more circumstantial, evidence derives from my experiences with my students. I often teach a course on the social psychology of social justice. After learning about the complexities of justice, the students begin to change their attitudes about a number of issues, including affirmative action. Of course, my students are as talented as any in sniffing out the professor's preferences and then presenting an image of themselves calculated to appeal. But some of the change appears to be genuine, as I hear from alumni who no longer have a reason to curry my favor.

Imperfections

Now that the Supreme Court in *Gratz v. Bollinger* and *Grutter v. Bollinger* has legitimated the use of race-conscious policies in college admissions, one challenge for proponents of affirmative action will be to convince people that affirmative action is a good vehicle for ensuring the reward of merit and not simply a good vehicle for creating diversity. The challenge, I think, can be met. But other, more troublesome issues lie ahead for those who wish to keep affirmative action functioning well.

For affirmative action law, the biggest single challenge, in my opinion, concerns the categories that are designated targeted classes. Historian John Skrentny thinks so too. "If affirmative action is dismantled on a national basis," writes Skrentny, "the policy's over- or un-derinclusiveness will likely be the reason."[21]

In 1965, when Lyndon Johnson signed Executive Order 11246, the federal government and federal contractors were enjoined to monitor the match between availability and utilization of four classes of ethnic minority citizens: African Americans, Hispanics, Asian Americans, and Native Americans. Over the years, the terminology has changed. And so have the nation's demographics.

Commentators have noted oddities about keeping the original four ethnic groups. One issue concerns Asian Americans. In education, where the scheme of affirmative action follows the same scheme put forward in employment, some groups of Asian Americans appear to have become "the model minority." Although Laotian Americans, Cambodian Americans, and Filipino Americans have not had notable successes in the United States, Chinese American, Japanese American, and Korean American citizens have been very successful in higher education and, to a lesser degree, in employment. Indian Americans and Pakistani Americans present yet another profile. Whether one thinks that affirmative action has been a boon or a bane for Asian Americans,[22] some attention needs to be paid to classification schemes.

Another historical challenge derives from changes in immigration patterns. As Skrentny points out, our laws allow a million immigrants a year. Three-quarters of the annual immigrants are Hispanics or Asians who, as soon as they are naturalized, may be considered to belong to the targeted classes. Already there are more Hispanic Americans than African Americans.[23]

It is also interesting to think about who is excluded from the targeted classes. Middle Easterners, including Turks, Egyptians, Afghanis, Iraqis, Iranians, Palestinians, and Israelis, are considered by law to be White. Perhaps they are, or have been, subject to as much discrimination in America as people who belong to the protected classes. Yet according to the federal code of regulations, no one need monitor their treatment.

For affirmative action, as for the census, the nation needs to think in a creative and responsible way about how to classify people of mixed heritage. How does one classify the person whose grandmother was Japanese American if all her other relatives are of European American stock? Perhaps she is Asian American only if she wishes to be. Is, then, ethnicity nothing more than a matter of self-definition?

Another issue concerns gender. Today women comprise one of the targeted classes. Yet women are not a minority. It may be that women, who are not residentially segregated from men the way people of color are segregated from White people, may be poised for equality in the foreseeable future.[24] If we do achieve sexual equity, should the law change so that it no longer includes gender as a dimension along which to assess fairness? And how many years of sexual equity in education and employment are needed for us to decide that sex discrimination is defunct?

Final Thoughts

My discomfort about the categories that are used in affirmative action mirrors the discomfort of many liberals. But my acknowledgment that the categories are imperfect and represent a form of pragmatic adjustment to reality does not mean that I wish to discard affirmative action. Indeed, in my view there are two major reasons why the policy is vital to the continued health of the nation.

The first reason America still needs affirmative action is its effectiveness in helping to diminish the large residue of sexual and racial prejudice and discrimination that still today pollute the moral atmosphere of the United States. For me the empirical evidence contained in Chapter 6 is overwhelming. Clearly, people of color are still subject to more unfair treatment than are White people and still, through no fault of their own, have less access to favorable life circumstances than do White people. Similarly, women today still have not achieved parity with men.

I must admit to some feelings of alarm at how women like Diana Furchtgott-Roth have managed to gain a following for their views of the contemporary levels of prejudice and discrimination. Furchtgott-Roth has gone so far as to cite the *Price Waterhouse* case, in which the Supreme Court upheld a plaintiff's allegation of sex discrimination, as evidence that "while some wage discrimination may persist, it does not appear to be pervasive in the American economy."[25] It is sheer sophistry to cite a landmark case showing blatant sex discrimination as evidence that discrimination does not exist. If Furchtgott-Roth and others at the American Enterprise Institute weren't so dangerous, they would be laughable. But they are indeed dangerous. As long as people like Furchtgott-Roth find a ready audience in the United States, Americans must continue to worry at the levels of prejudice and discrimination, levels so high that they require active measures to neutralize them.

The second reason why the United States shall continue to need affirmative action has more to do with continuing aspects of human information processing than it does with current aspects of prejudice. Without the aid of elaborate devices for observation and deduction, human beings are poor information processors. Two decades of social psychological research have been devoted to documenting the fallacies in information processing. The only social psychologist ever to win a Nobel Prize, Daniel Kahneman of Princeton University, has spent his career documenting the nature of problems in people's processing of information. People require special training to learn how to make the connection between data about individuals and data about groups, including large groups called societies.

Thus while the specific categories used in affirmative action may need some revision, the process underlying the policy does not. Many liberals have portrayed affirmative action as a policy that should self-destruct as soon as racial and gender equality have been attained. I no longer think of affirmative action as a time-delimited policy. Monitoring, in my opinion, will always be needed. As long as human beings love their own families more than other families—which, I believe, will be forever—biases and injustices will arise. A strong democracy is one with well-developed means for minimizing the effects of human bias and prejudice. Traditionally, as a nation, Americans have been successful, relative to many other nations, in terms of the procedures used to correct injustices that have occurred. Affirmative action takes the operation a step further. By insisting that people monitor their outcomes to see whether their processes are as unbiased as they hope, affirmative action helps ensure evolutionary change and, through small steps, avoid revolution.

In monitoring outcomes, do we run the risk of letting equality of results supplant equality of opportunity? Perhaps. And, of course, we run the risk that some may implement the policy of affirmative action in ways that subvert its purpose. Yet the risk of distortion seems no greater with affirmative action than with any other policy.

Good intentions and pure motives are not enough to ensure the successful operation of democracy. Even when the vast majority of Americans reach a place of truly diminished prejudice and hostility toward women and people of color, monitoring will continue to be a necessary aspect of the nation's economic, social, and political life. Thomas Jefferson observed that the price of democracy is eternal vigilance. Those who take a simplistic view of justice might assume that the vigilance of which Jefferson spoke concerns only foreign forces that might attack the nation from outside or through infiltration. But those who take a more mature view understand that vigilance must be applied to the self, for justice-loving though Americans be, they must always watch that their behaviors and their structures match their hopes, their dreams, and their own good intentions. That is why long after the categories of affirmative action are dead and gone, the monitoring process will need to live on.

Notes

Chapter 1: The Nature of the Beast

1. Gratz et al. v. Bollinger et al., 2003, *Daily Journal Daily Appellate Report* 6783.

2. Some legal scholars had predicted that the cases would hinge on whether the university could build a persuasive case that its drive for diversity constituted a compelling state interest. For a particularly prescient analysis see R. A. Epstein, "A Rational Basis for Affirmative Action: A Shaky but Classical Liberal Defense," *Michigan Law Review* 100 (2002).

3. Grutter v. Bollinger et al., 2003, *Daily Journal Daily Appellate Report* 6800.

4. J. Hurwitz and M. Peffley, "Introduction," *Perception and Prejudice: Race and Politics in the United States,* ed. J. Hurwitz and M. Peffley (New Haven: Yale University Press, 1998), 3. See also, as an exemplar of such thinking, H. Belz, *Equality Transformed: A Quarter Century of Affirmative Action* (New Brunswick, N.J.: Transaction, 1991).

5. See P. C. Roberts and L. M. Stratton, *The New Color Line: How Quotas and Privilege Destroy Democracy* (Washington, D.C.: Regnery, 1995).

6. See M. Foschi, "Status, Affect, and Multiple Standards for Competence," and C. L. Ridgeway, "Where Do Status Value Beliefs Come From? New Developments," in *Status, Network, and Structure: Theory Development in Group Process,* ed. J. Szmatka, J. Skvoretz, and J. Berger (Stanford: Stanford University Press, 1997); R. J. Steinberg, "Social Construction of Skill: Gender, Power and Comparable Worth," *Work and Occupations* 17 (1990).

7. See F. J. Crosby et al., "Affirmative Action: Psychological Data and the Policy Debates," *American Psychologist* 58 (2003), and M. J. T. Vasquez, "Leveling the Playing Field—Toward the Emancipation of Women," *Psychology of Women Quarterly* 25 (2001).

8. For an interesting analysis of some of the different meanings of affirmative action, see R. K. Robinson, J. G. P. Paolillo, and B. Reithel, "Race-Based Preferential Treatment Programs: Raising the Bar for Establishing Compelling Government Interests," *Public Personnel Management* 27 (1998). For a thoughtful historical, philosophical, and theoretical analysis of affirmative action and its many meanings, see W. G. Tierney, "The Parameters of Affirmative Action: Equity and Excellence in the Academy," *Review of Educational Research* 67 (1997). Another piece that also creates an interesting set of categories is the philosophical book by W. R. Gray, *The Four Faces of Affirmative Action: Fundamental Answers and Actions* (Westport: Greenwood, 2001).

9. American Psychological Association, *Affirmative Action: Who Benefits?* (Washington, D.C.: American Psychological Association, 1996), 2.

10. See Crosby, "Understanding Affirmative Action," *Basic and Applied Social Psychology* 15 (1994). For the difference between equal opportunity and affirmative action see also F. A. Holloway, "What Is Affirmative Action?" in *Affirmative Action in Perspective,* ed. F. A. Blanchard and F. J. Crosby (New York: Springer Verlag, 1989); and A. M. Konrad and F. Linnehan, "Affirmative Action: History, Effects, and Attitudes," in *Handbook*

of Gender and Work, ed. Gary N. Powell (Thousand Oaks, Calif.: Sage, 1999). For a fascinating discussion of the connections between affirmative action and disparate-impact
law, see R. Stryker, "Disparate Impact and Quota Debates: Law, Labor Market Sociology, and Equal Employment Practices," *Sociological Quarterly* 42 (2001). Of special interest is an analysis by Nicholas Pedriana and Robin Stryker, showing that affirmative action can be and has been framed as essentially coterminus with equal opportunity. The
Nixon administration was able to create the Philadelphia plan, which established staffing
goals in the construction industry in twenty cities around the country by demonstrating
the extent of discrimination in the construction industry and arguing that goals were
necessary to establish equal opportunity; see N. Pedriana and R. Stryker, "Political Culture Wars 1960s Style: Equal Employment Opportunity-Affirmative Action Law in the
Philadelphia Plan," *American Journal of Sociology* 103 (1997).

11. C. V. Dale, *Congressional Research Service Report to Robert Dole: Compilation and
Overview of Federal Laws and Regulations Establishing Affirmative Action Goals or Other
Preferences Based on Race, Gender, and Ethnicity* (Washington, D.C.: Congressional Re-
search Service, Library of Congress, 1995).

12. F. J. Crosby and D. I. Cordova, "Words Worth of Wisdom: Toward an Understanding of Affirmative Action," *Journal of Social Issues* 52, no. 2 (1996).

13. Dale, *Congressional Research Service Report to Robert Dole.*

14. Crosby and Cordova, "Words Worth of Wisdom."

15. For facts and figures about affirmative action in employment, consult the
OFCCP Web site at www.dol.gov/dol/esa/public/regs/compliance/offcp/aa.htm.

16. See W. Thomas and M. Garrett, "U.S. and California Affirmative Action Policies,
Laws, and Programs," in *Impacts of Affirmative Action: Policies and Consequences in California,* ed. P. Ong (Walnut Creek, Calif.: Altamira, 1999).

17. See Konrad and Linnehan, "Affirmative Action: History, Effects, and Attitudes."

18. See F. J. Crosby and C. VanDeVeer, eds., *Sex, Race, and Merit: Debating Affirmative Action in Education and Employment* (Ann Arbor: University of Michigan Press,
2000), pt. 4.

19. In 1965 California adopted its Master Plan for Education, in which the University
of California agreed to admit the top 12.5 percent of graduating high school seniors.
Since that time, various formulas, giving differing weights to grades and standardized test
scores, have evolved for determining what constitutes that top 12.5 percent.

20. Various social and political forces determine who is classified as a member of a minority. Characteristics such as sex, age, and religion are sometimes used to designate minority status. However, in contemporary U.S. society, race and ethnicity are the characteristics used most often to define the minority and majority populations. For more
information on this topic, see D. S. Eitzen and M. B. Zinn, *Social Problems,* 8th ed.
(Boston: Allyn and Bacon, 2000). Census data have been key in determining racial minority classification. As the United States changes and its racial makeup fluctuates, the
number of racial categories used in the census has also changed in the attempt to reflect
these fluctuations. Since 1970, the racial categories used in the census have grown from
four to thirteen. The most important factor in census data collection is the purpose for
which race data are used. Federal agencies and affirmative action employers utilize the revised racial and ethnic census data in determining who is classified as a minority member.
For example, the Bureau of Census works directly with the Equal Employment Opportunity Commission (EEOC) and the Office of Federal Contract Compliance Programs

(OFCCP) on Affirmative Action Plans. It is evident that in order for a particular racial or ethnic group to be protected by Affirmative Action Plans, census data must be collected and recorded for that particular group. While some groups in the United States experience economic or social hardship because they are a minority, unless the Bureau of Census adds their racial category to the census they will not benefit from affirmative action programs.

21. Rehnquist joined Justice Stewart's dissent in *Fullilove v. Klutznick* (448 U.S. 448 [1980]), writing, "The equal protection standard of the Constitution has one clear and central meaning—it absolutely prohibits invidious discrimination by government. That standard must be met by every State under the Equal Protection Clause of the Fourteenth Amendment. . . . The rule cannot be any different when the persons injured by a racially biased law are not members of a racial minority." Similar sentiments were expressed even more adamantly by Justice Scalia in his separate concurring opinion in *Richmond v. Croson Co.* (488 U.S. 469 [1998]).

22. See G. A. Spann, *The Law of Affirmative Action: Twenty-Five Years of Supreme Court Decisions on Race and Remedies* (New York: New York University Press, 2000).

23. The law has its own Web site at www.ed.gov/offices/OESE/esea/factsheet.html.

24. The classic source on the need to believe in a just world is Melvin Lerner, *The Belief in a Just World: The Fundamental Delusion* (New York: Plenum, 1980). For a comprehensive review of the literature on procedural, as distinct from distributive, justice, see Tom R. Tyler et al., *Social Justice in a Diverse Society* (Boulder, Colo.: Westview, 1997).

25. See C. Dalbert, "Coping with an Unjust Fate: The Case of Structural Unemployment," *Social Justice Research* 10 (1997). See also S. E. Taylor and J. D. Brown, "Illusion and Well-Being: A Social Psychological Perspective on Mental Health," *Psychological Bulletin* 103 (1988); T. Postmes et al., "Comparative Processes in Personal and Group Judgments: Resolving the Discrepancy," *Journal of Personality and Social Psychology* 76 (1999); and L. A. Baker and R. E. Emery. "When Every Relationship Is Above Average: Perceptions and Expectations of Divorce at the Time of Marriage," *Law and Human Behavior* 17 (1993).

26. F. J. Crosby et al., "Cognitive Biases in the Perception of Discrimination: The Importance of Format," *Sex Roles* 14 (1986).

27. See D. I. Cordova, "Cognitive Limitations and Affirmative Action: The Effects of Aggregate Versus Sequential Data in the Perception of Discrimination," *Social Justice Research* 5 (1992).

28. C. Twiss, S. Tabb, and F. J. Crosby, "Affirmative Action and Aggregate Data: The Importance of Patterns in the Perception of Discrimination," in *Affirmative Action in Perspective,* ed. F. Blanchard and F. J. Crosby (New York: Springer-Verlag, 1989).

29. C. G. Rutte et al., "Organizing Information and the Detection of Gender Discrimination," *Psychological Science* 5 (1994).

30. In one study we also showed that the process works in reverse: it is hard for people to make inferences about individuals on the basis of information about groups. See F. J. Crosby et al., "Two Rotten Apples Spoil the Justice Barrel," in *Justice in Social Relations,* ed. H. Bierhoff, R. Cohen, and J. Greenberg (New York: Plenum, 1986). For the difficulty of switching between information about individuals and information about groups, see R. M. Dawes, "Affirmative Action Programs: Discontinuities Between Thoughts About Individuals and Thoughts About Groups," in *Applications of Heuristics and Biases to Social Issues,* ed. R. S. Tindale et al. (New York: Plenum, 1994).

31. S. T. Fiske and S. E. Taylor, *Social Cognition,* 2d ed. (New York: McGraw-Hill, 1991).

32. L. L. Chavez, "Promoting Racial Harmony," in *The Affirmative Action Debate,* ed. G. E. Curry (Cambridge: Perseus, 1998), 315.

33. R. E. Miller and A. Sarat, "Grievances, Claims, and Disputes: Assessing the Adversary Culture," *Law and Society Review* 15, nos. 3/4 (1980–81).

34. K. Bumiller, "Victims in the Shadow of the Law: A Critique of the Model of Legal Protection," *Signs: Journal of Women in Culture and Society* 12 (1987).

35. C. L. Kaiser and C. T. Miller, "Stop Complaining! The Social Costs of Making Attributions to Discrimination," *Personality and Social Psychology Bulletin* 27 (2001).

36. F. J. Crosby, *Relative Deprivation and Working Women* (New York: Oxford University Press, 1982). Also see F. J. Crosby, "The Denial of Personal Discrimination," *American Behavioral Scientist* 27 (1984), and F. J. Crosby, "Relative Deprivation in Organizational Settings," in *Research in Organizational Behavior,* ed. B. Staw and L. L. Cummings (Greenwich: JAI Press, 1984).

37. C. L. Hafer and J. M. Olson, "Beliefs in a Just World, Discontent, and Assertive Actions by Working Women," *Personality and Social Psychology Bulletin* 1 (1993).

38. K. L. Dion and K. Kawakami, "Ethnicity and Perceived Discrimination in Toronto: Another Look at the Personal/Group Discrimination Discrepancy," *Canadian Journal of Behavioural Science* 28, no. 3 (1996).

39. D. M. Taylor et al., "Interpreting and Coping with Threat in the Context of Intergroup Relations," *Journal of Social Psychology* 2 (1982).

40. D. M. Taylor, S. C. Wright, and L. E. Porter, "Dimensions of Perceived Discrimination: The Personal/Group Discrimination Discrepancy," in *The Psychology of Prejudice: The Ontario Symposium,* ed. M. P. Zanna and J. M. Olson (Hillsdale, N.J.: Erlbaum, 1994).

41. D. M. Taylor et al., "The Personal/Group Discrimination Discrepancy: Perceiving My Group, but Not Myself, to Be a Target of Discrimination," *Personality and Social Psychology Bulletin* 16 (1990).

42. D. L. Ford, "Minority and Non-Minority MBA Progress in Business," in *Ensuring Minority Success in Corporate Management,* ed. D. E. Thompson and N. DiTomaso (New York: Plenum, 1988).

43. M. D. Foster and K. Matheson, "Double Relative Deprivation: Combining the Personal and the Political," *Personality and Social Psychology Bulletin* 21 (1995); F. M. Moghaddam and L. S. Hutcheson, "A Generalized Personal/Group Discrepancy: Testing the Domain Specificity of a Perceived Higher Effect of Events on One's Group Than on Oneself," *Personality and Social Psychology Bulletin* 7 (1997); D. Operario and S. T. Fiske, "Ethnic Identity Moderates Perceptions of Prejudice: Judgments of Personal Versus Group Discrimination and Subtle Versus Blatant Bias," *Personality and Social Psychology Bulletin* 27 (2001).

44. J. M. Olson et al., "The Preconditions and Consequences of Relative Deprivation: Two Field Studies," *Journal of Applied Social Psychology* 11 (1995).

45. C. M. Birt and K. L. Dion, "Relative Deprivation Theory and Responses to Discrimination in a Gay Male and Lesbian Sample," *British Journal of Social Psychology* 26 (1987); F. J. Crosby et al., "The Denial of Personal Disadvantage Among You, Me and All the Other Ostriches," in *Gender and Thought,* ed. M. Crawford and M. Gentry (New York: Springer-Verlag, 1989); J. D'Emilio, *Sexual Politics, Sexual Communities: The Mak-*

ing of a Homosexual Minority in the United States, 1940–1970 (Chicago: University of Chicago Press, 1983).

46. D. E. Lewis, "Study Finds Views on Race Diverge," *Boston Globe,* Jan. 20, 2002.

47. Indeed, people think of themselves as immune from many negative attributes as well as from discrimination. See G. Hudson and V. M. Esses, "A New Perspective on the Personal/Group Discrimination Discrepancy" (paper presented at the biannual meeting of the Society for the Psychological Study of Social Issues, Minneapolis, June 2000).

48. L. Harris, "Unequal Terms," *Columbia Journalism Review* 30, no. 5 (1992).

49. M. Marable, "Staying on the Path to Racial Equality," in *The Affirmative Action Debate,* ed. G. E. Curry (Cambridge: Perseus, 1998), 8. A national survey conducted by the *Los Angeles Times* on March 15–19, 1995, had roughly the same results. Interestingly, the *Times* poll showed no difference in the level of support for gender-based affirmative action, race-based affirmative action, or disadvantage-based affirmative action. See L. Sigelman, "The Public and Disadvantaged-Based Affirmative Action: An Early Assessment," *Social Science Quarterly* 78 (1997).

50. Princeton Survey Research Associates conducted the poll with 752 adults nationwide in July 2000. The results are available from the Roper Center at the University of Connecticut, accession number 0363565.

51. The results of a Gallup Poll of 1,523 adults conducted in August 2001 are available from the Roper Center at the University of Connecticut, accession numbers 0391286, 0391287, 0391288, and 0391289.

52. J. Chait, "Pol Tested—Why Politicians Love Affirmative Action," *New Republic,* Feb. 3, 2003, 14.

53. See D. A. Kravitz, "Attitudes Toward Affirmative Action Plans Directed at Blacks: Effects of Plan and Individual Differences," *Journal of Applied Social Psychology* 25 (1995); M. P. Bell, D. A. Harrison, and M. E. McLaughlin, "Forming, Changing, and Acting on Attitude Toward Affirmative Action Programs in Employment: A Theory-Driven Approach," *Journal of Applied Psychology* 85 (2000). See Chapter 3 for a more in-depth discussion of student opinions.

54. L. R. Truax et al., "Undermined? Affirmative Action from the Targets' Point of View," in *Prejudice: The Target's Perspective,* ed. J. K. Swim and C. Stagnor (New York: Academic, 1997).

55. L. Van Boven, "Pluralistic Ignorance and Political Correctness: The Case of Affirmative Action," *Political Psychology* 21 (2000). Van Boven also found pluralistic ignorance among the participants. Students, especially if they were opposed to affirmative action, generally thought that most other students supported affirmative action.

56. Marc Hetherington and Suzanne Globetti make the argument that affirmative action and related policies (e.g., school integration, aid to Blacks) present special cases because, in essence, such policies ask Whites to make sacrifices in the present in the belief that society in the future will benefit. Analyzing panel data from the National Election Studies, Hetherington and Globetti find that trust in the government at time 1 (e.g., 1990) tends to predict support for affirmative action and related policies at time 2 (e.g., 1992). It seems to me that many government policies, from taxation to smoking bans to seat belt laws, have the same underlying dynamic of asking people to give up a present privilege or to incur a present cost in the hope of future benefit to society. See M. J. Hetherington and S. Globetti, "Political Trust and Racial Policy Preferences," *American Journal of Political Science* 46 (2002).

57. See C. Winkelman and F. J. Crosby, "Affirmative Action: Setting the Record Straight," *Social Justice Research* 7 (1994).

58. See S. T. Fiske and S. E. Taylor, *Social Cognition,* 2d ed. (New York: McGraw-Hill, 1991).

59. See T. Cox, Jr., and S. Blake, "Managing Cultural Diversity: Implications for Organizational Competitiveness," *Executive* 5, no. 3 (1991); C. C. Hoffman, "Reopening the Affirmative Action Debate," *Personnel Administrator* (1986); and L. R. Davis, "Racial Diversity in Higher Education," *Journal of Applied Behavioral Science* 38 (2002). Also important is the external pressure brought to bear by various pressure groups, as Vivian Price makes clear in her case study of women's employment in highway construction in Boston, Los Angeles, and Oakland ("Race, Affirmative Action, and Women's Employment in US Highway Construction," *Feminist Economics* 8 [2002]).

60. R. L. Warner and B. S. Steele, "Affirmative Action in Times of Fiscal Stress and Changing Value Priorities: The Case of Women in Policing," *Public Personnel Management* 18 (1989). For a fascinating in-depth study contrasting how two Southern communities implemented affirmative action between 1975 and 1986, see J. Augustus Jones, *Affirmative Talk, Affirmative Action: A Comparative Study of the Politics of Affirmative Action* (New York: Praeger, 1991).

61. K. C. Naff, "Progress Toward Achieving a Representative Federal Bureaucracy: The Impact of Supervisors and Their Beliefs," *Public Personnel Management* 27 (1998).

62. J. W. Button and B. A. Rienzo, "The Impact of Affirmative Action: Black Employment in Six Southern Cities," *Social Science Quarterly* 84 (2003).

63. M. E. Banks II, "The Significance of Race in Urban Elite Political Behavior: A Case Study of the Atlanta Airport Affirmative Action Controversy, 1973–1980," *Western Journal of Black Studies* 25 (2001).

64. J. Fleming, G. R. Gill, and D. H. Swinton, *The Case for Affirmative Action for Blacks in Higher Education* (Washington, D.C.: Institute for the Study of Educational Policy, Howard University, published for ISEP by Howard University Press, 1978), 91.

65. For a discussion on the misapplications of affirmative action, see R. L. Woodson, Sr., "Personal Responsibility," in *The Affirmative Action Debate,* ed. G. E. Curry (Cambridge: Perseus, 1996).

66. The quotation appears in the majority decision of the *Grutter v. Bollinger* case and is itself a quotation from the famous *Brown v. Board of Education* decision (347 U.S. 483, 493 [1954]).

Chapter 2: Reverse Discrimination?

1. See J. Greenberg, "Approaching Equity and Avoiding Inequality in Groups and Organizations," in *Equity and Justice in Social Behavior,* ed. J. Greenberg and R. L. Cohen (New York: Academic, 1982); T. R. Tyler, *Social Justice in a Diverse Society* (Boulder, Colo.: Westview, 1997).

2. Kinley Larntz, a statistics professor at the University of Minnesota, estimated the odds of being accepted at the Law School of the University of Michigan between 1995 and 2000 using records from the school. The figure is reported in S. Dalmia, "The Diversity Defense: The University of Michigan's Excuse for Racial Discrimination," *Weekly Standard,* Mar. 26, 2001.

3. See K. R. Thomas and S. G. Weinrach, "Multiculturalism, Cultural Diversity and Affirmative Action Goals: A Reconsideration," *Rehabilitation Education* 12 (1998); P. H. Schuck, "Affirmative Action: Don't Mend It or End It—Bend It," *Brookings Review* 20 (2002).

4. William Bowen and Derek Bok, for example, have undertaken a massive study of race-sensitive admissions policies. In the resulting book and related publications and speeches, these two prominent educators discuss diversity but not fairness. Similarly, Gary Orfield emphasizes diversity in education but has little to say about issues of merit. See W. G. Bowen and D. C. Bok, *The Shape of the River: The Long-Term Consequences of Considering Race in College and University Admissions* (Princeton, N.J.: Princeton University Press, 1998). See also G. Orfield and E. Miller, eds., *Chilling Admissions: The Affirmative Action Crisis and the Search for Alternatives* (Cambridge: Harvard University Civil Rights Project, 1998).

5. See S. D. Clayton and S. S. Tangri, "The Justice of Affirmative Action," in *Affirmative Action in Perspective,* ed. F. A. Blanchard and F. J. Crosby (New York: Springer-Verlag, 1989).

6. J. Rawls, *A Theory of Justice,* rev. ed. (Cambridge: Belknap, 1999). See also J. Rawls and E. Kelly, *Justice as Fairness: A Restatement* (Cambridge: Harvard University Press, 2001).

7. The biggest criticism is against the concept of the "veil of ignorance." Each of us joins a preexisting society, in which everyone is already situated at birth. Thus, no one can hope to have the "original position."

8. See M. Lerner, *The Belief in a Just World: A Fundamental Delusion* (New York: Plenum, 1980); C. Dalbert, *The Justice Motive as a Personal Resource: Dealing with Challenges and Critical Life Events* (New York: Kluwer Academic/Plenum, 2001); C. L. Hafer, "Why We Reject Innocent Victims," in *The Justice Motive in Everyday Life,* ed. M. Ross and D. T. Miller (New York: Cambridge University Press, 2002); C. L. Hafer and J. M. Olson, "Individual Differences in the Belief in a Just World and Responses to Personal Misfortune," in *Responses to Victimizations and Belief in a Just World: Critical Issues in Social Justice,* ed. L. Montada and M. J. Lerner (New York: Plenum, 1998); C. L. Hafer and J. M. Olson, "Beliefs in a Just World, Discontent, and Assertive Actions by Working Women," *Personality and Social Psychology Bulletin* 1 (1993); and C. L. Hafer and J. M. Olson, "Beliefs in a Just World and Reactions to Personal Deprivation," *Journal of Personality and Social Psychology* 57 (1989).

9. See E. H. Walster and G. W. Walster, "Equity and Social Justice," *Journal of Social Issues* 31, no. 3 (1975); W. Austin and E. H. Walster, "Participants' Reactions to 'Equity with the World,'" *Journal of Experimental Social Psychology* 10 (1974); and E. H. Walster, E. Berschied, and G. W. Walster, "New Directions in Equity Research," *Journal of Personality and Social Psychology* 25 (1973). See also J. S. Adams, "Inequity in Social Exchange," in *Advances in Experimental Social Psychology,* vol. 2, ed. L. Berkowitz (New York: Academic, 1965).

10. The equity formula is usually applied—with or without conscious awareness—in impersonal or business situations. In other situations, such as family life where some members of the group are responsible for others, equity may not be the determining factor of feelings of fairness. Instead, other norms, such as the norm of fulfilling needs, can determine judgments of fairness. A business associate does not expect to be given new shoes simply because he needs them, but it seems fair to give a child the new shoes she needs. It does not matter that the child makes no contribution to the family's income (in-

puts). Among friends, equality operates as the justice norm. Friends may, for example, share a meal and divide the bill more or less equally, without making minute calculations. For more detail, see M. Deutsch, "Equity, Equality, and Need: What Determines Which Value Will Be Used as the Basis of Distributive Justice?" *Journal of Social Issues* 31, no. 3 (1975); and D. Prentice and F. J. Crosby, "The Importance of Context for Assessing Deservingness," in *Social Comparison, Social Justice, and Relative Deprivation,* ed. J. C. Masters and W. P. Smith (Hillsdale, N.J.: Erlbaum, 1987).

11. There is a large empirical literature, guided by a model of procedural justice. See E. A. Lind and T. R. Tyler, *The Social Psychology of Procedural Justice: Critical Issues in Social Justice* (New York: Plenum, 1988); T. Tyler and E. A. Lind, "A Relational Model of Authority in Groups," in *Advances in Experimental Social Psychology,* vol. 25, ed. M. P. Zanna (1992); and T. Tyler, P. Degoey, and H. Smith, "Understanding Why the Justice of Group Procedures Matters: A Test of the Psychological Dynamics of the Group-Value Model," *Journal of Personality and Social Psychology* 70 (1996).

12. See F. J. Crosby and J. Franco, "Anger as a Function of Rule Change" (paper presented at the 25th annual meeting of the International Society of Political Psychology, July 2002).

13. See, for instance, R. Folger, "Distributive and Procedural Justice: Combined Impact of Voice and Improvement on Experienced Inequity," *Journal of Personality and Social Psychology* 35 (1977); and E. A. Lind, R. Kanfer, and P. C. Earley, "Voice, Control, and Procedural Justice: Instrumental and Noninstrumental Concerns in Fairness Judgments," *Journal of Personality and Social Psychology* 59 (1990).

14. W. Connerly, "U.C. Must End Affirmative Action," *San Francisco Chronicle,* May 3, 1995. Reprinted in F. J. Crosby and C. VanDeVeer, *Sex, Race, and Merit: Debating Affirmative Action in Education and Employment* (Ann Arbor: University of Michigan Press, 2000), 30.

15. Connerly, quoted in J. Klein, "The End of Affirmative Action," *Newsweek,* Feb. 13, 1995. Also see K. Jose, "Rethinking Affirmative Action," *Congressional Quarterly,* Apr. 28, 1995.

16. The CIR Web site is www.cir-usa.org.

17. R. Perloff and F. B. Bryant, "Identifying and Measuring Diversity's Payoffs: Light at the End of the Affirmative Action Tunnel," *Psychology, Public Policy, and Law* 6 (2000), 102.

18. L. Marinoff, "Equal Opportunity Versus Equity," *Sexuality and Culture* 4 (2000), 24.

19. S. Steele, *The Content of Our Character: A New Vision of Race in America* (New York: St. Martin's, 1990), 119.

20. Ibid.

21. P. C. Roberts and L. M. Stratton, *The New Color Line: How Quotas and Privilege Destroy Democracy* (Washington, D.C.: Regnery, 1995).

22. C. T. Canady, "The Meaning of American Equality," in *The Affirmative Action Debate,* ed. G. E. Curry (Cambridge: Perseus, 1998), 280.

23. E. Blum and M. Levin, "Racial Profiling: Wrong for Police, Wrong for Universities," *Washington Times,* May 17, 1999. Reprinted in Crosby and VanDeVeer, *Sex, Race, and Merit,* 67–69.

24. See M. A. Fletcher, "For Asian Americans, a Barrier or a Boon," *Washington Post,* June 20, 1998.

25. S. A. Holmes, "Defining Disadvantages Up to Preserve Preferences," *Los Angeles Times,* Aug. 24, 1997. Reprinted in Crosby and VanDeVeer, *Sex, Race, and Merit,* 31–33, quotation on 31.

26. S. Steele, "The New Sovereignty," *Harper's,* July 1992.

27. L. S. Gottfredson, "The Science and Politics of Race-Norming," *American Psychologist* 29 (1994), and L. S. Gottfredson, "Racially Gerrymandering the Content of Police Tests to Satisfy the U.S. Justice Department: A Case Study," *Psychology, Public Policy, and Law* 2 (1996).

28. F. R. Lynch and W. R. Beer, "You Ain't the Right Color, Pal: White Resentment of Affirmative Action," *Policy Review* 51 (1990): 67. For a fuller treatment, see W. R. Beer, "Affirmative Action: Social Policy as Shibboleth," in *Psychology and Social Policy,* ed. P. Suedfeld and P. E. Tetlock (New York: Hemisphere, 1992).

29. M. P. Bell, D. A. Harrison, and M. E. McLaughlin, "Forming, Changing, and Acting on Attitude Toward Affirmative Action Programs in Employment: A Theory-Driven Approach," *Journal of Applied Psychology* 85 (2000).

30. J. R. Kluegel and E. R. Smith, "Whites' Beliefs About Blacks' Opportunity," *American Sociological Review* 47 (1982).

31. S. D. Verhovek, "In Poll, Americans Reject Means but Not Ends of Racial Diversity," *New York Times,* Dec. 14, 1997.

32. Quoted in J. Fraser and E. Kick, "The Interpretive Repertoires of Whites on Race-Targeted Policies: Claims of Reverse Discrimination," *Sociological Perspectives* 43 (2000), 23.

33. Quoted in M. Chesler and M. Peet, "White Student Views of Affirmative Action on Campus," *Diversity Factor* 10, no. 2 (2002): 23.

34. W. R. Lynch and W. R. Beer, "You Ain't the Right Color, Pal," 64.

35. C. Steeh and M. Krysan, "Poll Trends: Affirmative Action and the Public, 1970–1995," *Public Opinion Quarterly* 60 (1996).

36. L. Bobo and S. A. Suh, *Surveying Racial Discrimination: Analyses from a Multi-Ethnic Labor Market.* Working Paper No. 75 (New York: Russell Sage Foundation, 1996).

37. For a brilliant treatment of the topic see chapter 5 in B. Reskin, *The Realities of Affirmative Action in Employment* (Washington, D.C.: American Sociological Association, 1998), from which I draw heavily here.

38. Ibid., 73.

39. P. Burstein, "'Reverse Discrimination' Cases in the Federal Courts: Mobilization by a Countermovement," *Sociological Quarterly* 32 (1991).

40. A. W. Blumrosen, "Declaration Statement Submitted to the Supreme Court of California in Response to Proposition 209," cited in Reskin, *Realities of Affirmative Action,* 98.

41. U.S. Department of Labor, Employment Standards Administration, *The Rhetoric and Reality About Affirmative Action at the OFCCP* (Washington, D.C., n.d.), cited in Reskin, *Realities of Affirmative Action,* 73.

42. G. Stephanopoulos and C. Edley, Jr., *Affirmative Action Review: Report to the President* (Washington, D.C.: Government Printing Office, 1995), sect. 6.3.

43. For some interesting philosophical treatments of these issues, see part 2 of F. J. Beckwith and T. E. Jones's anthology *Affirmative Action: Social Justice or Reverse Discrimination?* (Amherst, N.Y.: Prometheus, 1997).

44. See C. Ridgeway, "The Social Construction of Status Value: Gender and Other Nominal Characteristics," *Social Forces* 70 (1991).

45. See F. D. Blau and J. W. Graham, "Black-White Differences in Wealth and Asset Composition," *Quarterly Journal of Economics* 105 (1990).

46. Students of color are well aware of the economic returns on education and see it as the way to achieve the American dream. See F. Miller and M. A. Clark, "Looking Toward the Future: Young People's Attitudes About Affirmative Action and the American Dream," *American Behavioral Scientist* 41 (1997).

47. F. J. Crosby, "Confessions of an Affirmative Action Mama," in *Off White: Readings on Race, Power, and Society,* ed. L. Weis et al. (New York: Routledge, 1997).

48. I am not certain we could have bought a house in the area known as Plandome because my mother is Jewish. Many Jews lived in our section, but I never knew of any living in Plandome in the 1950s.

49. D. M. Stewart, "Meanings of Merit: Higher Education as a Lens on Public Culture," *American Behavioral Scientist* 42 (1999), 1057. The study of high school experiences was conducted by S. M. Dornbusch, and published in Dornbusch, *Off the Track* (Ann Arbor: Society for Research on Adolescence, 1994).

50. J. C. Edwards, F. G. J. Maldonado, and J. A. Calvin, "The Effects of Differently Weighting Interview Scores on the Admission of Underrepresented Minority Medical Students," *Academic Medicine* 74 (1999).

51. See also A. Tekian, "Minority Students, Affirmative Action, and the Admission Process: A Literature Review, 1987–1998," *Teaching and Learning in Medicine* 12 (2000); and H. T. Everson, "A Principled Design Framework for College Admissions Tests: An Affirming Research Agenda," *Psychology, Public Policy, and Law* 6 (2000).

52. See L. F. Wightman, "An Examination of Sex Differences in LSAT Scores from the Perspective of Social Consequence," *Applied Measurement in Education* 11 (1998). Women generally outperform men 0.5 standard deviation on UGPA while men generally outperform women 0.1 standard deviation on the LSAT. See also K. Hattrup, J. Rock, and C. Scalia, "The Effects of Varying Conceptualizations of Job Performance on Adverse Impact, Minority Hiring, and Predicted Performance," *Journal of Applied Psychology* 82 (1997).

53. F. J. Crosby, "A Rose by any Other Name," in *Quoten und Gleichstellung von Frau und Mann,* ed. K. Arioli (Basel: Helberg and Lichtenhan, 1996).

54. See L. Reisberg, "A Top University Wonders Why It Has No Black Freshman," *Chronicle of Higher Education,* Apr. 28, 2000; and J. Selingo, "Why Minority Recruiting Is Alive and Well in Texas," *Chronicle of Higher Education,* Nov. 19, 1999.

55. After the University of Maryland was forced to abandon its special scholarships for African American students after the decision in the *Podberesky* case, other state universities also dropped race-conscious scholarships and fellowships. See Podberesky v. Kirwin, 38 F.3d 147 (4th Cir. 1994).

56. See A. Murrell, F. J. Crosby, and R. Ely, eds., *Mentoring Dilemmas: Developmental Relationships Within the Multicultural Organization* (Mahwah, N.J.: Erlbaum, 1999); and D. Clutterbuck and D. B. R. Ragins, *Mentoring and Diversity: An International Perspective* (Boston: Butterworth and Heinemann, 2002).

57. See N. W. Jabbra, "Affirmative Action and the Stigma of Gender and Ethnicity: California in the 1990s," *Journal of Asian and African Studies* 36 (2001).

58. Griggs v. Duke Power Co., 401 U.S. 424 (1971). See also J. D. Newman, "Affirmative Action and the Courts," in Blanchard and Crosby, *Affirmative Action in Perspective;* and R. M. Hendrickson, "Rethinking Affirmative Action: Redefining Compelling State Interest and Merit in Admission," *Peabody Journal of Education* 76 (2001).

59. See W. E. Norris and M. Reardon, "Employment Screening, Qualifications, and Gender Discrimination: A Case Study of the New York City Firefighters," in Blanchard and Crosby, *Affirmative Action in Perspective.*

60. For more information, refer to the Educational Testing Service Web site at www.ets.org.

61. See J. A. Hartigan and A. K. Wigdor, *Fairness in Employment Testing: Validity, Generalization, Minority Issues, and the General Aptitude Test Battery* (Washington, D.C.: National Academy Press, 1989).

62. C. Jencks and M. Phillips, ed., *The Black-White Test Score Gap* (Washington D.C.: Brookings Institution Press, 1998).

63. *Psychology, Public Policy, and Law* 6 (2000).

64. See, for example, P. R. Sackett and S. L. Wilk, "Within-Group Norming and Other Forms of Score Adjustment in Pre-Employment Testing," *American Psychologist* 49 (1994); and P. R. Sackett et al., "High-Stakes Testing in Employment, Credentialing, and Higher Education," *American Psychologist* 56 (2001).

65. For a similar argument, see R. Dworkin, "The Court and the University," *New York Review of Books,* May 15, 2003.

66. For an extremely provocative debate among scholars about the issues of affirmative action and meritocracy, see L. Guinier and S. Sturm, *Who's Qualified?* (Boston: Beacon, 2001).

67. R. J. Herrnstein and C. A. Murray, *The Bell Curve: Intelligence and Class Structure in American Life* (New York: Free Press, 1994). There have been numerous debates concerning the details of *The Bell Curve,* specifically information provided in chapter 13, which discusses the heritability of intelligence. Herrnstein and Murray concluded that the reason that Blacks score lower than Whites on I.Q. tests is that Blacks are genetically inferior to Whites in terms of the traits that I.Q. tests measure. At the core of their conclusion is the assertion that most people inherit their intelligence from their parents. Offspring of intelligent people tend to be intelligent. Offspring of unintelligent people tend to be unintelligent. The assertion about inheritance of intelligence is, in turn, based on the observed correlation between parents' scores and children's scores. Thus, if you invited a group of a hundred mothers to your laboratory and told each to bring one child, and if you then lined up the mothers so that the most intelligent stood on the left and the least intelligent stood on the right, you could predict with imperfect accuracy where their children would stand if you lined them up as you had lined up the mothers. The child of the woman on the far left end might not be in the left-most spot, but she or he would be close to it. In Herrnstein and Murray's theoretical lineups most of the Black mothers and their offspring would stand near the right.

By changing the analogy slightly, it is possible to see the flaw in Herrnstein and Murray's logic. Imagine that you are dealing with plants, not people. Plant height is inherited: tall plants produce tall plants; short plants produce short plants. You can line up the parent plants from tallest on the left to shortest on the right, and their seedlings will line up in exactly the same order. Now pretend that you have two seedlings each from five plants (A through E), arranged from left to right in terms of the height of the parent plants. You place one seedling from each of the five sets in Hatch A and one in Hatch B. Hatch A has enriched potting soil in it and is well watered. Hatch B has rocks and is poorly watered. The seedlings in Hatch A produce plants that are arranged in height exactly according to the parent plants, with A the tallest and E the shortest. So do the seedlings in Hatch B. But the plants in Hatch A are all 4 inches taller than the plants in Hatch B.

Conclusion? Variations within a group are not sufficient evidence of innate differences between groups.

If the picture is still not clear, change plants to Dutch and Japanese people. Even though it is true that the height of all people, including Dutch people and Japanese people, is largely determined by the height of their parents, we cannot conclude that the Dutch are genetically programmed to be taller than the Japanese. In recent years, a change in the Japanese diet has meant a gain in their height.

The issues raised in *The Bell Curve* have provoked debates among academics and policymakers focused on dissenting opinions about whether the I.Q. gap between Whites and Blacks is genetic or environmental in nature. Aside from the measured gap itself, there is little evidence of an inherited difference. Because part of the measured gap has already been shown to be the result of environmental differences, it is plausible to assume that the rest of the gap is also the result of environment. For more , see S. Fraser, *The Bell Curve Wars: Race, Intelligence, and the Future of America* (New York: Basic, 1995); and B. Leone et al., *Genetics and Intelligence: Current Controversies* (San Diego: Greenhaven, 1996).

68. One of the best treatments of the question is the book edited by Christopher Jencks and Meredith Phillips, *The Black-White Test Score Gap*. Another informative source is R. Valencia and L. A. Suzuki, *Intelligence Testing and Minority Students: Foundations, Performance Factors, and Assessment Issues* (Thousand Oaks, Calif.: Sage, 2000).

69. A. R. Jensen, *Bias in Mental Testing* (New York: Free Press, 1980).

70. Valencia and Suzuki, *Intelligence Testing and Minority Students.*

71. See Sackett and Wilk, "Within-Group Norming."

72. R. J. Sternberg, "Implicit Theories of Intelligence as Exemplar Stories of Success: Why Intelligence Test Validity Is in the Eye of the Beholder," *Psychology, Public Policy, and Law* 6 (2000).

73. See C. Jencks, "Racial Bias in Testing," in Jencks and Phillips, *Black-White Test Score Gap*. For a different perspective, see Valencia and Suzuki, *Intelligence Testing and Minority Students.*

74. F. E. Vars and W. G. Bowen, "Scholastic Aptitude Test Scores, Race, and Academic Performance in Selective Colleges and Universities," in Jencks and Phillips, *Black-White Test Score Gap.*

75. M. N. Cohen, *The Culture of Intolerance: Chauvinism, Class, and Racism in the United States* (New Haven: Yale University Press, 1998), 216.

76. Valencia and Suzuki, *Intelligence Testing and Minority Students,* 143.

77. Jencks refers to the results of the study by the National Academy of Science: "Racial Bias in Testing," 78.

78. See Williams, "Perspectives on Intelligence Testing.

79. Jencks, "Racial Bias in Testing," 77.

80. Note that we are following here exactly the logic of the Supreme Court in the 1971 case *Griggs v. Duke Power Company,* cited earlier.

81. Jencks and Phillips, *Black-White Test Score Gap,* 14–15.

82. Indeed, a meta-analysis of studies that looked at scores on the GATB and objective measures of job performance found one standard deviation difference (with Blacks scoring worse than Whites) on the GATB but only one-third of a standard deviation dif-

ference in terms of work performance. See G. A. Chung-Yan and S. F. Cronshaw, "A Critical Re-examination and Analysis of Cognitive Ability Tests Using the Thorndike Model of Fairness," *Journal of Occupational and Organizational Psychology* 75 (2002).

83. J. Amirkhan et al., "Reflections on Affirmative Action Goals in Psychology Admissions," *Psychological Science* 6 (1995), 140.

84. M. Bendick, Jr., and M. L. Egan, "Adding Testing to the Nation's Portfolio of Information on Employment Discrimination," in *A National Report Card on Discrimination in America: The Role of Testing,* ed. M. Fix and M. A. Turner (Washington, D.C.: Urban Institute, 1999).

85. D. Bell, "Love's Labor Lost? Why Racial Fairness Is a Threat to Many White Americans," in Guinier and Storm, *Who's Qualified?* 42. Bell has a good point. A study of freshmen at the University of California showed that, system-wide, the SAT scores lost their ability to predict freshmen year grades if one took into account the socioeconomic status of the student. See J. Fernald, "Preliminary Findings on the Relationship Between SAT Scores, High School GPA, Socioeconomic Status, and UCSC Freshman GPA," retrieved Nov. 15, 2002, from www.senate.ucsc.edu/cafa/SATGP.htm. One hopes that such studies will be fed to the media to correct, for example, the opinion that appeared in the British publication *The Economist* on February 24, 2001. The writer questioned whether the University of California's president Atkinson might be getting rid of the SATs not because they are uninformative but because they are too informative, consistently giving lower marks to Blacks and Hispanics than to Asians and Whites ("Disabling the National Educational Defence System," 36).

86. The data are not clear. On the one hand a team in Montreal sent a questionnaire to all employees of a large printing and publishing company in Canada that used Canada's version of affirmative action. Analysis of the 1,440 questionnaires showed that the same people who envisioned affirmative action as an assault on justice also had the most sexist and racist attitudes. Justice concerns seemed to be little more than an acceptable justification for a resistance to integrate the workforce. See J. D. Leck, M. D. Saunders, and M. Charbonneau, "Affirmative Action Programs: An Organizational Justice Perspective," *Journal of Organizational Behavior* 17 (1996). On the other hand, another study, also conducted in Canada, showed a somewhat different pattern. Resistance to some forms of affirmative action signaled racism, but resistance to other forms reflected a genuine concern with justice issues. See D. R. Bobocel and M. Debeyer, "Explaining Controversial Organizational Decisions: To Legitimize the Means or the Ends?" *Social Justice Research* 11 (1998). See also D. R. Bobocel and A. C. Farrell, "Sex-Based Promotion Decisions and Interactional Fairness: Investigating the Influence of Managerial Accounts," *Journal of Applied Psychology* 81 (1996). I shall return to the issue in Chapter 7.

Chapter 3: Semantics Versus Substance

1. See G. Stephanopoulos and C. Edley, Jr., *Affirmative Action Review: Report to the President* (Washington, D.C.: Government Printing Office, 1995).

2. The figure of 27 percent comes from exit polls and is cited on page 46 of J. Karabel, "No Alternative: The Effects of Color-Blind Admissions in California," in *Chilling Admissions: The Affirmative Action Crisis and the Search for Alternatives,* ed. G. Orfield and E. Miller (Cambridge: Harvard University Civil Rights Project, 1998).

3. See "Proposition 209" in F. J. Crosby and C. VanDeVeer, *Sex, Race, and Merit: Debating Affirmative Action in Education and Employment* (Ann Arbor: University of Michigan Press, 2000). Note that section (e) reads, "Nothing in this section shall be interpreted as prohibiting action which must be taken to establish or maintain eligibility for any federal program, where ineligibility would result in a loss of federal funds to the state" (230–31). In other words, nothing in Proposition 209 should interfere with the operation of classical affirmative action as established by Executive Order 11246.

4. For excellent, comprehensive analyses of the Michigan cases, consult the articles by Peter Schmidt in the *Chronicle of Higher Education*, especially P. Schmidt and J. Selino, "A Supreme Court Showdown," *Chronicle of Higher Education*, Dec. 13, 2002.

5. S. Steele, *The Content of Our Character: A New Vision of Race in America* (New York: St. Martin's, 1990); S. L. Carter, *Reflections of an Affirmative Action Baby* (New York: Basic, 1991); S. Thernstrom and A. M. Thernstrom, *America in Black and White: One Nation, Indivisible* (New York: Simon and Schuster, 1997).

6. P. Williams, *The Alchemy of Race and Rights* (Cambridge: Harvard University Press, 1991); B. R. Bergmann, *In Defense of Affirmative Action* (New York: Basic, 1996); B. F. Reskin, *The Realities of Affirmative Action in Employment* (Washington, D.C.: American Sociological Association, 1998); C. F. Edley, *Not All Black and White: Affirmative Action, Race, and American Values* (New York: Hill and Wang, 1996); W. G. Bowen and D. C. Bok, *The Shape of the River: Long-Term Consequences of Considering Race in College and University Admissions* (Princeton: Princeton University Press, 1998). Bowen and Bok avoid the term "affirmative action," using instead the phrase "race-sensitive policies." J. D. Skrentny, *The Ironies of Affirmative Action: Politics, Culture, and Justice in America* (Chicago: University of Chicago Press, 1996).

7. F. L. Pincus, "Test of Affirmative Action Knowledge," *Current World Leaders: International Issues* 39, no. 2 (1996). Pincus is an authority on affirmative action. See F. L. Pincus, "The Social Construction of Reverse Discrimination: The Impact of Affirmative Action on Whites," *Journal of Intergroup Relations* 38, no. 4 (Winter 2001–2), and F. L. Pincus, "Reverse Discrimination vs. White Privilege: An Empirical Study of Alleged Victims of Affirmative Action," *Race and Society* 3 (2000). The table is reprinted with permission from Fred Pincus. For full explanations of the correct answers to Pincus's table, see his "Test of Affirmative Action Knowledge."

8. A. Noble and R. A. Winett, "Chairpersons' and Hirees' Opinions, Knowledge, and Experiences with Affirmative Action Guidelines," *Journal of Community Psychology* 6 (1978).

9. P. Huckle, "A Decade's Difference: Mid-Level Managers and Affirmative Action," *Public Personnel Management Journal* 12 (1983), 251.

10. Ibid.

11. N. Goldsmith et al., "Reactions to Affirmative Action: A Case Study," in *Affirmative Action in Perspective*, ed. F. A. Blanchard and F. J. Crosby (New York: Springer-Verlag, 1989).

12. A second rater graded a subset of the answers for reliability. The ratings were reliable.

13. $r = .49$

14. D. A. Kravitz and J. Platania, "Attitudes and Beliefs About Affirmative Action: Effects of Target and of Respondent Sex and Ethnicity," *Journal of Applied Psychology* 78 (1993).

15. H. Golden, S. Hinkle, and F. J. Crosby, "Reactions to Affirmative Action: Substance and Semantics," *Journal of Applied Social Psychology* 31 (2001).

16. C. Steeh and M. Krysan, "Poll Trends: Affirmative Action and the Public, 1970–1995," *Public Opinion Quarterly* 60 (1996).

17. See Study 1 in D. A. Kravitz et al., "Attitudes Toward Affirmative Action: Correlations with Demographic Variables and with Beliefs About Targets, Actions, and Economic Effects," *Journal of Applied Social Psychology* 30 (2000).

18. K. R. Jacob Arriola and E. R. Cole, "Framing the Affirmative Action Debate: Attitudes Toward Out-Group Members and White Identity," *Journal of Applied Social Psychology* 31 (2001).

19. The dislike of quotas and preferences is shared by Canadians, as three studies have shown: the first with undergraduate business majors and MBA students in Halifax (R. J. Summers, "Attitudes Toward Different Methods of Affirmative Action," *Journal of Applied Social Psychology* 25 [1995]); the second with 185 Canadian undergraduates (G. J. Nosworthy, J. A. Lea, and C. L. Lindsay, "Opposition to Affirmative Action: Racial Affect and Traditional Value Predictors Across Four Programs," *Journal of Applied Social Psychology* 25 [1995]); and the third with undergraduate women (K. Matheson et al., "Women's Attitudes Toward Affirmative Action: Putting Action in Context," *Journal of Applied Social Psychology* 24 [1994]).

20. Kravitz and Platania also divided the group into three parts or conditions: a third of the participants learned about programs for women, a third for minorities, and a third for people with disabilities. They found that the same components were liked or disliked in all three conditions. Other researchers have confirmed that students much prefer "soft" affirmative action plans over preferential treatment. See, for example, K. A. Quinn, E. A. Ross, and V. M. Esses, "Attributions of Responsibility and Reactions to Affirmative Action: Affirmative Action as Help," *Personality and Social Psychology Bulletin* 27 (2001). One especially rare sample, alas with a low response rate, came from the student membership of the National Society of Black Engineers, as reported in J. E. Slaughter, E. F. Sinar, and P. D. Bachiochi, "Black Applicants' Reactions to Affirmative Action Plans: Effects of Plan Content and Previous Experience with Discrimination," *Journal of Applied Psychology* 87 (2002).

21. In the social sciences, an experiment is seen as superior to a survey for drawing causal inferences. An experiment involves manipulation and measurement with subjects randomly assigned to the experimental and control conditions. A survey can be in the form of an interview or a questionnaire, and it involves asking people their opinions. The experiment was reported in D. A. Kravitz, "Attitudes Toward Affirmative Action Plans Directed at Blacks: Effects of Plan and Individual Differences," *Journal of Applied Social Psychology* 25 (1995).

22. Ibid., 2204.

23. M. P. Bell, D. A. Harrison, and M. E. McLaughlin, "Forming, Changing, and Acting on Attitude Toward Affirmative Action Programs in Employment: A Theory-Driven Approach," *Journal of Applied Psychology* 85 (2000), 792.

24. "Gallup Short Subjects," *Gallup Poll Monthly* 358 (July 1995): 34–61.

25. Ibid. The percentages of Whites to endorse the various options were: option 1—80 %; option 2—73 %; option 3—71 %; option 4—47 %; option 5—44 %; option 6—35 %; option 7—30 %; option 8—27 %; option 9—11 %. For Blacks in the sample, the endorsement figures were: option 1—94 %; option 2—90 %; option 3—81 %; option 4—51 %; option 5—73 %; option 6—70 %; option 7—66 %; option 8—51 %; option 9—22 %.

26. L. Harris, "Unequal Terms," *Columbia Journalism Review* 30, no. 5 (1992).

27. P. M. Sniderman and E. G. Carmines, *Reaching Beyond Race* (Cambridge: Harvard University Press, 1997), chap. 2. Sniderman tends to equate affirmative action with preferences and quotas and ignores the monitoring function of the policy. But his voice has been an important one in the debates, and he has spearheaded many of the major efforts at data collection.

28. D. R. Kinder and L. M. Sanders, *Divided by Color: Racial Politics and Democratic Ideals, American Politics and Political Economy* (Chicago: University of Chicago Press, 1996). Also see D. R. Kinder, and L. M. Sanders, "Mimicking Political Debate with Survey Questions: The Case of White Opinion on Affirmative Action for Blacks," *Social Cognition* 8 (1990); and T. S. Fine, "Public Opinion Toward Equal Opportunity Issues: The Role of Attitudinal and Demographic Forces Among African Americans," *Sociological Perspectives* 35 (1992).

29. Kinder and Sanders, *Divided by Color,* 18.

30. Ibid., 25.

31. Ibid., 26.

32. College students may be even less representative of Juan and Juanita America than of Joe and Josephine. White Americans are still more likely to have a college education than Americans of color.

33. In the Chicago sample studied by Golden, Hinkle, and Crosby, more women than men and more Blacks than Whites thought affirmative action was a monitoring system. Another study, conducted among college students at Smith College and Yale University, found the same split along ethnic lines. Truax and colleagues report that 40 percent of White students, but only 16 percent of underrepresented students, think that affirmative action involves quotas (L. R. Truax et al., "Undermined? Affirmative Action from the Targets' Point of View," in *Prejudice: The Target's Perspective,* ed. J. K. Swim and C. Stagnor [New York: Academic, 1997]).

34. Kravitz et al., "Attitudes Toward Affirmative Action." The investigators also found that the more politically liberal the participants, the less likely they were to see affirmative action as including set-asides. Racial minorities were less likely than Whites to see affirmative action as including preferential hiring and set-asides.

35. Jacob Arriola and Cole, "Framing the Affirmative Action Debate."

36. M. Rose, "An Interview with the Intervenors," *AAAA News* (Winter 2002), 8.

37. F. J. Crosby and D. I. Cordova, "Words Worth of Wisdom: Toward an Understanding of Affirmative Action," *Journal of Social Issues* 52, no. 2 (1996). Of course, there are differences among newspapers. Robin Stryker and colleagues conducted a close content analysis of editorials, news articles, and letters to the editors that appeared in the *Wall Street Journal* and the *New York Times* during the debates over the Civil Rights Acts of 1990–91. The *Wall Street Journal* characterized the civil rights legislation as relying on quotas, while the *New York Times* argued the opposite. The *Journal* also linked affirmative action and quotas. See R. Stryker, M. Scarpellino, and M. Holtzman, "Political Culture Wars 1990s Style: The Drum Beat of Quotas in Media Framing of the Civil Rights Act of 1991," *Research in Social Stratification and Mobility* 17 (1999).

38. Stephanopoulos and Edley, *Affirmative Action Review.*

39. Media critic Todd Gitlin believes that the media's fascination with the idea of "political correctness" has little to do with selling papers, especially when "the world is brimming with potential subjects of media frenzy." Journalists, says Gitlin, care about ideo-

logical battles at colleges and universities because they "have a stake in the legitimacy of the sorts of activities that go on there. To the degree that the university loses face or devalues the disinterested pursuit of knowledge, their own credentials are devalued" ("The Demonization of Political Correctness," *Dissent* 42 [1995], 493). Even more cynical than Gitlin is Jesse Jackson, who wrote: "Four o'clock every day, when editors meet with their staffs to discuss the next day's news consumption, is perhaps the most segregated hour in this nation" ("The 1996 Presidential Campaign," in *The Affirmative Action Debate,* ed. G. E. Curry [Cambridge: Perseus, 1998], 295). In 1996, 5 percent of newsroom employees were African American, 3 percent Hispanic, 2 percent Asian American, and less than one-half of 1 percent Native American. One study of African American newspaper journalists found them to be pessimistic about social change. See J. S. McCleneghan, "How African-American Journalists View America's Social Institutions into the Twenty-first Century," *Social Science Journal* 38 (2001).

40. S. L. Klineberg and D. A. Kravitz, "Ethnic Differences in Predictors of Support for Municipal Affirmative Action Contracting," *Social Science Quarterly* 84 (2003).

41. A large empirical literature exists in social psychology on what is known as the actor-observer difference. Basically, people are more generous to themselves than to others in terms of the causal explanations they construct. For the classic paper, see L. Ross, "The Intuitive Psychologist and His Shortcomings: Distortions in the Attribution Process," in *Advances in Experimental Social Psychology,* vol. 10, edited L. Berkowitz (New York: Academic, 1977). For typical empirical studies see D. A. Gioia and H. P. Sims, Jr., "Self-Serving Bias and Actor-Observer Differences in Organizations: An Empirical Analysis," *Journal of Applied Social Psychology* 15 (1985); R. E. Nisbett et al., "Behavior as Seen by the Actor and as Seen by the Observer," *Journal of Personality and Social Psychology* 27 (1973); and M. D. Storms, "Videotape and the Attribution Process: Reversing Actors' and Observers' Points of View," *Journal of Personality and Social Psychology* 27 (1973). As could be predicted from the theory, studies of people who are differently situated in organizations show that these people have different perceptions. For example, one study of the University of Colorado system found that professors of color were less satisfied with their jobs and felt more excluded from nonminority campus events than did White professors. The former also were less likely than the latter to think that majority faculty understood the positive aspects of affirmative action and were sensitive to the need for cultural diversity (A. Aguirre, Jr., R. Martinez, and A. Hernandez, "Majority and Minority Faculty Perceptions in Academe," *Research in Higher Education* 34 [1993]).

42. D. M. Truxillo and T. N. Bauer, "Applicant Reactions to Test Scores Banding in Entry-Level and Promotional Contexts," *Journal of Applied Psychology* 84 (1999).

43. K. J. Matheson et al., "Reactions to Affirmative Action: Seeking the Bases for Resistance," *Journal of Applied Social Psychology* 30 (2000).

44. K. Matheson et al., "Women's Attitudes Toward Affirmative Action," 1021.

45. Ibid. There were actually two "preferential treatment" groups, one that received the explanation given here and one that was also given a justification concerning the need for diversity. A fourth experimental condition also existed which made no reference to sex.

46. See J. D. Newman, "Affirmative Action and the Courts," in Blanchard and Crosby, *Affirmative Action in Perspective.*

47. D. A. Kravitz and S. L. Klineberg, "Reactions to Two Versions of Affirmative Action Among Whites, Blacks, and Hispanics," *Journal of Applied Psychology* 85 (2000).

People of color liked each plan better than Whites did. Blacks and Hispanics also had a different understanding of what is involved in a "typical" affirmative action plan from Whites'. Whites thought typical plans involved preferential treatment, which explains why they preferred the tie break. People of color thought that discrimination persists unless action is taken to erase it, which is why they preferred typical affirmative action programs. Blacks thought that Blacks suffered more discrimination than Hispanics, while Hispanics thought their group suffered more discrimination than Blacks. Other survey researchers also find evidence of self-interest.

Russell Summers also found concrete evidence of the importance of self-interest. Summers questioned eighty continuing-education students at the MBA and undergraduate levels at Saint Mary's University in Halifax. His survey opened with a general definition of affirmative action and an explanation of affirmative action for targeted groups, including women and Blacks. Next the participants were asked how they thought affirmative action would affect their careers. The women expected to derive some benefit from affirmative action while the men expected to be harmed by the policy. In the third part of the questionnaire, Summers asked participants to evaluate special training programs, differential scoring methods, and quotas. For each method, the men expressed less-positive opinions than the women did. When Summers used a statistical procedure to reanalyze the attitude scores while taking into account self-interest, the gender differences disappeared, showing that differences in self-interest were the driving force behind the apparent gender differences. In other words, male-female differences in levels of support for affirmative action were all about what they stood to gain or lose from it. See Summers, "Attitudes Toward Different Methods of Affirmative Action."

48. See H. Schuman et al., *Racial Attitudes in America: Trends and Interpretations,* rev. ed. (Cambridge: Harvard University Press, 1997); and J. M. Glaser, "The Preference Puzzle: Educational Differences in Racial-Political Attitudes," *Political Behavior* 23 (2001).

49. D. M. Truxillo and T. N. Bauer, "The Roles of Gender and Affirmative Action Attitudes in Reactions to Test Score Use Methods," *Journal of Applied Social Psychology* 30 (2000).

50. Ibid., 1818.

51. Ibid., 1818–19.

52. Ibid., 1819.

53. These analyses were limited to White subjects.

54. Truxillo and Bauer's 1999 study was much more comprehensive than their 2000 study.

55. Kinder and Sanders, *Divided by Color.* See also T. S. Fine, "The Impact of Issue Framing on Public Opinion: Toward Affirmative Action Programs," *Social Science Journal* 29 (1992); and D. R. Kinder and L. M. Sanders, "Mimicking Political Debate with Survey Questions: The Case of White Opinion on Affirmative Action for Blacks," *Social Cognition* 8 (1990).

56. Kinder and Sanders, "Mimicking Political Debate with Survey Questions," 78.

57. Ibid.

58. For gender differences see M. P. Bell, D. A. Harrison, and M. E. McLaughlin, "Asian American Attitudes Toward Affirmative Action in Employment: Implications for the Model Minority Myth," *Journal of Applied Behavioral Science* 33 (1997); Goldsmith et al., "Reactions to Affirmative Action; A. M. Konrad and F. Linnehan, "Race and Sex Dif-

ferences in Line Managers' Reactions to Equal Employment Opportunity and Affirmative Action Interventions," *Group and Organizational Management* 20 (1995); Kravitz et al., "Attitudes Toward Affirmative Action"; Kravitz and Platania, "Attitudes and Beliefs About Affirmative Action"; J. C. Latack et al., "Carpenter Apprentices: Comparison of Career Transitions for Men and Women," *Journal of Applied Psychology* 72 (1987); K. Ozawa, M. Crosby, and F. J. Crosby, "Individualism and Resistance to Affirmative Action: A Comparison of Japanese and American Samples," *Journal of Applied Social Psychology* 26 (1996); Summers, "Attitudes Toward Different Methods of Affirmative Action"; A. Tickamyer et al., "Affirmative Action in Higher Education Administration," in Blanchard and Crosby, *Affirmative Action in Perspective;* Truxillo and Bauer, "Roles of Gender and Affirmative Action Attitudes in Reactions to Test Score Use Methods." For ethnic or racial differences see A. Aguirre, Jr., R. Martinez, and A. Hernandez, "Majority and Minority Faculty Perceptions in Academe," *Research in Higher Education* 34 (1993); W. Arthur, D. Doverspike, and R. Fuentes, "Recipients' Affective Responses to Affirmative Action," *Behavioral Sciences and the Law* 10 (1992); Bell, Harrison, and McLaughlin, "Asian American Attitudes Toward Affirmative Action in Employment"; L. Bobo and J. R. Kluegel, "Opposition to Race-Targeting: Self-Interest, Stratification Ideology, or Racial Attitudes?" *American Sociological Review* 58 (1993); L. Bobo and R. A. Smith, "Antipoverty Policies, Affirmative Action, and Racial Attitudes," in *Confronting Poverty: Prescriptions for Change,* ed. G. D. Sandefur, S. H. Danziger, and D. H. Weinberg (Cambridge: Harvard University Press, 1994); J. Citrin, "Affirmative Action in the People's Court," *Public Interest* 122 (1996); Fine, "Public Opinion Toward Equal Opportunity Issues"; Fine, "Impact of Issue Framing on Public Opinion"; J. R. Kluegel and E. R. Smith, *Beliefs About Inequality: Americans' Views of What Is and What Ought to Be, Social Institutions and Social Change* (New York: De Gruyter, 1986); S. L. Klineberg and D. A. Kravitz, "Ethnic Differences in Predictors of Support of Municipal Affirmative Action Contracting," *Social Science Quarterly* 84 (2003); Kravitz et al., "Attitudes Toward Affirmative Action"; L. Sigelman and S. Welch, *Black Americans' Views of Racial Inequality: The Dream Deferred* (Cambridge: Cambridge University Press, 1991); and G. Wilson, "Support for Redistributive Policies Among the African American Middle Class: Race and Class Effects," *Research in Social Stratification and Mobility* 18 (2001).

59. For a technical but very readable account of how gender affects the perceptions of attorneys and judges in Illinois see S. Riger et al., "Gender Bias in Courtroom Dynamics," *Law and Human Behavior* 19 (1995).

60. See Y. Fried et al., "The Relation Between Political Ideology and Attitudes Toward Affirmative Action Among African-Americans: The Moderating Effect of Racial Discrimination in the Workplace," *Human Relations* 54 (2001).

61. For a look at national survey data from the 1940s to the late 1990s, see Schuman et al., *Racial Attitudes in America.* See also the Web site kept by Maria Krysan which is updated regularly: www.tigger.cc.uic.edu/krysan/racialattitudes.htm.

62. Steeh and Krysan, "Poll Trends."

63. See the results of the survey conducted by Barbara Bergmann and reported in her *In Defense of Affirmative Action,* 152–59.

64. Kinder and Sanders, "Mimicking Political Debate with Survey Questions"; Kinder and Sanders, *Divided by Color.*

65. Kinder and Sanders, *Divided by Color,* 30.

66. A. M. Konrad and F. Linnehan, "Formalized HRM Structures: Coordinating

Equal Employment Opportunity or Concealing Organizational Practices?" *Academy of Management Journal* 38 (1995).

67. See A. R. Pratkanis and M. E. Turner, "Nine Principles of Successful Affirmative Action: Mr. Branch Rickey, Mr. Jackie Robinson, and the Integration of Baseball," *NINE: A Journal of Baseball History and Social Policy Perspectives* 3 (1994); Konrad and Linnehan, "Formalized HRM Structures"; Konrad and Linnehan, "Race and Sex Differences in Line Managers' Reactions"; and A. M. Konrad and F. Linnehan, "Affirmative Action: History, Effects, and Attitudes," in *Handbook of Gender and Work,* ed. Gary N. Powell (Thousand Oaks, Calif.: Sage, 1999).

Chapter 4: Effectiveness

1. See S. Kelman, *Procurement and Public Management: The Fear of Discretion and the Quality of Government Performance* (Washington, D.C.: American Enterprise Institute, 1990). The 10 percent figure is cited in T. Larson, "Affirmative Action Programs for Minority- and Women-Owned Businesses," in *The Impacts of Affirmative Action: Policies and Consequences in California,* ed. P. Ong (Walnut Creek, Calif.: Altamira, 1999).

2. A. A. Robinson, "The Business of Affirmative Action," in *The Affirmative Action Debate,* ed. G. E. Curry (Cambridge: Perseus, 1998).

3. D. L. Williams, "The California Civil Rights Initiative: Which Firms Stand to Lose and How Much?" in Ong, *Impacts of Affirmative Action.*

4. T. Larson, "Affirmative Action Programs for Minority- and Women-Owned Businesses," in Ong, *Impacts of Affirmative Action.*

5. See Larson's appendixes in ibid.

6. *Final Report: City of Tallahassee MBE Disparity Fact-Finding Report* (Tallahassee, Fla.: MGT of America, 1990), cited in ibid.

7. Larson, "Affirmative Action Programs for Minority- and Women-Owned Businesses," 148.

8. M. E. Enchautegui et al., *Do Minority-Owned Businesses Get a Fair Share of Government Contracts?* (Washington, D.C.: Urban Institute, 1998).

9. N. Munk, "Fighting over the Spoils," *Forbes,* Aug. 15 1994.

10. Ibid.

11. M. Bendick, Jr., "The Croson Decision Mandates That Set-Aside Programs Be Tools of Business Development," *George Mason University Civil Rights Law Journal* 1 (1990).

12. T. Bates, *Banking on Black Enterprise: The Potential of Emerging Firms for Revitalizing Urban Economies* (Washington, D.C.: Joint Center for Economic Studies, 1993).

13. T. Bates and D. Williams, "Preferential Procurement Programs and Minority-Owned Businesses," *Journal of Urban Affairs* 17 (1995).

14. K. Mfume, "Why America Needs Set-Aside Programs," in Curry, *Affirmative Action Debate.*

15. I. Ayres, *Pervasive Prejudice? Unconventional Evidence of Race and Gender Discrimination* (Chicago: University of Chicago Press, 2002).

16. B. F. Reskin, *The Realities of Affirmative Action in Employment* (Washington, D.C.: American Sociological Association, 1998).

17. R. Blank, "An Analysis of Workers' Choices Between Employment in the Public and Private Sectors," *Industrial and Labor Relations Review* 38 (1985).

18. A. M. Konrad and J. Pfeffer, "Understanding the Hiring of Women and Minorities in Educational Institutions," *Sociology of Education* 664 (1991). While the public-private distinction influenced minority hiring, it did not influence hiring on the basis of gender.

19. A. M. Konrad and F. Linnehan, "Affirmative Action: History, Effects, and Attitudes," in *Handbook of Gender and Work,* ed. G. N. Powell (Thousand Oaks, Calif.: Sage, 1999).

20. M. V. L. Badgett, "The Impact of Affirmative Action on Public-Sector Employment in California, 1970–1990," in Ong, *Impacts of Affirmative Action.*

21. Ibid., 97. Meanwhile, other states show similar changes. In New York, minorities captured only 1 percent of the state's official and administrative-level jobs in 1984 but 8 percent a decade later. See M. Durr and J. R. Logan, "Racial Submarkets in Government Employment: African American Managers in New York State," *Sociological Forum* 12 (1997).

22. S. P. Smith, "Government Wage Differentials by Sex," *Journal of Human Resources* 11 (1976).

23. J. M. Firestone, "Occupational Segregation: Comparing the Civilian and Military Workforce," *Armed Forces and Society* 18 (1992).

24. See S. Martin, "The Effectiveness of Affirmative Action: The Case of Women in Policing," *Justice Quarterly* 8 (1991).

25. See T. Sass and J. L. Troyer, "Affirmative Action, Political Representation, Unions, and Female Police Employment," *Journal of Labor Research* 20 (1999). It did not matter whether there were women on the town councils. In addition, the greater the concentration of men on the force, the greater the continued resistance over time.

26. According to Jonathan Leonard, 35 percent of federal contractors are in the manufacturing sector, compared to 27 percent of noncontractors; and 31 percent of contractors are in the retail trade, while 53 percent of noncontractors are ("Women and Affirmative Action," *Journal of Economic Perspectives* 3 [1989]).

27. Since 1966 every employer with more than a hundred employees has had to file an EEO-1 form with the Equal Employment Opportunity Commission.

28. M. V. L. Badgett and H. I. Hartmann, "The Effectiveness of Equal Employment Opportunity Policies," in *Economic Perspectives on Affirmative Action,* ed. M. C. Simms (Washington, D.C.: Joint Center for Political and Economic Studies, 1995); and H. I. Hartmann, "Who Has Benefited from Affirmative Action in Employment?" in Curry, *Affirmative Action Debate.*

29. O. Ashenfelter and J. Heckman, "Measuring the Effect of an Anti-Discrimination Program," in *Evaluating the Labor Market Effects of Social Programs,* ed. J. Blum and O. Ashenfelter (Princeton: Princeton University Press, 1976).

30. One should, however, be cautious of data collected over a short period of time. As an interesting study by A. H. Beller shows, sometimes gains are lost a few years later; see "Occupational Segregation by Sex: Determinants and Changes," *Journal of Human Resources* 17 (1982).

31. M. Goldstein and R. S. Smith, "The Estimated Impact of the Anti-Discrimination Program Aimed at Federal Contractors," *Industrial and Labor Relations Review* 29 (1976).

32. J. J. Heckman and K. I. Wolpin, "Does the Contract Compliance Program Work? An Analysis of Chicago Data," *Industrial and Labor Relations Review* 29 (1976).

33. J. J. Heckman and B. S. Payner, "Determining the Impact of Federal Antidiscrimination Policy on the Economic Status of Blacks: A Study of South Carolina," *American Economic Review* 79 (1989).

34. Leonard has been a prolific writer on the topic of affirmative action in the late 1970s and the 1980s. See his "Anti-Discrimination or Reverse Discrimination: The Impact of Changing Demographics, Title VII, and Affirmative Action or Productivity," *Journal of Human Resources* 19 (1984); "Employment and Occupational Advance Under Affirmative Action," *Review of Economics and Statistics* 66 (1984); and "The Impact of Affirmative Action on Employment," *Journal of Labor Economics* 2 (1984); "What Promises Are Worth: The Impact of Affirmative Action Goals," *Journal of Human Resources* 20, no. 1 (1985); "The Effectiveness of Equal Employment Law and Affirmative Action Regulation," in *Research in Labor Economics,* ed. R. A. Ehrenberg (Greenwich, Conn.: JAI, 1986); "The Impact of Affirmative Action Regulation and Equal Employment Law on Black Employment," *Journal of Economic Perspectives* 4 (1990); *Use of Enforcement Techniques in Eliminating Glass Ceiling Barriers: Report to the Glass Ceiling Commission* (Washington, D.C.: Department of Labor, 1994); and "Women and Affirmative Action."

35. Leonard, "Impact of Affirmative Action on Employment."

36. For details on the Reagan-Bush attack on the OFCCP see L. F. Williams, "Tracing the Politics of Affirmative Action," in Curry, *Affirmative Action Debate,* especially pages 251–52.

37. Leonard "Women and Affirmative Action," 73.

38. Leonard, "Impact of Affirmative Action Regulation and Equal Employment Law on Black Employment." Black male employment growth was 17 percent in the late 1970s among federal contractors, but 10 percent after 1980. Among noncontractors, the Black male employment growth was 12 percent in the late 1970s and 11 percent after 1980.

39. See L. B. Edelman and S. Petterson, "Symbols and Substance in Organizational Response to Civil Rights Law" (paper presented at the annual meeting of the American Sociological Association, Miami Beach, Florida, August 1993). Data reported in Reskin, *Realities of Affirmative Action in Employment,* 47.

40. See W. M. Rodgers III and W. E. Spriggs, "The Effect of Federal-Contractor Status on Racial Differences in Establishment-Level Employment Shares: 1979–1992," *American Economic Review* 86 (1996); and W. M. Rodgers III, "Racial Differences in Employment Shares—New Evidence from the EEO-1 Files," in *Civil Rights and Race Relations in the Post-Reagan-Bush Era,* ed. S. L. Meyers (Westport, Conn.: Praeger, 1997).

41. W. M. Rodgers III, "Federal-Contractor Status and Minority Employment: A Case Study of California, 1979–1994," in Ong, *Impacts of Affirmative Action.*

42. B. R. Bergmann, *In Defense of Affirmative Action* (New York: Basic, 1996).

43. C. Herring and S. M. Collins, "Retreat from Opportunity? The Case of Affirmative Action," in *The Bubbling Cauldron: Race, Ethnicity, and the Urban Crisis,* ed. M. P. Smith and J. R. Feagin (Minneapolis: University of Minnesota Press, 1995).

44. Ibid., 170.

45. H. J. Holzer and D. Neumark, *Assessing Affirmative Action* (Cambridge: National Bureau of Economic Research, 1999), 539. See also H. Holzer and D. Neumark, "What Does Affirmative Action Do?" *Industrial and Labor Relations Review* 53 (2000).

46. Bureau of National Affairs, *Affirmative Action Today: A Legal and Practical Analysis* (Washington, D.C.: Bureau of National Affairs, 1986).

47. U.S. Department of Labor, *OFCCP Egregious Discrimination Cases* (Washington, D.C.: Department of Labor, 1996), cited in Reskin, *Realities of Affirmative Action in Employment.*

48. Bureau of National Affairs, *EEO Policies and Programs. Personnel Policies Forum* survey No. 141 (Washington, D.C.: Bureau of National Affairs, 1986), cited in Reskin, *Realities of Affirmative Action in Employment.*

49. A. M. Konrad and F. Linnehan, "Formalized HRM Structures: Coordinating Equal Employment Opportunity or Concealing Organizational Practices?" *Academy of Management Journal* 38 (1995).

50. K. B. Rai and J. W. Critzer, *Affirmative Action and the University: Race, Ethnicity, and Gender in Higher Education Employment* (Lincoln: University of Nebraska Press, 2000).

51. G. Simpson, "The Plexiglass Ceiling: The Careers of Black Women Lawyers," *The Career Development Quarterly* 45 (1996). The women noted that they could not have accomplished their professional goals without affirmative action in education. Thirty-one percent claimed that affirmative action helped them gain admission to their undergraduate institution; 55 percent said it helped them get into law school. About a third of the women received a minority scholarship at college, and 45 percent had such a scholarship in law school.

52. Quoted in J. Leonard, "Anti-Discrimination or Reverse Discrimination," 145.

53. See W. H. Truesdell, *The Secrets of Affirmative Action Compliance,* 5th ed. (Walnut Creek, Calif.: Management Advantage, 2001).

54. Leonard, "Women and Affirmative Action," 68.

55. Leonard, "Anti-Discrimination or Reverse Discrimination," 168.

56. See C. A. Conrad, "The Economic Cost of Affirmative Action," in Simms, *Economic Perspectives on Affirmative Action.*

57. G. Stephanopoulos and C. Edley, Jr., *Affirmative Action Review: Report to the President* (Washington, D.C.: Government Printing Office, 1995).

58. For a discussion of the thin line employers have to walk to avoid reverse-discrimination suits, see C. R. Gullett, "Reverse Discrimination and Remedial Affirmative Action in Employment: Dealing with the Paradox of Nondiscrimination," *Public Personnel Management* 29 (2000).

59. On the myth of the angry White man, see L. Harris, "The Future of Affirmative Action," in Curry, *Affirmative Action Debate.*

60. E. H. Norton, "Affirmative Action in the Workplace," in Curry, *Affirmative Action Debate,* 45. Speaking of an unspecified period, Louis Harris gives a higher figure: 3.6 percent (in Curry, ibid.). That's still just a trickle.

61. Norton, "Affirmative Action in the Workplace," 45.

62. For various forms of this argument, see P. S. Greenlaw and S. S. Jensen, "Race-Norming and the Civil Rights Act of 1991," *Public Personnel Management* 25 (1996); and J. J. Silva and R. R. Jacobs, "Performance as a Function of Increased Minority Hiring," *Journal of Applied Psychology* 78 (1993).

63. Conrad, "Economic Cost of Affirmative Action," 41.

64. P. Osterman, "Affirmative Action and Opportunity: A Study of Female Quit Rates," *Review of Economics and Statistics* 64, no. 4 (1982).

65. Leonard, "Anti-Discrimination or Reverse Discrimination."

66. Conrad, "Economic Cost of Affirmative Action."

67. Holzer and Neumark, "What Does Affirmative Action Do?"

68. P. Wright, S. P. Ferris, J. S. Hiller, and M. Kroll, "Competitiveness Through Management of Diversity: Effect on Stock Price Valuation," *Academy of Management Journal* 38 (1995).

69. Hersch found that the negative impact of EEO lawsuits on stock prices was short-lived. See J. Hersch, "EEO Law and Firm Profitability," *Journal of Human Resources* 26 (1991).

70. Glass Ceiling Commission, *Good for Business: Making Full Use of the Nation's Human Capital* (Washington, D.C.: Department of Labor, 1995).

71. "Equal Opportunity Pays," *Wall Street Journal,* June 4, 1993, 1. In a similar vein, companies with diversified boards tend to have higher investor returns than companies with fewer women and people of color. See L. Bellinger and A. J. Hillman, "Does Tolerance Lead to Better Partnering?" *Business and Society* 39 (2000).

72. M. Kilson, "Affirmative Action," *Dissent* (1995), 470.

73. Ibid., 469.

74. These are all cited in Conrad, "Economic Cost of Affirmative Action."

75. D. D'Souza, *Illiberal Education: The Politics of Race and Sex on Campus* (Detroit: Free Press, 1991); C. A. Murray, and R. J. Herrnstein, *The Bell Curve: Intelligence and Class Structure in American Life* (New York: Free Press, 1994).

76. Herring and Collins, "Retreat from Opportunity?" 178.

77. See D. Card and A. B. Krueger, "Labor Market Effects of School Quality: Theory and Evidence," in *Does Money Matter? The Effects of School Resources on Student Achievement and Adult Success,* ed. G. Burtless (Washington, D.C.: Brookings Institution Press, 1996).

78. I do not mean to minimize the distinctiveness of racial politics in America. Given the scar of racial injustice in the United States, the fact that affirmative action in education is more about race than about gender may help explain some of the vehemence of feelings regarding educational issues. But while the reactions may differ, the logic behind the policy is the same in education as in employment.

79. See R. Downing et al., "Affirmative Action in Higher Education," *Diversity Factor* 10, no. 2 (2002).

80. The Master Plan is being revised at present, but the major contours remain in place; see www.sen.ca.gov/masterplan/.

81. C. Tien, "In Defense of Affirmative Action," *USA Today* 126, no. 2630 (1997), reprinted in F. J. Crosby and C. VanDeVeer, *Sex, Race, and Merit: Debating Affirmative Action in Education and Employment* (Ann Arbor: University of Michigan Press, 2000), 34–39.

82. Asian Americans, meanwhile, are a heterogeneous group. Japanese Americans, Chinese Americans, and Korean Americans tend to live in affluent districts, while Filipino Americans, Cambodian Americans, Laotian Americans, and other recent immigrants are less well off. Educational attainment among the different groups tends to correspond to economic prosperity.

83. Of course, with the passage of SP 1 by the California Board of Regents in July 1995, it became impermissible for the university to take account of the sex or ethnicity of applicants, thereby ending affirmative action in admissions. In 2002, the Regents ended SP 1.

84. Recently, in contrast to the *Bakke* case decided by the Supreme Court in 1978,

most Circuit Courts have decided that schools must abandon race-conscious policies. One exception is the 2002 decision of the Sixth Circuit that the University of Michigan's law school had a compelling interest in ensuring diversity.

85. D. K. Detterman, "Tests, Affirmative Action in University Admissions, and the American Way," *Psychology, Public Policy, and Law* 6 (2000), 53.

86. Ibid.

87. W. G. Bowen and D. C. Bok, *The Shape of the River: Long-Term Consequences of Considering Race in College and University Admissions* (Princeton: Princeton University Press, 1998).

88. T. J. Kane, "Racial and Ethnic Preferences in College Admissions," in *The Black-White Test Score Gap,* ed. C. Jencks and M. Phillips (Washington D.C.: Brookings Institution Press, 1998). At 60 percent of the U.S. colleges, being Black or Hispanic offers no advantage because, in essence, all who apply are admitted.

89. See L. F. Wightman, "The Threat to Diversity in Legal Education: An Empirical Analysis of the Consequences of Abandoning Race as a Factor in Law School Admissions Decisions," *New York University Law Review* 72 (1997); American Council on Education, *Making the Case for Affirmative Action in Higher Education* (Washington D.C.: American Council on Education, 1996); R. Gandara, *Over the Ivy Walls: The Educational Mobility of Low-Income Chicanos* (Albany: State University of New York Press, 1995); M. S. Moses, "Affirmative Action and the Creation of More Favorable Contexts of Choice," *American Educational Research Journal* 38 (2001); and J. J. Cohen, "The Consequences of Premature Abandonment of Affirmative Action in Medical School Admissions," *Journal of the American Medical Association* 289 (2003).

90. See D. Karen, "'Achievement' and 'Ascription' in Admission to an Elite College: A Political-Organizational Analysis," *Sociological Forum* 6 (1991). See also E. S. Chen and T. R. Tyler, "Cloaking Power: Legitimizing Myths and the Psychology of the Advantaged," in *The Use and Abuse of Power: Multiple Perspectives on the Causes of Corruption,* ed. A. Y. Lee-Chai and J. A. Bargh (Philadelphia: Taylor and Francis, 2001).

91. S. Steele, *The Content of Our Character: A New Vision of Race in America* (New York: St. Martin's, 1990).

92. S. Thernstrom and A. M. Thernstrom, *America in Black and White: One Nation, Indivisible* (New York: Simon and Schuster, 1997). See also Bowen and Bok, *Shape of the River,* 258.

93. These opinion data were also collected from the class entering in 1976.

94. Quoted in M. Chesler and M. Peet, "White Student Views of Affirmative Action on Campus," *Diversity Factor* 10, no. 2 (2002), 25.

95. Ibid.

96. P. Gurin, R. Nagda, and G. Lopez, "Preparation for Citizenship: The Benefits of Diversity" (2001). Available from the authors at the Psychology Department, University of Michigan, Ann Arbor, MI 48106.

97. P. Gurin et al., "Diversity and Higher Education: Theory and Impact on Educational Outcomes," *Harvard Educational Review* 72 (2002).

98. Ibid.

99. L. S. Gottfredson, "Racially Gerrymandering the Content of Police Tests to Satisfy the U.S. Justice Department: A Case Study," *Psychology, Public Policy, and Law* 2 (1996).

100. Ibid., 421.

101. Ibid., 422.

102. Ibid., 423.

103. J. R. Lott, Jr., "Does a Helping Hand Put Others at Risk? Affirmative Action, Police Departments, and Crime," *Economic Inquiry* 38 (2000).

104. B. S. Steel and N. P. Lovrich, "Equality and Efficiency Tradeoffs in Affirmative Action—Real or Imagined? The Case of Women in Policing," *Social Science Journal* 24 (1987).

105. Another investigator found that affirmative action in employment produced tensions among the employees of San Quentin Prison. See B. Owen, "Race and Gender Relations Among Prison Workers," *Crime and Delinquency* 31 (1985).

106. W. J. Wilson, *When Work Disappears: The World of the New Urban Poor* (New York: Knopf, 1996); W. J. Wilson, "Race-Neutral Programs and the Democratic Coalition," in *Affirmative Action: Social Justice or Reverse Discrimination,* ed. F. J. Beckwith and T. J. Jones (Amherst, N.Y.: Prometheus, 1997); G. C. Loury, *The Anatomy of Racial Inequality* (Cambridge: Harvard University Press, 2001). See also A. Moro and P. Norman, "Affirmative Action in a Competitive Economy," *Journal of Public Economics* 87 (2003), for an example of how econometric modeling can be used to predict that affirmative action might actually harm the minority community. Blau has extended the wedge issue to gender (F. D. Blau, "Trends in the Well-Being of American Women, 1970–1995," *Journal of Economic Literature* 36 [1998]).

107. R. L. Woodson, Sr., "Personal Responsibility," in Curry, *Affirmative Action Debate,* 112.

108. F. J. Crosby, B. Allen, and S. Opotow, "Changing Patterns of Income Among Blacks and Whites Before and After E.O. 11246," *Social Justice Research* 5 (1992).

109. Loury, *Anatomy of Racial Inequality.*

110. R. O. Lempert, D. A. Chambers, and T. K. Adams, "Michigan's Minority Graduates in Practice: The River Runs Through Law School," *Law and Social Inquiry* 25 (2000). For a fascinating analysis, see L. Guinier, "Commentary," *Law and Social Inquiry* 25 (2000).

111. N. E. Penn, P. J. Russell, and H. J. Simon, "Affirmative Action at Work: A Survey of Graduates of the University of California, San Diego Medical School," *American Journal of Public Health* 76 (1986).

112. M. Komaromy et al., "The Role of Black and Hispanic Physicians in Providing Health Care for Underserved Populations," *New England Journal of Medicine* 334 (1996).

113. G. E. Fryer, Jr., et al., "Hispanic Versus White, Non-Hispanic Physician Medical Practices in Colorado," *Journal of Health Care for the Poor and Underserved* 12 (2001). Another study, meanwhile, showed that Black patients are more satisfied with the care given them by Black physicians than with the care given them by White physicians (T. A. LaViest and T. Carroll, "Race of Physician and Satisfaction with Care Among African-American Patients," *Journal of the National Medical Association* 94 [2002]).

114. A. F. Brimmer, "The Economic Cost of Discrimination Against Black Americans," in Simms, *Economic Perspectives of Affirmative Action.*

Chapter 5: Does the Medicine Kill the Patient?

1. W. R. Beer, "Affirmative Action: Social Policy as Shibboleth," in *Psychology and Social Policy,* ed. P. Suedfeld and P. E. Tetlock (New York: Hemisphere, 1992), 137.

2. See "*H. Earl Fullilove et al., Petitioners v. Philip M. Klutznick, Secretary of Com-*

merce of the United States, et al.," in *Sex, Race and Merit: Debating Affirmative Action in Education and Employment,* ed. F. J. Crosby and C. VanDeVeer (Ann Arbor: University of Michigan Press, 2000), 267.

3. Ibid., 264.

4. In judgments, justices may write their own decisions, even if they concur with the majority decision. As Jim Newman has noted, affirmative action cases tend to be even more divisive than other cases. See J. D. Newman, "Affirmative Action and the Courts," in *Affirmative Action in Perspective,* ed. F. A. Blanchard and F. J. Crosby (New York: Springer-Verlag, 1989). None of the justices who were in the majority opinion in *Fullilove* is still on the bench. All of the dissenters are.

5. *"Fullilove,"* in Crosby and VanDeVeer, *Sex, Race and Merit,* 275.

6. Ibid.

7. Ibid., 277.

8. Ibid., 276.

9. Ibid., 278.

10. See, e.g., Board of Regents v. Bakke, 438 U.S. 265 (1978); Gratz v. Bollinger, 277 F.3d 803 (2003); Grutter v. Bollinger, 137 F. Supp, 2d 821 (2003); Hopwood v. Texas, 861 F. Supp 551 (W.D. Tex. 1994); Johnson v. Board of Regents of University of Georgia, 106 F. Supp 2d 1362 (2000); Smith v. University of Washington Law School, 233 F. 3d. 1188 (4th Cir. 2000).

11. *"Cheryl Hopwood v. University of Texas,"* in Crosby and VanDeVeer, *Sex, Race and Merit,* 315.

12. Ibid., 316.

13. *Grutter v. Bollinger,* dissent by Justice Thomas.

14. Both are reported in M. E. Heilman, C. J. Block, and J. A. Lucas, "Presumed Incompetent? Stigmatization and Affirmative Action Efforts," *Journal of Applied Psychology* 77 (1992).

15. Ibid., 540.

16. Ibid.

17. M. E. Heilman, W. F. McCullough, and D. Gilbert, "The Other Side of Affirmative Action: Reactions of Nonbeneficiaries to Sex-Based Preferential Selection," *Journal of Applied Psychology* 81 (1996).

18. M. E. Heilman, C. J. Block, and P. Stathatos, "The Affirmative Action Stigma of Incompetence: Effects of Performance Information Ambiguity," *Academy of Management Journal* 40 (1997).

19. M. E. Heilman et al., "Type of Affirmative Action Policy: A Determinant of Reactions to Sex-Based Preferential Selection?" *Journal of Applied Psychology* 83 (1998).

20. Heilman, McCullough, and Gilbert, "Other Side of Affirmative Action," 353. In a follow-up study (Heilman et al., "Type of Affirmative Action Policy," study 3), Heilman and her associates replicated the findings with a new group of undergraduates. They also found in the follow-up study that the men who had been "passed over" were less willing to volunteer labor to the experimenter when the woman was ostensibly selected to be leader on the basis of any kind of preference (even with equivalent scores to the man) rather than on the basis of straight merit.

21. Heilman, Block, and Stathatos, "Affirmative Action Stigma of Incompetence."

22. Heilman et al., "Type of Affirmative Action Policy."

23. M. B. Jacobson and W. Koch, "Women as Leaders: Performance Evaluation as a

Function of Method of Leader Selection," *Organizational Behavior and Human Performance* 20 (1977).

24. L. T. Garcia et al., "The Effect of Affirmative Action on Attributions About Minority Members," *Journal of Personality and Social Psychology* 49 (1981). Garcia and colleagues looked at reactions to supposed applicants to graduate school. See also G. B. Northcraft and J. Martin, "Double Jeopardy: Resistance to Affirmative Action from Potential Beneficiaries," in *Sex Role Stereotyping and Affirmative Action Policy,* ed. B. Gutek (Los Angeles: University of California Institute of Industrial Relations, 1982).

25. B. Rosen and M. F. Mericle, "Influence of Strong Versus Weak Fair Employment Policies and Applicant's Sex on Selection Decisions and Salary Recommendations in a Management Simulation," *Journal of Applied Psychology* 64 (1979). The strength of the affirmative action program had no effect on the decision to hire.

26. G. R. Maio and V. M. Esses, "The Social Consequences of Affirmative Action: Deleterious Effects on Perceptions of Groups," *Personality and Social Psychology Bulletin* 24 (1998), 68.

27. Ibid.

28. Ibid., 72.

29. Both are reported in M. G. Resendez, "The Stigmatizing Effects of Affirmative Action: An Examination of Moderating Variables," *Journal of Applied Social Psychology* 32 (2002).

30. J. Gilbert and B. A. Stead, "Stigmatization Revisited: Does Diversity Management Make a Difference in Applicant Success?" *Group and Organization Management* 24 (1999).

31. D. C. Evans, "A Comparison of the Other-Directed Stigmatization Produced by Legal and Illegal Forms of Affirmative Action," *Journal of Applied Psychology* 88 (2003).

32. Ibid., 124.

33. Ibid.

34. Ibid.

35. P. M. Sniderman and T. Piazza, *The Scar of Race* (Cambridge: Harvard University Press, 1993), chap. 4.

36. Ibid., 102.

37. We cannot, however, conclude, as Sniderman and Piazza do, that the set of findings "further strengthens the argument that the central problem of racial politics is *not* the problem of prejudice" (ibid., 107). Hiring quotas should not be equated with affirmative action, and a study which draws on people's fears about their livelihood would be considered by some a clear indicator of racially coded materials. Following the line of reasoning of John Dovidio about aversive racism, one could argue that the provocative phrasing of the survey question essentially gave permission to covert racists to voice their dislike of Blacks.

38. C. P. Parker, B. B. Baltes, and N. D. Christiansen, "Support for Affirmative Action, Justice Perceptions, and Work Attitudes: A Study of Gender and Racial-Ethnic Group Differences," *Journal of Applied Psychology* 82 (1997), 381.

39. Ibid. As shown in their table 4, all the correlations controlled for the effects of age, education, hierarchical level, and tenure on the job. Parker and his colleagues found that the associations were stronger among the White women, Black and Hispanic workers, and Asian workers than they were among the White men.

40. A. M. Konrad and F. Linnehan, "Formalized HRM Structures: Coordinating

Equal Employment Opportunity or Concealing Organizational Practices?" *Academy of Management Journal* 38 (1995). See also A. M. Konrad and F. Linnehan, "Race and Sex Differences in Line Managers' Reactions to Equal Employment Opportunity and Affirmative Action Interventions," *Group and Organizational Management* 20 (1995).

41. Heilman, Block, and Stathatos, "Affirmative Action Stigma of Incompetence."

42. See A. R. Pratkanis and M. E. Turner, "Nine Principles of Successful Affirmative Action: Mr. Branch Rickey, Mr. Jackie Robinson, and the Integration of Baseball," *NINE: A Journal of Baseball History and Social Policy Perspectives* 3 (1994); M. E. Turner and A. R. Pratkanis, "Affirmative Action as Help: A Review of Recipient Reactions to Preferential Selection and Affirmative Action," *Basic and Applied Social Psychology* 15 (1994); and A. R. Pratkanis and M. E. Turner, "The Year Cool Papa Bell Lost the Batting Title: Mr. Branch Rickey and Mr. Jackie Robinson's Plea for Affirmative Action," *NINE: A Journal of Baseball History and Social Policy Perspectives* 2 (1994).

43. Heilman, Block, and Lucas, "Presumed Incompetent?" The authors did not actually say that there were no gender effects, but custom dictates that they would have reported it if women and men had differed in the preliminary analyses.

44. Heilman, Block, and Stathatos, "Affirmative Action Stigma of Incompetence."

45. Heilman et al., "Type of Affirmative Action Policy," study 2.

46. See M. E. Heilman and J. M. Herlihy, "Affirmative Action, Negative Reaction? Some Moderating Conditions," *Organizational Behavior and Human Performance* 33 (1984).

47. R. Rodriguez, *Hunger of Memory: The Education of Richard Rodriguez, an Autobiography* (Boston: Godine, 1982), 146–47.

48. Ibid., 170–71.

49. See R. Rodriguez, *Brown: The Last Discovery of America* (New York: Viking Penguin, 2002).

50. S. Steele, *The Content of Our Character: A New Vision of Race in America* (New York: St. Martin's, 1990), 111, 116.

51. Ibid., 116–117.

52. Ibid., 135.

53. S. L. Carter, *Reflections of an Affirmative Action Baby* (New York: Basic, 1991), 74, 79.

54. Ibid., 12, 14, 21.

55. Ibid., 86.

56. G. C. Loury, "Performing Without a Net," in *The Affirmative Action Debate,* ed. G. E. Curry (Cambridge: Perseus, 1998), 53–54; G. C. Loury, *The Anatomy of Racial Inequality* (Cambridge: Harvard University Press, 2001).

57. M. E. Heilman, M. C. Simon, and D. P. Repper, "Intentionally Favored, Unintentionally Harmed? Impact of Sex-Based Preferential Selection on Self-Perceptions and Self-Evaluations," *Journal of Applied Psychology* 72 (1987), 64.

58. Ibid.

59. M. E. Heilman, J. C. Rivero, and J. F. Brett, "Skirting the Competence Issue: Effects of Sex-Based Preferential Selection on Task Choices of Women and Men," *Journal of Applied Psychology* 76 (1991), 91.

60. A more recent pair of experiments has shown the self-limiting effects for women of knowing that a male teammate assumes that a woman was given a job simply on the basis of sex. When women learn about the sexist opinions of a male teammate whom

they do not expect to meet, the women feel dispirited. When women learn about the sexist opinions of a male teammate whom they do expect to meet, on the other hand, they strive harder, presumably in an effort to overcome the negative opinion. See M. E. Heilman and V. B. Alcott, "What I Think You Think of Me: Women's Reactions to Being Viewed as Beneficiaries of Preferential Selection," *Journal of Applied Psychology* 86 (2001).

61. M. E. Heilman et al., "When Similarity Is a Liability: Effects of Sex-Based Preferential Selection on Reactions to Like-Sex and Different-Sex Others," *Journal of Applied Psychology* 78 (1993), study 1.

62. Care was taken to counterbalance the materials presented in the dossiers so that, on average, the subjects saw the same materials for the female and male job candidates.

63. M. E. Heilman, J. A. Lucas, and S. R. Kaplow, "Self-Derogating Consequences of Sex-Based Preferential Selection: The Moderating Role of Initial Self-Confidence," *Organizational Behavior and Human Decision Processes* 46 (1990). Meanwhile, for male subjects the crippling effects were negated by positive feedback and also by neutral or no information. Only when men had been preferentially selected and then failed at a task were their self-estimations damaged.

64. Heilman et al., "When Similarity Is a Liability," study 2.

65. Heilman et al., "Type of Affirmative Action Policy," study 1.

66. Heilman and Alcott, "What I Think You Think of Me."

67. B. Blaine, J. Crocker, and B. Major, "The Unintended Negative Consequences of Sympathy for the Stigmatized," *Journal of Applied Social Psychology* 25 (1995).

68. M. E. Turner and A. R. Pratkanis, "Effects of Preferential and Meritorious Selection on Performance: An Examination of Intuitive and Self-Handicapping Perspectives," *Personality and Social Psychology Bulletin* 19 (1993).

69. B. Major, J. Feinstein, and J. Crocker, "Attributional Ambiguity of Affirmative Action," *Basic and Applied Social Psychology* 15 (1994), 94.

70. R. W. Nacoste, "Affirmative Action and Self-Evaluation," in Blanchard and Crosby, *Affirmative Action in Perspective.*

71. J. T. Kulas and L. M. Finkelstein, "Preferential Selection Independent of Race and Gender: Effects on Self-Evaluations and Newcomer Information-Seeking Behavior," *Social Justice Research* 15 (2002).

72. O. C. Richard and S. L. Kirby, "African Americans' Reactions to Diversity Programs: Does Procedural Justice Matter?" *Journal of Black Psychology* 23 (1997); O. C. Richard and S. L. Kirby, "Women Recruits' Perceptions of Workforce Diversity Program Selection Decisions: A Procedural Justice Examination," *Journal of Applied Social Psychology* 28 (1998).

73. S. Brutus and A. N. Ryan, "A New Perspective on Preferential Treatment: The Role of Ambiguity and Self-Efficacy," *Journal of Business and Psychology* 13 (1998).

74. R. P. Brown et al., "Putting the 'Affirm' into Affirmative Action: Preferential Selection and Academic Performance," *Journal of Personality and Social Psychology* 79 (2000), study 1.

75. S. Highhouse et al., "Effects of Advertised Human Resource Management Practices on Attraction of African American Applicants," *Personnel Psychology* 52 (1999).

76. W. Arthur, D. Doverspike, and R. Fuentes, "Recipients' Affective Responses to Affirmative Action," *Behavioral Sciences and the Law* 10 (1992).

77. D. Doverspike and W. Arthur, "Race and Sex Differences in Reactions to a Simulated Selection Decision Involving Race-Based Affirmative Action," *Journal of Black Psychology* 21 (1995), 95.

78. P. Stanush, W. Arthur, and D. Doverspike, "Hispanic and African American Reactions to a Simulated Race-Based Affirmative Action Scenario," *Hispanic Journal of Behavioral Sciences* 20 (1998).

79. M. M. Stewart and D. L. Shapiro, "Selection Based on Merit Versus Demography: Implications Across Race and Gender Lines," *Journal of Applied Psychology* 85 (2000).

80. T. I. Chacko, "Women and Equal Employment Opportunity: Some Unintended Effects," *Journal of Applied Psychology* 67 (1982).

81. M. C. Taylor, "Impact of Affirmative Action on Beneficiary Groups: Evidence from the 1990 General Social Survey," *Basic and Applied Social Psychology* 15 (1994).

82. Ibid., 158.

83. T. S. Fine, "Public Opinion Toward Equal Opportunity Issues: The Role of Attitudinal and Demographic Forces Among African Americans," *Sociological Perspectives* 35 (1992).

84. Ibid., 712.

85. "Gallup Short Subjects," *Gallup Poll Monthly* 358 (July 1995): 34–61.

86. Taylor, "Impact of Affirmative Action on Beneficiary Groups." The same was true for men in the study: the more they saw affirmative action as working on behalf of men, the more satisfied they felt.

87. However, Parker et al., "Support for Affirmative Action, Justice Perceptions, and Work Attitudes," found that for Asian American employees, work attitudes were not reliably related to perceptions of affirmative action.

88. F. Tougas et al., "Reactions of Beneficiaries to Preferential Treatment: A Reality Check," *Human Relations* 49 (1996).

89. L. R. Ayers, "Perceptions of Affirmative Action Among Its Beneficiaries," *Social Justice Research* 5 (1992).

90. Ibid., 232.

91. As Madeline Heilman pointed out to me in email correspondence, some people worry about self-selection biases in the correlational data. Maybe, for example, it is only the Blacks who feel good about themselves who chose to work for an affirmative action employer.

92. J. G. Ponterotto, F. M. Martinez, and D. C. Hayden, "Student Affirmative Action Programs: A Help or Hindrance to Development of Minority Graduate Students," *Journal of College Student Personnel* 27 (1986).

93. E. Margolis and A. Romero, "'The Department Is Very Male, Very White, Very Old, and Very Conservative': The Functioning of the Hidden Curriculum in Graduate Sociology Departments," *Harvard Educational Review* 68 (1998), 12–13.

94. L. R. Truax et al., "Undermined? Affirmative Action from the Targets' Point of View," in *Prejudice: The Target's Perspective,* ed. J. K. Swim and C. Stagnor (New York: Academic, 1997).

95. Smith College is a women's school.

96. Truax et al., "Undermined?" 184.

97. A. Schmermund et al., "Attitudes Toward Affirmative Action as a Function of

Racial Identity Among African American College Students," *Political Psychology* 22 (2001).

98. S. Sincharoen, F. J. Crosby, and R. Sellers, "Varied Support of Affirmative Action Among Black College Students: Who Supports and Who Opposes Affirmative Action?" (paper presented at the 26th Annual Conference of the American Association for Affirmative Action, Washington D.C., Apr. 7, 2000).

99. Subsequent research conducted at UCLA has shown that ethnic minority students who join fraternities and sororities tend to have a pronounced sense of ethnic identity and to support affirmative action and similar policies. Membership in such organizations did not decrease the likelihood of minority students making friends with members of other ethnic groups. See J. Sidanius et al., "Ethnic Enclaves on the College Campus: The Good, the Bad, and the Ugly" (Russell Sage Foundation Working Paper 194, 2002).

100. E. Elizondo and L. Hu, "Extending Latino Identity Among a Sample of College Students" (paper presented at the Annual Meeting of the International Society of Political Psychology, Amsterdam, 1999). E. Elizondo and F. J. Crosby, "Attitudes Toward Affirmative Action as a Function of the Strength of Ethnic Identity Among Latino College Students," *Journal of Applied Social Psychology,* in press.

101. D. D'Souza, *Illiberal Education: The Politics of Race and Sex on Campus* (Detroit: Free Press, 1991), 40.

102. Brown et al., "Putting the 'Affirm' into Affirmative Action."

103. Brown and colleagues were also able to statistically rule out the possibility that suspicion was just a proxy for self-confidence or for preparation as measured by the SATs (ibid.).

104. C. van Laar and S. Levin, "Social and Personal Identity in Stereotype Threat: Is Affirmative Action Stigmatizing?" (paper presented at the Biannual Meeting of the Society for the Psychological Study of Social Issues, Minneapolis, June 2000).

105. C. M. Steele, "A Threat in the Air: How Stereotypes Shape Intellectual Identity and Performance," *American Psychologist* 52 (1997).

106. J. Aronson et al., "When White Men Can't Do Math: Necessary and Sufficient Factors in Stereotype Threat," *Journal of Experimental Social Psychology* 35 (1999).

107. Van Laar and Levin carry through empirically the distinction between stereotype threat of a personal nature and stereotype threat to the group. For minority students who are not highly identified with their group, personal stereotype threat is the important moderator between the consciousness of being an affirmative action admit and scholastic performance. For those who are highly identified, group stereotype threat matters more.

108. Brown et al., "Putting the 'Affirm' into Affirmative Action," 745–46.

109. Ibid., 746.

110. W. G. Bowen and D. C. Bok, *The Shape of the River: Long-Term Consequences of Considering Race in College and University Admissions* (Princeton: Princeton University Press, 1998).

111. M. E. Heilman and S. L. Blader, "Assuming Preferential Selection When the Admissions Policy Is Unknown: The Effects of Gender Rarity," *Journal of Applied Psychology* 86 (2001).

112. B. R. Bergmann, *In Defense of Affirmative Action* (New York: Basic, 1996), 28.

Chapter 6: The Ugly Underbelly

1. I do not, of course, think that our demographic characteristics determine our politics and recognize that we should not essentialize women and men or White people and people of color. See K. F. Wyche and F. J. Crosby, *Women's Ethnicities: Journeys Through Psychology* (Boulder: Westview, 1996. Some of the strongest feminists are men; some of the greatest supporters of ethnic justice are White. Yet there is a tendency for people to understand social issues from the perspective of their own experience. For a fascinating exchange in which worldviews are relevant and only partially influenced by demographic characteristics, see G. V. Barrett and S. B. Morris, "The American Psychological Association's Amicus Curiae Brief in *Price Waterhouse v. Hopkins*," *Law and Human Behavior* 17 (1993). See also S. T. Fiske et al., "What Constitutes a Scientific Review? A Majority Retort to Barrett and Morris," *Law and Human Behavior* 17 (1993).

2. For an example of a comparative study of earnings (only a small indicator of well-being), see F. D. Blau and L. M. Kahn, "Wage Structure and Gender Earnings Differentials: An International Comparison," *Economica* 63 (1996), and F. D. Blau and L. M. Kahn, "Gender Differences in Pay," *Journal of Economic Perspectives* 14 (2000).

3. Note the United Nation's Development Programme keeps an index called the Gender Empowerment Measure. The United States compares favorably to many other nations on the index. See United Nations Development Programme, *Human Development Report 2001* (New York: Oxford University Press, 2001). The report can be accessed at www.undp.org/hdr2001/.

4. For an analysis of the past twenty-five years in economic terms, see F. D. Blau, "Trends in the Well-Being of American Women, 1970–1995," *Journal of Economic Literature* 36 (1998). See also F. D. Blau and L. M. Kahn, "Swimming Upstream: Trends in Gender Wage Differential in the 1980s," *Journal of Labor Economics* 15 (1997). It is vital to remember that not all women have shared in the economic advantage. There may be more poor women today than in the past.

5. The sweet irony was that I was delivering a talk on sex discrimination.

6. More precisely, in 1961 Section 51 of the California Civil Code was amended to read, "All persons within the jurisdiction of this State are free and equal, and no matter what their race, color, religion, ancestry, or national origin are entitled to the full and equal accommodations, advantages, facilities, privileges, or services in all business establishments of every kind whatsoever."

7. D. Furchtgott-Roth and C. Stolba, *Women's Figures: An Illustrated Guide to the Economic Progress of Women in America* (Washington D.C.: AEI Press, 1999), 3–4. The authors make some dramatic claims in their book. For example, they claim that statistics show that women aged 25–34 now earn 95 percent of what men earn, if one adjusts for the factors that contribute to salary. The source they cite for this is J. O'Neill, "Affirmative Action," *Wall Street Journal,* Oct. 7, 1994, which, in turn, references J. O'Neill and S. Polacheck, "Why the Gender Gap in Wages Narrowed in the 1980s," *Journal of Labor Economics* 11, no. 1 (1993).

8. See S. Riger et al., "Gender Bias in Courtroom Dynamics," *Law and Human Behavior* 19 (1995). Also see F. M. Haemmerlie and R. L. Montgomery, "Goldberg Revisited: Pro-Female Evaluation Bias and Changed Attitudes toward Women by Engineering

Students," *Journal of Social Behavior and Personality* 6 (1991). These studies show that women may overvalue women while men undervalue them. For how different sensitivities or insensitivities affect the way female and male scholars assess the existence of sex discrimination and the need for affirmative action, see the interesting exchange in *American Psychologist:* P. Bronstein and J. L. Pfennig, "Misperceptions of Women and Affirmative Action Principles in Faculty Hiring," *American Psychologist* 43 (1988); R. Elliot, "Preferential Hiring of Women in Psychology Is Unwarranted and Unwise: Reply to Bronstein and Pfennig," *American Psychologist* 44 (1989). P. Bronstein and J. L. Pfennig, "Beliefs Versus Realities: Response to Elliot," *American Psychologist* 44 (1989).

9. See W. Kahn and F. J Crosby, "Discrimination Between Attitudes and Discriminatory Behavior: Change and Stasis," in *Women and Work: An Annual Review,* ed. L. Larwood, B. A. Gutek, and A. H. Stromberg (Beverly Hills, Calif.: Sage, 1985), 217.

10. P. Glick and S. T. Fiske, "The Ambivalent Sexism Inventory: Differentiating Hostile and Benevolent Sexism," *Journal of Personality and Social Psychology* 70 (1996).

11. Ibid., 512.

12. Ibid.

13. Psychologist Alice Eagly has written extensively about the myths and realities of women in leadership positions. See A. H. Eagly and B. T. Johnson, "Gender and Leadership Style: A Meta-Analysis," *Psychological Bulletin* 108 (1990); A. H. Eagly, S. J. Karau, and M. G. Makhijani, "Gender and Effectiveness of Leaders: A Meta-Analysis," *Psychological Bulletin* 117 (1995); A. H. Eagly, M. G. Makhijani, and B. G. Klonsky, "Gender and the Evaluation of a Meta-Analysis," *Psychological Bulletin* 111 (1992). In 2001, Eagly and Linda Carli edited an issue of the *Journal of Social Issues* (vol. 57, no. 4) entitled *Gender, Hierarchy, and Leadership.*

14. P. Glick et al., "Beyond Prejudice as Simple Antipathy: Hostile and Benevolent Sexism Across Cultures," *Journal of Personality and Social Psychology* 79 (2000).

15. P. Goldberg, "Are Women Prejudiced Against Women?" *Transaction* 5 (1968).

16. I. Broverman et al., "Sex-Role Stereotypes: A Reappraisal," *Journal of Social Issues* 28, no. 2 (1972), 70.

17. J. Swim et al., "Joan Mckay Versus John Mckay: Do Gender Stereotypes Bias Evaluations?" *Psychological Bulletin* 105 (1989).

18. J. Swim and L. J. Sanna, "He's Skilled, She's Lucky: A Meta-Analysis of Observer's Attributions for Women's and Men's Successes and Failures," *Personality and Social Psychology Bulletin* 22 (1996). In a meta-analysis, the researchers look at the results of many different studies of the same topic to see if findings hold up across time and place.

19. A. H. Eagly and S. J. Karau, "Gender and the Emergence of Leaders: A Meta-Analysis," *Journal of Personality and Social Psychology* 60 (1991); Eagly, Makhijani, and Klonsky, "Gender and the Evaluation of a Meta-Analysis." Eagly, Karau, and Makhijani, "Gender and Effectiveness of Leaders."

20. M. Biernat and D. Kobrynowicz, "Gender and Race-Based Standards of Competence: Lower Minimum Standards but Higher Standards for Devalued Groups," *Journal of Personality and Social Psychology* 72 (1997).

21. The example is drawn from a study of sex stereotyping conducted by one of the major investigators using the reaction-time technique, Mahzarin Banaji. See M. Banaji and C. T. Hardin, "Automatic Stereotyping," *Psychological Science* 7 (1996).

22. D. C. Johnston, "As Salary Grows, So Does a Gender Gap," *New York Times,* May 12, 2002.

23. Blau, "Trends in the Well-Being of American Women."

24. S. W. Raudenbush and R. M. Kasim, "Cognitive Skill and Economic Inequality: Findings from the National Adult Literacy Survey," *Harvard Educational Review* 68 (1998).

25. L. K. Stroh, J. M. Brett, and A. H. Reilly, "All the Right Stuff: A Comparison of Female and Male Managers' Career Progression," *Journal of Applied Psychology* 77 (1992).

26. R. G. Wood, M. E. Corcoran, and P. N. Courant, "Pay Differences Among the Highly Paid: The Male-Female Earnings Gap in Lawyers' Salaries," *Journal of Labor Economics* 11 (1993). The equation used to produce the finding also assumed that differences in job settings were "voluntary," but as Wood et al. point out in a footnote, they have data showing that the choices were not voluntary. Those data include the stated workplace choices of graduates on the day of graduation from law school.

27. E. Becker, "Study Finds a Growing Gap Between Managerial Salaries for Men and Women," *New York Times,* Jan. 24, 2002.

28. L. Billard, "Twenty Years Later: Is There Pay Equity for Academic Women?" *Thought and Action* 10 (1994). See also L. H. Collins, "Competition and Contact: The Dynamics Behind Resistance to Affirmative Action in Academe," in *Career Strategies for Women in Academe: Arming Athena,* ed. L. H. Collins and J. C. Chrisler (Thousand Oaks, Calif.: Sage, 1998).

29. I. H. Frieze, J. E. Olson, and D. C. Good, "Perceived and Actual Discrimination in the Salaries of Male and Female Managers," *Journal of Applied Social Psychology* 20 (1990).

30. T. D. Stanley and S. B. Jarrell, "Gender Wage Discrimination Bias? A Meta-Regression Analysis," *Journal of Human Resources* 33 (1998).

31. A good source for summaries of Department of Labor statistics and commentaries on their implications is the Institute for Women's Policy Research in Washington, D.C., which maintains a good Web site at www.iwpr.org/.

32. J. P. Jacobsen, "Sex Segregation at Work: Trends and Predictions," *Social Science Journal* 31 (1994). Similar statistics are reported by Blau, "Trends in the Well-Being of American Women, 1970–1995."

33. D. Tomaskovic-Devey, "Sex Composition and Gendered Earnings Inequality: A Comparison of Job and Occupational Models," in *Gender Inequality at Work,* ed. J. A. Jacobs (Thousand Oaks, Calif.: Sage, 1995).

34. U.S. Department of Labor, Bureau of Labor Statistics, *Highlights of Women's Earnings in 2000,* Report 952 (Washington, D.C.: Government Printing Office 2001).

35. Becker, "Study Finds a Growing Gap Between Managerial Salaries for Men and Women."

36. A. Tsui, T. Egan, and C. O'Reilly, "Being Different: Relational Demography and Organizational Attachment," *Administrative Science Quarterly* 37 (1992); and A. Wharton and J. Baron, "So Happy Together? The Impact of Gender Segregation on Men at Work," *American Sociological Review* 52 (1987).

37. S. J. South et al., "Sex Differences in Support for Organizational Advancement," *Work and Occupations* 14 (1987).

38. C. Negrey, *Working First, but Working Poor* (Washington, D.C.: Institute for Women's Policy Research, 2001).

39. D. Neumark, "Sex Discrimination in Restaurant Hiring: An Audit Study," *Quarterly Journal of Economics* 111 (1996).

40. Economists debate the point frequently. For one side of the issue see Blau, "Trends in the Well-Being of American Women"; Blau and Kahn, "Wage Structure and Gender Earnings Differentials"; Blau and Kahn, "Swimming Upstream"; M. J. Budig and P. England, "The Wage Penalty for Motherhood," *American Sociological Review* 66 (2001); D. A. MacPherson and B. T. Hirsch, "Wages and Gender Composition: Why Do Women's Jobs Pay Less?" *Journal of Labor Economics* 13 (1995). For the opposing point of view, see O'Neill and S. Polacheck, "Why the Gender Gap in Wages Narrowed in the 1980s." Psychologists also debate the point. For example, Richard Lippa has found that women's vocational interests deal with people and feelings, while men's deal with things and how they work. See R. Lippa, "Gender-Related Individual Differences and the Structure of Vocational Interests: The Importance of the People-Things Dimension," *Journal of Personality and Social Psychology* 74 (1998). For how experience and social structures affect women's and men's expectations (entitlements), see S. Desmarais and J. Curtis, "Gender and Perceived Pay Entitlement: Testing for Effects of Experience with Income," *Journal of Personality and Social Psychology* 72 (1997). Psychologists and sociologists also deal with the iterative nature of personality and social structure. Generally, women's personality characteristics seem to reflect the social opportunities open to them. See J. M. Twenge, "Changes in Women's Assertiveness in Response to Status and Roles: A Cross-Temporal Meta-Analysis, 1931–1993," *Journal of Personality and Social Psychology* 81 (2001); B. F. Reskin and C. E. Ross, "Jobs, Authority, and Earnings Among Managers—The Continuing Significance of Sex," *Work and Occupations* 19 (1992); and C. L. Ridgeway and L. Smith-Lovin, "Interaction in the Gender System: Theory and Research," *Annual Review of Sociology* 25 (1999).

41. B. A. Done and R. Gutek, "Sexual Harassment," in *Handbook of the Psychology of Women and Gender,* ed. R. K. Unger (New York: Wiley, 2001). See also B. Gutek, "Working Environments," in *Encyclopedia of Women and Gender,* ed. J. Worell (New York: Academic, 2001).

42. B. Gutek, *Sex and the Workplace: Impact of Sexual Behavior and Harassment on Women, Men, and Organizations* (San Francisco: Jossey-Bass, 1985).

43. Cited in G. Horne, *Reverse Discrimination: The Case for Affirmative Action* (New York: International, 1992), 73; also reported in *Washington Post,* Feb. 18, 1992.

44. The variation derives from the different types of harassment from colleagues, superiors, and clients. See American Bar Association, *Unfinished Business: Overcoming the Sisyphus Factor: A Report on the Status of Women in the Legal Profession* (Chicago: American Bar Association, 1995). The report also notes many other aspects of gender inequity such as salary differentials and a chilly atmosphere for women in law schools.

45. D. N. Laband and B. F. Lentz, "The Effects of Sexual Harassment on Job Satisfaction, Earnings, and Turnover Among Female Lawyers," *Industrial and Labor Relations Review* 51 (1998).

46. F. Tougas et al., "Men's Attitudes Toward Affirmative Action: Justice and Intergroup Relations at the Crossroads," *Social Justice Research* 8 (1995). See also F. Tougas and F. Veilleux, "The Response of Men to Affirmative Action Strategies for Women: The Study of a Predictive Model," *Canadian Journal of Behavioural Science* 22 (1990).

47. F. Tougas et al., "Neosexism Among Women: The Role of Personally Experienced Social Mobility Attempts," *Personality and Social Psychology Bulletin* (1999).

48. Barnett, quoted in D. R. Kinder and L. M. Sanders, *Divided by Color: Racial Politics and Democratic Ideals, American Politics and Political Economy* (Chicago: University of Chicago Press, 1996), 221.

49. H. J. Harrington and N. Miller, "Overcoming Resistance to Affirmative Action in Industry: A Social Psychological Perspective," in *Psychology and Social Policy,* ed. P. Suedfeld and P. E. Tetlock (Washington, D.C.: Hemisphere, 1992), 127. Other scholars report somewhat different figures. According to Jon Hurwitz and Mark Peffley, in 1964 80 percent of Whites thought Blacks were as intelligent as Whites. See J. Hurwitz and M. Peffley, *Perception and Prejudice: Race and Politics in the United States* (New Haven: Yale University Press, 1998).

50. S. Thernstrom and A. M. Thernstrom, *America in Black and White: One Nation, Indivisible* (New York: Simon and Schuster, 1997).

51. Ibid., 196, table 7.

52. Ibid., 224–30.

53. Ibid., 242. Such a statement might seem quite misleading to some. Census figures show, for example, that 75–80 percent of poor families include at least part-time workers in them. Numerous reports are available at the Web site www.census.gov.

54. Thernstrom and Thernstrom, *America in Black and White,* 264.

55. Ibid., 273.

56. Ibid., 250.

57. Ibid., 256.

58. Ibid., 259.

59. Ibid., 256–57.

60. Ibid., 534.

61. An interesting and respectful rebuttal of aspects of the Thernstroms' argument is made by W. G. Bowen and D. C. Bok, *The Shape of the River: Long-Term Consequences of Considering Race in College and University Admissions* (Princeton: Princeton University Press, 1998).

62. Quoted in M. Chesler and M. Peet, "White Student Views of Affirmative Action on Campus," *The Diversity Factor* 10, no. 2 (2002), 22.

63. The phrase belongs to Jonathan Kozol, but the idea is shared by many. J. Kozol, *Savage Inequalities: Children in America's Schools* (New York: Crown, 1991).

64. See P. Gurin, A. H. Miller, and G. Gurin, "Stratum Identification and Consciousness," *Social Psychology Quarterly* 43 (1980).

65. Kinder and Sanders, *Divided by Color,* 287.

66. See D. Lewis, "Out in the Field," *Boston Sunday Globe,* Jan. 20, 2002.

67. Most people of color are aware of White racism and prejudice. But that is not to say that they, or scholars documenting racial prejudice, think that people of color are free of prejudice. See, for example, R. E. Hall, "Occupational Aspiration Among African-Americans: A Case for Affirmative Action," *Journal of Sociology and Social Welfare* 23 (1996).

68. Researchers and other scholars are, ultimately, human beings with biases like other people. For a fascinating account of how bias can be hidden and then uncovered, see R. B. Darlington, "On Race and Intelligence: A Commentary on Affirmative Action, the Evolution of Intelligence, the Regression Analyses in the Bell Curve, and Jensen's Two-Level Theory," *Psychology, Public Policy, and Law* 2 (1996).

69. See L. Bobo, "Attitudes Toward Black Political Movement: Trends, Meaning and Effects on Racial Policy Preferences," *Social Psychology Quarterly* 51, no. 4 (1988). See also L. Bobo, "Race, Interest, and Beliefs About Affirmative Action: Unanswered Questions and New Directions," *American Behavioral Scientist* 41 (1998); L. Bobo, "Race and Beliefs

About Affirmative Action: Assessing the Effects of Interests, Group Threat, Ideology, and Racism," in *Racialized Politics: The Debate About Racism in America,* ed. D. O. Sears, J. Sidanius, and L. Bobo (Chicago: University of Chicago Press, 2000); L. Bobo and V. L. Hutchings, "Perceptions of Racial Group Competition: Extending Blumer's Theory of Group Position to a Multiracial Social Context," *American Sociological Review* 61 (1996); and W. A. Gamson and A. Modigliani, "The Changing Culture of Affirmative Action," in *Research in Political Sociology,* ed. R. D. Braungart (Greenwich, Conn.: JAI, 1987).

70. J. F. Dovidio and S. L. Gaertner, "Affirmative Action, Unintentional Racial Biases, and Intergroup Relations," in *Intergroup Relations: Essential Readings,* ed. M. A. Hogg and D. Abrams (Philadelphia: Psychology Press/Taylor and Francis, 2001).

71. G. Simpson, "The Plexiglass Ceiling: The Careers of Black Women Lawyers," *Career Development Quarterly* 45 (1996).

72. R. K. Caputo, " Discrimination and Human Capital: A Challenge to Economic Theory and Social Justice," *Journal of Sociology and Social Welfare* 29 (2002).

73. B. Staples, "When a Law Firm Is Like a Baseball Team," in *Sex, Race, and Merit: Debating Affirmative Action in Education and Employment,* ed. F. J. Crosby and C. Van-DeVeer (Ann Arbor: University of Michigan Press, 2000).

74. Horne, *Reverse Discrimination,* 93.

75. A. Munnell et al., *Mortgage Lending in Boston: Interpreting HDMA Data; Federal Reserve Bank of Boston,* Working Paper 92-07 (Boston: Federal Reserve Bank of Boston, 1992), cited in F. Pratto, "The Puzzle of Continuing Group Inequality: Piecing Together Psychological, Social, and Cultural Forces in Social Dominance Theory," *Advances in Experimental Social Psychology* 31 (1999).

76. M. Janofsky, "Report Finds Bias in Lending Hinders Home Buying in Cities," *New York Times,* Feb. 23, 1998.

77. T. Bates, *Banking on Black Enterprise: The Potential of Emerging Firms for Revitalizing Urban Economies* (Washington, D.C.: Joint Center for Economic Studies, 1993), 83.

78. Horne, *Reverse Discrimination,* 89. See also M. F. Berry, "Affirmative Action: Why We Need It, Why It Is Under Attack," in *The Affirmative Action Debate,* ed. G. E. Curry (Cambridge: Perseus, 1998).

79. T. Hsien and F. H. Wu, "Beyond the Model Minority Myth," in Curry, *Affirmative Action Debate.*

80. B. F. Reskin, *The Realities of Affirmative Action in Employment* (Washington, D.C.: American Sociological Association, 1998).

81. Dovidio and Gaertner, "Affirmative Action, Unintentional Racial Biases, and Intergroup Relations," 152.

82. L. B. Shaw et al., *The Impact of Restructuring and the Glass Ceiling on Minorities and Women. Report to the Glass Ceiling Commission* (Washington, D.C.: Department of Labor, 1993).

83. C. W. Reimers, "Hispanic Earnings and Employment in the 1980s," in *Hispanics in the Workplace,* ed. P. Rosenfeld, S. B. Knouse, and A. L. Culbertson (Newbury Park, Calif.: Sage, 1992). The statistics were provided by L. Chavez and cited on page 46.

84. Hsien and Wu, "Beyond the Model Minority Myth."

85. M. M. Elvira and C. D. Zatzick, "Who's Displaced First? The Role of Race in Layoff Decisions," *Industrial Relations* 41 (2002).

86. Horne, *Reverse Discrimination,* 51.

87. W. Kriesel, T. J. Centner, and A. G. Keeler, "Neighborhood Exposure to Toxic

Releases: Are There Racial Inequities?" *Growth and Change* 27 (1996). Not all states studied showed the difference. In Georgia toxic sites were not necessarily more likely to be placed near Black neighborhoods, but in Ohio they were. Concerning the extent of and the effects of residential segregation along racial lines generally, see D. S. Massey and N. A. Denton, *American Apartheid: Segregation and the Making of the Underclass* (Cambridge: Harvard University Press, 1993).

88. S. G. Stolberg, "Race Gap Seen in Health Care of Equally Insured Patients," *New York Times,* Mar. 21, 2002.

89. I. Ayres, *Pervasive Prejudice? Unconventional Evidence of Race and Gender Discrimination* (Chicago: University of Chicago Press, 2002).

90. D. Baldus, G. Woodworth, and C. Pulaski, *Equal Justice and the Death Penalty: A Legal and Empirical Analysis* (Boston: Northeastern University Press, 1990).

91. Ibid.

92. T. K. T. Kuran, *Private Truths, Public Lies* (Cambridge: Harvard University Press, 1995). Kuran presents the figure as proof of the deleterious effects of affirmative action. Says Kuran, "Duke's covert supporters undoubtedly included some genuine racists. But it is hard to believe that all were bigots. Many must have been nonracist citizens attracted to his anti-affirmative action message" (142). Why Kuran has a hard time believing Duke's supporters bigots is never explicated.

93. J. Yinger, "Access Denied, Access Constrained: Results and Implications of the 1989 Housing Discrimination Study," in *Clear and Convincing Evidence: Measurement of Discrimination in America,* ed. M. Fix and R. J. Struyk (Washington, D.C.: Urban Institute, 1992).

94. M. A. Turner, "Limits on Neighborhood Choice: Evidence of Racial and Ethnic Steering in Urban Housing Markets," in Fix and Struyk, *Clear and Convincing Evidence.*

95. Reskin, *Realities of Affirmative Action in Employment.*

96. P. Moss and C. Tilly, *Stories Employers Tell: Race, Skill, and Hiring in America* (New York: Russell Sage, 2001). The information appears on page 7 and is taken from M. Bendick, Jr., C. W. Jackson, and V. A. Reinoso, "Measuring Employment Discrimination through Controlled Experiments," *Review of Black Political Economy* (Summer 1994). The Urban Institute did a series of studies and found anti-Black and anti-Hispanic discrimination. Meanwhile, around the same time, the University of Colorado conducted studies that revealed a bias in favor of Hispanics. For a comparison of the methods and findings of the studies, see W. Zimmerman, "Summary of the Urban Institute's and the University of Colorado's Hiring Audits," in Fix and Struyk, *Clear and Convincing Evidence.* Also see M. Bendick, Jr., "A National Report Card on Discrimination in America: The Role of Testing," in *A National Report Card on Discrimination in America: The Role of Testing,* ed. M. Fix and M. A. Turner (Washington, D.C.: Urban Institute, 1999).

97. Ayres, *Pervasive Prejudice?* The Chicago study is described on page 12, and the Atlanta study is described on page 100.

98. See C. Steeh and M. Krysan, "Poll Trends: Affirmative Action and the Public, 1970–1995," *Public Opinion Quarterly* 60 (1996).

99. L. Bobo and S. A. Suh, *Surveying Racial Discrimination: Analyses from a Multi-Ethnic Labor Market.* Working Paper 75 (New York: Russell Sage Foundation, 1996), cited in Reskin, *Realities of Affirmative Action in Employment,* 72.

100. J. F. Dovidio et al., "Cognitive and Motivational Bases of Bias: Implications of

Aversive Racism for Attitudes Toward Hispanics," in Rosenfeld, Knouse, and Culbertson, *Hispanics in the Workplace.*

101. H. Schuman, C. Steeh, and L. Bobo, *Racial Attitudes in America: Trends and Interpretations* (Cambridge: Harvard University Press, 1988). A more recent study, using cohort analysis, showed that Whites born between 1961 and 1981 are more liberal than previous generations on interracial matters, but still are opposed to government aid to minorities and are more likely than not to think that the nation has "gone too far" in pushing equal rights. See M. W. Andolina and J. D. Mayer, "Demographic Shifts and Racial Attitudes: How Tolerant Are Whites in the Most Diverse Generation?" *Social Science Journal* 40 (2003).

102. M. Krysan et al., "Response Rates and Response Content in Mail Versus Face-to-Face Surveys," *Public Opinion Quarterly* 58 (1994).

103. M. O. Emerson, G. Yancey, and K. J. Chai, "Does Race Matter in Residential Segregation? Exploring the Preferences of White Americans," *American Sociological Review* 66 (2001).

104. J. H. Kuklinski and M. D. Cobb, "When White Southerners Converse About Race," in Hurwitz and M. Peffley, *Perception and Prejudice.*

105. F. J. Crosby, S. Bromley, and L. Saxe, "Recent Unobtrusive Studies of Black and White Discrimination and Prejudice: A Literature Review," *Psychological Bulletin* 87 (1980). The more public the behavior, the less the discrimination. In one experiment, for example, a confederate of the experimenter who was either White or Black left a grocery store carrying a bag of groceries which she then dropped. White shoppers tended to offer the same amount of help whether the klutzy confederate was White or Black. The grocery store experiment, and others like it, involved behaviors that were more or less anonymous but public nonetheless.

106. J. F. Dovidio and S. L. Gaertner, "Aversive Racism and Selection Decisions: 1989 and 1999," *Psychological Science* 11 (2000), 104.

107. J. F. Dovidio and S. L. Gaertner, "Affirmative Action, Unintentional Racial Biases, and Intergroup Relations," in *Intergroup Relations: Essential Readings,* ed. M. A. Hogg and D. Abrams (Philadelphia: Psychology Press/Taylor and Francis, 2001), 148.

108. Dovidio and Gaertner, "Aversive Racism and Selection Decisions."

109. J. F. Dovidio et al., "Racial Attitudes and the Death Penalty," *Journal of Applied Social Psychology* 27 (1997). See also S. R. Summers and P. C. Ellsworth, "Race and the Courtroom: Perceptions of Guilt and Dispositional Attributions," *Personality and Social Psychology Bulletin* 26 (2000).

110. See, for example, M. Biernat and T. K. Vescio, "Categorization and Stereotyping: Effects of Group Context on Memory and Social Judgment," *Journal of Experimental Social Psychology* 29 (1993).

111. J. F. Dovidio and S. L. Gaertner, "Stereotypes and Evaluative Intergroup Bias," in *Affect, Cognition, and Stereotyping: Interactive Processes in Group Perception,* ed. D. M. Mackie and D. L. Hamilton (San Diego: Academic, 1993); and S. L. Gaertner and J. P. McLaughlin, "Racial Stereotypes: Associations and Ascriptions of Positive and Negative Characteristics," *Social Psychology Quarterly* 46 (1983).

112. J. S. Thompson, W. G. Stephan, and R. W. Schvaneveldt, "The Organization of Social Stereotypes in Semantic Memory" (paper presented at the Annual Meeting of the Rocky Mountain Psychological Association, Tucson, March 1980). Cited in Dovidio et al., "Cognitive and Motivational Bases of Bias," 91.

113. J. F. Dovidio et al., "Racial Bias and the Role of Implicit and Explicit Attitudes" (paper presented at the Annual meeting of the Eastern Psychological Association, Providence, R.I., April 1994), cited in Dovidio and Gaertner, "Affirmative Action, Unintentional Racial Biases, and Intergroup Relations."

114. A. J. Murrell et al., "Aversive Racism and Resistance to Affirmative Action: Perceptions of Justice Are not Necessarily Color Blind," *Basic and Applied Social Psychology* 15 (1994). In 2001 researchers in Canada found essentially the same dislike of programs for visible minorities and women relative to programs for the disabled. The researchers also found that the more subjects see affirmative action as a threat to nonbeneficiaries, the less they like affirmative action. See A. M. Beaton and F. Tougas, "Reactions to Affirmative Action: Group Membership and Social Justice," *Social Justice Research* 14 (2001).

115. S. Clayton, "Reactions to Social Categorizations: Evaluating One Argument Against Affirmative Action," *Journal of Applied Social Psychology* 26 (1996).

116. S. B. Malos, "The New Affirmative Action: Socioeconomic Preference Criteria in College Admissions," *Journal of Applied Behavioral Science* 36 (2000), 9.

117. E. Costantini and J. King, "Affirmative Action: The Configuration, Concomitants, and Antecedents of Student Opinion," *Youth and Society* 16 (1985).

118. S. Steele, *The Content of Our Character: A New Vision of Race in America* (New York: St. Martin's, 1990).

119. P. MacIntosh, "White Privilege: Unpacking the Invisible Knapsack," in *Revisioning Family Therapy: Race, Culture, and Gender in Clinical Practice,* ed. M. McGoldrick (New York: Guilford, 1998).

120. L. Bobo and J. R. Kluegel, "Opposition to Race-Targeting: Self-Interest, Stratification Ideology, or Racial Attitudes?" *American Sociological Review* 58 (1993).

121. D. A. Kravitz et al., "Attitudes Toward Affirmative Action: Correlations with Demographic Variables and with Beliefs About Targets, Actions, and Economic Effects," *Journal of Applied Social Psychology* 30 (2000).

122. Horne, *Reverse Discrimination.*

123. Quoted in D. Ward, "Generations and the Expression of Symbolic Racism," *Political Psychology* 6 (1985), 9.

124. Quoted in ibid., 10.

125. L. Stoker, "Understanding Whites' Resistance to Affirmative Action: The Role of Principled Commitments and Racial Prejudice," in Hurwitz and Peffley, *Perception and Prejudice: Race and Politics in the United States,* 140.

126. As Stoker is at pains to point out, the pattern of results for the admissions experiment differs slightly from that for the hiring experiment in the Race and Politics data set.

127. J. B. McConahay, "Modern Racism, Ambivalence and the Modern Racism Scale," in *Prejudice, Discrimination, and Racism,* ed. S. L. Gaertner and J. F. Dovidio (New York: Academic, 1983).

128. D. R. Williams et al., "Traditional and Contemporary Prejudice and Urban Whites' Support for Affirmative Action and Government Help," *Social Problems* 46 (1999).

129. Ibid.

130. C. K. Jacobson, "Resistance to Affirmative Action: Self-Interest or Racism?" *Journal of Conflict Resolution* 29 (1985).

131. P. M. Sniderman and T. Piazza, *The Scar of Race* (Cambridge: Harvard University Press, 1993). The correlations appear on page 94. However, Sniderman and Piazza do not

interpret the association as an indication that racial prejudice influences attitudes toward affirmation action. Because some racial prejudices (e.g., the belief that Blacks are born with less ability than Whites) show only a small correlation, Sniderman and Piazza conclude that racial prejudice plays only a small role in anti–affirmative action opinions.

132. Bobo and Kluegel, "Opposition to Race-Targeting."

133. Bobo, "Race, Interest, and Beliefs About Affirmative Action."

134. See D. O. Sears et al., "Is It Really Racism? The Origins of White Americans' Opposition to Race-Targeted Policies," *Public Opinion Quarterly* 61 (1997).

135. M. Peffley and J. Hurwitz, "Whites' Stereotypes of Blacks: Sources and Political Consequences," in Hurwitz and Peffley, *Perception and Prejudice: Race and Politics in the United States.*

136. E. Hayes-James et al., "Prejudice Matters: Understanding Reactions of Whites to Affirmative Action Programs Targeted to Benefit Blacks," *Journal of Applied Psychology* 86 (2001).

137. B. L. Little, W. D. Murry, and J. C. Wimbush, "Perceptions of Workplace Affirmative Action Plans: A Psychological Perspective," *Group and Organizational Management* 23 (1998).

138. J. N. Sawires and M. J. Peacock, "Symbolic Racism and Voting Behavior on Proposition 209," *Journal of Applied Social Psychology* 30 (2000).

139. D. A. Mack et al., "Motivation to Control Prejudice as a Mediator of Identity and Affirmative Action Attitudes," *Journal of Applied Social Psychology* 32 (2002).

140. K. R. Jacob Arriola and E. R. Cole, "Framing the Affirmative Action Debate: Attitudes Toward Out-Group Members and White Identity," *Journal of Applied Social Psychology* 31 (2001).

141. See D. A. Kravitz et al., *Affirmative Action: A Review of Psychological and Behavioral Research* (Bowling Green: Society for Industrial and Organizational Psychology, 1997). See also F. J. Crosby, B. M. Ferdman, and B. R. Wingate, "Addressing and Redressing Discrimination: Affirmative Action in Social Psychological Perspective," in *Blackwell Handbook of Social Psychology: Intergroup Processes,* ed. R. Brown and S. Gaertner (Malden: Blackwell, 2001). In a related vein, Bobo and Kluegel, "Opposition to Race-Targeting," 446–74, and Williams, "Traditional and Contemporary Prejudice and Urban Whites' Support for Affirmative Action and Government Help," 504–6, also review the not-inconsequential literature showing that Whites with anti-Black bias tend to give limited support to a range of race-targeted policies including busing and government support for Blacks. How racism and conservatism differ is discussed in P. M. Sniderman et al., "The New Racism," *American Journal of Political Science* 35 (1991).

142. Studies show how the belief in individual meritocracy shapes attitudes. See M. Kemmelmeier, "The Individualist Self and Attitudes Toward Affirmative Action: Evidence from Priming Experiments" (paper presented at the Biannual Conference of the Society for the Psychological Study of Social Issues, Minneapolis, June 2000). On the issue of individualism and American distrust of affirmative action–like solutions to discrimination, see also K. Ozawa, M. Crosby, and F. J. Crosby, "Individualism and Resistance to Affirmative Action: A Comparison of Japanese and American Samples," *Journal of Applied Social Psychology* 26 (1996).

143. E. G. Carmines and C. G. Layman, "When Prejudice Matters: The Impact of Racial Stereotypes on the Racial Policy Preferences of Democrats and Republicans," in Hurwitz and Peffley, *Perceptions and Prejudice.*

144. See H. J. Smith and T. R. Tyler, "Justice and Power: When Will Justice Concerns Encourage the Advantaged to Support Policies Which Redistribute Economic Resources and the Disadvantaged to Willingly Obey the Law?" *European Journal of Social Psychology* 26 (1996).

145. One study of the reasoning of professors showed the importance of competing conceptions of justice, relative to racial prejudice, in determining people's reactions to affirmative action. E. C. Vozzola and A. Higgins-D'Alessandro, "Competing Conceptions of Justice: Faculty Moral Reasoning About Affirmative Action," *Journal of Adult Development* 7 (2000). In another series of experiments, Ramona Bobocel and associates showed that prejudice generally predicted opposition to nonpreferential policies (e.g., mentoring) while adherence to strong justice norms predicted opposition to preferential treatment. However, when participants were aware of high levels of discrimination, those with a strong adherence to justice norms were much less likely to oppose preferences than participants without that adherence. See D. R. Bobocel et al., "Justice-Based Opposition to Social Policies: Is It Genuine?" *Journal of Personality and Social Psychology* 75 (1998); and D. R. Bobocel et al., "Policies to Redress Social Injustice: Is the Concern for Justice a Cause Both of Support and of Opposition?" in *The Justice Motive in Everyday Life,* ed. M. Ross and D. Miller (New York: Cambridge University Press, 2002). See also L. S. Son Hing, D. R. Bobocel, and M. P. Zanna, "Meritocracy and Opposition to Affirmative Action: Making Concessions in the Face of Discrimination," *Journal of Personality and Social Psychology* 83 (2002).

146. J. R. Kluegel and E. R. Smith, "Affirmative Action Attitudes: Effects of Self-Interest, Racial Affect, and Stratification Beliefs on Whites' Views," *Social Forces* 61 (1983).

147. F. Pratto et al., "Social Dominance Orientation: A Personality Variable Predicting Social and Political Attitudes," *Journal of Personality and Social Psychology* 67 (1994).

148. See J. Sidanius, *Social Dominance: An Intergroup Theory of Social Hierarchy and Oppression* (New York: Cambridge University Press, 1999); J. Sidanius, F. Pratto, and L. Bobo, "Racism, Conservatism, Affirmative Action, and Intellectual Sophistication: A Matter of Principled Conservatism or Group Dominance?" *Journal of Personality and Social Psychology* 70 (1996); and J. T. Jost and E. P. Thompson, "Group-Based Dominance and Opposition to Equality as Independent Predictors of Self-Esteem, Ethnocentrism, and Social Policy Attitudes Among African Americans and European Americans," *Journal of Experimental Social Psychology* 36 (2000).

149. Blind adherence to the principles of (individualistic) meritocracy helps preserve the status quo. See A. Hurtado, C. Haney, and E. E. Garcia, "Becoming the Mainstream: Merit, Changing Demographics, and Higher Education in California," *La Raza Law Journal* 10 (1998); and M. S. Moses, "Affirmative Action and the Creation of More Favorable Contexts of Choice," *American Educational Research Journal* 38 (2001).

150. C. Federico and J. Sidanius, "Racism, Ideology, and Affirmative Action Revisited: The Antecedents and Consequences of 'Principled Objections' to Affirmative Action," *Journal of Personality and Social Psychology* 82 (2002). C. Federico and J. Sidanius, "Sophistication and the Antecedents of Whites' Racial-Policy Attitudes: Racism, Ideology, and Affirmative Action in America," *Public Opinion Quarterly* 66 (2002). The fact that the association between conservatism and racism is stronger among the well-educated and politically sophisticated than among the poorly educated and politically unsophisticated is in direct contradiction to the predictions made by Paul Sniderman. Such a pattern undermines the claim that opposition to affirmative action is principled reasoning.

151. A number of researchers have documented that support for affirmative action bears an inverse relationship to perceptions of discrimination. Those who think that discrimination is not a serious problem tend not to like affirmative action. See J. R. Kluegel and E. R. Smith, *Beliefs About Inequality : Americans' Views of What Is and What Ought to Be, Social Institutions and Social Change* (New York: de Gruyter, 1986). For commentary, see A. M. Konrad and F. Linnehan, "Race and Sex Differences in Line Managers' Reactions to Equal Employment Opportunity and Affirmative Action Interventions," *Group and Organizational Management* 20 (1995).

152. See M. B. Brewer, "In-Group Bias in the Minimal Intergroup Situation: A Cognitive-Motivational Analysis," *Psychological Bulletin* 86 (1979); M. B. Brewer, "Ingroup Identification and Intergroup Conflict: When Does Ingroup Love Become Outgroup Hate?" in *Social Identity, Intergroup Conflict, and Conflict Reduction.* Rutgers Series on Self and Social Identity, ed. R. D. Ashmore and L. Jussim (London: Oxford University Press, 2001); M. Hewstone, F. Fincham, and J. Jaspars, "Social Categorization and Similarity in Intergroup Behaviour: A Replication with "Penalties," *European Journal of Social Psychology* 11, no. 1 (1981); M. Hewstone, M. Argyle, and A. Furnham, "Favouritism, Fairness and Joint Profit in Long-Term Relationships," *European Journal of Social Psychology* 12 (1982); and M. Hewstone, M. Rubin, and H. Willis, "Intergroup Bias," *Annual Review of Psychology* 53, no. 1 (2002).

153. Stereotypes that are learned do not relate only to the "other" or to "out-groups." A former student told me that he learned to feel ashamed of being poor and Jewish by noticing that his father attempted to put on airs whenever Gentiles were around.

154. Representative publications by Devine and her colleagues include P. Devine, "Stereotypes and Prejudice: Their Automatic and Controlled Components," *Journal of Personality and Social Psychology* 56 (1989); P. G. Devine et al., "Prejudice with and Without Compunction," *Journal of Personality and Social Psychology* 60 (1991); P. G. Devine and M. J. Monteith, "The Role of Discrepancy-Associated Affect in Prejudice Reduction," in Mackie and Hamilton, *Affect, Cognition, and Stereotyping;* P. G. Devine and A. J. Elliot, "Are Racial Stereotypes Really Fading? The Princeton Trilogy Revisited," *Personality and Social Psychology Bulletin* 21 (1995); J. R. Zywerink et al., "Prejudice Toward Blacks: With and Without Compunction? *Basic and Applied Social Psychology* 18 (1996); M. J. Monteith, J. W. Sherman, and P. G. Devine, "Suppression as a Stereotype Control Strategy," *Personality and Social Psychology Review* 2 (1998); E. A. Plant and P. G. Devine, "Internal and External Motivation to Respond Without Prejudice," *Journal of Personality and Social Psychology* 75 (1998); E. A. Plant and P. G. Devine, "Responses to Other-Imposed Pro-Black Pressure: Acceptance or Backlash?" *Journal of Experimental Social Psychology* 37 (2001).

Chapter 7: Conclusions and Speculations

1. C. M. Swain, *The New White Nationalism: Its Threat to Integration* (New York: Cambridge University Press, 2002).

2. In contrast, Justice Ginsberg's dissent in *Adarand,* joined by Justice Breyer, was much more explicit. It specifically mentioned the conviction that "a carefully designed affirmative action program" may help the nation finally realize the dreams of the Equal Protection Clause of the Fourteenth Amendment.

3. E. Blum and M. Levin, "Racial Profiling: Wrong for Police, Wrong for Universities," *Washington Times,* May 17, 1999, reprinted in F. J. Crosby and C. VanDeVeer, *Sex, Race, and Merit: Debating Affirmative Action in Education and Employment* (Ann Arbor: University of Michigan Press, 2000), quote on 67.

4. Ibid.

5. See G. Ezorsky, *Racism and Justice: The Case for Affirmative Action* (Ithaca, N.Y.: Cornell University Press, 1991). Also see A. Perlo, "The Digital Divide and Institutional Racism," *Political Affairs* 80 (2001). For an interesting case study of how White people can be blind to the forces of institutional racism and to their role in perpetuating racism, see J. L. Pierce, "'Racing for Innocence': Whiteness, Corporate Culture, and the Backlash Against Affirmative Action," *Qualitative Sociology* 26 (2003).

6. See M. Marable, "Staying on the Path to Racial Equality," in *The Affirmative Action Debate,* ed. G. E. Curry (Cambridge: Perseus, 1998).

7. J. L. Lichtman, J. C. Frye and H. Norton, "Why Women Need Affirmative Action," in Curry, *Affirmative Action Debate,* 179.

8. R. L. Woodson, Sr., "Personal Responsibility," in Curry, *Affirmative Action Debate,* 113.

9. M. F. Berry, "Affirmative Action: Why We Need It, Why It Is Under Attack" in Curry, *Affirmative Action Debate,* 311.

10. Marable, "Staying on the Path to Racial Equality," 12.

11. S. Steele, *The Content of Our Character: A New Vision of Race in America* (New York: St. Martin's, 1990).

12. S. Fish, "Reverse Racism, or How the Pot Got to Call the Kettle Black," *Atlantic Monthly,* November 1993.

13. G. W. Allport, *The Nature of Prejudice* (New York: Addison-Wesley, 1954).

14. Ibid., 218.

15. L. S. Son Hing, D. R. Bobocel, and M. P. Zanna, "Meritocracy and Opposition to Affirmative Action: Making Concessions in the Face of Discrimination," *Journal of Personality and Social Psychology* 83 (2002). One particularly noteworthy aspect of the work is that the researchers conducted both experimental and survey studies, thereby allowing for both strong causal inferences and generalizability.

16. J. Amirkhan et al., "Reflections on Affirmative Action Goals in Psychology Admissions," *Psychological Science* 6 (1995).

17. See B. W. Pelham and J. J. Hetts, "Underworked and Overpaid: Elevated Entitlement in Men's Self-Pay," *Journal of Experimental Social Psychology* 37 (2001). For an analysis of the two "angry white men" who started Proposition 209, see N. Lemann, "Taking Affirmative Action Apart," *New York Times Magazine,* June 11, 1995.

18. N. R. Branscombe, "Thinking About One's Gender Group's Privileges or Disadvantages: Consequences for Well-Being in Women and Men," *British Journal of Social Psychology* 37 (1998). See also D. Kobrynowicz and N. R. Branscombe, "Who Considers Themselves Victims of Discrimination? Individual Difference Predictors of Perceived Discrimination in Women and Men," *Psychology of Women Quarterly* 21 (1997); and H. S. Shorey, G. Cowan, and M. P. Sullivan, "Predicting Perceptions of Discrimination Among Hispanics and Anglos," *Hispanic Journal of Behavioral Sciences* 24 (2002).

19. Stephen Hawking, delivering a lecture on string theory and the Ekpyrotic Universe Model at California Institute of Technology on Mar. 15, 2002, noted: "We can have several different descriptions of the universe, all of which predict the same observations.

We cannot say that one description is more correct than another, just that it may be more convenient for a particular situation." (T. Ma, "Hawking Visit," *California Tech,* March 18, 2002, 1). This point of view is highly unusual and goes against the predominant positivist norms in the sciences and social sciences. Hawking was speaking of speculations about the origins of the universe. It would not be appropriate to permit ourselves the same explanatory liberties we accord to Hawking.

20. There are measures that test how people approach issues of justice. In 1975 Rubin and Peplau developed an instrument called the Just World Scale. See Z. Rubin and L. Peplau, "Who Believes in a Just World?" *Journal of Social Issues* 31, no. 3 (1975). Claudia Dalbert has updated the scale and adapted it for international use. See Claudia Dalbert, *The Justice Motive as a Personal Resource: Dealing with Challenges and Critical Life Events* (New York: Kluwer Academic/Plenum, 2001).

21. J. D. Skrentny, "Inventing Race," *The Public Interest* 40 (2002), 112.

22. See M. A. Fletcher, "For Asian Americans, a Barrier or a Boon," *Washington Post,* June 20, 1998, reprinted in Crosby and VanDeVeer, *Sex, Race, and Merit.*

23. Skrentny, "Inventing Race."

24. See C. Deitch, "Gender, Race, and Class Politics and the Inclusion of Women in Title VII of the 1964 Civil Rights Act," *Gender and Society* 7 (1993).

25. Furchtgott-Roth does acknowledge that in *Price Waterhouse v. Hopkins,* "the Supreme Court ruled that Anne Hopkins, who had been denied a partnership at a major accounting firm, had been the subject of unfair discrimination" and then concludes that sex discrimination is dead because the courts uphold the laws which, according to Furchtgott-Roth, are anti-discriminatory. See D. Furchtgott-Roth and C. Stolb, *Women's Figures: An Illustrated Guide to the Economic Progress of Women in America* (Washington D.C.: AEI, 1999). Also see the case Price Waterhouse v. Hopkins, 490 U.S. 228 (1989).

Bibliography

Adams, J. S. "Inequity in Social Exchange." In *Advances in Experimental Social Psychology*, ed. L. Berkowitz, 2:267–99. New York: Academic, 1965.

Affirmative Action Today: A Legal and Practical Analysis. Washington, D.C.: Bureau of National Affairs, 1986.

Aguirre, A., Jr., Martinez, R., and Hernandez, A. "Majority and Minority Faculty Perceptions in Academe." *Research in Higher Education* 34 (1993): 371–85.

Allport, G. W. *The Nature of Prejudice.* New York: Addison-Wesley, 1954.

American Bar Association. *Unfinished Business: Overcoming the Sisyphus Factor; A Report on the Status of Women in the Legal Profession.* Chicago: American Bar Association, 1995.

American Psychological Association. *Affirmative Action: Who Benefits?* Washington, D.C.: American Psychological Association, 1996.

Amirkhan, J., Betancourt, H., Graham, S., Lopez, S. R., and Weiner, B. "Reflections on Affirmative Action Goals in Psychology Admissions." *Psychological Science* 6 (1995): 140–48.

Andolina, M. W., and Mayer, J. D. "Demographic Shifts and Racial Attitudes." *Social Science Journal* 40 (2003): 19–31.

Aronson, J., Lustina, M., Keough, K., Brown, J. L., and Steele, C. M. "When White Men Can't Do Math: Necessary and Sufficient Factors in Stereotype Threat." *Journal of Experimental Social Psychology* 35 (1999): 29–46.

Arthur, W., Doverspike, D., and Fuentes, R. "Recipients' Affective Responses to Affirmative Action." *Behavioral Sciences and the Law* 10 (1992): 229–43.

Austin, W., and Walster, E. H. "Participants' Reactions to 'Equity with the World.'" *Journal of Experimental Social Psychology* 10 (1974): 528–48.

Ayres, I. *Pervasive Prejudice? Unconventional Evidence of Race and Gender Discrimination.* Chicago: University of Chicago Press, 2002.

Ayers, L. R. "Perceptions of Affirmative Action Among Its Beneficiaries." *Social Justice Research* 5 (1992): 223–38.

Baker, L. A., and Emery, R. E. "When Every Relationship Is Above Average: Perceptions and Expectations of Divorce at the Time of Marriage." *Law and Human Behavior* 17 (1993): 439–50.

Baldus, D., Woodworth, G., and Pulaski, C. *Equal Justice and the Death Penalty: A Legal and Empirical Analysis.* Boston: Northeastern University Press, 1990.

Banaji, M., and Hardin, C. T. "Automatic Stereotyping." *Psychological Science* 7 (1996): 136–41.

Banks, M. E. "The Significance of Race in Urban Elite Political Behavior." *Western Journal of Black Studies* 25 (2001): 117.

Barrett, G. V., and Morris, S. B. "The American Psychological Association's Amicus Curiae Brief in *Price Waterhouse v. Hopkins*." *Law and Human Behavior* 17 (1993): 201–15.

Bates, T. *Banking on Black Enterprise: The Potential of Emerging Firms for Revitalizing Urban Economies* (Washington, D.C.: Joint Center for Economic Studies, 1993).

Bates, T., and Williams, D. "Preferential Procurement Programs and Minority-Owned Businesses." *Journal of Urban Affairs* 17 (1995): 1–17.

Beaton, A. M., and Tougas, F. "Reactions to Affirmative Action: Group Membership and Social Justice." *Social Justice Research* 14 (2001): 61–78.

Becker, E. "Study Finds a Growing Gap Between Managerial Salaries for Men and Women." *New York Times,* Jan. 24, 2002, A24.

Beckwith, F. J., and Jones, T. E., eds. *Affirmative Action: Social Justice or Reverse Discrimination?* Amherst, N.Y.: Prometheus, 1997.

Bell, M. P., Harrison, D. A., and McLaughlin, M. E. "Forming, Changing, and Acting on Attitude Toward Affirmative Action Programs in Employment: A Theory-Driven Approach." *Journal of Applied Psychology* 85 (2000): 784–98.

Beller, A. H. "Occupational Segregation by Sex: Determinants and Changes." *Journal of Human Resources* 17 (1982): 371–92.

Bellinger, L., and Hillman, A. J. "Does Tolerance Lead to Better Partnering?" *Business and Society* 39 (2000): 323–37.

Belz, H. *Equality Transformed: A Quarter Century of Affirmative Action.* New Brunswick, N.J.: Transaction, 1991.

Bendick, M., Jr., "The Croson Decision Mandates That Set-Aside Programs Be Tools of Business Development," *George Mason University Civil Rights Law Journal* 1 (1990): 87–104.

Bendick, M., Jr., Jackson, C. W., and Reinoso, V. A. "Measuring Employment Discrimination Through Controlled Experiments." *Review of Black Political Economy* (Summer 1994): 24–28.

Bergmann, B. R. *In Defense of Affirmative Action.* New York: Basic, 1996.

Bielby, W. T. "Minimizing Workplace Gender and Racial Bias." *Contemporary Sociology* 29 (2000): 120–29.

Biernat, M., and Kobrynowicz, D. "Gender and Race-Based Standards of Competence: Lower Minimum Standards but Higher Standards for Devalued Groups." *Journal of Personality and Social Psychology* 72 (1997): 544–57.

Biernat, M., and Vescio, T. K. "Categorization and Stereotyping: Effects of Group Context on Memory and Social Judgment." *Journal of Experimental Social Psychology* 29 (1993): 166–202.

Billard, L. "Twenty Years Later: Is There Pay Equity for Academic Women?" *Thought and Action* 10 (1994): 115–44.

Birt, C. M., and Dion, K. L. "Relative Deprivation Theory and Responses to Discrimination in a Gay Male and Lesbian Sample." *British Journal of Social Psychology* 26 (1987): 139–45.

Blaine, B., Crocker, J., and Major, B. "The Unintended Negative Consequences of Sympathy for the Stigmatized." *Journal of Applied Social Psychology* 25 (1995): 889–905.

Blanchard, F. A., and F. J. Crosby, eds. *Affirmative Action in Perspective.* New York: Springer-Verlag, 1989.

Blank, R. "An Analysis of Workers' Choices Between Employment in the Public and Private Sectors." *Industrial and Labor Relations Review* 38 (1985): 211–24.

Blau, F. D. "Trends in the Well-Being of American Women, 1970–1995." *Journal of Economic Literature* 36 (1998): 112–65.

Blau, F. D., and Graham, J. W. "Black-White Differences in Wealth and Asset Composition." *Quarterly Journal of Economics* 105 (1990): 321–29.

Blau, F. D., and Kahn, L. M. "Gender Differences in Pay." *Journal of Economic Perspectives* 14 (2000): 75–99.

———. "Swimming Upstream: Trends in Gender Wage Differential in the 1980s." *Journal of Labor Economics* 15 (1997): 1–42.

———. "Wage Structure and Gender Earnings Differentials: An International Comparison." *Economica* 63 (1996): 829–62.

Blum, E., and Levin, M. "Racial Profiling: Wrong for Police, Wrong for Universities." *Washington Times,* May 17, 1999.

Blum, J., and Ashenfelter, O., eds. *Evaluating the Labor Market Effects of Social Programs.* Princeton: Princeton University Press, 1976.

Bobo, L. "Attitudes Toward Black Political Movement: Trends, Meaning and Effects on Racial Policy Preferences." *Social Psychology Quarterly* 51, no. 4 (1988): 287–302.

———. "Race, Interest, and Beliefs About Affirmative Action: Unanswered Questions and New Directions." *American Behavioral Scientist* 41 (1998): 985–1003.

Bobo, L., and Hutchings, V. L. "Perceptions of Racial Group Competition: Extending Blumer's Theory of Group Position to a Multiracial Social Context." *American Sociological Review* 61 (1996): 951–72.

Bobo, L., and Kluegel, J. R. "Opposition to Race-Targeting: Self-Interest, Stratification Ideology, or Racial Attitudes?" *American Sociological Review* 58 (1993): 443–64.

Bobo, L., and Suh, S. A. *Surveying Racial Discrimination: Analyses from a Multi-Ethnic Labor Market.* Working Paper 75. New York: Russell Sage Foundation, 1996.

Bobocel, D. R., and Debeyer, M. "Explaining Controversial Organizational Decisions: To Legitimize the Means or the Ends?" *Social Justice Research* 11 (1998): 21–40.

Bobocel, D. R., and Farrell, A. C. "Sex-Based Promotion Decisions and Inter-actional Fairness: Investigating the Influence of Managerial Accounts." *Journal of Applied Psychology* 81 (1996): 22–35.

Bobocel, D. R., Son Hing, L. S., Davey, L. M., Stanley, D. J., and Zanna, M. P. "Justice-Based Opposition to Social Policies: Is It Genuine?" *Journal of Personality and Social Psychology* 75 (1998): 653–69.

Bowen, W. G., and Bok, D. C. *The Shape of the River: Long-Term Consequences of Considering Race in College and University Admissions.* Princeton: Princeton University Press, 1998.

Branscombe, N. R. "Thinking About One's Gender Group's Privileges or Dis-advantages: Consequences for Well-Being in Women and Men." *British Journal of Social Psychology* 37 (1998): 167–84.

Brewer, M. B. "In-Group Bias in the Minimal Intergroup Situation: A Cogni-tive-Motivational Analysis." *Psychological Bulletin* 86 (1979): 307–24.

———. "Ingroup Identification and Intergroup Conflict: When Does Ingroup Love Become Outgroup Hate?" In *Social Identity, Intergroup Conflict, and Conflict Reduction.* Rutgers Series on Self and Social Identity, ed. R. D. Ashmore and L. Jussim, 17–41. London: Oxford University Press, 2001.

Bronstein, P., and Pfennig, J. L. "Beliefs Versus Realities: Response to Elliot." *American Psychologist* 44 (1989): 1550.

———. "Misperceptions of Women and Affirmative Action Principles in Fac-ulty Hiring." *American Psychologist* 43 (1988): 668–69.

Broverman, I., Vogel, S., Broverman, D., Clarkson, F., and Rosenkrantz, P. "Sex-Role Stereotypes: A Reappraisal." *Journal of Social Issues* 28, no. 2 (1972): 59–78.

Brown, R. P., Charnsangavej, T., Keough, K. A., Newman, M. L., and Rent-frow, P. J. "Putting the "Affirm" into Affirmative Action: Preferential Se-lection and Academic Performance." *Journal of Personality and Social Psy-chology* 79 (2000): 736–47.

Brutus, S., and Ryan, A. N. "A New Perspective on Preferential Treatment: The Role of Ambiguity and Self-Efficacy." *Journal of Business and Psychology* 13 (1998): 157–78.

Budig, M. P., and England, P. "The Wage Penalty for Motherhood." *American Sociological Review* 66 (2001): 204–25.

Bumiller, K. *The Civil Rights Society: The Social Construction of Victims.* Balti-more: Johns Hopkins University Press, 1988.

———. "Victims in the Shadow of the Law: A Critique of the Model of Legal Protection." *Signs: Journal of Women in Culture and Society* 12 (1987): 421–39.

Burstein, P. "'Reverse Discrimination' Cases in the Federal Courts: Mobiliza-tion by a Countermovement." *Sociological Quarterly* 32 (1991): 511–28.

Button, J. W., and Rienzo, B. A. "The Impact of Affirmative Action on Blacks." *Social Science Quarterly* 84 (2003): 1–14.

Caputo, R. K. "Discrimination and Human Capital." *Journal of Sociology and Social Welfare* 29 (2002) 105–20.

Card, D., and Krueger, A. B. "Labor Market Effects of School Quality: Theory and Evidence." In *Does Money Matter? The Effects of School Resources on Student Achievement and Adult Success,* ed. G. Burtless, 97–140. Washington, D.C.: Brookings Institution Press, 1996.

Carter, S. L. *Reflections of an Affirmative Action Baby.* New York: Basic, 1991.

Chacko, T. I. "Women and Equal Employment Opportunity: Some Unintended Effects." *Journal of Applied Psychology* 67 (1982): 119–23.

Chen, E. S., and Tyler, T. R. "Cloaking Power: Legitimizing Myths and the Psychology of the Advantaged." In *The Use and Abuse of Power: Multiple Perspectives on the Causes of Corruption,* ed. A. Y. Lee-Chai and J. A. Bargh, 241–61. Philadelphia: Taylor and Francis, 2001.

Chesler, M., and Peet, M. "White Student Views of Affirmative Action on Campus." *Diversity Factor* 10, no. 2 (2002): 21–27.

Chung-Yan, G. A., and Cronshaw, S. F. "A Critical Examination and Analysis of Cognitive Ability Tests Using Thorndike Model of Fairness." *Journal of Occupational and Organizational Psychology* 75 (2002): 489–521.

Citrin, J. "Affirmative Action in the People's Court." *Public Interest* 122 (1996): 39–48.

Clayton, S. D. "Reactions to Social Categorizations: Evaluating One Argument Against Affirmative Action." *Journal of Applied Social Psychology* 26 (1996): 1472–93.

Clutterbuck, D., and Ragins, B. R. *Mentoring and Diversity: An International Perspective.* Boston: Butterworth and Heinemann, 2002.

Cohen, J. J. "The Consequences of Premature Abandonment of Affirmative Action in Medical School Admissions." *Journal of the American Medical Association* 289 (2003): 1143–49.

Cohen, M. N. *The Culture of Intolerance: Chauvinism, Class, and Racism in the United States.* New Haven: Yale University Press, 1998.

Collins, L. H. "Competition and Contact: The Dynamics Behind Resistance to Affirmative Action in Academe." In *Career Strategies for Women in Academe: Arming Athena,* ed. L. H. Collins and J. C. Chrisler. Thousand Oaks, Calif.: Sage, 1998.

Connerly, W. "U.C. Must End Affirmative Action." *San Francisco Chronicle,* May 3, 1995.

Cordova, D. I. "Cognitive Limitations and Affirmative Action: The Effects of Aggregate Versus Sequential Data in the Perception of Discrimination." *Social Justice Research* 5 (1992): 319–33.

Costantini, E., and King, J. "Affirmative Action: The Configuration, Concomitants, and Antecedents of Student Opinion." *Youth and Society* 16 (1985): 499–525.

Cox, T., Jr., and Blake, S. "Managing Cultural Diversity: Implications for Organizational Competitiveness." *Executive* 5, no. 3 (1991): 45–56.

Crosby, F. J. "Confessions of an Affirmative Action Mama." In *Off White: Readings on Race, Power, and Society,* ed. L. Weis, M. Fine, L. C. Powell, and L. M. Wong, 179–86. New York: Routledge, 1997.

———. "The Denial of Personal Discrimination." *American Behavioral Scientist* 27 (1984): 371–86.

———. *Relative Deprivation and Working Women.* New York: Oxford University Press, 1982.

———. "Relative Deprivation in Organizational Settings." In *Research in Organizational Behavior,* ed. B. Staw and L. L. Cummings, 51–93. Greenwich, Conn.: JAI, 1984.

———. "A Rose by Any Other Name." In *Quoten und Gleichstellung von Frau und Mann,* ed. K. Arioli, 151–67. Basel: Helberg and Lichtenhan, 1996.

———. "Understanding Affirmative Action." *Basic and Applied Social Psychology* 15 (1994): 13–41.

Crosby, F. J., Allen, B., and Opotow, S. "Changing Patterns of Income Among Black and Whites Before and After E.O. 11246." *Social Justice Research* 5 (1992): 335–41.

Crosby, F. J., Bromley, S., and Saxe, L. "Recent Unobtrusive Studies of Black and White Discrimination and Prejudice: A Literature Review." *Psychological Bulletin* 87 (1980): 546–63.

Crosby, F. J., Burris, L., Censor, C., and MacKethan, E. R. "Two Rotten Apples Spoil the Justice Barrel." In *Justice in Social Relations,* ed. H. Bierhoff, R. Cohen, and J. Greenberg, 267–81. New York: Plenum, 1986.

Crosby, F. J., Clayton, S., Alksnis, O., and Hemker, K. "Cognitive Biases in the Perception of Discrimination: The Importance of Format." *Sex Roles* 14 (1986): 637–46.

Crosby, F. J., and Cordova, D. I. "Words Worth of Wisdom: Toward an Understanding of Affirmative Action." *Journal of Social Issues* 52, no. 2 (1996): 33–49.

Crosby, F. J., Ferdman, B. M., and Wingate, B. R. "Addressing and Redressing Discrimination: Affirmative Action in Social Psychological Perspective." In *Blackwell Handbook of Social Psychology: Intergroup Processes,* ed. R. Brown and S. Gaertner, 495–513. Malden, Mass.: Blackwell, 2001.

Crosby, F. J., and Franco, J. "Anger as a Function of Rule Change." Paper presented at the 25th Annual Meeting of the International Society of Political Psychology, July 2002.

Crosby, F. J., Iyer, A., Clayton, S., and Downing, R. A. "Affirmative Action: Psychological Data and the Policy Debates." *American Psychologist* 58 (2003): 93–115.

Crosby, F. J., and Konrad, A. M. "Affirmative Action in Employment." *Diversity Factor* 10, no. 2 (2002): 5–9.

Crosby, F. J., Pufall, A., Snyder, R. C., O'Connell, M., and Whalen, P. "The Denial of Personal Disadvantage Among You, Me and All the Other Ostriches." In *Gender and Thought,* ed. M. Crawford and M. Gentry, 79–99. New York: Springer-Verlag, 1989.

Crosby, F. J., and VanDeVeer, C. *Sex, Race, and Merit: Debating Affirmative Action in Education and Employment.* Ann Arbor: University of Michigan Press, 2000.

Curry, G. E., ed. *The Affirmative Action Debate.* Cambridge, Mass.: Perseus, 1998.

D'Emilio, J. *Sexual Politics, Sexual Communities: The Making of a Homosexual Minority in the United States, 1940–1970.* Chicago: University of Chicago Press, 1983.

D'Souza, D. *Illiberal Education: The Politics of Race and Sex on Campus.* Detroit: Free Press, 1991.

Dalbert, C. "Coping with an Unjust Fate: The Case of Structural Unemployment." *Social Justice Research* 10 (1997): 175–89.

———. *The Justice Motive as a Personal Resource: Dealing with Challenges and Critical Life Events.* New York: Kluwer Academic/Plenum, 2001.

Dale, C. V. *Congressional Research Service Report to Robert Dole: Compilation and Overview of Federal Laws and Regulations Establishing Affirmative Action Goals or Other Preferences Based on Race, Gender, and Ethnicity.* Washington, D.C.: Congressional Research Service, Library of Congress, 1995.

Dalma, S. "The University of Michigan's Excuse for Racial Discrimination." *Weekly Standard,* Mar. 26, 2001, 26–29

Darlington, R. B. "On Race and Intelligence: A Commentary on Affirmative Action, the Evolution of Intelligence, the Regression Analyses in the Bell Curve, and Jensen's Two-Level Theory." *Psychology, Public Policy, and Law* 2 (1996): 635–45.

Davis, L. R. "Racial Diversity in Higher Education." *Journal of Applied Behavioral Science* 38 (2002): 137–55.

Dawes, R. M. "Affirmative Action Programs: Discontinuities Between Thoughts About Individuals and Thoughts About Groups." In *Applications of Heuristics and Biases to Social Issues,* ed. R. S. Tindale, L. Heath, J. Edwards, E. J. Posavac, F. B. Bryant, E. Henderson-King, Y. Suarez-Balcazar, and J. Myers, 223–39. New York: Plenum, 1994.

"Death Penalty Sentencing: Research Indicates Pattern of Racial Disparities." Report to Senate and House Committee on the Judiciary, 101st Congress, 2d Session. Washington D.C.: Government Accounting Office, 1990.

Deitch, C. "Gender, Race, and Class Politics and the Inclusion of Women in Title VII of the 1964 Civil Rights Act." *Gender and Society* 7 (1993): 183–203.

Desmarais, S., and Curtis, J. "Gender and Perceived Pay Entitlement: Testing for Effects of Experience with Income." *Journal of Personality and Social Psychology* 72 (1997): 141–50.

Detterman, D. K. "Tests, Affirmative Action in University Admissions, and the American Way." *Psychology, Public Policy, and Law* 6 (2000): 44–55.

Deutsch, M. "Equity, Equality, and Need: What Determines Which Value Will Be Used as the Basis of Distributive Justice?" *Journal of Social Issues* 31, no. 3 (1975): 137–49.

Devine, P. G. "Stereotypes and Prejudice: Their Automatic and Controlled Components." *Journal of Personality and Social Psychology* 56 (1989): 5–18.

Devine, P. G., and Elliot, A. J. "Are Racial Stereotypes Really Fading? The Princeton Trilogy Revisited." *Personality and Social Psychology Bulletin* 21 (1995): 1139–50.

Devine, P. G., Monteith, M. J., Zywerink, J. R., and Elliot, A. J. "Prejudice with and Without Compunction." *Journal of Personality and Social Psychology* 60 (1991): 817–30.

Dion, K. L., and Kawakami, K. "Ethnicity and Perceived Discrimination in Toronto: Another Look at the Personal/Group Discrimination Discrepancy." *Canadian Journal of Behavioural Science* 28, no. 3 (1996): 203–13.

"Disabling the National Education Defence System." *The Economist*, Feb. 24, 2001.

Dornbusch, S. M. *Off the Track*. Ann Arbor: Society for Research on Adolescence, 1994.

Doverspike, D., and Arthur, W. "Race and Sex Differences in Reactions to Assimilated Selection Decision Involving Race-Based Affirmative Action." *Journal of Black Psychology* 21 (1995): 181–200.

Dovidio J. F., and Gaertner, S. L. "Affirmative Action, Unintentional Racial Biases, and Intergroup Relations." In *Intergroup Relations: Essential Readings,* ed. M. A. Hogg and D. Abrams, 146–61. Philadelphia: Psychology Press/Taylor and Francis, 2001.

———. "Aversive Racism and Selection Decisions: 1989 and 1999." *Psychological Science* 11 (2000): 315–19.

Dovidio, J. F., Johnson, C., Gaertner, S. L., Validzic, A., Ho, A., and Eisinger, N. "Racial Bias and the Role of Implicit and Explicit Attitudes." Paper presented at the Annual Meeting of the Eastern Psychological Association, Providence, R.I., April 1994.

Dovidio, J. F., Smith, J. K., Donnella, A. G., and Gaertner, S. L. "Racial Attitudes and the Death Penalty." *Journal of Applied Social Psychology* 27 (1997): 1468–87.

Downing, R., Lubensky, M. E., Sincharoen, S., Gurin, P., Crosby, F. J., Quierolo, S., and Franco, J. "Affirmative Action in Higher Education." *Diversity Factor* 10, no. 2 (2002): 15–20.

Durr, M., and Logan, J. R. "Racial Submarkets in Government Employment:

African American Managers in New York State." *Sociological Forum* 12 (1997): 353–70.

Dworkin, R. "The Court and the University." *New York Review of Books,* May 15, 2003.

Eagly, A. H., and Johnson, B. T. "Gender and Leadership Style: A Meta-Analysis." *Psychological Bulletin* 108 (1990): 233–56.

Eagly, A. H., and Karau, S. J. "Gender and the Emergence of Leaders: A Meta-Analysis." *Journal of Personality and Social Psychology* 60 (1991): 685–710.

Eagly, A. H., Karau, S. J., and Makhijani, M. G. "Gender and Effectiveness of Leaders: A Meta-Analysis." *Psychological Bulletin* 117 (1995): 125–45.

Eagly, A. H., Makhijani, M. G., and Klonsky, B. G. "Gender and the Evaluation of a Meta-Analysis." *Psychological Bulletin* 111 (1992): 3–22.

Edelman, L. B., and Petterson, S. "Symbols and Substance in Organizational Response to Civil Rights Law." Paper presented at the Annual Meeting of the American Sociological Association, Miami Beach, Fla., August 1993.

Edley, C. F. *Not All Black and White: Affirmative Action, Race, and American Values.* New York: Hill and Wang, 1996.

Edwards, J. C., Maldonado, F. G. J., and Calvin, J. A. "The Effects of Differently Weighting Interview Scores on the Admission of Underrepresented Minority Medical Students." *Academic Medicine* 74 (1999): 59–61.

"EEO Policies and Programs." Personnel Policies Forum Survey 141. Washington, D.C.: Bureau of National Affairs, 1986.

Eitzen, D. S., and Zinn, M. B. *Social Problems.* 8th ed. Boston: Allyn and Bacon, 2000.

Elizondo, E., and Crosby, F. J., "Attitudes Toward Affirmative Action as a Function of the Strength of Ethnic Identity Among Latino College Students." *Journal of Applied Social Psychology.* In press.

Elizondo, E., and Hu, L. "Extending Latino Identity Among a Sample of College Students." Paper presented at the Annual Meeting of the International Society of Political Psychology, Amsterdam, 1999.

Elliot, R. "Preferential Hiring of Women in Psychology Is Unwarranted and Unwise: Reply to Bronstein and Pfennig." *American Psychologist* 44 (1989): 1549–50.

Elvira, M. M., and Zatzick, C. D. "Who's Displaced First? The Role of Race in Layoff Decisions." *Industrial Relations* 41 (2002): 329–60.

Emerson, M. O., Yancey, E., and Chai, K. J. "Does Race Matter in Residential Segregation? Exploring the Preferences of White Americans." *American Sociological Review* 66 (2001): 922–35.

Enchautegui, M. E., Fix, M., Loprest, P., von der Lippe, S. C., and Wissocker, D. *Do Minority-Owned Businesses Get a Fair Share of Government Contracts?* Washington, D.C.: Urban Institute, 1998.

Epstein, R. A. "A Rational Basis for Affirmative Action." *Michigan Law Review* 100 (2002): 2036–61.

Evans, D. C. "A Comparison of the Other-Directed Stigmatization Produced by Legal and Illegal Forms of Affirmative Action." *Journal of Applied Psychology* 88 (2003): 121–30.

Everson, H. T. "A Principled Design Framework for College Admissions Tests: An Affirming Research Agenda." *Psychology, Public Policy, and Law* 6 (2000): 112–20.

Ezorsky, G. *Racism and Justice: The Case for Affirmative Action.* Ithaca, N.Y.: Cornell University Press, 1991.

Federico, C., and Sidanius, J. "Racism, Ideology, and Affirmative Action Revisited: The Antecedents and Consequences of 'Principled Objections' to Affirmative Action." *Journal of Personality and Social Psychology* 82 (2002): 488–502.

———. "Sophistication and the Antecedents of Whites' Racial-Policy Attitudes: Racism, Ideology, and Affirmative Action in America." *Public Opinion Quarterly* 66 (2002): 145–76.

Final Report: City of Tallahassee MBE Disparity Fact-Finding Report. Tallahassee, Fla.: MGT of America, 1990.

Fine, T. S. "The Impact of Issue Framing on Public Opinion: Toward Affirmative Action Programs." *Social Science Journal* 29 (1992): 323–34.

———. "Public Opinion Toward Equal Opportunity Issues: The Role of Attitudinal and Demographic Forces Among African Americans." *Sociological Perspectives* 35 (1992): 705–20.

Firestone, J. M. "Occupational Segregation: Comparing the Civilian and Military Workforce." *Armed Forces and Society* 18 (1992): 363–81.

Fish, S. "Reverse Racism, or How the Pot Got to Call the Kettle Black." *Atlantic Monthly,* November 1993, 128–36.

Fiske, S. T., Bersoff, D. N., Borgida, E., Deaux, K., and Heilman, M. E. "What Constitutes a Scientific Review? A Majority Retort to Barrett and Morris." *Law and Human Behavior* 17 (1993): 217–33.

Fiske, S. T., and Taylor, S. E. *Social Cognition.* 2d ed. New York: McGraw-Hill, 1991.

Fix, M., and Struyk, R. J. *Clear and Convincing Evidence: Measurement of Discrimination in America.* Washington, D.C.: Urban Institute, 1992.

Fix, M., and Turner, M. A. eds. *A National Report Card on Discrimination in America: The Role of Testing.* Washington, D.C.: Urban Institute, 1999.

Fleming, J., Gill, G. R., and Swinton, D. H. *The Case for Affirmative Action for Blacks in Higher Education.* Washington, D.C.: Institute for the Study of Educational Policy, Howard University, 1978.

Fletcher, M. A. "For Asian Americans, a Barrier or a Boon." *Washington Post,* June 20, 1998.

Folger, R. "Distributive and Procedural Justice: Combined Impact of Voice and

Improvement on Experienced Inequity." *Journal of Personality and Social Psychology* 35 (1977): 108–19.

Ford, D. L. "Minority and Non-Minority MBA Progress in Business." In *Ensuring Minority Success in Corporate Management,* ed. D. E. Thompson and N. DiTomaso, 57–69. New York: Plenum, 1988.

Foster, M. D., and Matheson, K. "Double Relative Deprivation: Combining the Personal and the Political." *Personality and Social Psychology Bulletin* 21 (1995): 1167–77.

Fraser, J., and Kick, E. "The Interpretive Repertoires of Whites on Race-Targeted Policies: Claims of Reverse Discrimination." *Sociological Perspectives* 43 (2000): 13–28.

Fraser, S. *The Bell Curve Wars: Race, Intelligence, and the Future of America.* New York: Basic, 1995.

Fried, Y., Levi, A. S., Billings, S. W., and Kinsley, R. B. "The Relation Between Political Ideology and Attitudes Toward Affirmative Action Among African-Americans: The Moderating Effect of Racial Discrimination in the Workplace." *Human Relations* 54 (2001): 561–84.

Frieze, I. H., Olson, J. E., and Good, D. C. "Perceived and Actual Discrimination in the Salaries of Male and Female Managers." *Journal of Applied Social Psychology* 20 (1990): 46–67.

Fryer, G. E., Jr., Green, L. A., Vojir, C. P., Krugman, R. D., Miyoshi, T. J., Stine, C., and Miller, M. E. "Hispanic Versus White, Non-Hispanic Physician Medical Practices in Colorado." *Journal of Health Care for the Poor and Underserved* 12 (2001): 342–51.

Furchtgott-Roth, D., and Stolba, C. *Women's Figures: An Illustrated Guide to the Economic Progress of Women in America.* Washington D.C.: AEI, 1999.

Gaertner, S. L., and McLaughlin, J. P. "Racial Stereotypes: Associations and Ascriptions of Positive and Negative Characteristics." *Social Psychology Quarterly* 46 (1983): 23–30.

Gamson, W. A., and Modigliani, A. "The Changing Culture of Affirmative Action." In *Research in Political Sociology,* ed. R. D. Braungart, 137–77: Greenwich, Conn.: JAI, 1987.

Gandara, R. *Over the Ivy Walls: The Educational Mobility of Low-Income Chicanos.* Albany: State University of New York Press, 1995.

Garcia, L. T., Erskine, N., Hawn, K., and Casmay, S. R. "The Effect of Affirmative Action on Attributions About Minority Members." *Journal of Personality and Social Psychology* 49 (1981): 427–37.

Gilbert, J., and Stead, B. A. "Stigmatization Revisited: Does Diversity Management Make a Difference in Applicant Success?" *Group and Organization Management* 24 (1999): 239–56.

Gioia, D. A., and Sims, H. P., Jr. "Self-Serving Bias and Actor-Observer Differences in Organizations: An Empirical Analysis." *Journal of Applied Social Psychology* 15 (1985): 547–63.

Gitlin, T. "The Demonization of Political Correctness." *Dissent* 42 (1995): 487–97.

Glaser, J. M., "The Preference Puzzle." *Political Behavior* 23 (2001): 313–33.

Glass Ceiling Commission. *Good for Business: Making Full Use of the Nation's Human Capital.* Washington, D.C.: Department of Labor, 1995.

Glick, P., and Fiske, S. T. "The Ambivalent Sexism Inventory: Differentiating Hostile and Benevolent Sexism." *Journal of Personality and Social Psychology* 70 (1996): 491–512.

Glick, P., Fiske, S. T., Mladinic, A., Saiz, J. L., Abrams, D., Basseer, B., Adetoun, B., Osagie, J. E., Akande, A., Alao, A., Brunner, A., Willemsen, T. M., Chipeta, K., Dardenne, B., Dijksterhuis, A., Wigboldus, D., Eckes, T., Six-Materna, I., Exposito, F., Mmoya, M., Foddy, M., Kim, H. J., Lamerias, M., Sotelo, M. J., Mucchi-Faina, A., Romani, M., Sakalli, N., Udegbe, B., Yamamoto, M., Ui, M., Ferreira, M. C., and Lopez, W. L. "Beyond Prejudice as Simple Antipathy: Hostile and Benevolent Sexism Across Cultures." *Journal of Personality and Social Psychology* 79 (2000): 763–75.

Goldberg, P. "Are Women Prejudiced Against Women?" *Transaction* 5 (1968): 28–30.

Golden, H., Hinkle, S., and Crosby, F. J. "Reactions to Affirmative Action: Substance and Semantics." *Journal of Applied Social Psychology* 31 (2001): 73–88.

Goldstein, M., and Smith, R. S. "The Estimated Impact of the Anti-Discrimination Program Aimed at Federal Contractors." *Industrial and Labor Relations Review* 29 (1976): 523–43.

Gottfredson, L. S. "Racially Gerrymandering the Content of Police Tests to Satisfy the U.S. Justice Department: A Case Study." *Psychology, Public Policy, and Law* 2 (1996): 418–46.

———. "The Science and Politics of Race-Norming." *American Psychologist* 29 (1994): 955–63.

Gray, W. R. *The Four Faces of Affirmative Action: Fundamental Answers and Actions.* Westport: Greenwood, 2001.

Greenberg, J. "Approaching Equity and Avoiding Inequality in Groups and Organizations." In *Equity and Justice in Social Behavior,* ed. J. Greenberg and R. L. Cohen, 339–435. New York: Academic, 1982.

Greenlaw, P. S., and Jensen, S. S. "Race-Norming and the Civil Rights Act of 1991." *Public Personnel Management* 25 (1996): 13–24.

Guinier, L. "Commentary." *Law and Social Inquiry* 25 (2000): 565.

Guinier, L., and Sturms, S. *Who's Qualified?* Boston: Beacon, 2001.

Gullett, C. R. "Reverse Discrimination and Remedial Affirmative Action in Employment: Dealing with the Paradox of Nondiscrimination." *Public Personnel Management* 29 (2000): 107–18.

Gurin, P., Dey, E. L., Hurtado, S., and Gurin, G. "Diversity and Higher Education: Theory and Impact on Educational Outcomes." *Harvard Educational Review* 72 (2002): 330–66.

Gurin, P., Miller, A. H., and Gurin, G. "Stratum Identification and Consciousness." *Social Psychology Quarterly* 43 (1980): 30–47.

Gutek, B. A. *Sex and the Workplace: Impact of Sexual Behavior and Harassment on Women, Men, and Organizations.* San Francisco: Jossey-Bass, 1985.

———. "Working Environments." In *Encyclopedia of Women and Gender,* ed. J. Worell, 1191–204. New York: Academic, 2001.

Gutek, B. A., ed. *Sex Role Stereotyping and Affirmative Action Policy.* Los Angeles: University of California Institute of Industrial Relations, 1982.

Gutek, B. A., and Done, R. "Sexual Harassment." In *Handbook of the Psychology of Women and Gender,* ed. R. K. Unger, 367–87. New York: Wiley, 2001.

Haemmerlie, F. M., and Montgomery, R. L. "Goldberg Revisited: Pro-Female Evaluation Bias and Changed Attitudes Toward Women by Engineering Students." *Journal of Social Behavior and Personality* 6 (1991): 179–94.

Hafer, C. L., and Olson, J. M. "Beliefs in a Just World and Reactions to Personal Deprivation." *Journal of Personality and Social Psychology* 57 (1989): 799–823.

———. "Beliefs in a Just World, Discontent, and Assertive Actions by Working Women." *Personality and Social Psychology Bulletin* 1 (1993): 30–38.

———. "Individual Differences in the Belief in a Just World and Responses to Personal Misfortune." In *Responses to Victimizations and Belief in a Just World: Critical Issues in Social Justice,* ed. L. Montada and M. J. Lerner, 65–86. New York: Plenum, 1998.

Hall, R. E. "Occupational Aspiration Among African-Americans: A Case for Affirmative Action." *Journal of Sociology and Social Welfare* 23 (1996): 117–28.

Harris L. "Unequal Terms." *Columbia Journalism Review* 30, no. 5 (1992): 20.

Hartigan, J. A., and Wigdor, A. K. *Fairness in Employment Testing: Validity, Generalization, Minority Issues, and the General Aptitude Test Battery.* Washington, D.C.: National Academy Press, 1989.

Hattrup, K., Rock, J., and Scalia, C. "The Effects of Varying Conceptualizations of Job Performance on Adverse Impact, Minority Hiring, and Predicted Performance." *Journal of Applied Psychology* 82 (1997): 656–64.

Hayes-James, E., Brief, A. P., Dietz, J., and Cohen, R. R. "Prejudice Matters: Understanding Reactions of Whites to Affirmative Action Programs Targeted to Benefit Blacks." *Journal of Applied Psychology* 86 (2001): 1120–28.

Healy, P. "Affirmative Action Survives at Colleges in Some States Covered by *Hopwood* Ruling." *Chronicle of Higher Education* 44, no. 33 (1998): A42–A43.

———. "A Lawsuit Against Georgia University System Attacks a Range of Race-Based Policies." *Chronicle of Higher Education* 43, no. 27 (1997): A25–A26.

Heckman, J. J., and Payner, B. S. "Determining the Impact of Federal Antidiscrimination Policy on the Economic Status of Blacks: A Study of South Carolina." *American Economic Review* 79 (1989): 138–77.

Heckman, J. J., and Wolpin, K. I. "Does the Contract Compliance Program Work? An Analysis of Chicago Data." *Industrial and Labor Relations Review* 29 (1976): 544–64.

Heilman, M. E., and Alcott, V. B. "What I Think You Think of Me: Women's Reactions to Being Viewed as Beneficiaries of Preferential Selection." *Journal of Applied Psychology* 86 (2001): 574–82.

Heilman, M. E., Battle, W. S., Keller, C. E., and Lee, R. A. "Type of Affirmative Action Policy: A Determinant of Reactions to Sex-Based Preferential Selection?" *Journal of Applied Psychology* 83 (1998): 190–205.

Heilman, M. E., and Blader, S. L. "Assuming Preferential Selection When the Admissions Policy Is Unknown: The Effects of Gender Rarity." *Journal of Applied Psychology* 86 (2001): 188–93.

Heilman, M. E., Block, C. J., and Lucas, J. A. "Presumed Incompetent? Stigmatization and Affirmative Action Efforts." *Journal of Applied Psychology* 77 (1992): 536–44.

Heilman, M. E., Block, C. J., and Stathatos, P. "The Affirmative Action Stigma of Incompetence: Effects of Performance Information Ambiguity." *Academy of Management Journal* 40 (1997): 603–25.

Heilman, M. E., and Herlihy, J. M. "Affirmative Action, Negative Reaction? Some Moderating Conditions." *Organizational Behavior and Human Performance* 33 (1984): 204–13.

Heilman, M. E., Kaplow, S. R., Amato, M. A., and Stathatos, P. "When Similarity Is a Liability: Effects of Sex-Based Preferential Selection on Reactions to Like-Sex and Different-Sex Others." *Journal of Applied Psychology* 78 (1993): 917–27.

Heilman, M. E., Lucas, J. A., and Kaplow, S. R. "Self-Derogating Consequences of Sex-Based Preferential Selection: The Moderating Role of Initial Self-Confidence." *Organizational Behavior and Human Decision Processes* 46 (1990): 202–16.

Heilman, M. E., McCullough, W. F., and Gilbert, D. "The Other Side of Affirmative Action: Reactions of Nonbeneficiaries to Sex-Based Preferential Selection." *Journal of Applied Psychology* 81 (1996): 346–57.

Heilman, M. E., Rivero, J. C., and Brett, J. F. "Skirting the Competence Issue: Effects of Sex-Based Preferential Selection on Task Choices of Women and Men." *Journal of Applied Psychology* 76 (1991): 99–105.

Heilman, M. E., Simon, M. C., and Repper, D. P. "Intentionally Favored, Unintentionally Harmed? Impact of Sex-Based Preferential Selection on Self-Perceptions and Self-Evaluations." *Journal of Applied Psychology* 72 (1987): 62–68.

Hendrickson, R. M. "Rethinking Affirmative Action." *Peabody Journal of Education* 76 (2001): 117–35.

Herring, C., and Collins, S. M. "Retreat from Opportunity? The Case of Affirmative Action." In *The Bubbling Cauldron: Race, Ethnicity, and the Urban Crisis,* ed. M. P. Smith and J. R. Feagin, 163–81. Minneapolis: University of Minnesota Press, 1995.

Herrnstein, R. J., and Murray, C. A. *The Bell Curve: Intelligence and Class Structure in American Life.* New York: Free Press, 1994.

Hersch, J. "EEO Law and Firm Profitability." *Journal of Human Resources* 26 (1991): 139–53.

Hetherington, M. J., and Globetti, S. "Political Trust and Racial Policy Preferences." *American Journal of Political Science* 46 (2002): 253–75.

Hewstone, M., Argyle, M., and Furnham, A. "Favouritism, Fairness and Joint Profit in Long-Term Relationships." *European Journal of Social Psychology* 12 (1982): 283–95.

Hewstone, M., Fincham, F., and Jaspars, J. "Social Categorization and Similarity in Intergroup Behaviour: A Replication with 'Penalties.'" *European Journal of Social Psychology* 11, no. 1 (1981): 101–7.

Hewstone, M., Rubin, M., and Willis, H. "Intergroup Bias." *Annual Review of Psychology* 53, no. 1 (2002): 575–604.

Highhouse, S., Stierwalt, S. L., Bachiochi, P., Elder, A. E., and Fisher, G. "Effects of Advertised Human Resource Management Practices on Attraction of African American Applicants." *Personnel Psychology* 52 (1999): 425–42.

Hoffman, C. C. "Reopening the Affirmative Action Debate." *Personnel Administrator* (1986): 31, 36, 38, and 40.

Holzer, H. J., and Neumark, D. *Assessing Affirmative Action.* Cambridge: National Bureau of Economic Research, 1999.

———. "What Does Affirmative Action Do?" *Industrial and Labor Relations Review* 53 (2000): 240–71.

Horne, G. *Reverse Discrimination: The Case for Affirmative Action.* New York: International, 1992.

Huckle, P. "A Decade's Difference: Mid-Level Managers and Affirmative Action." *Public Personnel Management Journal* 12 (1983): 249–57.

Hudson, G., and Esses, V. M. "A New Perspective on the Personal/Group Discrimination Discrepancy." Paper presented at the Biannual Meeting of the Society for the Psychology Study of Social Issues, Minneapolis, June 2000.

Hurtado, A., Haney, C., and Garcia, E. E. "Becoming the Mainstream: Merit, Changing Demographics, and Higher Education in California." *La Raza Law Journal* 10 (1998): 645–90.

Hurwitz, J., and Peffley, M., eds. *Perception and Prejudice: Race and Politics in the United States.* New Haven: Yale University Press, 1998.

Jabbra, N. W., "Affirmative Action and the Stigma of Gender and Ethnicity." *Journal of Asian and African Studies* 36 (2001): 253–74.

Jacob Arriola, K. R., and Cole, E. R., "Framing the Affirmative-Action Debate." *Journal of Applied Social Psychology* 31 (2001): 2462–83.

Jacobsen, J. P. "Sex Segregation at Work: Trends and Predictions." *Social Science Journal* 31 (1994): 153–69.

Jacobson, C. K. "Resistance to Affirmative Action: Self-Interest or Racism?" *Journal of Conflict Resolution* 29 (1985): 306–29.

Jacobson, M. B., and Koch, W. "Women as Leaders: Performance Evaluation as a Function of Method of Leader Selection." *Organizational Behavior and Human Performance* 20 (1977): 149–57.

Janofsky, M. "Report Finds Bias in Lending Hinders Home Buying in Cities." *New York Times,* Feb. 23, 1998, A13.

Jencks, C., and Phillips, M., eds. *The Black-White Test Score Gap.* Washington, D.C.: Brookings Institution Press, 1998.

Jensen, A. R. *Bias in Mental Testing.* New York: Free Press, 1980.

Johnston, D. C. "As Salary Grows, So Does a Gender Gap." *New York Times,* May 12, 2002, 8.

Jones, A. J. *Affirmative Talk, Affirmative Action: A Comparative Study of the Politics of Affirmative Action.* New York: Praeger, 1991.

Jose, K. "Rethinking Affirmative Action." *Congressional Quarterly,* Apr. 28, 1995, 369–92.

Jost, J. T., and Thompson, E. P. "Group-Based Dominance and Opposition to Equality as Independent Predictors of Self-Esteem, Ethnocentrism, and Social Policy Attitudes Among African Americans and European Americans." *Journal of Experimental Social Psychology* 36 (2000): 209–32.

Kahn, W., and Crosby, F. "Discrimination Between Attitudes and Discriminatory Behavior: Change and Stasis." In *Women and Work: An Annual Review,* ed. L. Larwood, B. A. Gutek, and A. H. Stromberg, 215–38. Beverly Hills, Calif.: Sage, 1985.

Karen, D. "'Achievement' and 'Ascription' in Admission to an Elite College: A Political-Organizational Analysis." *Sociological Forum* 6 (1991): 349–80.

Kasinitz, P., and Rosenberg, J. "Missing the Connection: Social Isolation and Employment on the Brooklyn Waterfront." *Social Problems* 43 (1996): 180–96.

Kelman, S. *Procurement and Public Management: The Fear of Discretion and the Quality of Government Performance.* Washington, D.C.: American Enterprise Institute, 1990.

Kemmelmeier, M. "The Individualist Self and Attitudes Toward Affirmative Action: Evidence from Priming Experiments." Paper presented at the Biannual Conference of the Society for the Psychological Study of Social Issues, Minneapolis, June 2000.

Kilson, M. "Affirmative Action." *Dissent* (1995): 469–70.

Kimura, D. "Affirmative Action Policies Are Demeaning to Women in Academia." *Canadian Psychology* 38 (1997): 238–43.

Kinder, D. R. "The Continuing American Dilemma: White Resistance to

Racial Change 40 Years After Myrdal." *Journal of Social Issues* 42, no. 2 (1986): 151–71.

Kinder, D. R., and Sanders, L. M. *Divided by Color: Racial Politics and Democratic Ideals, American Politics and Political Economy.* Chicago: University of Chicago Press, 1996.

———. "Mimicking Political Debate with Survey Questions: The Case of White Opinion on Affirmative Action for Blacks." *Social Cognition* 8 (1990): 73–103.

Klein, J. "The End of Affirmative Action." *Newsweek,* Feb. 13, 1995, 36.

Klineberg, S. L., and Kravitz D. A. "Ethnic Differences in Predictors of Support for Municipal Affirmative Action Contracting." *Social Science Quarterly* 84 (2003): 425–40.

Kluegel, J. R., and Smith, E. R. "Affirmative Action Attitudes: Effects of Self-Interest, Racial Affect, and Stratification Beliefs on Whites' Views." *Social Forces* 61 (1983): 707–824.

———. *Beliefs About Inequality: Americans' Views of What Is and What Ought to Be, Social Institutions and Social Change.* New York: A. de Gruyter, 1986.

———. "Whites' Beliefs About Blacks' Opportunity." *American Sociological Review* 47 (1982): 518–32.

Kobrynowicz, D., and Branscombe, N. R. "Who Considers Themselves Victims of Discrimination? Individual Difference Predictors of Perceived Discrimination in Women and Men." *Psychology of Women Quarterly* 21 (1997): 347–63.

Komaromy, M., Grumbach, K., Drake, M., Vranizan, K., Lurie, N., Keane, D., and Bindman, A. B. "The Role of Black and Hispanic Physicians in Providing Health Care for Underserved Populations." *New England Journal of Medicine* 334 (1996): 1305–10.

Konrad, A. M., and Linnehan, F. "Affirmative Action: History, Effects, and Attitudes." In *Handbook of Gender and Work,* ed. G. N. Powell, 429–52. Thousand Oaks, Calif.: Sage, 1999.

———. "Formalized HRM Structures: Coordinating Equal Employment Opportunity or Concealing Organizational Practices?" *Academy of Management Journal* 38 (1995): 787–820.

———. "Race and Sex Differences in Line Managers' Reactions to Equal Employment Opportunity and Affirmative Action Interventions." *Group and Organizational Management* 20 (1995): 409–39.

Konrad, A. M., and Pfeffer, J. "Understanding the Hiring of Women and Minorities in Educational Institutions." *Sociology of Education* 664 (1991): 141–57.

Kozol, J. *Savage Inequalities: Children in America's Schools.* New York: Crown, 1991.

Kravitz, D. A. "Attitudes Toward Affirmative Action Plans Directed at Blacks:

Effects of Plan and Individual Differences." *Journal of Applied Social Psychology* 25 (1995): 2192–20.

Kravitz, D. A., Harrison, D. A., Turner, M. E., Levine, E. L., Chaves, W., Brannick, M. T., Denning, D. L., Russell, C. J., and Conrad, M. A. *Affirmative Action: A Review of Psychological and Behavioral Research.* Bowling Green: Society for Industrial and Organizational Psychology, 1997.

Kravitz, D. A., and Klineberg, S. L. "Reactions to Two Versions of Affirmative Action Among Whites, Blacks, and Hispanics." *Journal of Applied Psychology* 85 (2000): 597–611.

Kravitz, D. A., Klineberg, S. L., Avery, D. R., Nguyen, C. L., Lund, C., and Fu, E. J. "Attitudes Toward Affirmative Action: Correlations with Demographic Variables and with Beliefs About Targets, Actions, and Economic Effects." *Journal of Applied Social Psychology* 30 (2000): 1109–36.

Kravitz, D. A., and Platania, J. "Attitudes and Beliefs About Affirmative Action: Effects of Target and of Respondent Sex and Ethnicity." *Journal of Applied Psychology* 78 (1993): 928–38.

Kriesel, W., Centner, T. J., and Keeler, A. G. "Neighborhood Exposure to Toxic Releases: Are There Racial Inequities?" *Growth and Change* 27 (1996): 479–90.

Krysan, M., Schuman, H., Scott, L. J., and Beatty, P. "Response Rates and Response Content in Mail Versus Face-to-Face Surveys." *Public Opinion Quarterly* 58 (1994): 381–99.

Kulas, J. T., and Finkelstein, L. M., "Preferential Selection Independent of Race and Gender." *Social Justice Research* 15 (2002): 147–62.

Kuran, T. *Private Truths, Public Lies.* Cambridge: Harvard University Press, 1995.

Laband, D. N., and Lentz, B. F. "The Effects of Sexual Harassment on Job Satisfaction, Earnings, and Turnover Among Female Lawyers." *Industrial and Labor Relations Review* 51 (1998): 594–607.

Latack, J. C., Josephs, S. L., Roach, B. L., and Levine, M. D. "Carpenter Apprentices: Comparison of Career Transitions for Men and Women." *Journal of Applied Psychology* 72 (1987): 393–400.

LaVeist, T. A., and Carrol, T., "Race of Physician and Satisfaction with Care Among African American Patients." *Journal of the National Medical Association* 94 (2002): 937–43.

Leck, J. D., Saunders, D. M., and Charbonneau, M. "Affirmative Action Programs: An Organizational Justice Perspective." *Journal of Organizational Behavior* 17 (1996): 79–89.

Lemann, N. "Taking Affirmative Action Apart." *New York Times Magazine*, June 11, 1995, 36–43.

Lempert, R. O., Chambers, D. A., and Adams, T. K. "Michigan's Minority Graduates in Practice: The River Runs Through Law School." *Law and Social Inquiry* 25 (2000): 395–505.

Leonard, J. S. "Anti-Discrimination or Reverse Discrimination: The Impact of Changing Demographics, Title VII, and Affirmative Action or Productivity." *Journal of Human Resources* 19 (1984): 145–74.

———. "The Effectiveness of Equal Employment Law and Affirmative Action Regulation." In *Research in Labor Economics,* ed. R. A. Ehrenberg, 319–50. Greenwich, Conn.: JAI, 1986.

———. "Employment and Occupational Advance Under Affirmative Action." *Review of Economics and Statistics* 66 (1984): 377–85.

———. "The Impact of Affirmative Action on Employment." *Journal of Labor Economics* 2 (1984): 439–63.

———. "The Impact of Affirmative Action Regulation and Equal Employment Law on Black Employment." *Journal of Economic Perspectives* 4 (1990): 47–63.

———. *Use of Enforcement Techniques in Eliminating Glass Ceiling Barriers. Report to the Glass Ceiling Commission.* Washington, D.C.: Department of Labor, 1994.

———. "What Promises Are Worth: The Impact of Affirmative Action Goals." *Journal of Human Resources* 20, no. 1 (1985): 3–20.

———. "Women and Affirmative Action." *Journal of Economic Perspectives* 3 (1989): 61–75.

Leone, B., Barbour, S., Stalcup, B., and Roleff, T. C. *Genetics and Intelligence: Current Controversies.* San Diego: Greenhaven, 1996.

Lerner, M. *The Belief in a Just World: A Fundamental Delusion.* New York: Plenum, 1980.

Lewis, D. E. "Study Finds Views on Race Diverge." *Boston Globe,* Jan. 20, 2002, 8.

Lind, E. A., Kanfer, R., and Earley, P. C. "Voice, Control, and Procedural Justice: Instrumental and Noninstrumental Concerns in Fairness Judgments." *Journal of Personality and Social Psychology* 59 (1990): 952–59.

Lind, E. A., and Tyler T. R. *The Social Psychology of Procedural Justice, Critical Issues in Social Justice.* New York: Plenum, 1988.

Lippa, R. "Gender-Related Individual Differences and the Structure of Vocational Interests: The Importance of the People-Things Dimension." *Journal of Personality and Social Psychology* 74 (1998): 996–1000.

Little, B. L., Murry, W. D., and Wimbush, J. C. "Perceptions of Workplace Affirmative Action Plans: A Psychological Perspective." *Group and Organizational Management* 23 (1998): 27–47.

Lott, J. R., Jr. "Does a Helping Hand Put Others at Risk?: Affirmative Action, Police Departments, and Crime." *Economic Inquiry* 38 (2000): 239–77.

Loury, G. C. *The Anatomy of Racial Inequality.* Cambridge: Harvard University Press, 2001.

Lynch, F. R., and Beer, W. R. "You Ain't the Right Color, Pal: White Resentment of Affirmative Action." *Policy Review* 51 (1990): 64–67.

MacIntosh, P. "White Privilege: Unpacking the Invisible Knapsack." In *Revisioning Family Therapy: Race, Culture, and Gender in Clinical Practice,* ed. M. McGoldrick, 147–52. New York: Guilford, 1998.

Mack, D. A., Johnson, C. D., Green, T. D., Parisi, A. G., and Thomas, K. M. "Motivation to Control Prejudice as a Mediator of Identity and Affirmative Action Attitudes." *Journal of Applied Social Psychology* 32 (2002): 934–64.

Mackie, D. M., and Hamilton, D. L., eds. *Affect, Cognition, and Stereotyping: Interactive Processes in Group Perception.* San Diego: Academic, 1993.

MacPherson, D. A., and Hirsch, B. T. "Wages and Gender Composition: Why Do Women's Jobs Pay Less?" *Journal of Labor Economics* 13 (1995): 426–71.

Maio, G. R., and Esses, V. M. "The Social Consequences of Affirmative Action: Deleterious Effects on Perceptions of Groups." *Personality and Social Psychology Bulletin* 24 (1998): 65–74.

Major, B., Feinstein, J., and Crocker, J. "Attributional Ambiguity of Affirmative Action." *Basic and Applied Social Psychology* 15 (1994): 113–41.

Making the Case for Affirmative Action in Higher Education. Washington D.C.: American Council on Education, 1996.

Malos, S. B. "The New Affirmative Action: Socioeconomic Preference Criteria in College Admissions." *Journal of Applied Behavioral Science* 36 (2000): 5–22.

Mangan, K. S. "The Unusual Rules for Affirmative Action in Medical Schools." *Chronicle of Higher Education* 47, no. 13 (2000): A57–A58.

Margolis, E., and Romero, A. "'The Department Is Very Male, Very White, Very Old, and Very Conservative': The Functioning of the Hidden Curriculum in Graduate Sociology Departments." *Harvard Educational Review* 68 (1998): 1–32.

Marinoff, L. "Equal Opportunity Versus Equity." *Sexuality and Culture: An Interdisciplinary Quarterly* 4 (2000): 23–43.

Martin, S. "The Effectiveness of Affirmative Action: The Case of Women in Policing." *Justice Quarterly* 8 (1991): 489–504.

Massey, D. S., and Denton, N. A. *American Apartheid: Segregation and the Making of the Underclass.* Cambridge: Harvard University Press, 1993.

Matheson, K., Echenberg, A., Taylor, D. M., Rivers, D., and Chow, I. "Women's Attitudes Toward Affirmative Action: Putting Action in Context." *Journal of Applied Social Psychology* 24 (1994): 2075–96.

Matheson, K. J., Warren, K. L., Foster, M. D., and Painter, C. "Reactions to Affirmative Action: Seeking the Bases for Resistance." *Journal of Applied Social Psychology* 30 (2000): 1013–38.

McCleneghan, S. J., "How African American Journalists View American's Social Institutions into the 21st Century." *Social Science Journal* 38 (2001): 251–84.

McConahay, J. B. "Modern Racism, Ambivalence and the Modern Racism Scale." In *Prejudice, Discrimination, and Racism,* ed. S. L. Gaertner and J. F. Dovidio, 91–125. New York: Academic, 1983.

Miller, F., and Clark, M.A. "Looking Toward the Future: Young People's Attitudes About Affirmative Action and the American Dream." *American Behavioral Scientist* 41 (1997): 262–71.

Miller, R. E., and Sarat, A. "Grievances, Claims, and Disputes: Assessing the Adversary Culture." *Law and Society Review* 15, nos. 3–4 (1980–81): 525–66.

Moghaddam, F. M., Stolkin, A. J., and Hutcheson, L. S. "A Generalized Personal/Group Discrepancy: Testing the Domain Specificity of a Perceived Higher Effect of Events on One's Group Than on Oneself." *Personality and Social Psychology Bulletin* 7 (1997): 743–50.

Monteith, M. J., Sherman, J. W., Devine, P. G. "Suppression as a Stereotype Control Strategy." *Personality and Social Psychology Review* 2 (1998): 63–82.

Moro, A., and Norman P. "Affirmative Action in a Competitive Economy." *Journal of Public Economics* 87 (2003): 567–94.

Moses, M. S. "Affirmative Action and the Creation of More Favorable Contexts of Choice." *American Educational Research Journal* 38 (2001): 3–36.

Moss, P., and Tilly, C. *Stories Employers Tell: Race, Skill, and Hiring in America.* New York: Russell Sage, 2001.

Munk, N. "Fighting over the Spoils." *Forbes,* Aug. 15, 1994, 50–51.

Munnell, A., Browne, L. E., McEneaney, J., and Tootsell, G. M. R. *Mortgage Lending in Boston: Interpreting HDMA Data; Federal Reserve Bank of Boston.* Working Paper 92-07. Boston: Federal Reserve Bank of Boston, 1992.

Murrell, A., Crosby, F., and Ely, R. *Mentoring Dilemmas: Developmental Relationships Within the Multicultural Organization.* Mahwah, N.J.: Erlbaum, 1999.

Murrell, A. J., Dietz-Uhler, B. L., Dovidio, J. F., and Gaertner, L. S. "Aversive Racism and Resistance to Affirmative Action: Perceptions of Justice Are not Necessarily Color Blind." *Basic and Applied Social Psychology* 15 (1994): 71–86.

Naff, K. C. "Progress Toward Achieving a Representative Federal Bureaucracy: The Impact of Supervisors and Their Beliefs." *Public Personnel Management* 27 (1998): 135–50.

Negrey, C. *Working First, but Working Poor.* Washington, D.C.: Institute for Women's Policy Research, 2001.

Neumark, D. "Sex Discrimination in Restaurant Hiring: An Audit Study." *Quarterly Journal of Economics* 111 (1996): 915–41.

Nisbett, R. E., Caputo, C., Legant, P., and Marecek, J. "Behavior as Seen by the Actor and as Seen by the Observer." *Journal of Personality and Social Psychology* 27 (1973): 154–64.

Noble, A., and Winett, R. A. "Chairpersons' and Hirees' Opinions, Knowledge, and Experiences with Affirmative Action Guidelines." *Journal of Community Psychology* 6 (1978): 194–99.

Nosworthy, G. J., Lea, J. A., and Lindsay, C. L. "Opposition to Affirmative Action: Racial Affect and Traditional Value Predictors Across Four Programs." *Journal of Applied Social Psychology* 25 (1995): 314–37.

OFCCP Egregious Discrimination Cases. Washington, D.C.: Department of Labor, 1996.

O'Neill, J. "Affirmative Action." *Wall Street Journal,* Oct. 7, 1994, 1.

O'Neill, J., and Polacheck, S. "Why the Gender Gap in Wages Narrowed in the 1980s." *Journal of Labor Economics* 11, no. 1 (1993): 205–28.

Olson, J. M., Roese, N. J., Meen, J., and Roberston, D. J. "The Preconditions and Consequences of Relative Deprivation: Two Field Studies." *Journal of Applied Social Psychology* 11 (1995): 944–64.

Ong, P., ed. *The Impacts of Affirmative Action: Policies and Consequences in California.* Walnut Creek, Calif.: Altamira, 1999.

Operario, D., and Fiske, S. T. "Ethnic Identity Moderates Perceptions of Prejudice: Judgments of Personal Versus Group Discrimination and Subtle Versus Blatant Bias." *Personality and Social Psychology Bulletin* 27 (2001): 550–61.

Orfield, G., and Miller, E., eds. *Chilling Admissions: The Affirmative Action Crisis and the Search for Alternatives.* Cambridge: Harvard Civil Rights Project, 1998.

Osterman, P. "Affirmative Action and Opportunity: A Study of Female Quit Rates." *Review of Economics and Statistics* 64, no. 4 (1982): 604–12.

Owen, B. "Race and Gender Relations Among Prison Workers." *Crime and Delinquency* 31 (1985): 147–59.

Ozawa, K., Crosby, M., and Crosby, F. "Individualism and Resistance to Affirmative Action: A Comparison of Japanese and American Samples." *Journal of Applied Social Psychology* 26 (1996): 1138–52.

Parker, C. P., Baltes, B. B., and Christiansen, N. D. "Support for Affirmative Action, Justice Perceptions, and Work Attitudes: A Study of Gender and Racial-Ethnic Group Differences." *Journal of Applied Psychology* 82 (1997): 376–89.

Pedriana, N., and Stryker, R. "Political Culture Wars, 1960s Style: Equal Employment Opportunity—Affirmative Action Law and the Philadelphia Plan." *American Journal of Sociology* 103 (1997): 633–91.

Pelham, B. W., and Hetts, J. J. "Underworked and Overpaid: Elevated Entitlement in Men's Self-Pay." *Journal of Experimental Social Psychology* 37 (2001): 93–103.

Penn, N. E., Russell, P. J., and Simon, H. J. "Affirmative Action at Work: A Survey of Graduates of the University of California, San Diego Medical School." *American Journal of Public Health* 76 (1986): 1144–46.

Perlo, A. "The Digital Divide and Institutional Racism." *Political Affairs* 80, no. 2 (2001): 4–9.

Perloff, R., and Bryant, F. B. "Identifying and Measuring Diversity's Payoffs: Light at the End of the Affirmative Action Tunnel." *Psychology, Public Policy, and Law* 6 (2000): 101–11.

Pierce, J. L. "Racing for Innocence." *Qualitative Sociology* 26 (2003): 53–69.

Pincus, F. L. "Reverse Discrimination vs. White Privilege: An Empirical Study of Alleged Victims of Affirmative Action." *Race and Society* 3 (2000): 1–22.

———. "The Social Construction of Reverse Discrimination: The Impact of Affirmative Action on Whites." *Journal of Intergroup Relations* 38, no. 4 (Winter 2001–2): 33–44.

———. "Test of Affirmative Action Knowledge." *Current World Leaders: International Issues* 39, no. 2 (1996): 94–104.

Plant, E. A., and Devine, P. G. "Internal and External Motivation to Respond Without Prejudice." *Journal of Personality and Social Psychology* 75 (1998): 811–32.

———. "Responses to Other-Imposed Pro-Black Pressure: Acceptance or Backlash?" *Journal of Experimental Social Psychology* 37 (2001): 486–501.

Ponterotto, J. G., Martinez, F. M., and Hayden, D. C. "Student Affirmative Action Programs: A Help or Hindrance to Development of Minority Graduate Students." *Journal of College Student Personnel* 27 (1986): 318–25.

Postmes, T., Branscombe, N. R., Spears, R., and Young, H. "Comparative Processes in Personal and Group Judgments: Resolving the Discrepancy." *Journal of Personality and Social Psychology* 76 (1999): 320–38.

Pratkanis, A. R., and Turner, M. E. "Nine Principles of Successful Affirmative Action: Mr. Branch Rickey, Mr. Jackie Robinson, and the Integration of Baseball." *NINE: A Journal of Baseball History and Social Policy Perspectives* 3 (1994): 36–65.

———. "The Year Cool Papa Bell Lost the Batting Title: Mr. Branch Rickey and Mr. Jackie Robinson's Plea for Affirmative Action." *NINE: A Journal of Baseball History and Social Policy Perspectives* 2 (1994): 260–76.

Pratto, F. "The Puzzle of Continuing Group Inequality: Piecing Together Psychological, Social, and Cultural Forces in Social Dominance Theory." *Advances in Experimental Social Psychology* 31 (1999): 191–263.

Pratto, F., Sidanius, J., Stallworth, L. M., and Malle, B. F. "Social Dominance Orientation: A Personality Variable Predicting Social and Political Attitudes." *Journal of Personality and Social Psychology* 67 (1994): 741–63.

Prentice, D., and Crosby, F. J. "The Importance of Context for Assessing Deservingness." In *Social Comparison, Social Justice, and Relative Deprivation*, ed. J. C. Masters and W. P. Smith, 165–82. Hillsdale, N.J.: Erlbaum, 1987.

Price, V. "Race, Affirmative Action, and Women's Employment in U.S. Highway Construction." *Feminist Economics* 8 (2002): 87–113.

Quinn, K. A., Ross, E. A., and Esses, V. M. "Attributions of Responsibility and Reactions to Affirmative Action: Affirmative Action as Help." *Personality and Social Psychology Bulletin* 27 (2001): 321–31.

Rai, K. B., and Critzer, J. W. *Affirmative Action and the University: Race, Ethnicity, and Gender in Higher Education Employment.* Lincoln: University of Nebraska Press, 2000.

Raudenbush, S. W., and Kasim, R. M. "Cognitive Skill and Economic Inequality: Findings from the National Adult Literacy Survey." *Harvard Educational Review* 68 (1998): 33–68.

Rawls, J. *A Theory of Justice.* Rev. ed. Cambridge: Belknap, 1999.

Rawls, J., and Kelly, E. *Justice as Fairness: A Restatement.* Cambridge: Harvard University Press, 2001.

Reisberg, L. "A Top University Wonders Why It Has No Black Freshman." *Chronicle of Higher Education,* Apr. 28, 2000, A52–A54.

Resendez, M. G., "The Stigmatization Effects of Affirmative Action." *Journal of Applied Social Psychology* 32 (2002): 185–206.

Reskin, B. F. *The Realities of Affirmative Action in Employment.* Washington, D.C.: American Sociological Association, 1998.

Reskin, B. F., and Ross, C. E. "Jobs, Authority, and Earnings Among Managers—The Continuing Significance of Sex." *Work and Occupations* 19 (1992): 342–65.

Richard, O. C., and Kirby, S. L. "African Americans' Reactions to Diversity Programs: Does Procedural Justice Matter?" *Journal of Black Psychology* 23 (1997): 388–97.

———. "Women Recruits' Perceptions of Workforce Diversity Program Selection Decisions: A Procedural Justice Examination." *Journal of Applied Social Psychology* 28 (1998): 183–88.

Ridgeway, C. L. "The Social Construction of Status Value: Gender and Other Nominal Characteristics." *Social Forces* 70 (1991): 367–386.

Ridgeway, C. L., and Smith-Lovin, L. "Interaction in the Gender System: Theory and Research." *Annual Review of Sociology* 25 (1999): 191–216.

Riger, S., Foster-Fishman, P., Nelson-Kuna, J., and Curran, B. "Gender Bias in Courtroom Dynamics." *Law and Human Behavior* 19 (1995): 465–80.

Roberts, P. C., and Stratton, L. M. *The New Color Line: How Quotas and Privilege Destroy Democracy.* Washington, D.C.: Regnery, 1995.

Robinson, R. K., Allen, B. M., and Yohannan, A. T. "Affirmative Action Plans in the 1990s: A Double-Edged Sword." *Public Personnel Management* 21 (1992): 261–72.

Robinson, R. K., Paolillo, J. G. P., and Reithel, B. "Race-Based Preferential Treatment Programs: Raising the Bar for Establishing Compelling Government Interests." *Public Personnel Management* 27 (1998): 349–60.

Robinson, R. K., Seydel, J., and Douglas, C. "Affirmative Action: The Facts, the

Myths, and the Future." *Employee Responsibilities and Rights Journal* 11 (1998): 99–115.

Rodgers, W. M. III. "Racial Differences in Employment Shares—New Evidence from the EEO-1 Files." In *Civil Rights and Race Relations in the Post-Reagan-Bush Era,* ed. S. L. Meyers, 60–97. Westport, Conn.: Praeger, 1997.

Rodgers, W. M. III, and Spriggs, W. E. "The Effect of Federal-Contractor Status on Racial Differences in Establishment-Level Employment Shares: 1979–1992." *American Economic Review* 86 (1996): 290–93.

Rodriguez, R. *Brown: The Last Discovery of America.* New York: Viking Penguin, 2002.

———. *Hunger of Memory: The Education of Richard Rodriguez, an Autobiography.* Boston: Godine, 1982.

Rose, M. "An Interview with the Intervenors." *AAAA News* (Winter 2002): 1, 8, 9.

Rosen, B., and Mericle, M. F. "Influence of Strong Versus Weak Fair Employment Policies and Applicant's Sex on Selection Decisions and Salary Recommendations in a Management Simulation." *Journal of Applied Psychology* 64 (1979): 435–39.

Rosenfeld, P., Knouse, S. B., and Culbertson, A. L., eds. *Hispanics in the Workplace.* Newbury Park, Calif.: Sage, 1992.

Ross, L. "The Intuitive Psychologist and His Shortcomings: Distortions in the Attribution Process." In *Advances in Experimental Social Psychology,* ed. L. Berkowitz, vol. 10. New York, Academic, 1977.

Ross, M., and Miller, D., eds. *The Justice Motive in Everyday Life.* New York: Cambridge University Press, 2002.

Ruark, J. K. "Texas A&M U. Withdraws Admissions Proposal That Was Criticized as Race-Based." *Chronicle of Higher Education,* Mar. 4, 2002, 3.

Rubin, Z., and Peplau, L. "Who Believes in a Just World?" *Journal of Social Issues* 31, no. 3 (1975): 65–89.

Rutte, C. G., Diekmann, K. A., Polzer, J. T., Crosby, F. J., and Messick, D. M. "Organizing Information and the Detection of Gender Discrimination." *Psychological Science* 5 (1994): 226–31.

Sackett, P. R., Schmitt, N., Ellingson, J. E., Kabin, M. B. "High-Stakes Testing in Employment, Credentialing, and Higher Education." *American Psychologist* 56 (2001): 302–18.

Sackett, P. R., and Wilk, S. L. "Within-Group Norming and Other Forms of Score Adjustment in Pre-Employment Testing." *American Psychologist* 49 (1994): 929–54.

Sandefur, G. D., Danziger, S. H., and Weinberg, D. H., eds. *Confronting Poverty: Prescriptions for Change.* Cambridge: Harvard University Press, 1994.

Sass, T., and Troyer, J. L. "Affirmative Action, Political Representation, Unions, and Female Police Employment." *Journal of Labor Research* 20 (1999): 571–87.

Sawires, J. N., and Peacock, M. J. "Symbolic Racism and Voting Behavior on Proposition 209." *Journal of Applied Social Psychology* 30 (2000): 2092–99.

Schmermund, A., Sellers, R., Mueller, B., and Crosby, F. J. "Attitudes Toward Affirmative Action as a Function of Racial Identity Among African American College Students." *Political Psychology* 22 (2001): 759–74.

Schmidt, P. "Appeals Court Upholds Affirmative Action at University of Michigan Law School." *Chronicle of Higher Education* 48, no. 37 (2002): A24.

———. "Debating the Benefits of Affirmative Action." *Chronicle of Higher Education* 47, no. 36 (2001): A25–A26.

———. "Report Accuses Virginia Law Schools of Bias Against Non-Black Applicants." *Chronicle of Higher Education*, Apr. 25, 2002, 4.

———. "U. of California Ends Affirmative Action Ban." *Chronicle of Higher Education* 47, no. 37 (2001): A23–A24.

Schmidt, P., and Selino, J. "A Supreme Court Showdown." *Chronicle of Higher Education* 49, no. 16 (2002): A20–26.

Schuck, P. H., "Affirmative Action." *Brookings Review* 20 (2002): 24.

Schuman, H., Steeh, C., and Bobo, L. *Racial Attitudes in America: Trends and Interpretations.* Cambridge: Harvard University Press, 1988.

Schuman, H., Steeh, C., Bobo, L., and Krysan, M. *Racial Attitudes in America: Trends and Interpretations.* Rev. ed. (Cambridge: Harvard University Press, 1997).

Sears, D. O., Sidanius, J., and Bobo, L., eds. *Racialized Politics: The Debate About Racism in America* (Chicago: University of Chicago Press, 2000).

Sears, D. O., van Laar, C., Carrillo, M., and Kosterman, R. "Is It Really Racism? The Origins of White Americans' Opposition to Race-Targeted Policies." *Public Opinion Quarterly* 61 (1997): 16–53.

Selingo, J. "A Quiet End to the Use of Race in College Admissions in Florida." *Chronicle of Higher Education* 46, no. 15 (1999): A31–A32.

———. "Why Minority Recruiting Is Alive and Well in Texas." *Chronicle of Higher Education* 46, no. 13 (1999): A34–A36.

Shaw, L. B., Champlain, D. P., Hartmann, H. I., and Spalter-Roth, R. M. *The Impact of Restructuring and the Glass Ceiling on Minorities and Women. Report to the Glass Ceiling Commission.* Washington, D.C.: Department of Labor, 1993.

Shorey, H. S., Cowan, G., and Sullivan, M. P. "Predicting Perceptions of Discrimination Among Hispanics and Anglos." *Hispanic Journal of Behavioral Sciences* 24 (2002): 3–22.

Sidanius, J. *Social Dominance: An Intergroup Theory of Social Hierarchy and Oppression.* New York: Cambridge University Press, 1999.

Sidanius, J., Pratto, F., and Bobo, L. "Racism, Conservatism, Affirmative Action, and Intellectual Sophistication: A Matter of Principled Conservatism or Group Dominance?" *Journal of Personality and Social Psychology* 70 (1996): 476–90.

Sidanius, J., van Laar, C., Levin, S., and Sinclair, S. "Ethnic Enclaves on the College Campus: The Good, the Bad, and the Ugly." Russell Sage Foundation Working Paper No. 194, 2002.

Sigelman, L. "The Public and Disadvantaged-Based Affirmative Action: An Early Assessment." *Social Science Quarterly* 78 (1997): 1011–22.

Sigelman, L., and Welch, S. *Black Americans' Views of Racial Inequality: The Dream Deferred.* Cambridge: Cambridge University Press, 1991.

Silva, J. J., and Jacobs, R. R. "Performance as a Function of Increased Minority Hiring." *Journal of Applied Psychology* 78 (1993): 591–601.

Simms, M. C., ed. *Economic Perspectives on Affirmative Action.* Washington, D.C.: Joint Center for Political and Economic Studies, 1995.

Simpson, G. "The Plexiglass Ceiling: The Careers of Black Women Lawyers." *Career Development Quarterly* 45 (1996): 173–88.

Sincharoen, S., Crosby, F. J., and Sellers, R. "Varied Support of Affirmative Action Among Black College Students: Who Supports and Who Opposes Affirmative Action?" Paper presented at the 26th Annual Conference of the American Association for Affirmative Action, Washington D.C., Apr. 7, 2000.

Skrentny, J. D., "Inventing Race." *Public Interest* 40 (2002): 97–113.

———. *The Ironies of Affirmative Action: Politics, Culture, and Justice in America.* Chicago: University of Chicago Press, 1996.

———. "Judges in the U. of Michigan Case Skirted the Thorniest Issues." *Chronicle of Higher Education* 48, no. 38 (2002): B20.

Slaughter, J. E., Sinar, E. F., Bachiochi, P. D. "Black Applicants' Reactions to Affirmative Action Plans." *Journal of American Psychology* 87 (2002): 333–44.

Smith, H. J., and Tyler, T. R. "Justice and Power: When Will Justice Concerns Encourage the Advantaged to Support Policies Which Redistribute Economic Resources and the Disadvantaged to Willingly Obey the Law?" *European Journal of Social Psychology* 26 (1996): 171–200.

Smith, S. P. "Government Wage Differentials by Sex." *Journal of Human Resources* 11 (1976): 185–99.

Sniderman, P. M., and Carmines E. G. *Reaching Beyond Race.* Cambridge: Harvard University Press, 1997.

Sniderman, P. M., and Piazza, T. *The Scar of Race.* Cambridge: Harvard University Press, 1993.

Sniderman, P. M., Piazza, T., Tetlock, P. E., and Kendrick, A. "The New Racism." *American Journal of Political Science* 35 (1991): 423–47.

Sniderman, P. M., Tetlock, P. E., Carmines, E. G., and Peterson, R. S. "The Politics of the American Dilemma: Issue Pluralism." In *Prejudice, Politics, and the American Dilemma,* ed. P. E. Tetlock, P. M. Sniderman, and E. G. Carmines, 212–36. Stanford: Stanford University Press, 1993.

Son Hing, L. S., Bobocel, D. R., and Zanna, M. P. "Meritocracy and Opposition to Affirmative Action: Making Concessions in the Face of Discrimination." *Journal of Personality and Social Psychology* 83 (2002): 493–509.

South, S. J., Markham, W. E., Bonjean, C. M., and Corder, J. "Sex Differences in Support for Organizational Advancement." *Work and Occupations* 14 (1987): 261–85.

Spann, G. A. *The Law of Affirmative Action: Twenty-Five Years of Supreme Court Decisions on Race and Remedies.* New York: New York University Press, 2000.

Stanley, T. D., and Jarrell, S. B. "Gender Wage Discrimination Bias? A Meta-Regression Analysis." *Journal of Human Resources* 33 (1998): 947–73.

Stanush, P., Arthur, W., and Doverspike, D. "Hispanic and African American Reactions to a Simulated Race-Based Affirmative Action Scenario." *Hispanic Journal of Behavioral Sciences* 20 (1998): 3–16.

Steeh, C., and Krysan, M. "Poll Trends: Affirmative Action and the Public, 1970–1995." *Public Opinion Quarterly* 60 (1996): 128–58.

Steel, B. S., and Lovrich, N. P. "Equality and Efficiency Tradeoffs in Affirmative Action—Real or Imagined? The Case of Women in Policing." *Social Science Journal* 24 (1987): 53–70.

Steele, C. M. "A Threat in the Air: How Stereotypes Shape Intellectual Identity and Performance." *American Psychologist* 52 (1997): 613–29.

Steele, S. *The Content of Our Character: A New Vision of Race in America.* New York: St. Martin's, 1990.

———. "The New Sovereignty." *Harper's Magazine,* July 1992, 47–54.

Stephanopoulos, G., and Edley, Jr., C. *Affirmative Action Review: Report to the President.* Washington, D.C.: Government Printing Office, 1995.

Steinberg, R. J. "Implicit Theories of Intelligence as Exemplar Stories of Success: Why Intelligence Test Validity Is in the Eye of the Beholder." *Psychology, Public Policy, and Law* 6 (2000): 367–78.

———. "Social Construction of Skill: Gender, Power and Comparable Worth." *Work and Occupations* 17 (1990): 449–82.

Stewart, D. M. "Meanings of Merit: Higher Education as a Lens on Public Culture." *American Behavioral Scientist* 42 (1999): 1052–63.

Stewart, M. M., and Shapiro, D. L. "Selection Based on Merit Versus Demography: Implications Across Race and Gender Lines." *Journal of Applied Psychology* 85 (2000): 219–31.

Stolberg, S. G. "Race Gap Seen in Health Care of Equally Insured Patients." *New York Times,* Mar. 21, 2002, A1, A30.

Storms, M. D. "Videotape and the Attribution Process: Reversing Actors' and Observers' Points of View." *Journal of Personality and Social Psychology* 27 (1973): 165–75.

Stroh, L. K., Brett, J. M., and Reilly, A. H. "All the Right Stuff: A Comparison of Female and Male Managers' Career Progression." *Journal of Applied Psychology* 77 (1992): 251–60.

Stryker, R. "Disparate Impact and Quota Debates: Law, Labor Market Sociology, and Equal Employment Policies." *Sociological Quarterly* 42 (2001): 13–46.

Stryker, R., Scarpellino, M., and Holtzman, M. "Political Culture Wars, 1990s Style: The Drum Beat of Quotas in Media Framing of the Civil Rights Act of 1991. *Research in Social Stratification and Mobility* 17 (1999): 33–106.

Suedfeld, P., and Tetlock, P. E., eds. *Psychology and Social Policy.* Washington, D.C.: Hemisphere, 1992.

Summers, R. J. "Attitudes Toward Different Methods of Affirmative Action." *Journal of Applied Social Psychology* 25 (1995): 1090–104.

Summers, S. R., and Ellsworth, P. C. "Race and the Courtroom: Perceptions of Guilt and Dispositional Attributions." *Personality and Social Psychology Bulletin* 26 (2000): 1367–79.

Swain, C. M. *The New White Nationalism: Its Threat to Integration.* New York: Cambridge University Press, 2002.

Swim, J., Borgida, E., Maruyama, G., and Meyers, D. G. "Joan Mckay Versus John Mckay: Do Gender Stereotypes Bias Evaluations?" *Psychological Bulletin* 105 (1989): 409–29.

Swim, J., and Sanna, L. J. "He's Skilled, She's Lucky: A Meta-Analysis of Observer's Attributions for Women's and Men's Successes and Failures." *Personality and Social Psychology Bulletin* 22 (1996): 507–19.

Szmatka, J., Skvoretz, J., and Berger, J., eds. *Status, Network, and Structure: Theory Development in Group Process.* Stanford: Stanford University Press, 1997.

Taylor, D. M., Wong-Rieger, D., McKirnan, D. J., and Bercusson, T. "Interpreting and Coping with Threat in the Context of Intergroup Relations." *Journal of Social Psychology* 2 (1982): 257–70.

Taylor, D. M., Wright, S. C., Moghaddam, F. M., and Lalonde, R. N. "The Personal/Group Discrimination Discrepancy: Perceiving My Group, but Not Myself, to Be a Target of Discrimination." *Personality and Social Psychology Bulletin* 16, no. 2 (1990): 254–62.

Taylor, D. M., Wright, S. C., and Porter, L. E. "Dimensions of Perceived Discrimination: The Personal/Group Discrimination Discrepancy." In *The Psychology of Prejudice: The Ontario Symposium,* ed. M. P. Zanna and J. M. Olson, 233–55. Hillsdale, N.J.: Erlbaum, 1994.

Taylor, M. C. "Impact of Affirmative Action on Beneficiary Groups: Evidence from the 1990 General Social Survey." *Basic and Applied Social Psychology* 15 (1994): 143–78.

Taylor, S. E., and Brown, J. D. "Illusion and Well-Being: A Social Psychological Perspective on Mental Health." *Psychological Bulletin* 103 (1988): 193–210.

Tekian, A. "Minority Students, Affirmative Action, and the Admission Process: A Literature Review, 1987–1998." *Teaching and Learning in Medicine* 12 (2000): 33–42.

Thernstrom, S., and Thernstrom, A. M. *America in Black and White: One Nation, Indivisible.* New York: Simon and Schuster, 1997.

Thomas, K. R., and Weinrach, S. G. "Multiculturalism, Cultural Diversity and Affirmative Action Goals: A Reconsideration." *Rehabilitation Education* 12 (1998): 65–75.

Thompson, J. S., Stephan, W. G., and Schvaneveldt, R. W. "The Organization of Social Stereotypes in Semantic Memory." Paper presented at the Annual Meeting of the Rocky Mountain Psychological Association, Tucson, March 1980.

Tien, C. "In Defense of Affirmative Action." *USA Today* 126, no. 2630 (1997): 58–60.

Tierney, W. G. "The Parameters of Affirmative Action: Equity and Excellence in the Academy." *Review of Educational Research* 67 (1997): 165–96.

Tomaskovic-Devey, D. "Sex Composition and Gendered Earnings Inequality: A Comparison of Job and Occupational Models." In *Gender Inequality at Work,* ed. J. A. Jacobs, 23–56. Thousand Oaks, Calif.: Sage, 1995.

Tougas, F., and Beaton, A. M. "Affirmative Action in the Work Place: For Better or for Worse." *Applied Psychology: An International Review* 42 (1993): 253–64.

Tougas, F., Brown, R., Beaton, A. M., St.-Pierre, L. "Neosexism Among Women: The Role of Personally Experienced Social Mobility Attempts." *Personality and Social Psychology Bulletin* (1999): 1487–97.

Tougas, F., Crosby, F. J., Joly, S., and Pelchat, D. "Men's Attitudes Toward Affirmative Action: Justice and Intergroup Relations at the Crossroads." *Social Justice Research* 8 (1995): 57–71.

Tougas, F., Joly, S., Beaton, A. M., and St.-Pierre, L. "Reactions of Beneficiaries to Preferential Treatment: A Reality Check." *Human Relations* 49 (1996): 453–64.

Tougas, F., and Veilleux, F. "The Response of Men to Affirmative Action Strategies for Women: The Study of a Predictive Model." *Canadian Journal of Behavioural Science* 22 (1990): 424–32.

Truax, L. R., Wood, A., Wright, E., Cordova, D. I., and Crosby, F. J. "Undermined? Affirmative Action from the Targets' Point of View." In *Prejudice: The Targets' Perspective,* ed. J. K. Swim and C. Stagnor, 171–88. New York: Academic, 1997.

Truesdell, W. H. *The Secrets of Affirmative Action Compliance,* 5th ed. Walnut Creek, Calif.: Management Advantage, 2001.

Truxillo, D. M., and Bauer, T. N. "Applicant Reactions to Test Scores Banding in Entry-Level and Promotional Contexts." *Journal of Applied Psychology* 84 (1999): 322–39.

———. "The Roles of Gender and Affirmative Action Attitudes in Reactions to Test Score Use Methods." *Journal of Applied Social Psychology* 30 (2000): 1812–28.

Tsui, A., Egan, T., and O'Reilly, C. "Being Different: Relational Demography and Organizational Attachment." *Administrative Science Quarterly* 37 (1992): 554–79.

Turner, M. E., and Pratkanis, A. R. "Affirmative Action as Help: A Review of Recipient Reactions to Preferential Selection and Affirmative Action." *Basic and Applied Social Psychology* 15 (1994): 43–69.

———. "Effects of Preferential and Meritorious Selection on Performance: An Examination of Intuitive and Self-Handicapping Perspectives." *Personality and Social Psychology Bulletin* 19 (1993): 47–58.

Twenge, J. M. "Changes in Women's Assertiveness in Response to Status and Roles: A Cross-Temporal Meta-Analysis, 1931–1993." *Journal of Personality and Social Psychology* 81 (2001): 133–45.

Tyler, T. R., Boeckmann, R. J., Smith, H. J., and Huo, Y. *Social Justice in a Diverse Society.* Boulder, Colo.: Westview, 1997.

Tyler, T., Degoey, P., and Smith, H. "Understanding Why the Justice of Group Procedures Matters: A Test of the Psychological Dynamics of the Group-Value Model." *Journal of Personality and Social Psychology* 70 (1996): 913–30.

Tyler, T., and Lind, E. A. "A Relational Model of Authority in Groups." In *Advances in Experimental Social Psychology,* ed. M. P. Zanna, 25:115–91. New York: Academic, 1992.

U.N. Development Programme. *Human Development Report, 2001.* New York: Oxford University Press, 2001.

U.S. Department of Labor, Bureau of Labor Statistics. *Highlights of Women's Earnings in 2000.* Report 952. Washington, D.C.: Government Printing Office 2001.

U.S. Department of Labor, Employment Standards Administration. *The Rhetoric and Reality About Affirmative Action at the OFCCP.* Washington, D.C., n.d.

Valencia, R., and Suzuki, L. A. *Intelligence Testing and Minority Students: Foundations, Performance Factors, and Assessment Issues.* Thousand Oaks, Calif.: Sage, 2000.

Van Boven, L. "Pluralistic Ignorance and Political Correctness: The Case of Affirmative Action." *Political Psychology* 21 (2000): 267–76.

van Laar, C., and Levin, S. "Social and Personal Identity in Stereotype Threat: Is Affirmative Action Stigmatizing?" Paper presented at the Biannual Meeting of the Society for the Psychological Study of Social Issues, Minneapolis, June 2000.

Vasquez, M. J. T. "1999 Division 35 Presidential Address." *Psychology of Women Quarterly* 25 (2001): 89–97.

Verhovek, S. D. "In Poll, Americans Rejects Means but Not Ends of Racial Diversity." *New York Times,* Dec. 14, 1997, 1, 32.

Vozzola, E. C., and Higgins-D'Alessandro, A. "Competing Conceptions of Justice: Faculty Moral Reasoning About Affirmative Action." *Journal of Adult Development* 7 (2000): 137–49.

Walster, E. H., Berscheid, E., and Walster, G. W. "New Directions in Equity Research." *Journal of Personality and Social Psychology* 25 (1973): 151–76.

Walster, E. H., and Walster, G. W. "Equity and Social Justice." *Journal of Social Issues* 31, no. 3 (1975): 21–43.

Ward, D. "Generations and the Expression of Symbolic Racism." *Political Psychology* 6 (1985): 1–18.

Warner, R. L., and Steele, B. S. "Affirmative Action in Times of Fiscal Stress and Changing Value Priorities: The Case of Women in Policing." *Public Personnel Management* 18 (1989): 291–309.

Wharton, A., and Baron, J. "So Happy Together? The Impact of Gender Segregation on Men at Work." *American Sociological Review* 52 (1987): 574–87.

Wightman, L. F. "An Examination of Sex Differences in LSAT Scores from the Perspective of Social Consequence." *Applied Measurement in Education* 11 (1998): 255–77.

———. "The Role of Standardized Admission Tests in the Debate About Merit, Academic Standards, and Affirmative Action." *Psychology, Public Policy, and Law* 6 (2000): 90–100.

———. "The Threat to Diversity in Legal Education: An Empirical Analysis of the Consequences of Abandoning Race as a Factor in Law School Admissions Decisions." *New York University Law Review* 72 (1997): 1–53.

Williams, D. R., Jackson, J. S., Brown, T. N., Torres, M., Forman, T. A., and Brown, K. "Traditional and Contemporary Prejudice and Urban Whites' Support for Affirmative Action and Government Help." *Social Problems* 46 (1999): 503–27.

Williams, P. *The Alchemy of Race and Rights.* Cambridge: Harvard University Press, 1991.

Williams, W. M. "Perspectives on Intelligence Testing, Affirmative Action, and Educational Policy." *Psychology, Public Policy, and Law* 6 (2000): 5–19.

Wilson, G., "Support for Redistributive Policies Among the African American Middle Class." *Research in Social Stratification and Mobility* 18 (2001): 97–115.

Wilson, L. V. E. "Affirmative Action: The Future of Race Based Preferences in Hiring." *Western Journal of Black Studies* 16 (1992): 173–79.

Wilson, W. J. *When Work Disappears: The World of the New Urban Poor.* New York: Knopf, 1996.

Winkelman, C., and Crosby, F. J. "Affirmative Action: Setting the Record Straight." *Social Justice Research* 7 (1994): 309–28.

Wood, R. G., Corcoran, M. E., and Courant, P. N. "Pay Differences Among the

Highly Paid: The Male-Female Earnings Gap in Lawyers' Salaries." *Journal of Labor Economics* 11 (1993): 417–41.

Wright, P., Ferris, S. P., Hiller, J. S., and Kroll, M. "Competitiveness Through Management of Diversity: Effect on Stock Price Valuation." *Academy of Management Journal* 38 (1995): 272–87.

Wyche, K. F., and Crosby, F. J., eds. *Women's Ethnicities: Journeys Through Psychology.* Boulder, Colo.: Westview, 1996.

Zywerink, J. R., Devine, P. G., Monteith, M. J., and Cook, D. "Prejudice Toward Blacks: With and Without Compunction?" *Basic and Applied Social Psychology* 18 (1996): 131–50.

Index

Academic performance, consequences of affirmative action on, 121, 169–72

Academy of Management Journal, 112

ACT (American College Test), 55

Actor-observer difference, 257n41

Adams, J. Stacy, 32–33

Adarand Constructors v. Pena, 9, 98–99, 134

Administrative costs of affirmative action hiring, 107–8

Admissions. *See* College admissions

Advanced-placement courses, 116, 117

Affirmative action: arguments against (*see* Reverse-discrimination claims); arguments in favor of, 46–58; in courts (*see* Courts; Michigan cases; Supreme Court decisions); definition of, 4–5, 71, 81–82; economic costs and benefits of, in employment, 112–15, 129; in education (*see* College admissions); in employment (*see* Employment, affirmative action in; Hiring practices; Set-aside procurement programs); versus equal opportunity, 5, 30; fairness of, 10–11, 30, 47, 58–60, 223–27; knowledge of, 64–73, 76, 93, 227–28, 229; laws (*see* Executive Order 11246; Laws and regulations); media coverage of, 2–3, 61, 63, 83–84, 228, 256–57n39; need for, 10–13, 229–30, 237–39; operation of, 6–10; psychological effects of (*see* Psychological effects of affirmative action); public opinion on (*see* Public opinion); scholarly studies of, 63–64; social benefits of, 127–29, 220; social costs of, 124–27

Affirmative Action: Who Benefits? (American Psychological Association), 5

African American employees: in affirmative action versus non–affirmative action firms, 104–5, 106, 158–59; on discrimination, 197; discrimination against, 198, 199–200, 230–31; in federal contractor jobs, 102–4; in govern-

ment jobs, 100–101, 107; pay differentials among, 186, 199; self-stigmatizing hypothesis of affirmative action and, 158–61, 230. *See also* Set-aside procurement programs

African Americans: crime rate for, 194–95; discrimination against, 198–202; economic progress of, 193–94; family income of, 113, 126, 193; social benefits of affirmative action, 127–29; social costs of affirmative action, 126–27. *See also* Racial differences; Racism

African American students: academic consequences of affirmative action, 170–71; stigmatizing effects of affirmative action, 164–66, 173, 174; support for affirmative action, 166–69, 173–74

Age-discrimination lawsuits, 109

"Aggregate Condition," 13–14

Alchemy of Race and Rights (Williams), 64

Alcott, Victoria, 154–55

Allport, Gordon, 231

Amato, S. R., 154

Ambition, of employees in affirmative action firms, 159

Ambivalent Sexism Scale, 181

America in Black and White (Thernstrom and Thernstrom), 63, 193

American Association for Affirmative Action, 83

American Bar Association, 190

American Enterprise Institute, 238

American Psychological Association (APA), definition of affirmative action, 5

American Psychologist, 51

Amirkhan, James, 58

Ashenfelter, Orley, 102

Asian Americans: attitude to affirmative action in college admissions, 166; attitude to affirmative action in employment, 160; classification as targeted class, 236; discrimination against, 199–